Technological Innovations for Business, Education and Sustainability

TECHNOLOGICAL INNOVATION AND SUSTAINABILITY FOR BUSINESS COMPETITIVE ADVANTAGE

Series Editors: Allam Hamdan and Reem Khamis

Innovation and sustainability are broad terms that describe many interdisciplinary sciences – business success and competitiveness may not be separated from social and cultural aspects that interfere with any future development prospects. Research in across areas would provide a better understanding of international experiences, bridging the gap between developing and developed nations. This series promotes new visions for business research prospects that work in favor of innovation and sustainability in terms of governance, environment, and ethics.

Technological Innovation and Sustainability for Business Competitive Advantage highlights business problems faced by institutions in a scientific way, finding possible practical solutions. Contributing to setting and improving business theories and practices and encouraging scientific research in technological innovation and sustainability, volumes activate dialogue between academics, practitioners, and individuals and provide recommendations to improve institutions.

Technological Innovations for Business, Education and Sustainability

EDITED BY

ALLAM HAMDAN

Ahlia University, Bahrain

United Kingdom – North America – Japan – India – Malaysia – China

Emerald Publishing Limited
Emerald Publishing, Floor 5, Northspring, 21-23 Wellington Street, Leeds LS1 4DL

First edition 2024

British Library Cataloguing in Publication Data
A catalogue record for this book is available from the British Library

ISBN: 978-1-83753-107-3 (Print)
ISBN: 978-1-83753-106-6 (Online)
ISBN: 978-1-83753-108-0 (Epub)

INVESTOR IN PEOPLE

Contents

Part II: Technological Education and Skills Development for Sustainable Practices

About the Editor

Allam Hamdan is a Full Professor; he is listed within the World's top 2% scientists list by Stanford University; he is the Dean of College of Business and Finance at Ahlia University, Bahrain. He is the author of many publications in regional and international journals that discussed several accountings, financial, and economic issues concerning the Arab world. In addition, he has interests in education-related issues in the Arab world universities like educational governance, investment in education, and economic growth. He was awarded the First Prize of Al-Owais Creative Award, UAE, 2019; 2017; the Second Prize of Rashid bin Humaid Award for Culture and Science, UAE, 2016; the Third Prize of Arab Prize for the Social Sciences and Humanities, 2015; and the First Prize of "Durrat Watan," UAE, 2013. He has achieved the highest (first) scientific research citation among the Arab countries according to Arcif 2018–2023; appointed as an external panel member as part of Bahrain Quality Assurance Authority and National Qualifications Framework NQF as a validator, and appeal committee, General Directorate of NQF, Kingdom of Bahrain. He is a member of Steering Committee in International Arab Conference of Quality Assurance of Higher Education. He is currently leading a mission-driven process for International Accreditation for College of Business and Finance by Association to Advance Collegiate Schools of Business (AACSB).

About the Editor

About the Contributors

Nawal Abdulla – Graduated from Ahlia University, Bahrain. He holds a Master's degree in Business Administration (MBA).

Mohamed Sayed Abou Elseoud holds a PhD in Economics. He is an Economics Professor at Sadat Academy for Management Sciences, Egypt and he currently works at the University of Bahrain's College of Business Administration, Department of Economics and Finance, and as a program coordinator for BSc in International Business and Economics. His areas of expertise include economic policies, econometrics, nonparametric models, and environmental economics. He has more than 50 research papers published in indexed journals worldwide and international conferences. Macroeconomic models, economic development, applied economics, financial markets, and sustainable development are among his research interests. Affiliation: Department of Economics and Finance, College of Business Administration University of Bahrain, Zallaq, Kingdom of Bahrain.

Walter Medrano Acuña is an Accountant and has completed Doctorate in Accounting. His research interests are competence of the public official, economic models of regional development, and business innovation. He is currently regional councilor of Ancash and University Professor of the Academic Department of Accounting at the National University Santiago Antunez de Mayolo, Huaraz, Peru.

Samar H. AlBagoury is an Economics Associate professor at Cairo University and director of centre of Nile basin studies. She had various studies in African economies and participated as an editor of various issues of African strategic report issued by Faculty of African postgraduate studies at Cairo University.

Hashim Al-Hashimi is in his 4th year of dental school at the tender age of 18, stands out as the youngest among his peers. He graduated with a high school diploma from the esteemed International School of Chouefiat (SABIS) at 16. Excelling in both academics and international board certified exams, he achieved an acceptance into Riyadh Elm University for a BDS in (Bachelor's Dentistry). Hashim's academic dedication led him to have the highest GPA in his class which awarded him with a partial scholarship.

Mukthar Al-Hashimi is a Bahraini national, who has four degrees: undergraduate, two Master's degrees, and a PhD from the well-reputed University of Utah and Indiana State University, USA. During the last 25 years, he has served as an academic, advisor, director, and executive member for a number of government and non-government organizations. He is currently working as an Academic Professor at Ahlia University, Bahrain. Professor Al-Hashmi's experiences are rich and a blend of academic, managerial, and administrative activities at both government and private organizations. He gained much recognition for the development of a comprehensive medical information system "Al-Care System."

Ahmad AL-Hawamleh is an Assistant Professor in Computer Science-Cybersecurity at the Institute of Public Administration-KSA, a Certified Trainer in Blackboard Education Technology and Services, and a Certified Trainer in the Zoom Meetings Platform. His research is situated in the fields of Information Security, Cybersecurity, and IoT.

Huthaifa Al-Hazaima is an Assistant Professor at the Department of Accounting, School of Business, The Hashemite University, Zarqa, Jordan.

Fahad K. Alkhaldi holds a PhD in Economics and Sustainability, with a significant focus on the nexus between Economic Growth and Climate Change. His expansive research interests also include "the Knowledge Economy, Resource Diversification, Economics of Energy, Circular Economy, and Security & Development Studies of The Middle East." Affiliation: Environment and Sustainable Development Program, College of Science, University of Bahrain, Zallaq, Kingdom of Bahrain.

Leena Abdelsalam Almajaly is a Researcher at Department of Accounting, Business School, The Hashemite University, Zarqa, Jordan.

Muneer Al Mubarak received his PhD in Business and Economic Studies (Marketing) from University of Leeds, UK, in early 2010. Al Mubarak's expertise is in strategic management, marketing management, and relationship marketing. He has over 34 years work experience as he contributed well in teaching and training in areas such as leadership, strategic management, relationship marketing, marketing management, marketing communications, sustainability, corporate social responsibility, customer relationship management, and service excellence. He has participated in many community activities over the years and is a reviewer of many reputable international journals.

Amer Al-Roubaie is a Professor of Economics at Ahlia University in Bahrain. He obtained his Doctorate in Economics from McGill University, Montreal, Canada. He taught Economics at Concordia University as an Adjunct Professor and also at other North American and Middle Eastern universities. He was also a research Fellow at ISTAC, kuala Lumpur, Malaysia, for a number of years. Besides economics, his expertise lies in the fields of knowledge-based development, Islamic banking and Finance, development economics and globalization, and international business.

Noor Alsayed – PhD holder from Brunel University – London and an Assistant Professor at College of Business and Finance, Ahlia University, Bahrain.

Mohannad Obeid Al Shbail is an Assistant Professor at the School of Business, Al al-Bayt University.

Hashem Alshurafat is an Assistant Professor at the Department of Accounting, School of Business, The Hashemite University, Zarqa, Jordan.

Marwan Altarawneh is an Assistant Professor in Accounting at the Faculty of Business Studies, Arab Open University-KSA. His research is currently focused on BI, blockchain technology. He has research papers published in journals indexed under data source Scopus.

Abdallah Bader Alzoubi is an Assistant Professor at Department of Accounting, Business School, The Hashemite University, Zarqa, Jordan.

Husam Ananzeh is an Assistant Professor of accounting at Irbid National University.

Luis Angulo-Cabanillas, PhD in Computer Science and Engineering from the Universidad Nacional Santiago Antúnez de Mayolo, is a Research Professor and Statistician specialized in the area of research methodology. He is an Associate Professor assigned to the Academic Department of Statistics at the Universidad Nacional Santiago Antúnez de Mayolo, Huaraz, Peru.

Omar Arabiat is an Assistant Professor in the Accounting Department of the Business School at Hashemite University in Jordan. He holds a PhD in Accounting and Financial Management from the Business Informatics, Systems, and Accounting Department of Henley Business School, University of Reading.

Arjun B. S., PhD, is an Assistant Professor in the School of Business and Management at Christ (Deemed to be University). He received his PhD degree in Finance and his current research interests include risk management, derivatives, volatility measurement, ESG investing, and sustainable finance.

Nilda Barrutia-Montoya, Master's in Tourism and Hotel Marketing, is a PhD student in Public Management and Governance, with more than 5 years of experience in the teaching and learning process in higher education. Her research interests are the management of tourism resources, tourism potential, development of new tourism products, and sustainability of tourism development. She currently teaches at the Universidad Tecnologica del Peru S.A.C., Ica, Peru.

Yeni Bullón-Miguel has a Doctorate in Public Management and Governance. She has more than 8 years of experience in the teaching and learning process of regular basic education. Her research interests are the management of the public education process, educational innovation, and the reduction of gaps and deficiencies in education. She currently teaches classes in education for work at the Institucion Educativa Javier Heraud – San Juan de Miraflores, Lima, Peru.

Jorge Castillo-Picon is a Senior Lecturer at Universidad Nacional Santiago Antunez de Mayolo; Master's in Economics with mention in Business Management; PhD in Economics. He is author of scientific articles published and indexed in Scopus and Web of Science. He has also published several essays and books on economics and development. His research interests are rural development and digital innovation. He is currently Dean of the Faculty of Economics and Accounting at the Universidad Nacional Santiago Antúnez de Mayolo, Huaraz, Peru.

Manuel Chenet-Zuta is a Senior Lecturer at the Universidad Nacional Tecnológica de Lima Sur UNTELS. He has been recognized as Doctor Honoris Causa, Honorary Professor, and Visiting Professor in several countries in Latin America and the United States. He holds a Postdoctoral degree in Diachronic and Synchronous Systems of Scientific Research and Postdoctorate in Educational Sciences; Postgraduate Unit in Education of the Universidad Nacional Mayor de San Marcos; Postgraduate of the Universidad del Golfo de México Rectoría Centro. He is a national and international Lecturer in University Management, University Internationalization, and Human Talent Management.

Deepika S. R. is an Assistant Professor at School of Business and Management, Christ (Deemed to be University), Bangalore. She holds a PhD in the area of Finance from Bharathiar University, Coimbatore. Her area of specialization is Finance and handles subjects such as Investment Analysis and Portfolio Management, Derivatives and Commodities Market, Financial markets and services, Fundamentals of Accounting, Business Statistics, Entrepreneurship Development, etc. She has also published research articles in refereed journals and has presented research papers at International Conferences. She is also a YouTuber, in the area of personal finance and investments and she is interested in public speaking.

Karin De la Cruz Inchicaqui, Economist, holds Master's in Finance, and is a PhD student in economics. Her research interests are knowledge society, econometric models, microfinance, and sustainable development. She currently teaches at the Academic Department of Economics of the Faculty of Economics and Accounting at the Universidad Nacional Santiago Antúnez de Mayolo, Huaraz, Peru.

William Dextre-Martinez holds Bachelor's in Management, Master's in Business Administration, and MBA. He has 12 years of experience in teaching and learning, as well as in writing scientific articles. He has four articles published and indexed in Scopus and Web of science. His research interests are information society, innovation in microfinance, and digital marketing. He is currently a full-time Assistant Professor in the Academic Department of Management at the Faculty of Management and Tourism – Universidad Nacional Santiago Antunez de Mayolo, Huaraz, Peru.

Alya Elfedawy is an Assistant Professor in Accounting at the Faculty of Business Studies, Arab Open University-KSA. Her research is currently focused on blockchain technology and AIS. She has research papers published in journals indexed under data source Scopus.

Abraham Jose García-Yovera, Industrial Engineer, holds Bachelor's in Administration and PhD in public management and governance. He has experience in recruitment and selection processes, hiring, training development, job analysis, and feedback. He currently holds the position of Coordinator of Research and Social Responsibility of the Universidad Señor de Sipan, Chicalyo, Peru.

Freddy David Zuluaga Guerrra, Chemical Engineer, holds a Master's degree in Digital Marketing. His research interests are the design of sustainable products, information society, innovation in microfinance, rural entrepreneurship, and digital business marketing. He is a Professor at the Universidad Industrial de Santander, Colombia.

Martha Esther Guerra Muñoz is a Full Professor at the Universidad Popular del Cesar, Valledupar, Colombia. She has a Doctorate in Administration and Social Sciences. She is a Research Professor recognized by the Ministry of Science, Technology and Innovation, Colombia. She has more than 20 years of experience in teaching and learning, as well as in writing scientific articles. She has articles published and indexed in Scopus and Web of science. She is currently the Director of the Graduate School of the Universidad Popular del Cesar, Colombia.

Heba Hikal is an Assistant Professor in Accounting at the Faculty of Business Studies, Arab Open University-KSA. Her research is currently focused on BI, blockchain technology and AIS. She has research papers published in journals indexed under data source Scopus.

Hober Huaranga-Toledo has a Doctorate in Public Management and Governance, with more than 15 years of experience in the public management. His research interests are public management, innovation in the public sector, and digital marketing. He currently teaches in different universities.

Mercedes Huerta-Soto is an Economist and holds an MBA. He is specialized in finance as regional credit manager; Researcher RENACYT qualified and recognized by the National Council of Science, Technology and Technological Innovation, Peru. He is the author of books, book chapters, and articles in journals indexed in Scopus and Web of science. He is currently teaching at the Academic Department of Economics at the Universidad Nacional Santiago Antúnez de Mayolo, Huaraz, Peru.

Rosario Huerta-Soto is an Economist and holds an MBA. He is a Researcher recognized by the National Council of Science, Technology and Technological Innovation, Peru. Her research interests are microfinance, regulation and innovation in the financial system. He has experience as regional credit manager at Financiera Confianza S.A. He is currently the Head of teaching and head of the formative research office at Universidad Cesar Vallejo, Huaraz, Peru.

Jaheer Mukthar K. P. holds PhD in economics. His research interests are econometrics, financial economics, monetary economics, capital markets, and foreign direct investment. He is a reviewer of Scopus indexed journals, chapter editor of Scopus indexed books, and editor of scientific journals in economics. He is currently an Assistant Professor of the Department of Economics, Kristu Jayanti College, Bangalore, India.

Zaid Jaradat is an Assistant Professor in the Department of Accounting at the Al al-Bayt University, where he earned his PhD in Managerial Accounting from Malaysia. His research is currently focused on E-accounting in SMEs and adoption of ERP and blockchain technology in industrial and banking sectors. He has research papers published in journals indexed under data source Scopus and Web of Science. ORCID: 0000-0002-1735-8346.

Orlando Leiva-Chauca has Bachelor's in Administration, Master's in Social Policies with mention in Project Management and Social Programs. His research interests are entrepreneurship, economic development models, microfinance for entrepreneurs, and social marketing. He currently teaches in the Academic Department of Administration at the Universidad Nacional Santiago Antúnez de Mayolo, Huaraz, Peru.

Ali Makhlooq graduated from George Washington University, USA and holds an MSc in Engineering Management.

Bashar Matoog graduated with honors from University of Bahrain. He also received an award for his high academic achievement from Ahlia University. Mr. Bashar Matooq joined Ahlia University as a part time Lecturer in the Accounting & Economics Department in 2007. He specializes in Economics, particularly microeconomics, macroeconomics, managerial economics, economic development, and mathematical economics.

Jenny Villacorta Miranda, Bachelor's in Economics, is a professional with experience in monitoring and evaluation of public investment. He is currently engaged in research on issues of competitiveness of the tourism sector, motivations of public servants, economic models of regional development, and business innovation. He has a spirit of self-improvement, capacity, responsibility, and aptitude to work under pressure.

Nagarjuna G. is an Assistant Professor in the Department of Tourism Management, School of Business and Management, Bannerghatta Campus, Christ (Deemed to be University). His research interests are sustainable tourism, cultural and heritage tourism, tourism education, and wildlife tourism. His doctoral research was on Sustainable Tourism Management: Issues and Challenges of Eco and Wildlife Resorts in Karnataka.

Emerson Norabuena-Figueroa has a BS in Statistics and Computer Science with a Master's degree in Science, and Engineering with a major in Information Technology and Computer Systems. His experience in research lines includes data mining, metaheuristics, production models, and decision-making. He is a university Professor attached to the Department of Mathematics at the Universidad Nacional Mayor de San Marcos (UNMSM), Lima, Peru.

Elia Ramirez-Asis, Master's in Educational Administration, is a Researcher recognized by the National Council of Science and Technology and Technological

Innovation of Peru. Her research interests are teaching competence, teaching–learning models, and innovation in higher education. She is currently a Professor at the National University Santiago Antunez de Mayolo, Huaraz, Peru.

Edwin Ramirez-Asis is a Research professor at Universidad Señor de Sipan, Chiclayo, Peru. He holds a PhD in administration and international Post-doctorate in Didactics of Scientific Research. He is a Researcher recognized by the National Council of Science, Technology and Technological Innovation, Peru. His research interests are the information society, innovation in micro-finance, and digital marketing. He is currently the Editor in Chief of the scientific journal Epistemia.

Edwin Hernan Ramirez Asis holds a Degree in Administration, Doctorate in Administration, and international Postdoctorate in Didactics of Scientific Research. He is a Researcher recognized by the National Council of Science, Technology and Technological Innovation, Peru. He has 15 years of experience in teaching and learning, as well as in writing scientific articles. He has 20 articles published and indexed in Scopus and Web of science. His research interests are the information society, innovation in microfinance and digital marketing. He is currently an Associate Professor in the Academic Department of Administration at the Universidad Nacional Santiago Antúnez de Mayolo, Huaraz, Peru.

Hernan Ramirez-Asis is a Research Professor at the Universidad Nacional Santiago Antunez de Mayolo, Huaraz, Peru. He has completed Doctorate in Administration and international Postdoctorate in Didactics of Scientific Research. He is a Researcher recognized by the National Council of Science, Technology and Technological Innovation, Peru. His research interests are the information society, innovation in microfinance, and digital marketing. He is currently the Editor in Chief of the Research Unit of the Faculty of Management and Tourism of the Universidad Nacional Santiago Antunez de Mayolo, Huaraz, Peru.

Eduardo Rocca-Espinoza is an Industrial Engineer from the Pontificia Universidad Católica del Perú (PUCP) with Master's in Business Administration at the Universidad del Pacífico. He completed his Doctoral studies at the Faculty of Economics and Business Administration of the University of Murcia, Spain. He is the Coordinator of Accreditation of the Department of Engineering of the PUCP. He has Participated in research with the universities of Murcia, Cantabria and the Polytechnic of Cartagena, member of the Faedpyme network, design and execution of research in the SME sector. He is currently an Associate Professor at the Engineering Department of the PUCP.

José Rodríguez Herrera is an Economist, Professor at the Universidad Nacional Santiago Antúnez de Mayolo, in the category of full-time associate, professional with spirit of improvement, ability, responsibility, and aptitude to work under pressure with full-time availability, able to perform in various fields related to the profession of economist. She is currently an Associate Professor of the Academic

Department of Economics of the Faculty of Economics and Accounting, Huaraz, Peru.

Jose Rodriguez-Kong is an Industrial Engineer with a Master's degree in Economic Sciences, mention: business management. He is responsible, perseverant, proactive, and efficient with initiative, ethics, analytical skills, and ability to interact with people and perform teamwork oriented to the achievement of objectives. He also has the ability to learn quickly, predisposition to work in a team and under pressure. He is currently teaching at the Universidad Señor de Sipan, Chicalyo, Peru.

Huber Rodriguez-Nomura is an Economist by profession, He holds a PhD in Economics and Industrial Development with experience in the area of university education and with management skills in both public and private sector by having democratic leadership. He seeks to transmit the knowledge and skills acquired throughout his career. He is currently Rector of the Universidad Señor de Sipan, Peru.

Hugo Marino Rodríguez-Orellana has Bachelor's in Statistics and Informatics, Master's in Public Management, specialist in sampling, with experience in spatial statistical analysis, SQL database management, and modeling with application in nonlinear physics. He currently teaches in the Academic Department of Mathematical Sciences at the Universidad Nacional Mayor de San Marcos, Lima, Peru.

Rober Trinidad Romero Ramirez is a lawyer with PhD in political science, specialist in public management, University Professor with undergraduate, graduate and Master's degree. He has served as deputy of the department of Cesar, councilman of the municipality of Valledupar, delegated prosecutor before the municipal criminal judges of Valledupar, Secretary of Municipal Government of Valledupar during the mayoralty of Luis Fabián Fernández, Dean of the law school of the Universidad Popular del Cesar in Valledupar Colombia, and currently Rector of the same institution.

Roger Rurush-Asencio is an Economist with Master's in Social Policies and PhD in public management and governance. He is a Professor at the Universidad Nacional Santiago Antúnez de Mayolo, in the category of full-time assistant, professional with a spirit of improvement, capacity, responsibility, and ability to work under pressure with full-time availability, able to work in various fields related to the profession of economist, law, and accounting that contribute to social welfare, institutional, and professional development.

Mallika Sankar is an Assistant Professor in the School of Business and Management at the Christ University in Bangalore, India. She received her PhD in Management from Bharathiar University. Her research interests are in the areas of higher education, ranging from scale development to design to implementation. She has co-authored a book in research methodology and is preferred as a resource person in several faculty development programs, conferences, and workshops. She has also served as trainer in the programs organized by AICTE and an invited speaker in many public events and academic institutions. She has also served in industry at various administrative positions for over 12 years. Her areas of teaching include research methodology, business analytics, and strategic management.

Maha Shehadeh is an Assistant Professor of FinTech at the Applied Science Private University in Jordan. She earned her PhD in Economics and Islamic Banking from Yarmouk University in 2021, focusing on digital transformation. Her research interests include FinTech, artificial intelligence (AI) and machine learning (ML), digital transformation in banking, and financial inclusion. Dr Shehadeh has been awarded the first place in the Al Qasimia University Research Award for Islamic Economics for her research on the dimensions of digital transformation. She also serves as an editor and reviewer for various academic journals. In her teaching role, she leverages her expertise in digital transformation, instructing a variety of courses in Financial Technology.

Fadi Shehab Shiyyab is an Assistant Professor at Department of Accounting, Business School, The Hashemite University, Zarqa, Jordan.

Walid Zakaria Siam is a Professor at Department of Accounting, Business School, The Hashemite University, Zarqa, Jordan.

Jose Sifuentes-Stratti is an Economist with Master's in Public Administration. His research interests are competence of the public official, economic models of regional development, and business innovation. Currently, he is the Head of the Statistics Unit and University Professor of the Academic Department of Economics at the Universidad Nacional Santiago Antúnez de Mayolo, Huaraz, Peru.

Jais V. Thomas is a Research Scholar at Christ University, Bangalore. He graduated in computer science and Philosophy and pursued an MBA specializing in finance. He has three years of industry experience in the Healthcare Sector in various capacities as Operating Manager and Finance Manager. He has served as director of a group of schools and presently working as an Assistant professor of Commerce and Management. He published four articles in various journals and was one of the guest editors of a book. His subject domains are financial management, organizational development, digital transformation, talent management, and strategic management.

Foreword

Technology innovation became essential in day-to-day operations; post COVID-19 governmental and organizational strategies have shifted toward digital transformation and green processes including education sector. The role of Business Education is crucial; business schools mission statements aim to produce graduates equipped with sustainable skills that could lead organizations from a technological aspect including digital transformation and use of technology innovation. International Accreditation Bodies including to Association to Advance Collegiate Schools of Business (AACSB) revised their standards with more emphasis on technology innovation to allow graduates to have the appropriate competency level to support business sustainability and impact. Technology Innovation including the use of Artificial Intelligence (AI), Big Data, and Data analytics supports various ways the businesses in terms of facilitating operational or strategic decision-making with a level of rationality, and evidence based on several studies highlighted the need to effectively utilize the technology for sustainable business operations including identification of risks and forecasting. In terms of business education, studies highlighted that 83 jobs will no longer be valid in the future due to technology innovation; therefore, education section must transform its teaching and learning methods to maintain the expedition of innovation and produce graduates with key competency in terms of ICT and digitalization. The question is "Technology Innovation" is it a blessing or a curse?

The answer is found in this book; a careful selection of the book chapters assures providing an insight for the readers that could be used by authors and policymakers. This book covers several chapters which highlight different innovative technology tools, education and teaching practices, and sustainability actions toward impact from multiple contexts. This book contributes to the United Nations Sustainable Development Goals (UNSDGs), particularly Education Quality (SDG4), Sustainable Cities and Communities (SDG11), and Partnership for the Goals (SDG17).

Esra AlDhaen, PFHEA
Associate Professor, Ahlia University, Manama, Bahrain
Executive Director Strategy, Quality and Sustainability

Preface

The world is rapidly changing, and technology is at the forefront of this transformation. Technological innovations have revolutionized every aspect of our lives, from the way we communicate, to how we learn, work, and do business. The impact of technology on business, education, and sustainability cannot be overstated, and this book serves as a testament to the crucial role of technology in shaping the future of these fields. The era of digital economy is no longer anticipated since we are currently living in it. Several frameworks are needed to be discussed to better understand how business, education, and technology could enable people contribute positively to the global digital transformation. Business and business education needs to beat the contradictory that always existed between the needs of labor market and outputs of universities. Educators need and employers should have some kind of similar perception for the skills needed to enhance employability. This book will clearly contribute to the growing need of aligning business strategy and educational curriculums with the changing needs and skills needed for business workplaces in different fields such as marketing, management information systems, and data analytics along with other business applications of AI.

The book's focus on sustainability is particularly relevant as it aligns with the United Nations' sustainable development goals (SDGs). The SDGs aim to create a better and more sustainable future for all, and technology is a key enabler in achieving these goals. This book's chapters explore the role of technology in promoting sustainable development and offer insights into how technology can be used to address the challenges facing the world today.

This book, entitled "Technological Innovations for Business, Education, and Sustainability," is a compilation of 19 chapters that have undergone rigorous double-blind peer review to ensure quality and accuracy. The chapters cover a range of topics that explore the intersection of technology, business, education, and sustainability.

This book is divided into three sections, each focusing on a different area of technology's impact on business, education, and sustainability. The sections are as follows:

Section I. Business Intelligence, Technology for Sustainability.
Section II. Technological Education and Skills Development for Sustainable Practices.

Section III. Digital technologies, Economic Diversification, Entrepreneurial Capacities, and Sustainability.

This book's chapters explore a range of topics within these sections, including the impact of digital transformation on business practices, the role of emotional intelligence in job satisfaction, and the relationship between board structure and financial performance. The chapters offer practical insights and solutions for leveraging technology to achieve sustainable development goals, improve business practices, and enhance the quality of education.

We hope that this book will inspire further research and innovation in this exciting and rapidly evolving field.

Allam Hamdan
Professor, Dean
College of Business and Finance, Ahlia University, Manama, Bahrain

Acknowledgment

We would like to express our sincere gratitude to Prof Abdulla Y. Al Hawaj the Founding President and the Chair of the Board of Trustees of Ahlia University, Bahrain, for his unwavering support and dedication to the advancement of scientific research. His invaluable guidance and expertise have been instrumental in the success of our research efforts. Also, we would like to thank all the chapter authors who contributed their time, knowledge, and expertise to make this book a reality. Lastly, I would like to thank the referee of our book for their insightful comments and constructive feedback, which have helped us to improve the quality of the book.

Part I

Business Intelligence, Technology for Sustainability

Chapter 1

Artificial Intelligence and Marketing: Challenges and Opportunities

Ali Makhlooq[a] *and Muneer Al Mubarak*[b]

[a]The George Washington University, USA
[b]Ahlia University, Bahrain

Abstract

It is important to implement artificial intelligence (AI) because it can simplify and solve complex problems faster than humans. Because AI learns about people and their behavior from the first purchase, AI marketing can boost marketing efforts by leveraging data to target extremely precise consumer groups. There is a debate about the efficacy of AI marketing due to the constraints and limits imposed by the system's nature. This chapter presents insights from published studies regarding the relationship of AI with marketing and how AI can affect marketing. A real-world example of Netflix's usage of AI in marketing has been demonstrated. Then, consumer attitudes regarding AI were revealed. Then, several ethical considerations concerning AI were highlighted. Finally, the anticipated future of AI marketing was addressed. This chapter demonstrated the significance of firms implementing AI marketing to get a competitive advantage. Although some of the difficulties mentioned in this study need to be resolved, AI marketing has a bright future. There are ethical concerns about bias and privacy that should be addressed further. This chapter will encourage firms to use AI systems in marketing, and it will open the door to concerns that will need to be investigated academically in the future.

Keywords: Marketing; artificial intelligence; marketing strategy; big data; machine learning; business technology

Technological Innovations for Business, Education and Sustainability, 3–16

Published under exclusive licence by Emerald Publishing Limited
doi:10.1108/978-1-83753-106-620241001

1. Introduction

The last few decades have seen great technological development, which has altered the course of human life. This technological advancement has helped in the betterment of human life by lowering borders between individuals and countries and making life easier. When talking about technological development, artificial intelligence (AI) must be mentioned as the basis for many developments in this era. The intelligence displayed by computers is known as AI. It is a branch of study concerned with competing with the ability of highly powered contemporary computer systems to handle difficulties by employing complicated competencies like as reasoning, learning, and self-correction. The concept of AI varies, but all center on the system's capacity to accurately read external input, learn from that data, and apply that knowledge to achieve specified objectives and activities through flexible adaptation.

From a marketing standpoint, AI can be defined as the development of AI that uses information available in the system about the company itself, consumers, and competitors to enable the organization to take or recommend marketing actions to achieve the best marketing result. Many businesses utilize AI to learn about people's preferences and inclinations in order to promote their products. Amazon, for example, use algorithms to understand what customers want and provide recommendations based on previously viewed and purchased things on their website.

1.1 The Relationship Between Marketing and AI

Marketing used to be restricted to marketing and advertising the products (such as placing advertisements in newspapers), but then a new marketing approach arose, focused on the consumer and creating a connection for long-term gain (through email communication or periodic visits to the customer). Currently, marketing is more reliant on technology and AI. As a result, new factors joined the competition, as well as tools that businesses should acquire. The quality of AI in data collection and analysis has become critical in the competition. Marketing with AI enables business owners and marketers to assess marketing data received via social media and the web in a reasonably short period of time. As a result, AI marketing is critical for all firms to be able to assess and address the demands of their clients. There are several areas where AI could aid enhanced marketing operations, such as:

- Automations, where AI assists in making marketing automation smarter, it may collaborate with marketing automation to translate data into meaningful choices and interactions, which benefits the organization.
- Reducing errors and boosting speed, as people are naturally prone to making mistakes, yet there is ongoing dispute regarding whether AI is a solution for human faults. There is consensus, however, that the purpose of creating AI is to enhance speed and minimize mistakes.

- Reducing expenses since AI can help reduce many of the resources that drain organizations' funds because it works faster and more efficiently. As a result, expenditures are reduced, and income is increased.
- Increasing the return on investment by targeting marketing to each consumer uniquely based on his preferences and orientation. This is accomplished by in-depth examination of client insights and requirements, as well as knowing what customers truly desire.

Social computing technology-based AI systems can be used to comprehend social networks on the internet. Different sorts of social networks can be analyzed using data mining techniques. This study assists the marketer in finding the prominent people or nodes inside the networks, which can then be used to adopt a civilized social marketing strategy. Based on the available data, customer behavior can be predicted when AI is used. When you anticipate the customer's behavior and vision, you may assess the market fit of the product and so aid in the choice to introduce or adjust the product. Marketers and salesmen do not need to comprehend how AI works because it is not their primary field. They are, however, expected to comprehend its mechanics and how they might use it in marketing for its greatest benefit.

1.2 Research Problem

The current state of AI technology is confined to intellectual domains such as picture recognition, speech recognition, and conversation response. In other words, AI has yet to collaborate with entire human brain functions such as self-awareness, self-control, self-consciousness, and self-motivation. As a result, while applying AI technology, there is a claim that there are various constraints for AI. Although recently created AI technology excels at extracting certain patterns, it has significant limits. Most models of information and communications technology are unduly reliant on big data, lack a self-idea function, and are complex. As a result, the computer or system is unable to read and evaluate data to make or assist in making a decision which led to a debate about the efficacy of AI marketing (Lu, Li, Chen, Kim, & Serikawa, 2017).

1.3 Contributions

There is a lack of study on the topic of marketing and its link to AI and how it will reflect on organizations, as there is a need to study to motivate organizations to modify their marketing strategy, how customer behaviors will be influenced, and policymaker difficulties (Davenport, Guha, Grewal, & Bressgott, 2019). The purpose of this study is to provide an update on the literature reviews about AI from the perspective of marketing and to discuss some of the challenges such as the ethical issues and the future of AI marketing. Certain expert-classified research may have some bias in some explanatory and descriptive respects. This study adds expert opinions to the published viewpoints, increasing the knowledge balance in this field. To update research on this topic, this study gathers, analyzes, and infers expert opinions.

1.4 Research Methodology

The research investigates some elements associated with the notion of AI marketing, which include limitations and opportunities. This chapter is a theoretical study in which instances are referenced based on citations from literature reviews and some from the author's individual opinions.

2. Literature Review

There are study articles that explore the limitations and opportunities of AI marketing. The goal of this literature review is to compile and discuss recent research on this issue.

2.1 AI Overview

As previously specified, AI is an area of computer science concerned with creating intelligent computers capable of thinking and responding in the same way as people do.

When we talk about AI, we should talk about machine learning (ML), which is a branch of AI that allows machines to automatically enhance and develop from practice. Customized systems are designed for this purpose, and no explicit programming is required to add new concepts to the system database. Deep learning is a branch of ML that consists of very large neural networks and a massive number of algorithms capable of simulating human intellect. Google, for example, is continually learning and mimicking human intellect without requiring people to enter all of the answers into its vast database (Villaronga, Kieseberg, & Li, 2018).

Algorithms, which are a collection of principles employed in problem-solving procedures, are at the heart of AI systems. When digital marketers hear the term "artificial intelligence," the first concept and term that comes to mind is "Rank Brain" Rank Brain is an ML -based search engine algorithm launched by Google in 2015 that assists Google in processing search results and providing more appropriate results to consumers. It makes use of AI to comprehend and answer to user enquiries in the same way that a human would. Furthermore, it offers a list of comparable inquiries that users frequently enter into Google. The precise findings of the answer, as well as a comparable set of questions, are backed by AI (Thiraviyam, 2018).

Because of their close relationship, two concepts are frequently associated with AI: big data and ML. These two terms can be defined as following:

- Big data is defined as data with greater variety that arrives in greater volumes and with higher velocity. This is also referred to as the three Vs (volume, velocity, and variety). Big data refers to greater, more complicated data volumes, particularly from new data sources. These data sets are so large that typical data processing technologies cannot handle them. However, these huge amounts of data may be leveraged to address business challenges that were previously unsolvable. The three Vs are defined in Table 1.1.

- ML is used to produce predictions or estimated solutions based on the study of massive volumes of data. The clearest illustrations are Netflix's algorithms, which recommend movies and series to customers based on previous viewings, and Amazon's algorithms, which propose products based on previous purchases or products whose pages have been recently viewed. ML is a branch of AI that allows programs to ingest enormous quantities of data and generate predictable algorithms that improve over time. Marketers may use ML to give consumers with personalized information as well as product ideas. When marketers have a vast database of data, ML has a better chance of delivering what customers want to buy. ML is multidisciplinary in nature, encompassing technology from a variety of disciplines such as computer science, statistics, mathematics, AI, and information systems. The fundamental benefit of ML is that it allows you to collect important data that was inferred from prior data by using algorithms based on computer vision, AI, and data mining.

Table 1.1. The 3 Vs Definiens.

The 3 Vs	Definition
Volume	It refers to the volume of data produced. By utilizing big data, the affiliate will be required to analyze massive volumes of unstructured data that is low in density. This might be unvalued data, such as a Netflix data stream, or the amount of hits on a certain web page. This might be dozens of terabytes of data for some corporations and tens of petabytes for others.
Velocity	It refers to the rate at which data is received and processed. Data often flows faster into memory versus slower rates when writing to hard drives. Some internet-enabled smart gadgets function in real time or near real time, necessitating real-time reaction and assessment.
Variety	The term "variety" refers to the number of different data kinds that have been entered. The data in big data stems from a number of sources, including new and unstructured data. Text, audio, and video are examples of unstructured and semi-structured data formats that require further preprocessing to get value from it.

Source: Authors' work.

2.2 AI and Marketing Strategy

In the past, a robot was created and tried to teach it certain fundamentals so that the robot could not comprehend anything you said or did, but with ML, the robot can learn on its own from people's actions and words. Like a tiny kid, this robot is still in the learning stage, but it can learn millions of pieces of information in a short period of time, and the more knowledge it learns, the stronger it grows and the closer it gets to the truth. This is something that large corporations are focusing on. A robot is being constructed to collect data on people's behavior. For example, Google can predict what a person will write in a Gmail message because other people have previously written the same sentence that you are attempting to write, and this is how the robot knows what you will write, and other people have purchased the same thing you purchased from Amazon, and then added another product, so Amazon displays related products that you are likely to purchase (Kumar, 2016).

The capacity to foresee what customers desire is aided by AI. One of the functions of AI is to assist in predicting what customers will purchase. The application of AI should result in significant gains in prediction capacity. Companies may radically adjust their business models based on degrees of predicted accuracy and outcomes, continually supplying goods and services to clients based on data and forecasts about their demands. As a result, several study possibilities on various client purchasing patterns and marketing methods emerge. AI may potentially play a larger part in anticipating not just what consumers want to buy but also what price they are willing to pay and whether price discounts should be made to entice the buyer. Because promotional pricing and discounts are significant marketing parts, it is one of the most important areas of future study to determine how to effectively utilize AI to anticipate ideal prices and whether price promotions should be provided (Davenport et al., 2019).

AI must comprehend the character of the consumer and what he desires. They have a part in deciding what a person can target in marketing, in addition to demographic criteria such as age, gender, and residential location. What appeals to the consumer in the Arab Gulf, for example, may not appeal to the individual in the United States. When addressing the phases of sales, AI may alter the traditional strategy used from the first stage, which is the search for a possible client, through follow-up, and the conclusion of delivering the product or service and collecting the customer's evaluation. Thus, there are components of AI that must be developed, such as the analysis of customer communications and customer information in order to make more compelling future messages or improve customer involvement, and thus boost sales volume. Another component is delivering real-time feedback to marketers to assist them enhance their sales offerings depending on customer replies. In addition to being an important component, it is the integration of many inputs such as client queries, comments, and real purchase orders. These present difficulties for AI in marketing and sales. According to Shankar (2018), although these issues necessitate massive technical advancements, AI can be considered to bring evolutionary benefits in the short term, but they will be large and revolutionary in the long run.

2.3 AI and Marketing: The Case of Netflix (Verganti, Vendraminelli, & Iansiti, 2020)

By using the power of big data and AI, Netflix has radically altered the media environment. Netflix's core is data, which is consumer input and an AI-centric operational model. AI is aided by software infrastructure that collects data and applies algorithms that aid in the preparation of content and the recommendation of information to clients. It is used at every level, from personalizing the user experience to picking winning movie themes for their next development. Netflix began deploying AI algorithms to enhance its search engine for user suggestions as early as 2010. Netflix broadened their strategy in 2014, spending much in studying user behavior and delivering a customized viewing experience for each customer. As user interfaces change from one user to the next, the screens of the program that the user sees today are developed in real time by AI. Many looks and content are originally determined by human designers, but selections on which films to show and how to show them, as well as other design decisions, are made by algorithms integrated in AI software.

When it comes to interface design and AI outputs, there are several fundamental issues that most AI systems attempt to tackle by predicting the outcome. Algorithms are the tools used to make this prediction. AI may incorporate a wide range of algorithms, some of which include an automatic update and optimization process. Netflix's algorithms, for example, dynamically adapt its user interface based on the user's real activity. While the number of applications has increased dramatically in the last decade, the fundamentals of algorithm design have been present for a long time. Existing neural networks were created in the 1960s and are just now being widely utilized with production-ready outputs. Most Netflix's production-ready AI systems employ one of three main techniques to creating accurate predictions based on statistical models, often known as ML.

When Netflix learned that its viewers had a wide range of likes and preferences, the Netflix team determined that each user should be provided with a user experience that is tailored to them. By displaying the covers of movies and television shows that he has already viewed. This system recommends movies that a person would like to see. The Netflix team had to determine which movie the user had viewed and then which artwork to mix with that movie to boost user match and recommendation. Designing artwork for each individual user based on their preferences would be difficult without AI due to differences in cinematic interests. Initially, Netflix organizes the movies at random and presents them to the user at random. Netflix then uses algorithms to provide a specific user a big number of recommendations depending on what they have already seen. Netflix suggestions, which are based on AI, continue to improve over time.

Netflix's first business premise, two decades ago, was to mail DVDs to consumers. Netflix could track the titles customers viewed and how long they remained on DVD via postal services, but they couldn't track actual viewing behavior. Although Netflix was previously aware of the need of leveraging data to improve consumer experience, their prior working concept limited its capacity to innovate. However, when Netflix put its services on its internet in 2007, it saw a chance to alter its operating model into an AI-enabled one. Netflix can trace the whole user experience down to the smallest detail from its website. For example, they may detect when viewers pause, rewind, or skip a certain scene or gadget. This enabled the development of various algorithms that dramatically increased Netflix's competitiveness. As a result of its early use of AI, Netflix is now one of the most powerful businesses in the film and television industries.

2.4 Customer Behavior and AI

When new technologies are brought into a service and interact with clients, it is normal to expect that their behavior will alter, which is the case with AI. Many customers have a negative perception of AI, which is an impediment to its implementation in marketing. This negative perception stems from consumers' beliefs that AI is incapable of emotion, that AI lacks empathy and the ability to share sentiments, and that AI is unable to recognize the customer's needs if they are not explicitly stated (Longoni, Bonezzi, & Morewedge, 2019). Many clients expect the vendor to grasp their wants and what they desire indirectly, as by changing the tone of voice while denying those things, which requires an advanced, complex AI system. One of the most recognizable applications of AI is its incorporation into robots, and as a result – as stated by Wirtz et al. (2018) – robots can play important roles in the lives of customers, as it is possible that they work to provide some services directly to customers (as a waiter in a restaurant, for example), babysitters, or alternatives to pets. This, however, would be impossible to do without putting some emotion into this intellect.

AI will also confront difficulties if client behavior changes. For example, if a customer's feeding pattern changes for a health system, AI may suggest foods based on the customer's previous history, or if the customer changes his sleep pattern to sleep early instead of staying up late, this affects the smartphone's suggestions for late-night activities based on the previous sleep pattern. Customers may be dissatisfied because of this disagreement. Customers may perceive AI as eroding their decision-making independence if AI can more consistently anticipate their preferences. Because it is based on the data that the consumer has previously searched for, AI improves the process of marketing relevant items that the customer demands. And this allows the consumer to see the things he or she is looking for faster and more easily. However, there is some selectivity in product display. The qualities of the items that are supplied may not be compatible with the consumer's invisible desires or offer him things that are not the best or that the customer can attain better products independently of AI. As a result, some buyers choose to search for their own goods without regard to what the AI system suggests (André et al., 2018).

It should be emphasized that there is a widespread worry that people will lose human connection if they build ties with robots utilizing AI. Some advancements in robot technology appear promising in this area since they can adopt diverse personalities and present various expressions. However, such robots might be considered to hurt society by increasing social isolation, limiting marriages, or diminishing social activities and connections, which is especially relevant for nations such as the Arab world, where communal communication is an intrinsic element of Arab culture.

2.5 AI and Ethical Issues

With the proliferation of AI at all levels and applications, data privacy, decision bias, and ethical difficulties are some of the ethical and legal challenges that must be addressed, where marketing firms should take it into account while building their marketing strategy. When marketers integrate AI with large amounts of client data, it means that businesses have a wealth of knowledge about their customers. Customers get worried because of the loss of their privacy. Privacy is a concern in today's contemporary technological environment for a variety of reasons, including the low cost of storage, which means that data may be present for much longer than intended. Furthermore, the amount of data acquired is significant and forms a big part of the consumer's lifestyle, and data may be recollected and repurposed. Data on a specific individual may contain information about other people or things that the consumer does not want to expose for reasons other than those for which it was created (Martin & Murphy, 2016). As a result, developing a data privacy strategy necessitates balancing two vital aspects of the business: privacy and successful marketing, which offers a significant difficulty. Large-scale data collection may result in more successful marketing, but at the expense of user privacy. On the other side, the limited amount of information collected allows the user more privacy, but also limits the capacity of AI to sell effectively.

Views differ on who is responsible for managing data privacy: internal marketing company policies with authorization for individuals to control the sharing of their information, or legal regulations that ensure the privacy of consumer data. This discrepancy is the outcome of cultural differences between people. People have different ideas about what privacy is and what it entails. In China, for example, there is an openness to data sharing and little restrictions on privacy because of cultural foundations that allow for this (Davenport et al., 2019). However, the Chinese experience cannot be applied to the rest of the world. Because, as previously stated, Arab culture places a high value on privacy. Furthermore, discussing one's religious background might help to determine the extent of privacy that can be shared with others.

As a result of the foregoing, there is a need for better insight and clarifications to acknowledge and address the concerns of individuals sharing their privacy at a time when a massive amount of data is being collected, and we also need to know how to manage data privacy failures such as information leakage through third-party hacking. Apple and other rivals in smartphones industry, for example, are integrating software in their smartphones that helps with health and exercise routines, suggests entertainment places based on prior journeys, and uses smart face ID recognition to unlock the device and other applications. Although it aids in guiding individuals, customers are concerned that firms would have access to data captured through these applications, which they may use or even sell to third parties. The concern is, does this suggest that people's privacy has been compromised? The records in these applications might be referred to by governmental authorities or accessed unlawfully by hackers. Such concerns point to future study subjects.

Customers themselves must balance privacy concerns with the benefits of tailored recommendations and offers. It is up to customers to strike a balance between the two issues in order to achieve the greatest benefit with the least amount of harm, especially when considering individual, social, and cultural differences, as well as situational variables that may influence their choices, as well as individuals' trust in the marketed company (Dirican, 2015). Bias is another ethical concern generated by algorithms in AI. It is conceivable that the output of the algorithms has an unintended bias as a result of programming for certain conditions. For example, Amazon had a difficulty with the usage of AI in one of its tools for filtering job prospects, which revealed a form of prejudice against the female category, forcing Amazon to withdraw this AI-based tool. This prejudice may be explained by the fact that algorithms, in addition to their dependence on historical data, employ unique situations, the majority of which are men-specific, which led to the formation of this problem (Davenport et al., 2019).

Due to the technological complexity of AI, it is impossible to identify the particular aspects that these algorithms take into account. Although it may arise on certain illuminations, it is unexpected since it seeks to evolve and learn on its own depending on prior inputs. AI bias research is important because AI aims to analyze details, link them, and reach a conclusion, which the human mind may not be able to do, but on the other hand, AI will deal with things that humans may consider to be red lines, such as attempting to link gender to a particular problem or a particular religion with a particular problem. On the commercial side, an illustrative example is that AI proposes a lower insurance amount for automobiles driven by males and a higher cost for cars driven by women because men have a lower accident rate than women. Another example is when a product or service is suggested to an individual based on the residential area in which he resides, but it does not correspond to what he wishes. For example, a movie may be recommended to a person on a digital platform based on the fact that many individuals in the same region have viewed the movie, which the individual may not desire.

It is critical that AI developers handle these ethical concerns. True, data privacy is important to a company's marketing plan, but there are ethical considerations that should not be neglected. Companies should research people's cultural background and distinctions, as well as have an ethical side, so that this privacy is not limited by written rules and regulations. Despite this, AI is still vulnerable to misuse, even by customers. What if people use data sharing apps to snoop on their friends or family, for example? It should be stated here that the use of AI is the duty of society, as well as the obligation of the state as represented by the government, businesses, and people.

2.6 The Future of AI Marketing

Organizations that create and use AI marketing appear to have a bright future in terms of gaining a competitive edge. The AI will go beyond merely making suggestions and displaying adverts based on your previous surfing activity. Rather, it will be a combination of forecasting the consumer's desire, touching the customer's sentiments, assessing the sensations, and communicating with the customer for marketing purposes. Since Amazon developed AI algorithms two decades ago to suggest products that customers want that they would not have found on their own, the algorithms have spread and been developed by companies like Google and have been adapted, modified, and developed to overcome their problems (Calabretta & Kleinsmann, 2017; More, 2023). However, there is still a lot of potential and a bright future for firms to create AI so that customer interactions are more realistic and bring delight to consumers' faces. As a result, a robot conversation becomes like a friend chat (Alshami, Mamun, Ahmed, & Rashid, 2021; Mathew, Brintha, & Jappes, 2023).

Marketers will gain from employing AI approaches in the future for the following benefits (Dimitrieska, Stankovska, & Efremova, 2018):

- Smarter and more complex search engines as technological solutions become more realistic and precise. It is true that the public has gotten more intelligent and particular in their needs, making them more difficult to fulfill. However, because to social media and quick search engines like Google, as well as their integration (for example, Google owns Facebook, YouTube, and many other platforms), users may locate what they need in a relatively short period by exchanging information between platforms. AI and big data can assess these research models and assist marketers in identifying the important areas on which they should focus their efforts, whether by employing AI marketing holistically or by relying on human assistance for decision-making.
- AI will create smarter marketing, as marketers strive to entice consumers with various adverts on social media today, but with AI, they will be able to do so faster and more efficiently. Online advertising will become smarter and more successful by gathering big data in databases and evaluating it with AI. AI may sift through data, social networks, personal files, and other internet information to discover solutions that a customer may not have considered.
- Before delivering solutions to the consumer, the AI will filter and evaluate the material. As a result of the use of AI, marketers' level of targeting to customers will be moved to a completely different level; by analyzing the target consumers more extensively, marketers will be able to understand the combination of demographic and individual characteristics of consumers on an individual basis more accurately. As a consequence, marketers will be able to leverage AI on two levels: recognizing actual consumers who are interested in a product or service and assisting in the delivery of the most appropriate solutions to their interests. This is accomplished through the use of big data, ML, and the combination of the two.

- Consumer care and retention is another area where AI can play a major role in the future, therefore reliance on robots will grow. AI robots will carry out duties such as communication, follow-up, seeking service feedback, and other direct interactions with customers. Companies that use this strategy will free up time for employees to accomplish more essential tasks, decrease employee stress, and save money for the organization. AI bots will get comprehensive access to the internet, databases, information, and search history in order to become more efficient than humans.
- AI will constantly learn to unearth hidden data, process, evaluate, and integrate it in order to produce new promotions and route them to the most appropriate clients. AI solutions will grow smarter, more efficient, and improve real-time decision-making over time.

3. Conclusion

AI in marketing is a successful bet if businesses are ready to take it seriously and include it into a comprehensive digital marketing and sales strategy. Although AI is still not perfect today, it really is just going to become better. With big data, ML, and optimal solutions, AI is already altering the corporate IT environment. Companies are modifying their business practices to become more reactive, efficient, and competitive. New marketing opportunities have always arisen as a result of technological advancements. As social media offered a new age of mass advertising and reach, and smartphones brought a new degree of targeting and context, AI will transform how humans communicate with media, technologies, companies, and services. AI is defined in this chapter as a branch of computer science concerned with constructing intelligent systems capable of thinking and responding in the same manner as humans do. The goal of AI is to make robots as intelligent or capable of solving problems as humans are. ML may be viewed as a novel approach to developing problem-solving systems and providing solutions in order to obtain a competitive edge. Previously, programmers created software that produced specific results depending on scenarios that were envisaged and designed in advance. However, ML is designed to enable the system to learn without the need to program it with a rigid set of rules, which restricts its potential.

Modern marketing and AI have a tight interaction. AI marketing, on the other hand, is one of the most recent data-driven marketing methods to sweep the digital world. AI enables marketers to create highly tailored experiences for customers at a fraction of the expense of traditional campaigns that can cost thousands of dollars. Many businesses have used AI to improve the customer experience. The Netflix experience is given as a real-world example in this study report. Netflix has an AI algorithm that compares the viewership of a certain work in different countries. For example, if the action is anticipated to perform well in Saudi Arabia, Netflix may not only increase its marketing efforts in the country, but it may also direct translations and dubbing to suit the Saudi audience. Because AI algorithm outputs are frequently reviewed by Netflix experts,

Netflix can keep track of the accuracy and quality of their marketing efforts. As a result, AI on Netflix has increased the company's marketing efforts, propelling it to the top of the market. Human acceptance of AI is a huge barrier, even though AI improves the lives of individuals and companies and increases employee productivity. However, some clients dislike working with AI because it lacks feeling and emotion. In this regard, AI is still lacking. However, owing to technology advancement, AI may be claimed to assist comprehend the markets and customers better and faster, which has a good impact on individuals. Marketers will be able to do what matters most using AI.

When using AI, there are several ethical considerations to consider, such as bias and privacy because these moral concerns have both legal and, more crucially, human aspects. In terms of bias, even if the intelligent system and the system that uses AI connect and conclude based on the input, and the result is based on relationships proven by AI, there is a philosophical debate about whether these reasons are valuable and reliable. It is illogical to relate the fate of humanity to the decisions of robots. This chapter also highlighted the future of AI marketing, as incorporating AI into marketing processes will provide marketers with deeper and actionable insights, as well as the ability to precisely forecast results. By incorporating AI into content marketing, marketers will be able to focus on higher value duties that effect business performance while AI software does lower value, repetitive tasks.

This chapter contributes to encouraging organizations to swiftly implement marketing strategies based on AI in order to gain a competitive advantage. The sooner they are used, the sooner they can gain from it and help them survive in today's competitive market climate. On the theoretical side, this study contributes to the existing literature by providing a review of the gathering and analyzing of concerns highlighted by AI marketing in the existing literature. Furthermore, this study addressed difficulties and questions about the capacity of AI to develop and issues that need to be improved to be more effective, and developers should take these into account and construct algorithms that solve these issues. The arguments highlighted centered on the requirement that AI be built on self-learning and ML so that it can improve itself, taking into consideration that this intelligence exhibits some emotions and sentiments for people. Ethical questions were raised that should be considered, debated, and cultural variations examined. These are the topics that should serve as the foundation for future research. The limitation of this chapter is that it is limited to studies published in the literature. The research can be expanded by studying the impact of marketing using AI in an empirical study.

References

Alshami, S., Mamun, A., Ahmed, E., & Rashid, N. (2021). Artificial intelligent towards hotels' competitive advantage: An exploratory study from the UAE. *Foresight*. doi:10.1108/FS-01-2021-0014

André, Q., Carmon, Z., Wertenbroch, K., Crum, A., Frank, D., & Goldstein, W. (2018). Consumer choice and autonomy in the age of artificial intelligence and big data. *Customer Needs and Solutions*, *5*(1), 28–37. doi:10.1007/s40547-017-0085-8

Calabretta, G., & Kleinsmann, M. (2017). Technology-driven evolution of design practices: Envisioning the role of design in the digital era. *Journal of Marketing Management*, *33*(3), 292–304. doi:10.1080/0267257X.2017.1284436

Davenport, T., Guha, A., Grewal, D., & Bressgott, T. (2019). How artificial intelligence will change the future of marketing. *Journal of the Academy of Marketing Science*, *48*(1), 24–42. doi:10.1007/s11747-019-00696-0

Dimitrieska, S., Stankovska, A., & Efremova, T. (2018). Artificial intelligence and marketing. *Entrepreneurship*, *6*(2), 298–304.

Dirican, C. (2015). The impacts of robotics, artificial intelligence on business and economics. *Procedia – Social and Behavioral Sciences*, *195*(1), 564–573. doi:10.1016/j.sbspro.2015.06.134

Kumar, M. (2016). An incorporation of artificial intelligence capabilities in cloud computing. *International Journal of Engineering and Computer Science*, *5*(11), 19070–19073. doi:10.18535/ijecs/v5i11.63

Longoni, C., Bonezzi, A., & Morewedge, C. (2019). Resistance to medical artificial intelligence. *Journal of Consumer Research*, *46*(4), 629–650. doi:10.1093/jcr/ucz013

Lu, H., Li, Y., Chen, M., Kim, H., & Serikawa, S. (2017). Brain intelligence: Go beyond artificial intelligence. *Mobile Networks and Applications*, *23*(2), 368–375. doi:10.1007/s11036-017-0932-8

Martin, K. D., & Murphy, P. E. (2016). The role of data privacy in marketing. *Journal of the Academy of Marketing Science*, *45*(2), 135–155. doi:10.1007/s11747-016-0495-4

Mathew, D., Brintha, N. C., & Jappes, J. T. W. (2023). Artificial Intelligence Powered Automation for Industry 4.0. In A. Nayyar, M. Naved, & R. Rameshwar (Eds.), *New Horizons for Industry 4.0 in Modern Business. Contributions to Environmental Sciences & Innovative Business Technology*. Cham: Springer. doi:10.1007/978-3-031-20443-2_1

More, A. B. (2023). Implementing Digital Age Experience Marketing to Make Customer Relations More Sustainable. In A. Nayyar, M. Naved, & R. Rameshwar (Eds.), *New Horizons for Industry 4.0 in Modern Business. Contributions to Environmental Sciences & Innovative Business Technology*. Cham: Springer. doi:10.1007/978-3-031-20443-2_5

Shankar, V. (2018). How artificial intelligence (AI) is reshaping retailing. *Journal of Retailing*, *94*(4), vi–xi. doi:10.1016/S0022-4359(18)30076-9

Thiraviyam, T. (2018). Artificial intelligence marketing. *International Journal of Recent Research Aspects*, *5*(1), 449–452.

Verganti, R., Vendraminelli, L., & Iansiti, M. (2020). Innovation and design in the age of artificial intelligence. *Journal of Product Innovation Management*, *37*(1), 212–227. doi:10.1111/jpim.12523

Villaronga, E. F., Kieseberg, P., & Li, T. (2018). Humans forget, machines remember: Artificial intelligence and the right to be forgotten. *Computer Law & Security Review*, *34*(2), 304–313. doi:10.1016/j.clsr.2017.08.007

Wirtz, J., Patterson, P. G., Kunz, W. H., Gruber, T., Lu, V. N., Paluch, S., & Martins, A. (2018). Brave new world: Service robots in the frontline. *Journal of Service Management*, *29*(5), 907–931. doi:10.1108/JOSM-04-2018-0119

Chapter 2

Digital Resources and Social Skills Development for Credit Analysts in Banks Focused on Green Finance

Nilda Barrutia-Montoya[a], *Huber Rodriguez-Nomura*[b], *Jaheer Mukthar K. P*[c], *Jose Rodriguez-Kong*[b] *and Abraham Jose García-Yovera*[b]

[a]Universidad Cesar Vallejo, Peru
[b]Universidad Señor de Sipán, Peru
[c]Kristu Jayanti College, Autonomous, India

Abstract

To predict the future of the business and implement successful changes, a credit analyst must make quick decisions about the economics and assets of their clients. Because the marketplace is constantly changing, companies that lack the interpersonal skills necessary to communicate with their customers run the risk of falling behind the competition and becoming obsolete. The objective of this research was to assess whether credit analysts in Peruvian banks that used digital resources also improved their communication and interpersonal skills. The study was quantitative in nature, with an applied and correlational design that lacked an experimental component. The sample consisted of 109 credit analysts from four different Peruvian banks (Interbank, Scotiabank, BBVA, and BCP). Two questionnaires were used in this survey; both were submitted to expert review for validation before being submitted for use, and their reliability was determined using Cronbach's alpha. In terms of use of digital resources (59.5%) and mastery of interpersonal skills (61.3%), credit analysts were at the average. Conclusions the *p*-value for the correlation between credit analysts' use of digital resources and their soft skills in Peruvian banks was less than 0.05, indicating a direct and strong link between these two factors. The Rho correlation coefficient was 0.738.

Technological Innovations for Business, Education and Sustainability, 17–27

doi:10.1108/978-1-83753-106-620241002

Keywords: Soft skills; initiative; digital resources; teamwork; green finance; sustainability

1. Introduction

The fight against climate change has become one of the most pressing issues of the modern era and of the 21st century. All major international organizations have climate change on their agendas as a top priority (Molina, 2019). The last G20 conference, held in Rome at the end of October, focused heavily on combating climate change. (The G20 countries are responsible for 80% of global GDP and 80% of greenhouse gas emissions.) They agreed to work together to keep global warming below 1.5°C above preindustrial levels, recognizing that achieving this goal will require significant and effective commitments and actions by all governments.

Sustainable finance, of which green finance is a subset, also takes into account ethical and social considerations in addition to environmental ones. In many contexts, environmental and social–ethical concerns are inextricably intertwined. Green finance and sustainable finance are defined and distinguished in this research (Marques, De Oliveira, Medeiros, Ferrando, & González, 2020). It is also essential to understand the history of the climate change movement, the Kyoto Protocol, the Paris Agreement, and the 2030 targets. In addition, "green bonds," one of the most significant financial vehicles used in green finance today, will be dissected for study. They represent a new type of investment security. In essence, they are bonds issued to support initiatives that improve environmental or climate conditions. Those wishing to direct their capital toward environmentally responsible investments can do so more easily thanks to a newly created class of securities. It also allows bonds to be compared with each other and with their environment in terms of environmental effect and valuation. In this research, I examine Green Bonds and their potential as a tool for financing sustainable investments (Galarza, Fossati, & Romo, 2021).

Especially in developed countries, everyday life has been revolutionized by the widespread availability of high-quality digital information. Access to data is crucial for the growth of various industries, such as health care, business, and education (Zapata-Sevilla, 2022). However, the greatest influence of digital technology is in alleviating poverty and improving health care and education worldwide (Castro & Cortés, 2022). The increased deployment of technology in the financial industry has led to improved educational opportunities and technical resources for training professionals. The introduction of new analytical methods that require the use of digital tools has modernized and expanded access to the financial system. Although the Peruvian financial sector is increasingly innovative, many institutions continue to rely on traditional and unimaginative methods (Mejía & Azar, 2021).

In this sense, the use of technology in the classroom can help foster a more inclusive and accepting work environment for people of all backgrounds. These funds allow for the development of novel strategies and methods of action that reduce the wealth gap and increase participation in a green finance system (Pérez-Caldentey & Titelman-Kardonsky, 2018; Soto, Asis, Figueroa, & Plasencia, 2023) committed to long-term sustainability. Rather than focusing solely on incorporating technological tools in the workplace, they want to adopt new methods that lead to greater long-term improvement in people's standard of living.

However, several authors have shown that digital resources can affect the performance outcomes of credit analysts, and Ríos, Pérez, Cruz, and Sánchez (2021) provide general evidence on the potential effects (positive or negative) of the availability and use of digital resources in financial sector activities. Many firms also consider soft skills training as an investment with a high potential return (Améstica-Rivas, King-Domínguez, Cornejo-Saavedra, & Romero-Romero, 2019). Credit analysts in banks would do well to work on their soft skills as many people lack them even though they are highly valued by employers. Because graduates with developed soft skills have an advantage in the hiring process and can more easily complete job responsibilities in lower management positions, financial institutions should integrate soft skills training into their training curriculum, according to the study by Guzmán-Fernández (2022).

The need for universities to instill "soft skills" in their students will only increase. University education continues to be valued for its ability to provide students with the hard skills they will need to succeed in their chosen fields, but it is increasingly clear that it is students' "soft skills" that will give them the greatest advantage in any workplace (Tualombo-Tituaña, Figueroa-Soledispa, & Moreno-Ponc, 2022). Soft skills, as defined by Álvarez-Diaz (2022), are the consequence of a person's intrinsic abilities, natural dispositions, learned information and personal values, and are manifested in their daily interactions with others. Transferable skills include those most in demand by employers, such as creativity, collaboration, communication skills, ethics, and time management. A person's ability to perform a particular job is proportional to their competence in that job. They are difficult enough that only people with exceptional skill and talent are able to perform them successfully (Castillo, Fernández, Camones, & Guerra, 2022; Pérez-Gómez, Borrero, & Pertúz, 2020).

This study builds on the work of researchers such as Zepeda-Hurtado, Cardoso, and Cortés (2019), whose study sought to demonstrate the connection between digital competencies and soft skills in university teachers, providing a basis for the present research. Credit analysts in health sciences and engineering were found to have the highest levels of digital competencies and soft skills (including the ability to make decisions and be aggressive) in research with 555 participants. Credit analysts' technological competence was shown to be correlated with their social competence at a level of $r = 0.681$. On the other hand, Pérez and Soto-Ortigoza (2021) investigated the relationship between bank workers' social skills and their independence in learning. The approaches used had positive effects, such as higher rates of self-directed learning and higher social competence among staff in the banking sector. This result is stable at the 5% significance level. Consequently, it improves the banking sector and helps students prepare for their future. It also provides data that can be used to influence educational policy so that emphasis is placed on helping children learn to manage their emotions in a way that does not interfere with their academic or social development.

Additionally, Lozano, Lozano, and Ortega (2022) analyzed how employees of municipal savings banks fared when assessed on their ability to study on their own. The sample size was 90 credit analysts, and the results showed that municipal savings bank employees had a positive relationship between soft skills and self-learning. A moderately significant association was found (rho $= 0.390, p = 0.000, p = 0.05$). On the other hand, Tsirkas, Chytiri, and Bouranta (2020) studied the effect of co-operative education in the working population of Lima, finding that it led to increased competence in both hard and soft skills. This study of 73 graduate credit analysts in health sciences found that 82% of respondents showed a high level of soft skills and 77% achieved a high level of collaborative learning. There is a substantial positive correlation (0.780), implying that students' gains in soft skills correspond to the intensity with which they engage in collaborative learning.

Collaborative learning and soft skills of bank credit analysts are the focus of the final research study by Singh and Jaykumar (2019). The sample size was 80 credit analysts. Soft skills and collaborative learning were shown to be correlated with a p-value below the 0.05 level of significance. Overall, the variables in the analysis had a fairly positive correlation ($r = 0.470$) according to Spearman's Rho. In light of the above, the main objective of this research is to investigate how credit analysts in Peruvian banks could use digital tools to improve their professional skills, particularly their interpersonal communication. The objectives were threefold: (1) to investigate the correlation between technological infrastructure and the development of credit analysts' interpersonal skills in Peruvian banks. It was postulated that credit analysts in a Peruvian bank can employ digital technologies to help them develop their interpersonal skills.

2. Materials and Methods

This study did not use an experimental design, as no efforts were made to manipulate the findings (Hernández & Mendoza, 2018). This work is considered "seminal," as its main purpose is to further our understanding of the underlying mechanisms at play (Ñaupas, Palacios, Valdivia, & Romero, 2018). Because its main purpose was to establish a link between the two variables, the study can also be classified as a correlational analysis.

One hundred nine credit specialists from four large Peruvian banks (Interbank, Scotiabank, BBVA, and BCP) participated in the study. Since the questionnaire served as both a research strategy and an instrument, it was necessary to create a question for each of the two variables. The 15-question, five-choice survey on the application of digital resources was developed taking into account technology, infrastructure, and technological equipment. It is assumed that 1 is never, 2 is rarely, 3 is occasionally, 4 is frequently, and 5 is always. Twenty five items measuring self-confidence, assertiveness in conversation, initiative, teamwork, and flexibility make up the five response options of the soft skills questionnaire. 1 represents "never," 2 "rarely," 3 "sometimes," 4 "often," and 5 "always."

To confirm the validity of the instruments, a validation method was applied in which three experts assessed the surveys based on criteria such as relevance, pertinence, and clarity. As both surveys were found to be credible by the expert panel, it was concluded that the study's data collection methods were effective. The instruments were assessed for consistency using Cronbach's alpha using SPSS. High levels of reliability (0.872 and 0.796, respectively) were identified for both the digital resource use survey and the social skills assessment.

3. Results

To achieve the objectives of the study, we first analyzed the demographics of the sample. The bulk of the 109 credit analysts who participated in the survey were male 55.2%, with women accounting for only 44.8%. The ages of the credit analysts surveyed show that 57.0% are between 24 and 27 years old, 19.3% are between 28 and 31 years old, 14.0% are between 32 and 35 years old, and 9.7% are 36 years old or older. This suggests that the majority of respondents are between 24 and 27 years old. According to the data, 59.3% of credit analysts have a bachelor's degree, while 25.7% have a professional degree, and 15.0% are graduate students.

Fig. 2.1 shows the descriptive results relating to the dimensions of the digital resource use variable; for example, in the software availability dimension, 46.7% of respondents indicated a moderate level, 24.9% reported a low level, and 28.4% indicated a high level; this indicates that credit analysts have the ability to

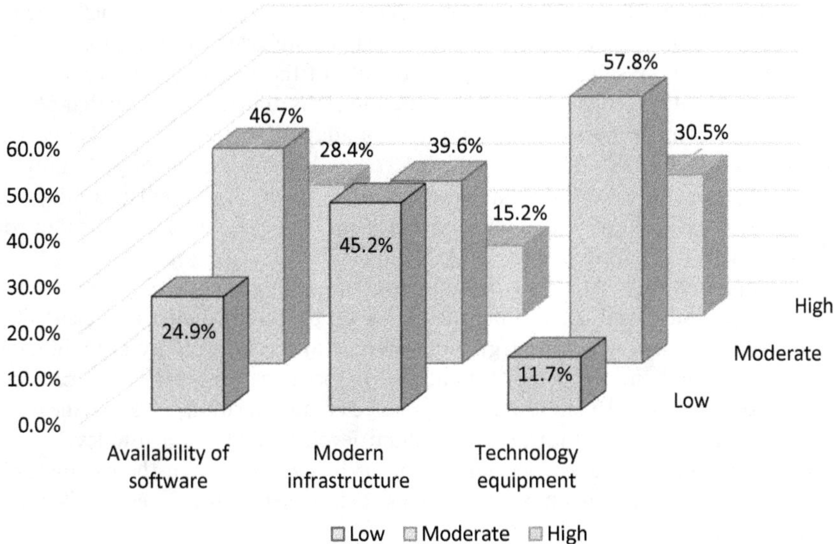

Fig. 2.1. Levels of Digital Resources. *Source:* Authors' work.

effectively use technological resources during the learning process, including software programs. They may, therefore, be able to put these resources to use in a wide range of academic contexts, from research to making presentations or interacting with colleagues and superiors.

Low levels predominated in the contemporary infrastructure component, with 39.6% of credit analysts reporting a moderate level, 45.2% reporting a low level, and 15.2% reporting a high level. According to these results, credit analysts have access to technological tools such as computers, mobile devices, and the internet, although they may experience difficulties with the accessibility and reliability of these tools. Credit analysts may have restricted access to technology if they do not have access to their own device or must share it with other family members. Internet connectivity problems may also prevent businesses from making full use of digital resources for customer service.

Credit analysts have access to technological devices and equipment such as computers, tablets, and mobile phones, but may not have access to more advanced or specialized equipment, with 57.8% of respondents indicating a moderate level, 11.7% indicating a low level and 30.5% indicating a high level. Credit analysts' access to quality technological tools may determine the extent to which they are able to use digital resources in their work. Therefore, a moderate level on this dimension indicates that credit analysts are able to use technological tools, although they may need more help to use more sophisticated or specialized tools.

In terms of their competence with a range of digital resources, the majority of credit analysts, 59.5% performed at a moderate level, while 27.4% performed at a low level, and 13.1% at a high level. These results suggest that credit analysts are proficient in the use of a variety of common computer applications and online communication tools, including email, social networking, and video conferencing sites. Credit analysts must be able to search for relevant information on the internet, filter the results, and assess the quality of the material they discover.

The descriptive results in Fig. 2.2 for the soft skills dimensions show that 56.8% of the respondents reported a medium level of adaptability, while 23.3% reported a low level, and 19.9% obtained a high level, with a medium level prevailing in this dimension; this suggests that credit analysts have some ability to adapt to changing situations and make effective decisions, but that there is still room for improvement in their ability to be flexible.

The majority (49.6%) have a medium level of initiative, while only 15.2% have a low level, and 35.2% have a high level. Based on these results, it is clear that credit analysts have a certain degree of initiative and responsibility but still have room for growth in terms of their ability to organize and carry out projects independently. Similarly, in terms of aggressive communication, 50.5% achieved a high level, while 37.8% indicated a medium level, and 11.7% a low level. This suggests that credit analysts are competent at being assertive in their communications, but may need to improve in areas such as articulating clearly, listening carefully, and mediating disagreements.

Similarly, in terms of collaboration, 43.1% rated a high level, 17.7% a medium level, and 39.2% a low level. These results suggest that credit analysts possess

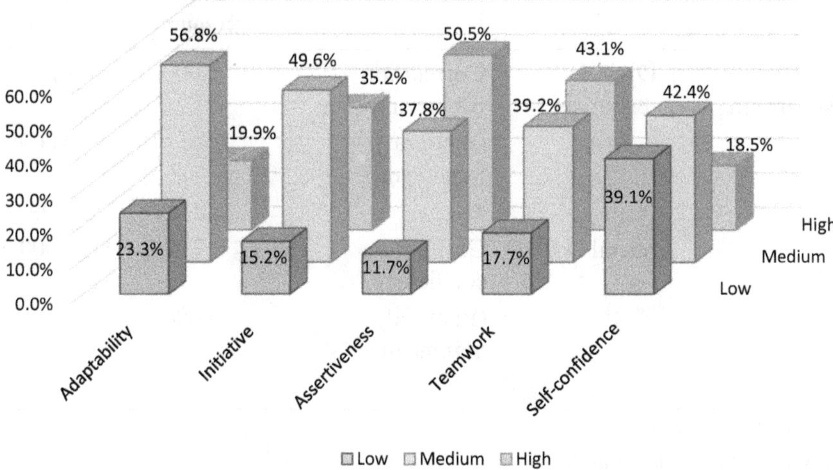

Fig. 2.2. Levels of Social Skills. *Source:* Authors' work.

above average teamwork skills, with room for development in areas such as communication, commitment to team goals, collaboration, and conflict resolution. Finally, self-confidence was the most popular response, with 42.4% indicating a medium level, 39.1% a low level, and 18.5% a high level. These results suggest that credit analysts have some self-confidence, but could benefit from honing their decision-making and problem-solving skills.

Descriptive analysis revealed that 61.3% of respondents indicated a medium level of soft skills, 21.9% a low level, and 16.8% a high level, with the medium level dominating the variable. These results suggest that credit analysts have room for improvement in their social and emotional skills and would benefit from specific programs and activities designed to foster such growth.

3.1 Inferential Results

The Kolmogorov–Smirnov test was used to check for normality and to be able to test hypotheses. If the sample has more than 50 components, this test can be applied to check whether the data follow a normal distribution. Therefore, a decision criterion was applied to determine that the null hypothesis should be rejected if the *p*-value is less than 0.05.

Spearman's correlation coefficient (Rho) was used to test the general hypothesis, the results of which are shown in Table 2.1. The acceptance of the HG was based on the criterion of a *p*-value of less than 0.05, which meant that the general hypothesis was rejected. As for the general hypothesis, a Spearman correlation coefficient (Rho) of 0.738 was found, suggesting a strong positive

Table 2.1. Hypothesis Testing of the Study.

			Digital Resources	**Social Skills**
Rho de Spearman	Digital resources	Correlation coefficient	1.000	0.738[a]
		(Bilateral) Significance		0.000
		N	109	109
	Social skills	Correlation coefficient	0.738[a]	1.000
		(Bilateral) Significance	0.000	
		N	109	109

Source: Authors' work.

[a]Correlation is significant at the 0.01 level (bilateral).

relationship between the use of digital resources by credit analysts in a Peruvian bank and the improvement of their soft skills. Also, the *p*-value was calculated to be 0.000, which means that the results obtained are statistically significant (because 0.000 is less than 0.05).

4. Discussion

Peruvian bank credit analysts who make intensive use of digital technologies also tend to have strong social skills, according to the results obtained in relation to the general premise. The *p*-value of 0.000 is strong evidence of this. Furthermore, the Rho correlation coefficient between the two variables was 0.738, showing a direct and strong association between them. Similarly, the descriptive data show that medium levels of both digital resource use (60.53%) and social competence (66.67%) predominate. In addition, moderate and medium levels predominated over low levels in all aspects of both variables.

Similarly, in the three objective hypotheses, we found that there is a direct and significant association between the characteristics of credit analysts' use of digital resources and their social skills in Peruvian banks (*p* 0.05). These findings are consistent with those of Soto, Avalos, Albornoz, and Aguilar (2022), who found a direct correlation between the digital competence of the recommended credit analysts and their soft skills with $r = 0.521$. They also agree with the findings of Ramirez et al. (2022), whose analysis revealed a positive correlation (Rho = 0.523) between the variables studied, demonstrating that the strategies adopted helped the credit analysts to grow both personally and professionally.

The findings of Saehu, Diah, Julca-Guerrero, Huerta-Soto, and Valderrama-Plasencia (2022) that credit analysts' soft skills correlate with their ability to work independently are consistent with these results. The results indicated a considerable and statistically significant association (rho = 0.390, p = 0.000 [p = 0.05]). In contrast, Huerta-Soto et al. (2023) found that a large percentage of their respondents (82%) also reported high levels of social skills and that a comparable percentage (77% of respondents) also achieved a high percentage (86%) of collaborative work. In summary, there is a strong positive connection (0.780), meaning that the effective implementation of collaborative work is positively correlated with higher soft skills development. There is a moderate positive correlation between the variables studied with a Spearman's Rho of 0.470, which is consistent with the findings of Huerta-Soto, Huaranga Toledo, Anaya Lopez, and Concepción Lázaro (2022), who found a relationship between social skills and collaborative performance when the p-value obtained was below the established significance level of 0.05.

5. Conclusion

A p-value of 0.000 was found, demonstrating a statistically significant association between credit analysts' use of digital resources and their improvement in soft skills in a Peruvian bank. Furthermore, rho was 0.738, demonstrating a direct and substantial link between the two variables. As a result, it is safe to assume that credit analysts' interpersonal competence will increase along with their computer skills.

The results show that credit analysts who use digital resources more frequently are more likely to improve their "soft skills," which include aspects such as their ability to communicate effectively, relate well with people, solve problems creatively, and so on. Educators and institutions could use these data to create programs to enhance the soft skills of credit analysts through the strategic application of digital resources. It is vital to remember that there are other factors that influence the development of soft skills, despite the strong link between the use of digital resources and the improvement of interpersonal competence. Therefore, it is suggested that banks use measures to improve credit analysts' interpersonal skills, such as communication, teamwork, problem-solving, empathy, and creativity.

Further studies are recommended to acquire a more comprehensive and detailed perspective on the relationship between the use of digital resources and soft skills in credit analysts in the financial system, taking into account the different institutions in the financial system, managers, and unit heads.

References

Álvarez-Diaz, L. J. (2022). Medición de la formación de habilidades blandas en artesanos, emprendedores y microempresarios de sectores vulnerables. Estudio de caso: Núcleo de asistencia empresarial de la facultad de ciencias económicas de la universidad nacional de Asunción. *Ciencia Latina Revista Científica Multidisciplinar*, *6*(6), 8158–8166. doi:10.37811/cl_rcm.v6i6.3989

Améstica-Rivas, L., King-Domínguez, A., Cornejo-Saavedra, E., & Romero-Romero, R. (2019). Aprendizaje activo a través del uso del software Excel en asignaturas de finanzas. *Revista Iberoamericana de Tecnología en Educación y Educación en Tecnología*, (23), 72–79. doi:10.24215/18509959.23.e08

Castillo, A., Fernández, C. E., Camones, O. G., & Guerra, M. E. (2022). Digitalización de la cadena de suministro y la competitividad de las empresas peruanas del sector minorista. *Revista Científica Epistemia*, *6*(2), 77–95. doi:10.26495/re.v6i2.2297

Castro, A. M., & Cortés, C. A. (2022). *Transformación digital en las empresas: Un enfoque desde la administración de la teoría a la práctica*. Columbia, SC: Ecoe Ediciones.

Galarza, G. T., Fossati, M. M., & Romo, M. D. C. G. (2021). Nuevos retos para la gestión administrativa pública y privada: Responsabilidad social y finanzas sostenibles. *Vinculatégica EFAN*, *7*(1), 856–867. doi:10.29105/vtga7.2-17

Guzmán-Fernández, C. (2022). Educación financiera: Impacto en las finanzas de la sociedad mexicana. *Revista de Investigaciones Universidad del Quindío*, *34*(2), 117–123. doi:10.33975/riuq.vol34n2.966

Hernández, R., & Mendoza, C. (2018). *Metodología de investigación. Las rutas cuantitativa, cualitativa y mixta*. New York, NY: McGraw-Hill.

Huerta-Soto, R., Huaranga Toledo, H., Anaya Lopez, C., & Concepción Lázaro, R. (2022). Marketing de influenciadores y su efecto en la intención de compra de los consumidores de prendas ecológicas. *Revista Científica Epistemia*, *6*(2), 113–127. doi:10.26495/re.v6i2.2299

Huerta-Soto, R., Ramirez-Asis, E., Tarazona-Jiménez, J., Nivin-Vargas, L., Norabuena-Figueroa, R., Guzman-Avalos, M., & Reyes-Reyes, C. (2023). Predictable inventory management within dairy supply chain operations. *International Journal of Retail & Distribution Management*. doi:10.1108/IJRDM-01-2023-0051

Lozano, M. A., Lozano, E. N., & Ortega, M. Y. (2022). Habilidades blandas una clave para brindar educación de calidad: Revisión teórica. *Conrado*, *18*(87), 412–420. Retrieved from https://conrado.ucf.edu.cu/index.php/conrado/article/view/2544

Marques, F., De Oliveira, G., Medeiros, M. I. M., Ferrando, T., & González, C. U. (2020). Finanzas verdes y hundimiento de la regulación ambiental al servicio de la extrema derecha en Brasil. *Ecología política*, (59), 57–66. Retrieved from https://www.jstor.org/stable/26947480

Mejía, D., & Azar, K. (2021). *Políticas de inclusión financiera y las nuevas tecnologías en América Latina*. Caracas: CAF. Retrieved from https://scioteca.caf.com/handle/123456789/1755

Molina, D. (2019). Las fintech y la reinvención de las finanzas. *Oikonomics. Revista de economía, empresa y sociedad*, *10*, 22–44. Retrieved from https://oikonomics.uoc.edu/divulgacio/oikonomics/es/numero10/dossier/digual.html

Ñaupas, H., Palacios, J., Valdivia, M., & Romero, H. (2018). *Metodología de la investigación Cuantitativa Cualitativa y redacción de la tesis*. Columbia, SC: DGP Editores.

Pérez-Caldentey, E., & Titelman-Kardonsky, D. (2018). *La inclusión financiera para la inserción productiva y el papel de la banca de desarrollo*. Cepal. Retrieved from https://hdl.handle.net/11362/44213

Pérez-Gómez, L. M., Borrero, C. P., & Pertúz, M. J. (2020). Identificación de habilidades blandas en directivos Pymes de Barranquilla. *Dictamen Libre*, (26), 153–168. doi:10.18041/2619-4244/dl.26.6193

Pérez, E., & Soto-Ortigoza, M. (2021). Habilidades blandas como herramienta competitiva de la gestión inteligente en tiempos de covid-19. Caso de estudio. *Revista de Economia, 9*(2), 30–42. Retrieved from https://revistas.unachi.ac.pa/index.php/pluseconomia/article/view/500

Ramirez, E. H., Rosario, H. S., Laura, N. V., Hober, H. T., Julio, V. A., & Victor, F. L. (2022). Distribution of Public Service and Individual Job Performance in Peruvian Municipality. *20*(10), 11–17. doi:10.15722/jds.20.10.202210.11

Ríos, M., Pérez, L., Cruz, M. D. L., & Sánchez, M. D. (2022). Entrepreneurship and technological innovation: The micro-entrepreneur in Mexico. *Contaduría y Administración, 67*(3), 54–84. doi:10.22201/fca.24488410e.2022.4561

Saehu, M. S., Diah, A. M., Julca-Guerrero, F., Huerta-Soto, R., & Valderrama-Plasencia, L. (2022). Environmental awareness and environmental management practices: Mediating effect of environmental data distribution. *Journal of Environmental Management & Tourism, 13*(5), 1339–1352. doi:10.14505/jemt.v13.5(61).11

Singh, A., & Jaykumar, P. (2019). On the road to consensus: Key soft skills required for youth employment in the service sector. *Worldwide Hospitality and Tourism Themes, 11*(1), 10–24. doi:10.1108/WHATT-10-2018-0066

Soto, R. H., Asis, E. H., Figueroa, R. P., & Plasencia, L. (2023). Autoeficacia emprendedora y desempeño de micro y pequeñas empresas peruanas. *Revista Venezolana de Gerencia: RVG, 28*(102), 751–768. doi:10.52080/rvgluz.28.102.19

Soto, R. M., Avalos, M., Albornoz, J. I., & Aguilar, S. J. (2022). Competencias digitales de los profesores universitarios durante la pandemia por covid-19 en el Perú. *Revista Electrónica Interuniversitaria de Formación del Profesorado, 25*(1), 49–60. doi:10.6018/reifop.500481

Tsirkas, K., Chytiri, A. P., & Bouranta, N. (2020). The gap in soft skills perceptions: A dyadic analysis. *Education + Training, 62*(4), 357–377. doi:10.1108/ET-03-2019-0060

Tualombo-Tituaña, J. J., Figueroa-Soledispa, M. L., & Moreno-Ponce, M. R. (2022). Habilidades directivas en el manejo de las finanzas de las pequeñas y medianas empresas. Caso: Sportmancar, Manabí-Ecuador. Revista Científica FIPCAEC (Fomento de la investigación y publicación científico-técnica multidisciplinaria). ISSN: 2588-090X. *Polo de Capacitación, Investigación y Publicación (POCAIP), 7*(1), 775–786. Retrieved from https://fipcaec.com/index.php/fipcaec/article/view/549

Zapata-Sevilla, J. (2022). Las lagunas del paquete de medidas sobre finanzas digitales de la UE. Especial referencia a las infraestructuras de los mercados. *Revista de Derecho del Sistema Financiero: Mercados, operadores y contratos*, (3), 9. 259–280. doi:10.32029/2695-9569.01.09.2022

Zepeda-Hurtado, M. E., Cardoso, E. O., & Cortés, J. A. (2019). El aprendizaje orientado en proyectos para el desarrollo de habilidades blandas en el nivel medio superior del IPN. *RIDE. Revista Iberoamericana para la Investigación y el Desarrollo Educativo, 10*(19). doi:10.23913/ride.v10i19.530

Chapter 3

Digital Transformation: A Catalyst for Sustainable Business Practices

Maha Shehadeh

Applied Science Private University, Jordan

Abstract

In an era where sustainability and digital transformation are becoming indispensable pillars of successful business operations, this chapter explores the potent synergy between these two paradigms. As businesses strive to align their operations with Environmental, Social, and Governance (ESG) goals, digital transformation emerges as a powerful enabler. This chapter delves into how digital technologies are not only revolutionizing traditional business models but are also paving the way toward more sustainable practices. From data-driven decision-making to improved resource management, this chapter discusses the diverse ways in which digital transformation contributes to sustainability. It also offers an in-depth analysis of real-world case studies, illustrating how businesses have successfully integrated digital transformation in their pursuit of sustainability. Recognizing the potential roadblocks, this chapter also addresses the challenges businesses may face in this journey, including cybersecurity risks, data privacy issues, and the need for technological literacy. It further presents strategies to navigate these challenges and underscores the importance of preparedness in managing potential risks. Finally, this chapter ventures into the future of digital transformation, evaluating current trends and predictions, and their potential impact on sustainable business practices.

Keywords: Digital transformation; sustainability; sustainable business practices; Environmental, Social, and Governance (ESG) factors; cybersecurity; data privacy; technological literacy; future trends

Technological Innovations for Business, Education and Sustainability, 29–45

Published under exclusive licence by Emerald Publishing Limited
doi:10.1108/978-1-83753-106-620241003

1. Introduction

In this chapter, the discussion centers on the transformative influence of digital technologies in restructuring business operations and promoting sustainable practices. This exploration navigates through an array of topics starting from the understanding of digital transformation to its multifaceted impact on sustainability. As the discourse progresses, readers will be introduced to the challenges businesses encounter in the digital transformation journey. The narrative concludes with a forward-looking perspective on the future of sustainable business practices, made possible through digital transformation.

Digital transformation is defined as the thorough integration of digital technology into all areas of a business (Almohtaseb, Shehadeh, & Aldehayyat, 2023). This transformation alters the foundational operations of organizations, thereby changing how they deliver value to their customers (Shehadeh, Almohtaseb, Aldehayyat, & Abu-AlSondos, 2023). However, it must be noted that digital transformation extends beyond a mere technological shift. It embodies a cultural change that demands businesses to persistently question their existing operations, experiment with new methods, and adapt to novel ways of functioning. In the face of an escalating digital revolution, businesses that resist this transformation risk trailing behind their more progressive counterparts.

In recent years, the shift toward sustainability has emerged as a crucial focus for businesses across the globe (Isaksson, 2021). This change is driven by the increasing demand from stakeholders for practices that are socially responsible and environmentally friendly. Digital transformation has surfaced as a critical facilitator of these sustainable practices. With the capability to provide insights for improved resource allocation through data analytics, to increasing efficiency and reducing waste via automation, digital technologies present a suite of solutions for businesses aiming to bolster their sustainability. Digital transformation holds the potential to redefine business models and value chains, setting the stage for a future where economic profitability and sustainability coexist harmoniously.

As we journey through this chapter, these aspects will be explored in detail, providing readers with a comprehensive understanding of how digital transformation operates as a catalyst for sustainable business practices.

2. Understanding Sustainable Business Practices

2.1 Definition and Importance of Sustainable Business Practices

Building upon our introductory chapter, we delve into understanding sustainable business practices in this section. It is a term that encapsulates strategies and methodologies that companies adopt to harmonize economic growth with societal welfare and environmental conservation.

Sustainable business practices inherently encapsulate strategies and methodologies that companies adopt to harmonize economic growth with societal welfare and environmental conservation. The vision is not to achieve an idealistic harmony between nature and humans but to construct a technologically advanced, modern economy buttressed by a conscious, educated, and cautious society. These practices acknowledge the broader responsibility of businesses extending beyond economic profitability, striving to create enduring value without jeopardizing future generations' ability to cater to their own needs (Erol & Kirpik, 2022).

The urgency for sustainable business practices is accentuated by several factors. Apart from enhancing a company's image, leading to improved customer loyalty and employee satisfaction, these practices often result in operational efficiencies through waste reduction and effective resource utilization. They also attract investors who increasingly consider sustainability a significant determinant in their investment decisions (Savastano, Zentner, Spremić, & Cucari, 2022).

The evaluation of business sustainability is often conducted through Environmental, Social, and Governance (ESG) factors, offering a comprehensive approach to gauging a company's ethical impact and sustainability. The Environmental aspect scrutinizes the company's ecological footprint, including its resource use, waste management, and efforts to incorporate renewable resources into its operations (Weber-Lewerenz, 2021). The Social element assesses the company's societal impact through its labor practices, interactions with local communities, and supply chain management. Governance concentrates on the company's leadership, strategy, corporate behavior, and the transparency of its operations (Long, Feng, & Chang, 2023).

In today's context, businesses need to transition toward more sustainable models, a critical requirement given our finite natural resources, climate change, and societal challenges. The market dynamics increasingly favor companies demonstrating sustainable practices. Customers' discerning choices, regulatory bodies' stringent environmental regulations, and operational efficiencies derived from sustainable practices emphasize this transition's necessity.

The Sustainable Development Goals (SDGs) approved by the United Nations General Assembly in 2015 embody an innovative approach toward sustainability. The 2030 Agenda for Sustainable Development based on five key concepts, people, prosperity, peace, partnership, and the planet, recognizes the unsustainability of the current development model, economically, socially, and environmentally. It necessitates a systemic approach to manage the three development dimensions. With 2020 marking the decade of action to achieve these goals, industries across the board, including the port industry, are striving to be more resilient by innovating management and planning systems to address environmental risk (Leal Filho et al., 2023; Secundo, Schena, Russo, Schiavone, & Shams, 2022).

A crucial aid in transitioning toward sustainability is the digital transformation, referring to the integration of digital technology into all business areas. This transformation, however, goes beyond merely digitizing existing services and demands a complete overhaul of processes, products, and services in a digital context. The implications of digital transformation are vast, enhancing decision-making capabilities, customer experiences, efficiency, and offering opportunities to innovate (Casciani, Chkanikova, & Pal, 2022).

Digital transformation and new technologies contribute significantly to achieving sustainable business practices. By reducing emission levels and optimizing resource utilization, they encourage a shift in the business model toward sustainability. Simultaneously, they bolster corporate competitiveness and foster a positive correlation between economic growth and sustainable yield. This holds particularly true in the ship-port interface, enhancing the efficiency of sea-land supply chain operations. Thus, technological innovation serves as a tool to weave sustainability into the business model, fostering long-term value creation.

By utilizing digital transformation, businesses can not only become more resilient but can also contribute effectively to the global goals of sustainable development, eventually leading us toward a future that is both sustainable and technologically advanced.

Thus, it becomes evident that sustainable business practices play a pivotal role in today's businesses' survival and success. In the Role of ESG Factors in Business Sustainability section, we will delve deeper into the role of ESG factors in driving business sustainability.

2.2 Role of ESG Factors in Business Sustainability

Having established the importance of sustainable business practices, it is crucial to understand the role of ESG criteria in shaping these practices. ESG criteria present a tripartite approach to measuring the sustainability and ethical impact of a company.

This tripartite approach has evolved over the past two decades from a specialized reporting system for financial investors to a generic term for how businesses consider the impact of these factors on their products, staff, and broader stakeholders (Ji, Sun, Liu, & Chiu, 2023).

The environmental component goes beyond focusing on the company's ecological footprint. In today's context, it encompasses the company's strategies toward climate change, energy use, carbon emissions, conservation of natural resources, and animal welfare, among others. It is the company's proactive approach toward mitigating environmental risks while seizing opportunities to contribute positively to the planet's well-being (Gao, 2023).

The social component scrutinizes the company's business relationships, stakeholder needs, and societal impact. It is not merely about labor practices and employee health and safety but also extends to the company's interactions with local communities, human rights stance, supply chain management, commitment to product safety, and customer treatment. It illustrates the company's awareness of its broader social implications and efforts to align its operations with societal expectations and needs (Kong & Liu, 2023).

Governance involves more than the company's leadership, strategy, and corporate behavior. It now also includes the company's accounting methods, transparency, shareholders' voting rights on important issues, and management of conflicts of interest. This component is central to the company's reputation, trustworthiness, and long-term sustainability. It underscores the importance of maintaining high standards of corporate governance while showing responsibility and accountability to shareholders and other stakeholders (Wang, 2023).

Moreover, today's digital transformation and sustainability trends are increasingly converging, making ESG factors more critical in shaping business strategies and operations. Digital transformation can support businesses in making sustainable investment decisions, developing ESG data sets systematically, and providing transparency, which could yield superior results over competitors in the long run (El Hilali, El Manouar, & Idrissi, 2020; Gomez-Trujillo & Gonzalez-Perez, 2022).

The benefits of robust ESG implementation include reducing the cost of capital and business risk, enhancing shareholder value, creating opportunities for accessing long-term capital, and improving operational efficiency and corporate reputation. Furthermore, this trend is gaining traction in the financial sector and banking strategies, reflecting the rising recognition of ESG factors in shaping sustainable and resilient business models.

In today's world, where consumers are presented with abundant choices, and sustainability-minded investors are urging enterprises to address their business, social, and governance issues transparently, ESG factors are no longer optional but essential for businesses aiming for sustainable growth and resilience (Yao, Tang, Boadu, & Xie, 2022).

Hence, the rising recognition of ESG factors underscores their importance in shaping sustainable and resilient business models. The subsequent section will underscore why transitioning toward sustainable business models is a current imperative and how companies are adapting to survive in an increasingly challenging global business environment.

2.3 The Need for Businesses to Transition to More Sustainable Models

After comprehending the role of ESG factors in business sustainability, it is important to understand why transitioning to more sustainable business models is essential in the current scenario. This is due to several factors including finite natural resources, climate change, and societal challenges.

Transitioning to more sustainable business models is an imperative in the current global business environment. As we face finite natural resources, climate change, and societal challenges, companies must adapt to survive. Market dynamics are increasingly favoring businesses that demonstrate commitment to sustainable practices. Consumers are becoming more discerning, often choosing to support businesses that align with their values.

Moreover, sustainable practices can lead to operational efficiencies and cost savings. Innovations can reduce waste and improve resource management. In the energy sector, for example, renewable energy technologies are not only more sustainable but are becoming increasingly cost-effective (Gil-Gomez, Guerola-Navarro, Oltra-Badenes, & Lozano-Quilis, 2020).

Regulatory bodies worldwide are also taking action. Environmental regulations are becoming more stringent, and companies are expected to demonstrate how they are reducing their environmental impact. Those who fail to transition risk not only reputational damage and financial penalties but may also find themselves outdated in a rapidly evolving business landscape (Hajiheydari, Kargar Shouraki, Vares, & Mohammadian, 2023).

Thus, the transition to more sustainable models is not only an environmental imperative but also a strategic move to ensure long-term business success. In the upcoming sections, we will explore how digital transformation serves as a catalyst in this transition, equipping businesses with the tools they need to adapt to these emerging paradigms.

3. Role of Digital Transformation in Driving Sustainability

3.1 Understanding Digital Transformation

Digital transformation is a multifaceted concept, understood and implemented in various ways depending on the economic or organizational context. In its core, digital transformation could be perceived as a fundamental technological infusion aimed to create new paradigms in business models, systems, and processes. This reinvention fosters amplified profitability, elevates efficiency, and provides a competitive advantage. This shift is achieved through evolution and innovation in business processes and models, improving workforce efficiency and delivering individualized customer experiences.

Moreover, digital transformation symbolizes the paradigm shifts instigated by digital technologies in a business's operational blueprint. These modifications could significantly transform products, restructure organizations, and automate processes. The changes are not merely limited to strategic adjustments, but they imply a significant overhaul influencing the basic structure of a business operation (El Hilali et al., 2020).

In addition, the new generation of digital technologies plays a crucial role in defining digital transformation. Technologies like mobile devices, artificial intelligence (AI), cloud computing, blockchain, and the Internet of Things (IoT) act as catalysts, fostering substantial advancements in business operations (Almahadin, Shehadeh, Al-Gasaymeh, Abu-AlSondos, & Atta et al., 2023). They augment customer experiences, streamline processes, and even trigger the birth of innovative business models.

Digital transformation is also an ongoing process where businesses continuously adapt to match the requirements of their customers and the market dynamics (Pappas, Mikalef, Dwivedi, Jaccheri, & Krogstie, 2023). This is facilitated by leveraging digital capabilities to innovate and develop novel business models, products, and services. The harmonious fusion of digital and physical business experiences enhances operational proficiency and boosts organizational performance. Digital transformation also refers to the application of pioneering digital technologies to execute significant improvements in business organizations, impacting processes, practices, or even the fundamental operational principles.

In essence, digital transformation is a dynamic process that evolves concurrently with technological advancements and changing customer expectations. Originating from digitizing manual processes, it has grown into a comprehensive integration of digital technology into every aspect of business. Ranging from transitioning from paper to digital records to complex applications like utilizing AI and machine learning (ML) for predictive analytics and decision-making, digital transformation is fundamentally linked to the progression of the Fourth Industrial Revolution. As the landscape of technology and customer expectations continues to evolve, digital transformation will consistently be a crucial aspect of business modernization strategies (Shehadeh, Almajali, Abu-AlSondos, Alkhwaldi, & Al-Gasaymeh, 2023).

This transformation brings extensive and diverse implications. For some businesses, it may involve deploying new technologies to enhance operational efficiency and productivity. For others (Belhadi, Kamble, Gunasekaran, & Mani, 2022), it could necessitate completely restructuring their business model to adapt to the opportunities and challenges brought about by Industry 4.0. Despite its advantages, such as improving decision-making capabilities, enhancing customer experiences, and creating opportunities for innovation, digital transformation also presents challenges like cybersecurity threats, regulatory compliance issues, and the requirement for a cultural shift within organizations.

3.2 The Role of Digital Transformation in Achieving SDGs

Digital transformation plays a crucial role in advancing the SDGs, providing the necessary tools and platforms to address global challenges across various sectors.

Digital transformation is proving instrumental in achieving SDG 1: No Poverty. It drives economic growth through digital entrepreneurship and stimulates innovation, shaping economies to be more resilient and adaptive (Marei, Abou-Moghli, Shehadeh, Salhab, & Othman, 2023). A prime example is the partnership between United Nations Development Program (UNDP) and Jumia in Uganda, which leveraged e-commerce to improve income-earning opportunities for informal market vendors. This initiative successfully provided economic opportunities to more than 4,000 vendors, a majority of whom were women, young people, and people with disabilities (Li & Pang, 2023).

The application of digital transformation strategies contributes significantly to SDG 5: Gender Equality. As in Cambodia, the strategic partnership between UNDP and the government has led to several programs that equipped more than 500,000 micro, small, and medium enterprises (MSMEs) and 2,500 young entrepreneurs with digital solutions for their businesses, enabling the empowerment of women in entrepreneurship (Leal Filho et al., 2023).

In terms of SDG 10: Reduced Inequalities, digital transformation fosters social inclusion. This can be seen in the Indian context, where UNDP's Accelerator Lab tested an IoT solution for precision agriculture. This system provided actionable insights to farmers, which helped them optimize water usage and manage irrigation challenges, promoting economic equality across the agricultural sector.

The digital revolution's potential in crisis management aligns with SDG 13: Climate Action. As an example, in Malawi, UNDP supported the deployment of advanced early warning systems, integrating solar-powered weather stations, lightning detection systems, and flood sensors (Savastano et al., 2022). This technology facilitated better climate resilience, effectively mitigating the negative impacts of climate change.

Furthermore, digital transformation fosters more inclusive societies, contributing to SDG 16: Peace, Justice, and Strong Institutions. The implementation of digital cash transfer systems in Afghanistan by UNDP provided greater financial inclusion, delivering critical assistance to 2,745 people across nine provinces.

In conclusion, the implementation and promotion of digital transformation strategies are pivotal in actualizing the SDGs. By adopting a proactive approach toward integrating digital technologies across all sectors, societies worldwide can effectively progress toward a more resilient, inclusive, and sustainable future. These concrete examples serve to emphasize the transformative power of digital technology in advancing global sustainability efforts.

3.3 Digital Transformation and Sustainability: A Synergistic Relationship

Digital transformation acts as a catalyst for sustainable business practices. It plays a pivotal role in driving informed data-driven decision-making, optimizing resource management, and achieving ESG goals, thereby helping companies forge a sustainable competitive advantage.

- Data-Driven Decision-Making: Data lie at the core of digital transformation, acting as a compass that guides businesses toward informed decision-making. For instance, businesses can leverage smart sensors and IoT devices to track energy consumption and waste production. Data analytics tools process these data to identify patterns in resource usage, allowing businesses to refine processes for greater efficiency and measure the effectiveness of their sustainability initiatives (Kumar, Vrat, & Shankar, 2022).
- Optimizing Resource Management: Digital transformation plays a crucial role in resource management, a key aspect of sustainable business practices. Advanced supply chain management systems and intelligent energy systems, powered by ML algorithms, enhance resource usage, reduce waste, and improve operational efficiency. By aligning production with predicted demand, companies can reduce overproduction and subsequent waste, thereby reducing their environmental impact while cutting costs.
- Achieving ESG Goals: Digital transformation is a critical ally for businesses striving to meet their ESG goals. Digital tools can track and reduce a company's carbon footprint, social networking platforms enhance internal communication and collaboration, blockchain can increase supply chain transparency, and data analytics can evaluate and enhance corporate governance practices.

3.4 Sustainability as a Competitive Advantage and Role of Leadership

The integration of digital technologies and sustainability can provide businesses with a considerable competitive advantage. Consumers today are increasingly conscious of the environmental and social impacts of their purchases. Consequently, companies that focus on sustainability are often perceived as more responsible, which can enhance their reputation and foster customer loyalty (Shehadeh, Al-Gasaymeh, Almahadin, Al Nasar, & Esra'a, 2023).

Innovation driven by sustainability can differentiate the company in the marketplace, giving it a competitive edge. For instance, a business might devise a more energy-efficient manufacturing process or create a product from recycled materials.

Leadership plays an instrumental role in advancing sustainable business practices. Leaders set the vision and strategic direction for the company and signal the company's values to employees, customers, and stakeholders. By fostering a culture of sustainability, leaders can inspire their employees to take the initiative and contribute their own ideas for sustainable practices. Moreover, by setting a positive example, they can potentially influence other companies, prompting industry-wide shifts toward sustainability.

The subsequent sections will explore specific case studies of businesses that have successfully harnessed digital transformation to drive sustainability, along with a discussion of potential challenges and strategies to overcome them.

4. Case Studies: Implementing Digital Transformation for Sustainability

In this section, we explore real-life examples of companies that have used digital transformation to enhance their sustainability efforts.

- Microsoft: Leveraging AI for Environmental Sustainability

Microsoft, a tech industry leader, exemplifies the successful implementation of digital transformation to drive sustainability. With its ambitious carbon negative pledge by 2030, the company harnesses digital technologies like AI and ML through its "AI for Earth" program to monitor and manage natural resources. The program includes projects like Wildbook for wildlife population tracking and FarmBeats for data-driven sustainable agriculture.

- Unilever: Enhancing Supply Chain Transparency through Digital Transformation

Unilever provides a case study of using digital transformation to promote sustainability within extensive supply chains. Responding to customers' demands for sustainable products, Unilever introduced blockchain technology into the supply chain of one of their tea brands, resulting in a transparent chain of custody that affirmed the sustainability of the product to customers.

- Vinamilk: Improving ESG Performance through Digital Transformation

Vinamilk, a leading dairy manufacturer in Vietnam, demonstrates how digital transformation can enhance ESG performance. The company has invested in technology to achieve international certifications, like Organic Europe and Global G.A.P, and used digital tools for data collection and analysis, ensuring transparent and efficient evaluation of their ESG performance. These efforts resulted in Vinamilk consistently ranking among the top 20 VNSI green stocks.

- The State Bank of Vietnam: Enforcing ESG Principles through Governance

The State Bank of Vietnam exemplifies the role of regulatory bodies in guiding a sector toward sustainable practices. Its Green Banking Development project increased awareness and social responsibility in banking and efforts to direct credit toward environmentally friendly finance projects underlined banks' role in supporting sustainable development.

The bank's use of digital transformation is illustrated by a large Vietnamese bank's use of the M-Office electronic office system to reduce paper waste and promote sustainable operations. The collaboration between a leading consumer finance company in Vietnam and Deutsche Bank to build an ESG lending facility further illustrates the integration of ESG principles into strategic and product management.

In the following sections, we will discuss potential challenges and strategies to navigate the transformation toward sustainability.

5. Navigating the Complex Landscape: Challenges and Ramifications of Digital Transformation on Sustainability

Digital transformation presents a plethora of opportunities to bolster sustainable business practices, as depicted by numerous case studies. However, understanding the complexities and potential roadblocks in its path is equally critical (Reis, Amorim, Melão, & Matos, 2018). Certain challenges may appear contradictory to the broader goals of sustainability, like the SDG of poverty eradication (Nieddu, Bertani, & Ponta, 2022).

5.1 Balancing Act: Job Displacement Risks

A major concern with the swift pace of digital transformation is the prospective displacement of jobs as a result of automation and AI technologies. These technologies offer improved efficiency and reduced environmental footprint, but they also potentially jeopardize specific job sectors, particularly those involving routine or manual tasks. This concern pertains especially to SDG 1: No Poverty and SDG 8: Decent Work and Economic Growth. Juggling the rewards of digital transformation with the potential socioeconomic repercussions is a multifaceted challenge, necessitating careful strategies and policies.

5.2 The Double-Edged Sword: Cybersecurity Threats

With increased reliance on digital platforms comes an escalated risk of cybersecurity threats. Such threats can undermine a company's data security and consumer trust, indirectly affecting SDG 16: Peace, Justice, and Strong Institutions, by potentially destabilizing businesses and economic frameworks.

5.3 Bridging the Gap: Unequal Access to Digital Technologies

Another obstacle is the digital divide or unequal access to digital resources. This issue directly affects SDG 10: Reduced Inequalities. While certain organizations and regions may thrive in their digital transformation efforts, others may lag due to inadequate access to necessary infrastructure, resources, or digital literacy.

5.4 Proficiency Gap: Inadequate Digital Competence in Workforce

To achieve sustainability in business operations, companies need a workforce that is proficient in digital skills. However, there is an existing shortfall of adequately trained professionals who comprehend and can exploit digital tools and technologies, obstructing the incorporation of sustainable digital solutions.

5.5 Trust Building in the Digital Era: Overcoming Skepticism

Sustainable business operations depend on customer trust. In the digital age, customers seek assurance about the security of their data and the reliability of digital processes. Hence, overcoming skepticism and apprehensions linked to digital services is vital for businesses to foster and maintain trust with their stakeholders.

5.6 Fiscal Limitations: Budget Constraints and Financing Capabilities

Implementing sustainable digital initiatives often calls for substantial financial investments. Budget restrictions and limited financing capabilities may discourage the adoption of eco-friendly technologies and other sustainability-oriented projects.

5.7 Absence of a Coherent Strategy: Lack of Clear Digital Transformation Roadmap

Without a well-articulated digital transformation strategy, businesses might find it challenging to channel their efforts toward sustainable objectives. A well-defined roadmap is indispensable to prioritize initiatives and effectively weave sustainability into digital transformation efforts.

5.8 Cultural Hurdles: Resistance to Change

The adoption of sustainable business practices often necessitates organizational and cultural changes. Resistance from employees and stakeholders to such shifts can slow or impede the adoption of sustainability-oriented digital solutions.

5.9 The Threat Landscape: Cybersecurity Risks

Cybersecurity threats pose a substantial challenge to sustainable business practices. Data breaches and cyberattacks can not only disrupt operations but also tarnish a company's reputation and its ability to maintain sustainable practices.

5.10 Privacy Dilemmas: Data Privacy Issues

In the pursuit of sustainability, businesses may need to collect and manage sensitive data related to environmental impact and social responsibility. Ensuring data privacy and compliance with regulations is paramount to maintain customer and stakeholder trust.

5.11 Digital Literacy Deficit: Technological Literacy and Workforce Skills

To fuel sustainable digital transformation, employees need to have the necessary digital literacy and skills. A lack of technological competence can hinder the adoption and effective use of eco-friendly technologies and practices.

5.12 Infrastructure Insufficiency: Inadequate Infrastructure and Internet Services

Sustainable businesses often depend on digital infrastructure and internet services for data collection, analytics, and communication. However, inadequate infrastructure and limited internet access in certain regions can impede the implementation of sustainable digital solutions.

Addressing these challenges is a critical task for businesses that are endeavoring to intertwine sustainability into their digital transformation journey. By confronting these obstacles head-on, they can harness the power of digital technologies and data-centric insights to advocate sustainable practices, lessen environmental impacts, and make a beneficial impact on society.

Given these challenges, it is evident that businesses should adopt a holistic and strategic perspective when it comes to the digital transformation for sustainability. This involves not only exploiting the advantages of digital technologies but also recognizing and mitigating potential risks and adverse effects. It necessitates a pledge to principles of accountable and inclusive digital transformation, which aligns perfectly with the broader ethos of the SDGs.

By incorporating these principles into their strategic blueprint, businesses can aid in cultivating a more sustainable and equitable digital future. This generates value not just for their stakeholders but also for the wider global community. As we venture deeper into the digital era, this commitment to responsible digital transformation will morph from being just a competitive edge to a prerequisite for sustained success.

In the subsequent sections, we will delve deeper into these strategies, providing tangible guidance on how to navigate the complexities and apparent contradictions of digital transformation for sustainability.

6. The Future of Digital Transformation and Sustainable Business Practices

6.1 The Evolution of Digital Transformation: Current Trends and Future Predictions

As we gaze into the crystal ball of the future, we see that digital transformation is not a static entity; it is continually evolving and redefining its own boundaries. Recent trends and future predictions suggest an exhilarating blend of digital technologies shaping the business landscape.

The Proliferation of AI and ML. According to the PwC's Global AI Study, AI could contribute up to $15.7 trillion to the global economy by 2030. Businesses across sectors are increasingly using AI and ML to analyze data, automate tasks, and streamline processes. As AI technology continues to evolve, we will likely see it being integrated into even more aspects of business, from customer service to supply chain management (Al-Gasaymeh, Almahadin, Shehadeh, Migdady, & Atta, 2023; Hatamlah, Allan, Abu-AlSondos, Shehadeh, & Allahham, 2023).

The Rise of Edge Computing. While cloud computing has dominated the digital landscape in recent years, the future points toward the rise of edge computing. Edge computing involves processing data near its source, reducing latency, and improving the speed of insights derived from these data. Gartner predicts that by 2025, 75% of data will be processed outside the traditional centralized data center or cloud, indicating the significant role edge computing will play.

The Era of Quantum Computing. Another trend that holds vast potential for the future of digital transformation is quantum computing. This technology harnesses quantum mechanics to process complex calculations at incredible speeds. IBM predicts that the 2020s will be the decade of quantum, suggesting a future where problems that are currently computationally impossible could be solved in seconds.

6.2 Shaping the Future of Sustainable Business Practices

AI and Sustainability. The proliferation of AI and ML could bring significant benefits for sustainable business practices. For example, AI algorithms can be used to analyze climate data and predict future environmental trends, enabling businesses to make proactive decisions about their environmental impact.

Additionally, ML can help optimize resource usage, reducing waste and promoting efficiency.

Edge Computing and Environmental Impact. The rise of edge computing could also have a positive impact on sustainability. By processing data closer to the source, businesses can reduce the energy consumption associated with data transfer, thus lessening their carbon footprint. Furthermore, edge computing could enable more effective monitoring and management of environmental conditions in real time, from tracking wildlife populations to monitoring air quality in cities.

Quantum Computing: A Quantum Leap for Sustainability? The advent of quantum computing could bring a paradigm shift in addressing complex sustainability challenges. For example, quantum computing could be used to design new materials for carbon capture or optimize logistics for reduced emissions. However, the true impact of quantum computing on sustainability remains to be seen, given the technology is still in its nascent stages.

In conclusion, the future of digital transformation paints a picture of promise for sustainable business practices. As these digital trends become more mainstream, businesses that successfully integrate these technologies into their sustainability strategies will be better positioned to meet the growing demands for a more sustainable and digitally empowered future.

7. Conclusion

As we draw this chapter to a close, let's reflect upon the critical themes that we have navigated in our exploration of the symbiosis between digital transformation and sustainable business practices. Our journey began with an understanding of digital transformation as the integration of digital technologies into all aspects of a business. This change fundamentally revolutionizes how businesses operate and deliver value to their customers, going beyond mere digitization to foster a paradigm shift in business operations and mentality.

Our attention then turned to the realm of sustainable business practices, which have become an increasingly significant element in today's business landscape. Sustainability has shifted from being a discretionary addition to a core component of any successful business model, impelled by a rising consumer, investor, and regulatory focus on ESG factors.

This discussion led us to uncover the dynamic interplay between digital transformation and sustainable business practices. We found that digital transformation catalyzes sustainability by enabling data-driven decision-making, improved resource management, and facilitating the accomplishment of ESG goals.

We also investigated real-world case studies, observing how trailblazing companies like Microsoft and Unilever have harnessed digital transformation to augment their sustainability efforts. Simultaneously, we explored potential challenges that businesses might encounter on this transformative journey, such as cybersecurity risks, data privacy issues, and technological literacy. Despite these potential obstacles, we found that with strategic planning and solutions, these hurdles can be successfully circumvented.

As we glanced toward the future, we discussed the potential impact of emerging trends in digital transformation on sustainable business practices. The pathway to sustainable business practices is increasingly laden with digital innovations. As we stand on the threshold of a new era of business, the role of digital transformation in achieving sustainability becomes ever more evident. Businesses are now employing technologies like AI, ML, and quantum computing not just for enhanced efficiency and profitability but to make a positive societal and environmental impact.

In conclusion, the alliance of digital transformation and sustainability is a powerful combination for businesses. By embracing this synergy, businesses can prepare for the future, create enduring value, and drive substantial change toward a more sustainable world. Therefore, the urgency and importance of digital transformation in realizing sustainable business practices cannot be overstated. As we cast our gaze toward the future, one thing is clear: digital transformation will be at the core of sustainable business practices, steering us toward a more sustainable and digitally powered future.

References

Al-Gasaymeh, A. S., Almahadin, H. A., Shehadeh, M., Migdady, H., & Atta, A. A. B. (2023, March). Investigating the Role of Artificial Intelligence in Embedded Finance on Improving a Nonfinancial Customer Experience. In *2023 International Conference on Business Analytics for Technology and Security (ICBATS)* (pp. 1–6). IEEE.

Almahadin, H. A., Shehadeh, M., Al-Gasaymeh, A. S., Abu-AlSondos, I. A., & Atta, A. A. B. (2023, March). Impact of Blockchain Technology and Fintech on Sustainable Performance. In *2023 International Conference on Business Analytics for Technology and Security (ICBATS)* (pp. 1–5). IEEE.

Almohtaseb, A., Shehadeh, M., & Aldehayyat, J. (2023). Psychological empowerment and organizational citizenship behavior in the information communications and technology (ICT) sector: A moderated-mediation model. *Cogent Business & Management*, *10*(1), 2200599.

Belhadi, A., Kamble, S., Gunasekaran, A., & Mani, V. (2022). Analyzing the mediating role of organizational ambidexterity and digital business transformation on industry 4.0 capabilities and sustainable supply chain performance. *Supply Chain Management: International Journal*, *27*(6), 696–711.

Casciani, D., Chkanikova, O., & Pal, R. (2022). Exploring the nature of digital transformation in the fashion industry: Opportunities for supply chains, business models, and sustainability-oriented innovations. *Sustainability: Science, Practice and Policy*, *18*(1), 773–795.

El Hilali, W., El Manouar, A., & Idrissi, M. A. J. (2020). Reaching sustainability during a digital transformation: A PLS approach. *International Journal of Innovation Science*, *12*(1), 52–79.

Erol, Y., & Kirpik, G. (2022). Sustainable digital business strategies. In *Conflict management in digital business: New strategy and approach* (pp. 259–280). Bingley: Emerald Publishing Limited.

Gao, Y. (2023). Unleashing the mechanism among environmental regulation, artificial intelligence, and global value chain leaps: A roadmap toward digital revolution and environmental sustainability. *Environmental Science and Pollution Research, 30*(10), 28107–28117.

Gil-Gomez, H., Guerola-Navarro, V., Oltra-Badenes, R., & Lozano-Quilis, J. A. (2020). Customer relationship management: Digital transformation and sustainable business model innovation. *Economic Research-Ekonomska istraživanja, 33*(1), 2733–2750.

Gomez-Trujillo, A. M., & Gonzalez-Perez, M. A. (2022). Digital transformation as a strategy to reach sustainability. *Smart and Sustainable Built Environment, 11*(4), 1137–1162.

Hajiheydari, N., Kargar Shouraki, M., Vares, H., & Mohammadian, A. (2023). Digital sustainable business model innovation: Applying dynamic capabilities approach (DSBMI-DC). *Foresight, 25*(3), 420–447.

Hatamlah, H., Allan, M., Abu-AlSondos, I., Shehadeh, M., & Allahham, M. (2023). The role of artificial intelligence in supply chain analytics during the pandemic. *Uncertain Supply Chain Management, 11*(3), 1175–1186.

Isaksson, R. (2021). Excellence for sustainability – Maintaining the license to operate. *Total Quality Management and Business Excellence, 32*(5–6), 489–500. doi:10.1080/14783363.2019.1593044

Ji, L., Sun, Y., Liu, J., & Chiu, Y. H. (2023). Environmental, social, and governance (ESG) and market efficiency of China's commercial banks under market competition. *Environmental Science and Pollution Research, 30*(9), 24533–24552.

Kong, D., & Liu, B. (2023). Digital technology and corporate social responsibility: Evidence from China. *Emerging Markets Finance and Trade*, 1–27.

Kumar, V., Vrat, P., & Shankar, R. (2022). Factors influencing the implementation of industry 4.0 for sustainability in manufacturing. *Global Journal of Flexible Systems Management, 23*(4), 453–478.

Leal Filho, W., Lange Salvia, A., Beynaghi, A., Fritzen, B., Ulisses, A., Avila, L. V., … Anholon, R. (2023). Digital transformation and sustainable development in higher education in a post-pandemic world. *The International Journal of Sustainable Development and World Ecology*, 1–16.

Li, W., & Pang, W. (2023). The impact of digital inclusive finance on corporate ESG performance: Based on the perspective of corporate green technology innovation. *Environmental Science and Pollution Research, 30*(24), 65314–65327.

Long, H., Feng, G. F., & Chang, C. P. (2023). How does ESG performance promote corporate green innovation? *Economic Change and Restructuring*, 1–25.

Marei, A., Abou-Moghli, A., Shehadeh, M., Salhab, H., & Othman, M. (2023). Entrepreneurial competence and information technology capability as indicators of business success. *Uncertain Supply Chain Management, 11*(1), 339–350.

Nieddu, M., Bertani, F., & Ponta, L. (2022). The sustainability transition and the digital transformation: Two challenges for agent-based macroeconomic models. *Review of Evolutionary Political Economy*, 1–34.

Pappas, I. O., Mikalef, P., Dwivedi, Y. K., Jaccheri, L., & Krogstie, J. (2023). Responsible Digital Transformation for a Sustainable Society. *Information Systems Frontiers*, 1–9.

Reis, J., Amorim, M., Melão, N., & Matos, P. (2018). Digital transformation: A literature review and guidelines for future research. In Á. Rocha, H. Adeli, L. P. Reis, & S. Costanzo (Eds.), *Trends and advances in information systems and technologies. WorldCIST'18 2018. Advances in Intelligent Systems and Computing* (pp. 411–421). Springer.

Savastano, M., Zentner, H., Spremić, M., & Cucari, N. (2022). Assessing the relationship between digital transformation and sustainable business excellence in a turbulent scenario. *Total Quality Management & Business Excellence*, 1–22.

Secundo, G., Schena, R., Russo, A., Schiavone, F., & Shams, R. (2022). The impact of digital technologies on the achievement of the Sustainable Development Goals: Evidence from the agri-food sector. *Total Quality Management & Business Excellence*, 1–17.

Shehadeh, M., Al-Gasaymeh, A. S., Almahadin, H. A., Al Nasar, M. R., & Esra'a, B. (2023, March). The blockchain technology integration with internet of things for digital supply chain transformation. In *2023 International Conference on Business Analytics for Technology and Security (ICBATS)* (pp. 1–5). IEEE.

Shehadeh, M., Almajali, D., Abu-AlSondos, I. A., Alkhwaldi, A. F., & Al-Gasaymeh, A. S. (2023, March). Digital transformation and its impact on operational efficiency and competitive advantage in Islamic Banks. In *2023 International Conference on Business Analytics for Technology and Security (ICBATS)* (pp. 1–6). IEEE.

Shehadeh, M., Almohtaseb, A., Aldehayyat, J., & Abu-AlSondos, I. A. (2023). Digital transformation and competitive advantage in the service sector: A moderated-mediation model. *Sustainability*, *15*(3), 2071–1050.

Wang, S. L. (2023). Digital technology-enabled governance for sustainability in global value chains: A framework and future research agenda. *Journal of Industrial and Business Economics*, *50*(1), 175–192.

Weber-Lewerenz, B. (2021). Corporate digital responsibility (CDR) in construction engineering—Ethical guidelines for the application of digital transformation and artificial intelligence (AI) in user practice. *SN Applied Sciences*, *3*, 1–25.

Yao, Q., Tang, H., Boadu, F., & Xie, Y. (2022). Digital transformation and firm sustainable growth: The moderating effects of cross-border search capability and managerial digital concern. *Journal of the Knowledge Economy*, 1–25.

Chapter 4

An Innovative Web Intelligence Data Clustering Algorithm for Human Resources Based on Sustainability

Emerson Norabuena-Figueroa[a], *Roger Rurush-Asencio*[b], *Jaheer Mukthar K. P.*[c], *Jose Sifuentes-Stratti*[b] *and Elia Ramírez-Asís*[b]

[a]Universidad Nacional Mayor de San Marcos, Perú
[b]Universidad Nacional Santiago Antunez de Mayolo, Peru
[c]Kristu Jayanti College, Autonomous, India

Abstract

The development of information technologies has led to a considerable transformation in human resource management from conventional or commonly known as personnel management to modern one. Data mining technology, which has been widely used in several applications, including those that function on the web, includes clustering algorithms as a key component. Web intelligence is a recent academic field that calls for sophisticated analytics and machine learning techniques to facilitate information discovery, particularly on the web. Human resource data gathered from the web are typically enormous, highly complex, dynamic, and unstructured. Traditional clustering methods need to be upgraded because they are ineffective. Standard clustering algorithms are enhanced and expanded with optimization capabilities to address this difficulty by swarm intelligence, a subset of nature-inspired computing. We collect the initial raw human resource data and preprocess the data wherein data cleaning, data normalization, and data integration takes place. The proposed K-C-means-data driven cuckoo bat optimization algorithm (KCM-DCBOA) is used for clustering of the human resource data. The feature extraction is done using principal component analysis (PCA) and the classification of human resource data is done using support vector machine (SVM). Other

Technological Innovations for Business, Education and Sustainability, 47–67

Published under exclusive licence by Emerald Publishing Limited
doi:10.1108/978-1-83753-106-620241004

approaches from the literature were contrasted with the suggested approach. According to the experimental findings, the suggested technique has extremely promising features in terms of the quality of clustering and execution time.

Keywords: Human resource; web intelligence; nature-inspired computing; spambase; sustainability; support vector machine

1. Introduction

Human resource management (HRM) has seen a dramatic transformation as a result of the widespread adoption of digital technologies in all facets of the field. HRM has figured out how to use technology like the computer and the internet to boost efficiency, cut costs, and boost the company's competitive edge. Web intelligence has been included in many tactical HR operations due to the large amount of organizational, human, and task-oriented data for which HR is responsible; this improves the viability of business models (Castillo, Fernández, Camones, & Guerra, 2022; Votto, Valecha, Najafirad, & Rao, 2021). The HR department now typically presents itself through an online portal rather than a live employee. In today's economy, companies can't afford to lose ground, therefore they need to invest in their workforce if they want to succeed. There is a widespread quest among the nation's largest corporations for the most qualified local workers. Staffing is a crucial part of HR development, and recruitment is one of the HR responsibilities included in the selection process. Changes in our economy, society, and culture have been substantial as a result of technological progress Veluchamy, Sanchari, and Gupta (2021). There have been numerous influences on HRM since the field's inception. The pressure was put on HR development to yield desirable results as a result of work shifts necessitated by the introduction of new, diverse technologies like online intelligence solutions. The future of the intelligent system will have a significant impact on human life, and it will be web intelligence (WI) (Hmoud & Laszlo, 2019). A type of meta-heuristic algorithm, "nature-inspired computing" (NIC) draws inspiration from the workings of the natural world. It draws its inspiration from the natural world and features a wide range of living things, including humans and animals. When it comes to translating the natural or biological cycle into machine intelligence, NIC is important. Understanding natural processes, designing patterns for nature processes, identifying the problem, and modeling it technologically are just a few of the steps involved in creating intelligent systems. Maintaining stability requires efficient management of scarce resources, and nature acts as a self-optimizing system in this regard (Asís, Figueroa, Quiñones, & Márquez Mázmela, 2022).

One of the most popular techniques for resolving practically all problems internationally is to apply algorithms that are inspired by nature. The dispersion of cloud services is analyzed and configured as part of cloud management to maximize the effectiveness of power applications, infrastructures, or workloads and minimize loss due to oversupply. The introduction of DevOps resulted in rapid distribution and frequent new code modifications. These algorithms draw their inspiration from nature and make use of how the world works to solve issues (Yahia et al., 2021). There have been numerous influences on HRM since the field's inception. The pressure was put on HR development to yield desirable results as a result of work shifts necessitated by the introduction of new, diverse technologies like online intelligence solutions. The future of the intelligent system will have a significant impact on human life, and it will be WI.

Wang (2022) applied WI and data analysis (DA) to the main parts of HRs, and then uses experimental simulation to get the data findings of the model. This chapter aims to construct and explain a WI and deep DA model for HRs within the context of the currently available theoretical framework. Mellal (2022) explained the fundamental ideas underlying several NIC methods and their applications, such as particle swarm optimization (PSO), a grey wolf optimization method, ant colony optimizations (ACOs), plant propagation techniques, cuckoo optimization algorithms, and artificial neural networks. Oral and Turgut (2018) evaluated the efficacy of the Flower Pollination Algorithm ("FPA"), the Forest Optimization Algorithm ("FOA"), and the Artificial Algae Algorithm ("AAA"), three relatively new nature-inspired computing ("NIC") algorithms. Ten widely used benchmark test functions, split into multimodal and unimodal categories, are used for the comparisons. Rui, Fong, Yang, and Deb (2019) explored the feasibility of using alternative optimization methods inspired by nature to carry out clustering using WI data. In this research, we claim that all of the recently developed clustering algorithms are superior to the industry standard, cuckoo particle swarm optimization (C-PSO). Dey et al. (2020) provided a state-of-the-art research methodology in the field of NIC. It introduces readers to a wide variety of algorithms, including multi-agent systems, genetic methods, particle optimization, the firefly method, flower pollination algorithms, collision-based optimization techniques, and the bat algorithm. Soto, Asis, Figueroa, and Plasencia (2023) and Shaikh et al. (2022) provided an overview of algorithms that are based on natural phenomena, including biologically inspired algorithms and swarm intelligence techniques. Optimization plays a crucial part in the success of many algorithms that take their inspiration from nature and are used to the solution of practical problems. Applications of computers inspired by nature for the wireless sensor network (WSN) are presented in this work. Even though WSN is becoming increasingly popular, it does have certain drawbacks, such as battery life, distraction, slow communication, and security. New forms of clever algorithms are required to solve these problems (Huerta-Soto et al., 2022).

Bharti, Biswas, and Shukla (2020) provided a high-level survey of recent developments and applications in the subject of nature-inspired computation focusing on their relevance to deep learning. Pallathadka et al. (2023) offered light on contemporary research trends. There is a brief list of algorithms followed by various variations of nature-inspired algorithms before it addresses the classifications of the algorithms. New optimization algorithms are occasionally created and altered using nature as their primary source of inspiration. HRM aims to optimize planned HR allocation by the organization's development requirements. The enthusiasm of the employees can be utilized through recruitment, training, assessment, incentive, and other areas of the staff to maximize benefits for the organization (Castro, Castillo, Camones, & Cochachin, 2022; Zhao, 2020). Sohrabi, Vanani, and Abedin (2018) employed text mining techniques applied to a comprehensive search of scholarly literature from across the world to examine emerging trends in the field of HRM in tandem with information systems. Herrera and delas Heras-Rosas (2020) examined developments in corporate social responsibility (CSR) and HRM-related scientific output. The connection between CSR, HRM and economic, environmental, and social sustainability has been the subject of numerous case studies. However, the groundwork for addressing the emerging competencies of CSR, HRM, and sustainable company management has yet to be laid. Ramirez-Asis, Maguina, Infantes, and Naranjo-Toro (2020) provided a comprehensive literature review of HR analytics to identify the present research trends and to establish future research agendas in this area. The purpose of this chapter is to provide a comprehensive overview of the topic, including its historical context, underlying theoretical principles and cutting-edge advancements. Human Resource Management and the Importance of Web Intelligence. As a result of globalization, traditional approaches to managing businesses are being put to the test. As the world becomes smaller because of technological advancements, businesses no longer have to compete solely with companies in their immediate geographic area (Vasantham, 2021). Li and Zhou (2022) investigated and enhanced the deep learning-based recommendation algorithm and applied it to the HR recommendation domain. The current recommendation system relies on a single, time-tested algorithm, and its efficacy in the field of HRM may benefit from a revamp. Venusamy, Rajagopal, and Yousoof (2020) identified the effects of chatbots in the modern day. This cutting-edge method orients the present HR executives toward a graphical viewpoint for analyzing candidates. Using a designated examination approach, the benefits and drawbacks of online intelligence have been analyzed, and the outcome of the investigation is certain. Statistical and analytical abilities are often lacking in HR departments, making it difficult to work with massive datasets (Yating et al., 2022). Inadequate infrastructure can prevent some businesses from gaining access to high-quality data.

Hence in this chapter, the novel clustering algorithm for HR WI data based on NIC was described. The further part of this chapter is categorized as follows: Part 2 provides the methods, Part 3 explains the experiments and results, and Part 4 explains the conclusion.

2. Methods

This section details the procedure that would be followed if the proposed approach were to be implemented. HR data collections, preprocessing including data cleaning, data normalization, data integration, a proposed technique of K-C-means-data driven cuckoo bat optimization algorithm (KCM-DCBOA) technique, a feature extraction utilizing principal component analysis (PCA),

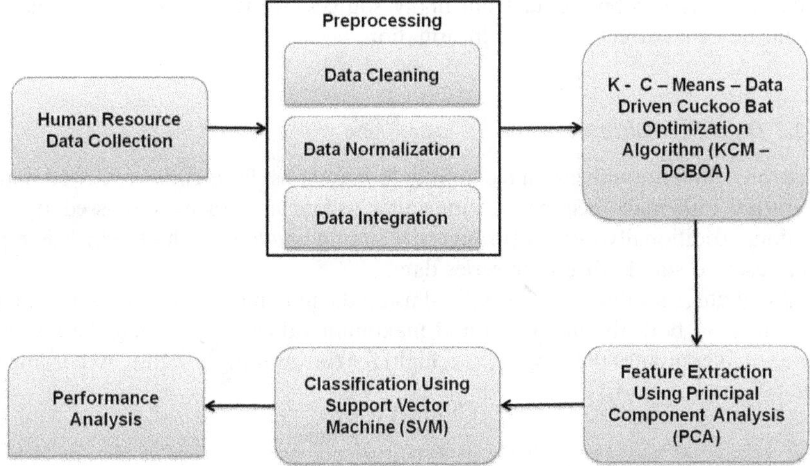

Fig. 4.1. Flow of the Suggested Methodology.

classifications utilizing support vector machines (SVMs), and so on are all depicted in the diagram. Fig. 4.1 depicts the flow of the suggested methodology.

2.1 HR Data Collection

At a large institution's part-time MBA program, executives were chosen by approaching HR-focused students. Since taking part in the study was entirely optional, only about 83% (n = 481) of executives were present for the first phase. These executives could have been away on vacation, personal leave, or business trips. The second portion of the study, which lasted around 14 weeks, involved the author hand administering a questionnaire to a subject to collect data on a density of job experience. Nearly 79% of this sample identified their managers and gave contact information for follow-up (n = 289), and approximately 76% of respondents showed up for the second phase of data collection (n = 366).

2.2 Preprocessing

Unstructured data are converted into a more understandable format during data preparation. Before using machine learning and data mining methods, it's important to make sure the data are of sufficient quality. Preprocessing consists of the following steps: data cleansing, data normalization, and data integration.

2.2.1 Data Cleaning

In computing, "data cleaning" relates to the process of correcting or removing incorrect, corrupted, incorrectly formatted, duplicate, or incomplete data from a dataset. If we combine data from many sources, we run the danger of having duplicate or incorrectly labeled information.

2.2.2 Data Normalization

The three data normalization techniques that are most frequently employed in the literature min–max, decimal scaling, and z-score are briefly discussed in this section. Additionally, we go through the sliding window method, which is typically used to standardize time series data.

Attribute A's values are normalized using the min–max technique, which takes into account both the minimum and maximum values of A. Using the given A value, a, it computes the ranges (low, high) for the resulting a' value. According to the following Eq. (4.1):

$$a' = (\text{high} - \text{low}) \times \frac{a - \min_A}{\max_A - \min_A} + \text{low} \tag{4.1}$$

Since the lowest and maximum values of the out-of-sample datasets are unknown, the min–max normalization approach cannot be used for time series forecasting. If we look at the minimum ($\min_A$) and maximum ($\max_A$) values in the in-sample datasets, we can easily solve this issue by assigning low and high to all out-of-sample values that fall between those ranges. This method, however, causes a dramatic drop in the quality of learning procedures and an over-concentration of values in a small portion of the normalized range.

Decimal scaling normalization is another popular normalization technique in which a decimal point of values of attribute A is shifted to correspond with its greatest absolute value. Thus, we convert an A value, a, to its normalized form, a', by the following Eq. (4.2):

$$a' = \frac{a}{(10^d)} \tag{4.2}$$

where d is the smallest positive integer such that $\text{Max}(|a'|) < 1$. Similar to min–max, this approach requires knowing the highest values in a time series and suffers from the same limitations when working with time series data.

Last but not least, the z-score normalization averages and standardizes the values of attribute A. To convert an A value, a, to a more universal value, a', we compute Eq. (4.3).

$$a' = \frac{a - \mu(A)}{\sigma(A)} \tag{4.3}$$

When the real minimum and maximum values for attribute A are unknown, this approach excels in stationary situations, but it struggles with nonstationary time series because the mean and standard deviations change with time.

2.2.3 Data Integration

Data integration is a preprocessing method that unifies disparate datasets from several sources into a cohesive database. Multiple data cubes, databases, or flat files could be among these resources.

2.3 K-C-Means-Data Driven Cuckoo Bat Optimization Algorithm

According to the K-C-means algorithm, data can be split into two or more groups with varying membership coefficients. Clustering with K-C-means is a recursive procedure. The first step is to build the initial partition matrix and determine the starting points for the clusters. At each iteration, an objective function is reduced and the cluster centers and membership cutoffs are recalculated to improve the solution. After a predetermined maximum number of iterations, or if the goal function doesn't improve by at least a user-specified threshold between two consecutive iterations, the procedure terminates. When the improvement of the objective function between two successive iterations is below the minimum quantity of improvement stated, or when a maximal number of iterations has been reached, the process terminates at a set point known as the threshold. The update in the iteration is performed using the membership degree and the center of the cluster, which are the two parameters changing. Additionally, a fuzziness coefficient denoted by "*m*," is selected; "*m*" can be any positive real integer higher than 1.

To divide a set of N vectors into C groups, an algorithm is available; this method is called KC-means clustering, or hard KC-means clustering. This algorithm determines the centroid of each cluster. Specifically, the dissimilarity function is minimized using this algorithm. Initially, the read function is used to import the image into the MATLAB workspace. Clustering is an approach to classifying collections of things. By default, KC-means clustering assumes that each item has a discrete spatial location. It finds clusterings where items are as close to each other as feasible inside their group, and as far away from other groups as possible. To use KC-means clustering, you must choose the distance metrics to measure how close items are to one another and the number of clusters into which they will be divided. Additionally, pixels are the building blocks of any image. The k-means clustering algorithm is used to assign labels to these pixels. KC-means provides an index representing a cluster for each object in the input. The KC-means cluster center output will be utilized in a subsequent demonstration stage. In Fuzzy K-C-Means, the goal is to achieve a best-case scenario with an iteration count equal to that of Fuzzy K-C-Means. This means that even with a reduced number of iterations, we will obtain a reliable result. In Fuzzy K-C-Means, the goal is to achieve a best-case scenario with an iteration count equal to that of Fuzzy K-C-Means. This means that even with a reduced number of iterations, we will obtain a reliable result.

A cuckoo algorithm (CA) has come a long way since its inception and has finally earned a place alongside other optimization techniques. This algorithm is inspired by observations of obligate brood parasitism in certain species of cuckoos and the Levy flight behavior observed in certain species of birds and fruit flies. The CA is a swarm-based metaheuristic algorithm that quickly finds a middle ground between exploiting the immediate environment and exploring the entire search space. A distinctive trait of the cuckoo is how it lays its eggs. Here are three simplified and idealized principles that characterize and explain the typical cuckoo search:

(1) Every time a cuckoo lays an egg, she chooses a nest at random and deposits it there.
(2) High-quality egg-laying nests will be passed down from generation to generation.
(3) There is a constant supply of host nests, and the cuckoo's egg has a likelihood of being found by the host bird of $P\alpha \in (0, 1)$. A host bird could either quit the nest and start over, or it can remove the egg. In addition, an n host nest can oust the additional nests using probability P.

The CA begins with a population of n host nests, similarly to other swarm-based algorithms. The cuckoos bearing eggs, as well as the random Levy flights, will attract these initial hosts' nests at random. Following this, the quality of the nest will be assessed and compared to that of a different host nest selected at random. The current host nests may be replaced by the new host nest if it proves to be superior. The cuckoo lays the egg for this novel approach. Host birds will either discard an egg or abandon it if they find it, given the probability $P\alpha \in (0, 1)$. In this step, new random solutions are substituted for the many existing ones. Since the cuckoo only lays a single egg, it can only signify a single answer. The goal is to get rid of the poorest solutions and bring in more novel ones that will hopefully be better. The CA, on the other hand, can be made more intricate by having numerous eggs in each nest to stand in for a group of answers.

Like a bat algorithm, the CA strikes a balance between probing and exploiting the environment. Integrating the local random walk is equivalent to the CA. The local random walk Eq. (4.4) can be written as:

$$x_i^{T+1} = x_i^t + \alpha s \otimes H(P\alpha - \varepsilon) \otimes \left(x_j^T - x_k^t\right) \tag{4.4}$$

If x_i^t and x_k^t are two solutions chosen at random by permutations, the Heaviside function $H(u)$ generates a random number between 0 and 1 with uniform probability, and s is a step size. It is also possible to give an expression for a worldwide random walk of exploration using Levy flights. According to the following Eqs. (4.5), (4.6):

$$x_i^{t+1} = x_i^t + \alpha L(s, \lambda), \tag{4.5}$$

And

$$L(s, \lambda) = \frac{\lambda \Gamma(\lambda) \sin(\lambda \pi / 2)}{\pi} \frac{1}{s^{1+\lambda}}, s \gg s0 > 010 \tag{4.6}$$

where L is the typical size at which a problem of interest occurs and $\alpha > 0$ is a size scaling factor. The formula for this number is $\alpha = O(L/10)$, while $\alpha = O(L/100)$ is more emotive. There is only one way to find the following location, x^{t+1}, which is represented by x^t in the equation above. Two well-known models for this situation are a random walk and a Markov chain. The second term is the transition probability, and it is denoted by $\alpha L(s, \lambda)$. Though the new solution should be created at a far enough distance from the best solution at the moment and some random aspects should be introduced to avoid early convergence and increase diversity (not just restricted to a local optimum). The search process of a CA is illustrated in Fig. 4.2.

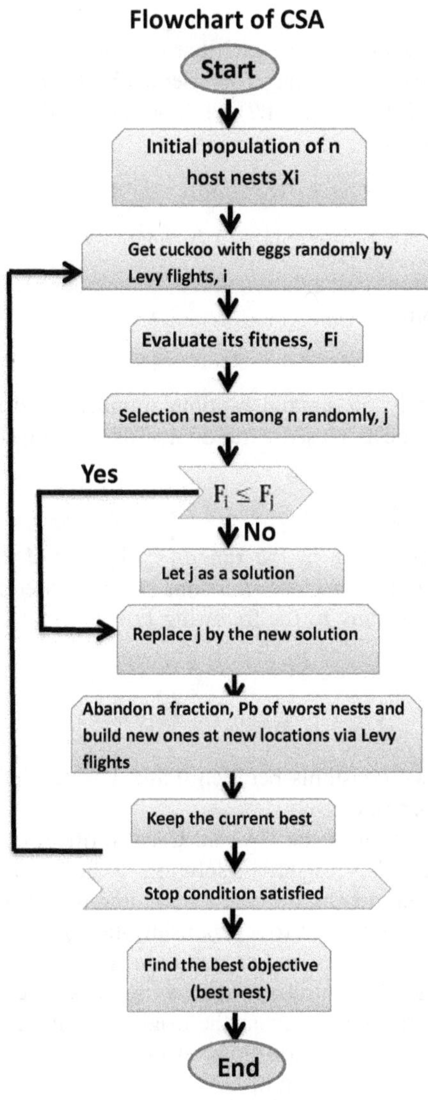

Fig. 4.2. Flowchart of Cuckoo Algorithm.

The bat algorithm (BA) takes its cues from the way bats use echolocation. In the wild, you can find a wide variety of bat species. Their navigational and hunting behaviors are similar, yet their physical characteristics vary greatly. Microbats rely heavily on echolocation, which helps them find food and avoid dangers even in total darkness. This cutting-edge optimization method can be applied to the study of microbat behavior.

Throughout the iterative process of the BA, the artificial bat's location vector, velocity vector, and frequency vector are modified to reflect the current state of play. The BA's position and speed vectors are useful for sifting through the search space.

In a d-dimensional search space, each bat occupies a certain location (represented by X_i), has a specific frequency (represented by F_i), and travels at a specific speed (represented by V_i). In Eqs. (4.7), (4.8), and (4.9), the velocities, positions, and frequencies are revised.

$$V_i(t+1) = v_i(t) + (x_i(t) - \text{Gbest}) \times F_i \tag{4.7}$$

$$X_i = (t+1) = X_i(t) + V_i(t+1) \tag{4.8}$$

where Gbest is the current best solution and F_i is the updated frequency of the ith bat after each iteration.

$$F_i = F_{\min} + (F_{\max} - F_{\min}) \times \beta \tag{4.9}$$

Where β is a uniformly distributed random number in [0,1]. To enhance its exploitative capacity, the BA used a random walk, the Eq. (4.10) as described below:

$$x_{\text{new}} = x_{\text{old}} + \varepsilon A_t \tag{4.10}$$

where ε is an arbitrary value in the range $[-1,1]$, and A is an output sound pressure level. The loudness or pulse emissions (r) are revised at each iteration in the following way. According to the following Eqs. (4.11), (4.12):

$$A_i(t+1) = \alpha A_i(t) \tag{4.11}$$

$$r_i\,(t+1) = r_i(0)\left(1 - e^{(-\gamma \times t)}\right) \tag{4.12}$$

Where α and γ are two constants between 0 and 1 which influence the rates of change for A_i and (r_i), respectively.

The combined algorithm of the BA and CA prioritizes exploitation to boost slow convergence and avoids low-fitness solutions to boost solution quality. Levy flight is used in optimization and optimal search, and it is effective at these tasks, with positive outcomes that point to a promising start. In this way, CA strikes a good balance between discovery and exploitation. In contrast, there are cases in which solutions are not fully utilized, such as when a large step yields a new solution that is either too distant from the original solution or falls outside the boundary. When the step size is too tiny, on the other hand, the effect is negligible. To get over this shortcoming of CA, the Cooperative bat searching Algorithm (CBA) is developed, which makes use of the benefits of BA; BA can give

Algorithm 1 Basic Bat-Inspired Algorithm

Set $X_i = (i = 1, 2, \ldots., n)$, V_i, and start the bat population.
Define pulse frequency F_i
Set the r_i pulse rate and A_i volume to initial values.
while $t <$ Max number of iterations *do*
  Create fresh ideas by varying the frequency,
  Changing speeds and locations
  if rand $> r_i$ *then*
    Choose at random one of the top solutions.
    Create a regional solution based on the best option.
  end if
  Create a fresh answer by flying at random
  if rand $< A_i$ and $f(X_i) < f(x')$ *then*
    Accept the innovative approaches.
    Raising r_i and lowering A_i
  end if
  Determine the current Gbest by ranking the best.
end while

fast convergence in the first stage by transitioning from exploration to exploitation. Consequently, the CBA's benefits include raising solution quality, improving performance, and avoiding being stuck in a cycle of local maxima.

The CBA flowchart, which is broken up into three sections, is depicted in Fig. 4.3. The initialization and comparison of the Levy flight and tournament selection solutions are shown in the first part before moving on to the second. A crimson band, which stands in for the BA component, surrounds the second component. On a basis of solutions *i* from the first phase, a new solution is constructed in this section. More so, Eqs. (4.9), (4.11), and (4.12) determine pulse frequencies F_i, loudness A_i, and pulse rate r_i, respectively. The updated coordinates and velocities (Eqs. 4.7 and 4.8) enable the search for all feasible solutions around the optimum solution.

2.4 Feature Extraction Using PCA

PCA is a method for easy identification and classification that can be used to deal with datasets built from a large number of noisy and highly correlated process observations. The idea behind PCA is to map the dataset onto a lower dimensional space. Collinearity between datasets is eliminated or considerably reduced in this compact representation. To do this, PCA re-explains the variance in the original data matrix $X_{m\times n}$, which had *m* observation of *n* variables $(m > N)$ in terms of a new set of independent factors. The Eq. (4.13) is calculated as follows:

$$X = TP^T + E = t_1p_1^T + \ldots + t_2p_2^T + \ldots t_ap_a^T + E \tag{4.13}$$

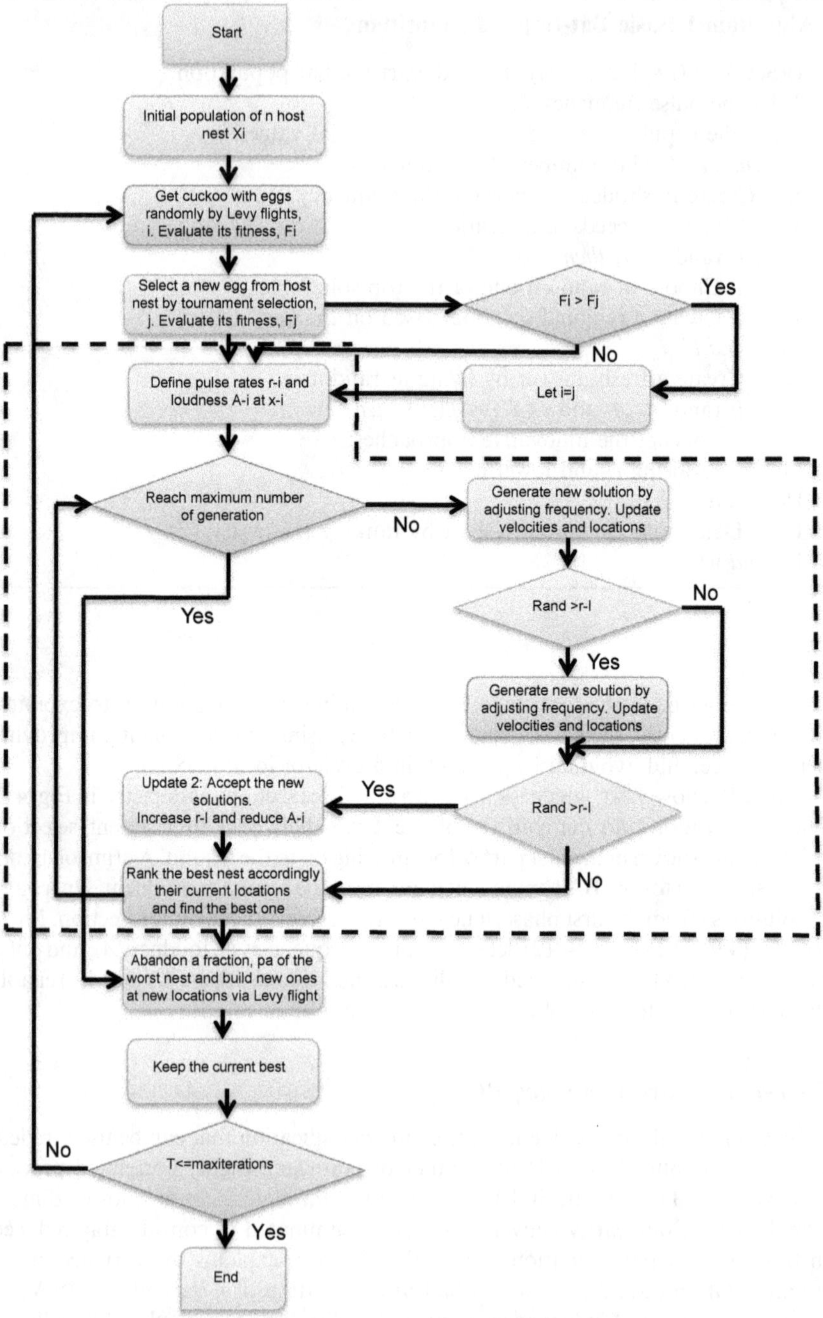

Fig. 4.3. Flowchart of CBA.

where P represents a loading matrix, E represents residual matrixes, and T represents a matrix containing the principal components' scores. The dimension $a \ll n$, a should ideally be selected so that it leaves no substantial process information in E. Since the matrix E represents a random error, adding another PC would only fit the noise, raising the prediction errors.

The loading vector is subject to $|p_i| = 1$ and is orthogonal to one another, implying that $p_i{}^T p_j = 0(i \neq j)$, $p_i{}^T p_j = 1(i \neq j)$. A new orthogonal basis is established by the PCs of an observation space of X. The score vectors $t_i = (i = 1, \ldots, a)$ locate each observation x_i on the PC subspace. The distances along each PC from the subspace's origin make up a score vector's elements. A loading vectors p_i and an actual observation are multiplied to arrive at the principal components scores t_i, which is then stated as follows. Following is an Eq. (4.14) that describes:

$$t_i = X_{pi}(i = 1, \ldots, a) \tag{4.14}$$

The PCA identifies the largest source of data variability, successive components account for progressively less variation. Significant variations are assumed to be related to feature space structure, and redundant features are eliminated with minimal accuracy loss.

Singular value decomposition is a well-liked method for determining PCs. It is straightforward since it is an eigenvalue problem of the covariance matrix, which can be easily solved. The Eq. (4.15) is given below:

$$C = \frac{1}{m} \sum_{i=1}^{m} \left(x_i - \overline{x}\right) \left(x_i - \overline{x}\right)^T \tag{4.15}$$

where $\overline{x}$ is the mean value of x_i.

Solving an eigenvalue equation is necessary to accomplish this. By utilizing this Eq. (4.16):

$$\lambda \mathrm{v} = \mathrm{Cv} \tag{4.16}$$

where C is the covariance matrix and v is its eigenvalue at $\lambda \geq 0$. The orthogonal projection onto the eigenvectors, denoted here as "new features," are new coordinates on an eigenvector basis and are represented by PCs. PC modeling is used to summarize the time-varying and interfeature correlations structure in the feature datasets in a single, digestible model. Three-dimensional and two-dimensional charts, often known as "windows into multidimensional features space," can be used for condition monitoring. Online, you can utilize a PC model to see the current process state against a historical background for known process states.

2.5 Classification Using SVM

In the domain of supervised learning, SVMs were a relatively recent tool for performing tasks like binary classification, regression, and outlier detection. SVM is superior to other classification algorithms because its structure is straightforward and it uses a modest set of features. According to statistical learning theory,

SVM is the best classifier algorithm for minimizing structural risk. Pattern regression and classification issues were the original motivation for developing SVMs.

The task is to assign a new data point to one of two groups, each of which is represented by a set of existing points. In SVMs, a data point is seen as an n-dimensional vector in an n-dimensional space R^n, and we want to know if we can separate these points with an $(n-1)$-dimensional hyperplane (Canonical plane). A linear classifier is a term for this type of system. The data could be classified along any number of hyperplanes. Due to the positive correlation between margin and generalization error, the hyperplane with the highest gap among the two classes is a strong candidate for the optimal hyperplane. It is possible to determine the hyperplane by utilizing the margins and support vectors. After "pushing against" two datasets, the canonical planes are used to construct two simultaneous supporting hyperplanes, one on either side of the plane to estimate the margin. To do this, we pick a hyperplane that is farthest away from the nearest data point on both sides. If such a hyperplane exists, we refer to it as a maximum margin hyperplane, and we refer to the linear classifier that it defines as a maximum margin classifier, also known as a perceptron because it achieves the highest levels of stability.

During its training phase, an SVM constructs spatial models of data points so that there is a sharp, maximally broad separation between the data points of different categories. Then, we anticipate which group a new set of instances belongs to dependent on which side of a divide they fall. Through the use of the kernel method, which implicitly maps their input into high-dimensional feature spaces, SVMs can easily conduct a nonlinear classification in addition to their more well-known linear classification capabilities. SVMs, in their most formal form, create a hyperplane or group of hyperplanes in a large or infinite dimensional space for classification, regression, and other tasks.

3. Experiments and Results

In this section, we discuss the recommended framework and its overall behavior. Figs. 4.4, 4.5, 4.6, 4.7, and 4.8 show the comparison of parameters, like accuracy, precision, specificity, recall, and F1 measure for existing and proposed methods. For example, among the approaches that may be utilized are the back propagation neural network (BPNN), PSO, ACO, confirmatory factor analysis (CFA), and KCM-DCBOA.

Neural network training relies fundamentally on a process called backpropagation. Finer tuning of a neural network's weights according to the error rate (loss) measured from the previous epoch's training (i.e., iteration). Reduced error rates and improved generalization are two benefits of fine-tuning the weights. The backpropagation algorithm has the potential downside of being very sensitive to irregularities and noisy data. Training data has a significant impact on backpropagation's final result. Training with backpropagation requires a significant amount of time. PSO is a method for optimizing a problem using a

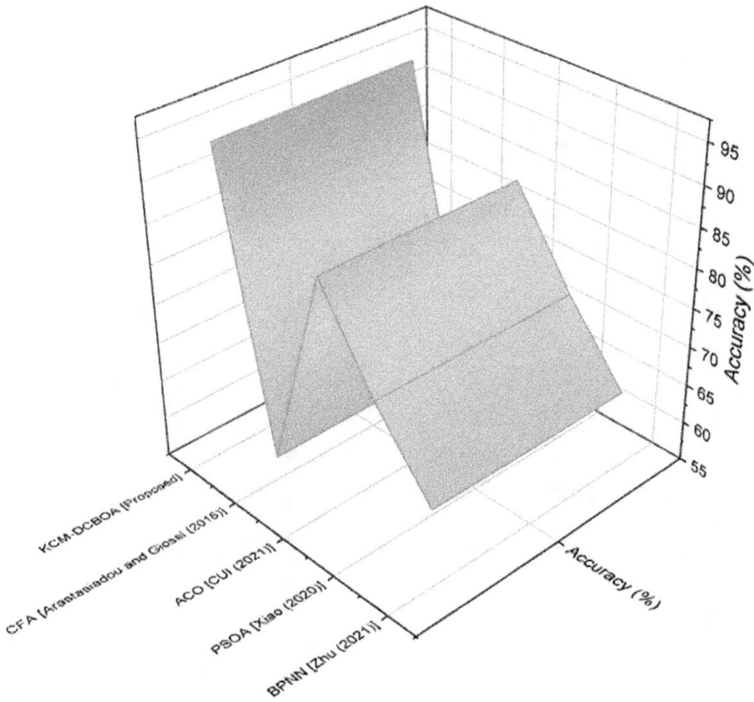

Fig. 4.4. Accuracy Results of Proposed and Existing Methodology.

computer by repeatedly searching for and testing improved versions of candidate solutions to the problem. Many benefits, including quick convergence, are associated with the basic PSO approach. One notable drawback, however, is that PSO algorithms frequently converge to local optimization. One population-based metaheuristic which can help with finding approximations to tough optimization issues is ACO. Artificial ACO is a technique where a colony of software agents, nicknamed "artificial ants," works to find optimal solutions to an optimization issue. If you want to use ACO, you'll need to first modify your optimization issue into one where you need to determine the optimal path via a weighted graph. To verify the observed dataset's factor structure, statisticians employ a technique called CFA. With CFA, the researcher can investigate the hypothesis that the observed variables are linked to latent constructs. One possible drawback of this often-used method is that factors that differ in quantity and substance from test scales may be generated due to excessive incidental item intercorrelations or the over or under of certain items. Therefore, in this work, we applied the KCM-DCBOA to address these challenges.

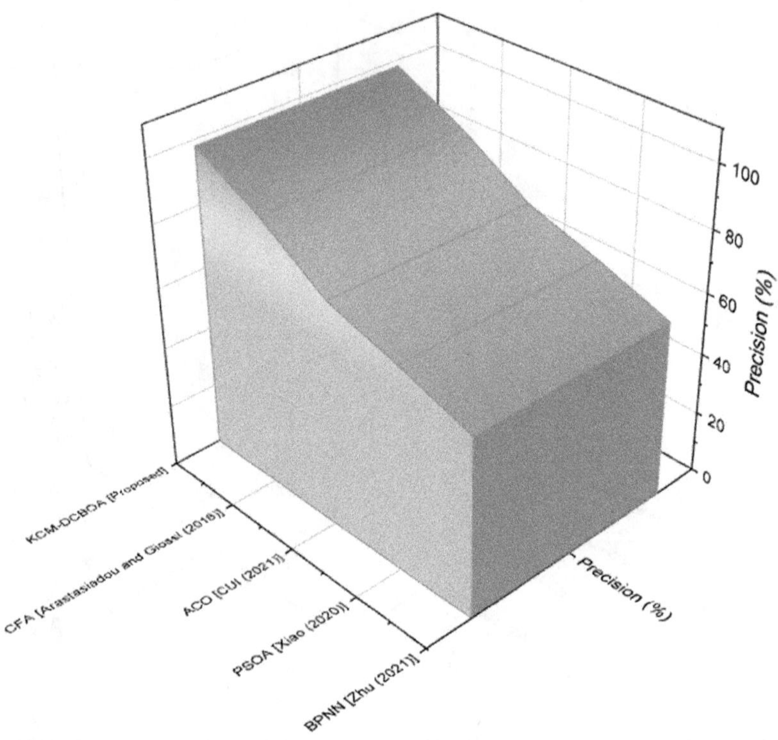

Fig. 4.5. Precision Results of Proposed and Existing Methodology.

To determine a test's accuracy, it must correctly distinguish between patient and healthy samples. Calculating the ratio of positive to negative results across all instances is a good way to get a sense of a test's reliability. The accuracy Eq. (4.17) is described given below:

$$\text{Accuracy} = \text{TP} + \text{TNTP} + \text{TN} + \text{FP} + \text{FN} \tag{4.17}$$

The results of suggested and existing approaches' accuracy calculations are shown in Fig. 4.4. According to the aforementioned graph, the proposed approach of KCM-DCBOA has a 94% higher accuracy level than the existing methods.

Precision is determined by dividing the total numbers of true positives and false positives by the imbalanced classification problem's two classes. According to the following Eq. (4.18):

$$\text{Precision} = \frac{\text{TP}}{\text{TP} + \text{FP}} \tag{4.18}$$

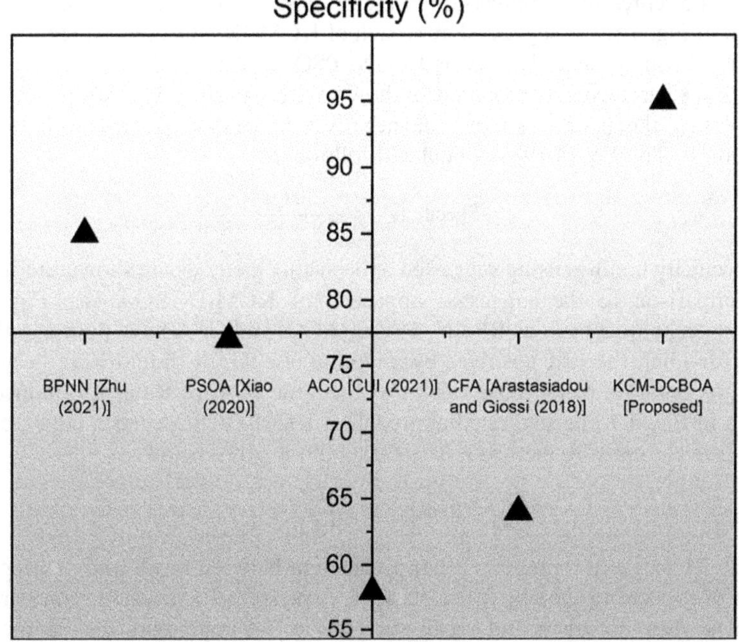

Fig. 4.6. Results of Proposed and Existing Methodologies' Specificity.

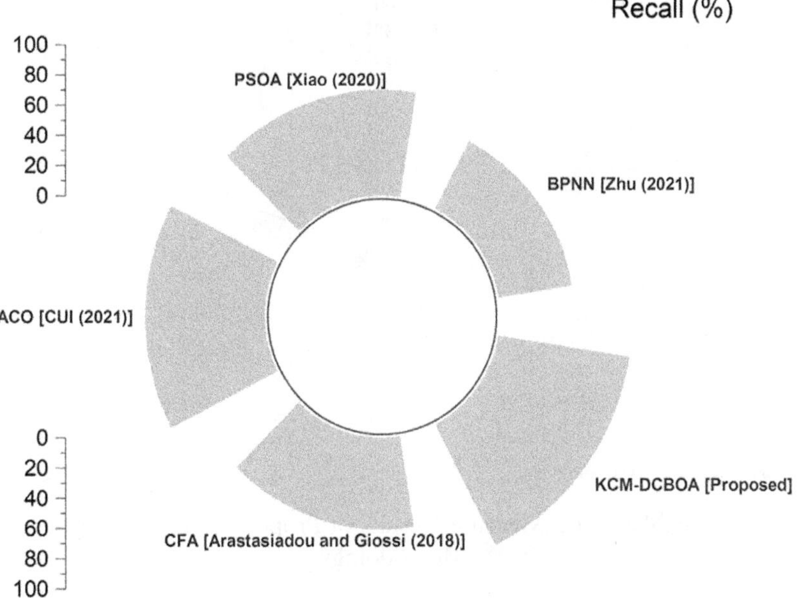

Fig. 4.7. Recall Results of Proposed and Existing Methodology.

Fig. 4.5 represents the precision of the proposed and existing methodology. As shown in Fig. 4.5, the suggested approach of KCM-DCBOA has a high precision than the existing methods such as BPNN, PSOA, ACO, and CFA.

A test's specificity is measured by how well it can identify healthy instances. Calculating the percentage of true negatives in healthy patients will help us estimate it. The Eq. (4.19) is calculated follows as:

$$\text{Specificty} = \frac{\text{TN}}{\text{TN} + \text{FP}} \tag{4.19}$$

Specificity findings using suggested and existing methods are shown in Fig. 4.6. In comparison to the suggested approach of KCM-DCBOA (see Fig. 4.6), existing techniques such as BPNN, PSOA, ACO, and CFA have poor specificity.

By dividing the real positives by anything else which should have been projected as positive, recall (also known as the True Positive Rate) is obtained. As shown in Fig. 4.7, the suggested approach of KCM-DCBOA has a high recall of 90% than the existing methods. The Eq. (4.20) is given below:

$$\text{Recall} = \frac{\text{TP}}{\text{TP} + \text{FN}} \tag{4.20}$$

The F1 measure represents a happy medium between recall and precision. In terms of measuring success, it is a statistic. A person's F1 measure represents the mean of their accuracy and recall scores. Fig. 4.8 represents the F1 measure results of the proposed and existing methodology. From Fig. 4.8, the proposed

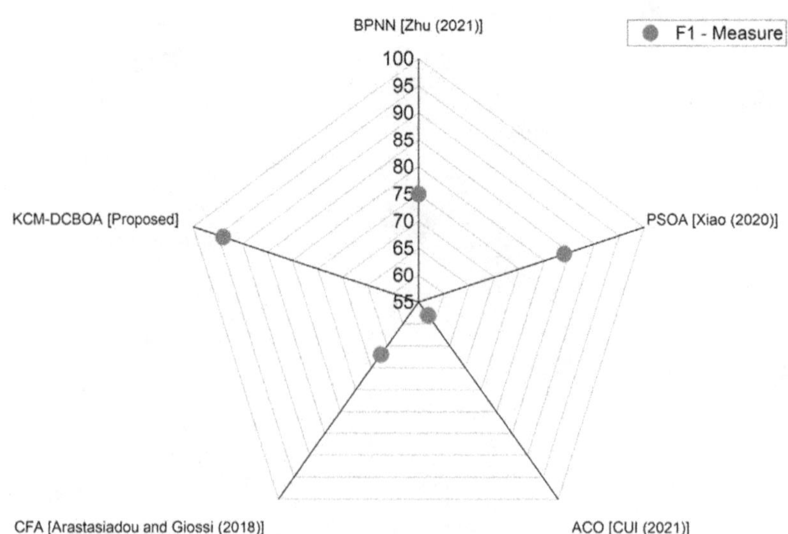

Fig. 4.8. F1-Measure Results of Proposed and Existing Methodology.

approach of KCM-DCBOA has a high F1 measure than the existing methods. Eq. (4.21) is described below:

$$\text{F1} - \text{measure} = \frac{\text{TP}}{\text{TP} + \frac{1}{2}(\text{FP} + \text{FN})} \tag{4.21}$$

4. Conclusion

The vitality of the business and the morale of its workers can both benefit from a well-organized HR department. Across a wide range of sectors, data derived by WI apps have become the norm. Some of the newest optimization algorithms modified from their natural world inspirations for clustering are presented and tested in the context of a WI scenario in this study. Comparisons are made to state-of-the-art methods in terms of accuracy, precisions, specificity, recall, and the F1 measure. Our future studies will incorporate a broader range of data types for the tests as well as more evaluation measures. Compared to other approaches now in use, our suggested method outperforms them.

References

Asís, E. H. R., Figueroa, R. P. N., Quiñones, R. E. T., & Márquez Mázmela, P. R. H. (2022). Validation of a cybercrime awareness scale in Peruvian university students. *Revista Científica General José María Córdova*, *20*(37), 208–224. doi:10.21830/19006586.791

Bharti, V., Biswas, B., & Shukla, K. K. (2020, January). Recent trends in nature inspired computation with applications to deep learning. In *2020 10th International Conference on Cloud Computing, Data Science & Engineering (Confluence)* (pp. 294–299). IEEE.

Castillo, A., Fernández, C. E., Camones, O. G., & Guerra, M. E. (2022). Digitalización de la cadena de suministro y la competitividad de las empresas peruanas del sector minorista. *Revista Cientifica Epistemia*, *6*(2), 77–95. doi:10.26495/re.v6i2.2297

Castro, J. A., Castillo, A., Camones, O. G., & Cochachin, L. F. (2022). Mejoramiento del servicio al cliente y ampliación de las oportunidades de venta mediante el uso de tecnología de punta en el comercio textil peruano. *Revista Cientifica Epistemia*, *6*(2), 35–49. doi:10.26495/re.v6i2.2294

Dey, N., Ashour, A. S., & Bhattacharyya, S. (Eds.). (2020). *Applied nature-inspired computing: algorithms and case studies*. Springer Singapore.

Herrera, J., & de las Heras-Rosas, C. (2020). Corporate social responsibility and human resource management: Towards sustainable business organizations. *Sustainability*, *12*(3), 841.

Hmoud, B., & Laszlo, V. (2019). Will artificial intelligence take over human resources recruitment and selection. *Network Intelligence Studies*, *7*(13), 21–30.

Huerta-Soto, R., Ramirez-Asis, H., Mukthar, K. J., Rurush-Asencio, R., Villanueva-Calderón, J., & Zarzosa-Marquez, E. (2022). Purchase intention based on the brand value of pharmacies in a locality of the Peruvian highlands. In *International*

Conference on Business and Technology (pp. 67–78). Cham: Springer International Publishing. doi:10.1007/978-3-031-26956-1_7

Li, J., & Zhou, Z. (2022). Design of human resource management system based on deep learning. Computational Intelligence and Neuroscience, 2022.

Mellal, M. A. (2022). Some words about nature-inspired computing. In *Applications of nature-inspired computing in renewable energy systems* (pp. 1–9). Hershey, PA: IGI Global.

Oral, M., & Turgut, S. S. (2018, October). Performance analysis of relatively new nature inspired computing algorithms. In *2018 Innovations in Intelligent Systems and Applications Conference (ASYU)* (pp. 1–6). IEEE.

Pallathadka, H., Wenda, A., Ramirez-Asís, E., Asís-López, M., Flores-Albornoz, J., & Phasinam, K. (2023). Classification and prediction of student performance data using various machine learning algorithms. *Materials Today Proceedings*, *80*, 3782–3785. doi:10.1016/j.matpr.2021.07.382

Ramirez-Asis, E., Maguina, M. E., Infantes, S. E., & Naranjo-Toro, M. (2020). Emotional intelligence, competencies and performance of the university professor: Using the SEM-PLS partial least squares technique. *Rev. Electron. Interuniv. Form. Profr*, *23*, 99–114. doi:10.6018/reifop.428261

Rui, T., Fong, S., Yang, X. S., & Deb, S. (2019, December). Nature-inspired clustering algorithms for web intelligence data. In *2012 IEEE/WIC/ACM International Conferences on Web Intelligence and Intelligent Agent Technology* (Vol. 3, pp. 147–153). IEEE.

Shaikh, A. A., Lakshmi, K. S., Tongkachok, K., Alanya-Beltran, J., Ramirez-Asis, E., & Perez-Falcon, J. (2022). Empirical analysis in analysing the major factors of machine learning in enhancing the e-business through structural equation modelling (SEM) approach. *International Journal of System Assurance Engineering and Management*, *13*(Suppl 1), 681–689. doi:10.1007/s13198-021-01590-1

Sohrabi, B., Vanani, I. R., & Abedin, E. (2018). Human resources management and information systems trend analysis using text clustering. *International Journal of Human Capital and Information Technology Professionals*, *9*(3), 1–24.

Soto, R. H., Asis, E. H., Figueroa, R. P., & Plasencia, L. (2023). Autoeficacia emprendedora y desempeño de micro y pequeñas empresas peruanas. *Revista Venezolana de Gerencia: RVG*, *28*(102), 751–768. doi:10.52080/rvgluz.28.102.19

Vasantham, S. T. (2021). The role of artificial intelligence in human resource management. doi:10.30726/ESIJ/V8.I2.2021.82013

Veluchamy, R., Sanchari, C., & Gupta, S. (2021). Artificial intelligence within recruitment: Eliminating biases in human resource management. *Artificial Intelligence*, *8*(3).

Venusamy, K., Rajagopal, N. K., & Yousoof, M. (2020, December). A study of human resources development through chatbots using artificial intelligence. In *2020 3rd International Conference on Intelligent Sustainable Systems (ICISS)* (pp. 94–99). IEEE.

Votto, A. M., Valecha, R., Najafirad, P., & Rao, H. R. (2021). Artificial intelligence in tactical human resource management: A systematic literature review. *International Journal of Information Management Data Insights*, *1*(2), 100047.

Wang, W. (2022). Design and simulation of human resource allocation model based on artificial intelligence and in-depth data analysis. In *International Conference on Multi-modal Information Analytics* (pp. 192–200). Cham: Springer.

Yahia, H. S., Zeebaree, S. R., Sadeeq, M. A., Salim, N. O., Kak, S. F., Adel, A. Z., . . . Hussein, H. A. (2021). Comprehensive survey for cloud computing based on nature-inspired algorithms optimization scheduling. *Asian Journal of Research in Computer Science*, *8*(2), 1–16.

Yating, Y., Mughal, N., Wen, J., Ngan, T. T., Ramirez-Asis, E., & Maneengam, A. (2022). Economic performance and natural resources commodity prices volatility: Evidence from global data. *Resources Policy*, *78*, 102879. doi:10.1016/j.resourpol.2022.102879

Zhao, Y. (2020, December). Application of K-means clustering algorithm in human resource data informatization. In *Proceedings of the 2020 International Conference on Cyberspace Innovation of Advanced Technologies* (pp. 12–16).

Part II

Technological Education and Skills Development for Sustainable Practices

Chapter 5

Blockchain Technology and Virtual Asset Accounting in the Metaverse

Heba Hikal[a], *Marwan Altarawneh*[a], *Ahmad AL-Hawamleh*[b], *Zaid Jaradat*[c] *and Alya Elfedawy*[a]

[a]Arab Open University, Saudi Arabia
[b]Department of Electronic Training, Institute of Public Administration, Saudi Arabia
[c]Al al-Bayt University, Jordan

Abstract

This research focuses on the Metaverse's evolving trend and the potential application of blockchain technology in the accounting of virtual assets in this digital domain. The Metaverse introduces a new economy in which users may earn real-world revenue through virtual activities, necessitating the need for efficient and dependable virtual asset accounting. Blockchain technology, with its decentralized and immutable record, appears to be a viable answer to these problems. This chapter discusses the present status of blockchain technology for accounting for virtual assets in the Metaverse as well as its potential role for businesses and the economy. It also determines the technology's issues and limits and makes recommendations for further development. The findings indicate that blockchain technology has the potential to transform virtual asset accounting in the Metaverse by improving security, transparency, and consistency. However, scalability and legal/regulatory issues must be overcome before it can completely achieve its promise. Accounting experts, developers, and stakeholders interested in the convergence of blockchain technology and the Metaverse economy will find this chapter useful.

Keywords: Metaverse; virtual asset accounting; blockchain technology; accounting education; business education; accounting profession

Technological Innovations for Business, Education and Sustainability, 71–78

Published under exclusive licence by Emerald Publishing Limited
doi:10.1108/978-1-83753-106-620241005

1. Introduction

The Metaverse, a virtual environment that blurs the boundaries between physical and digital domains, has attracted millions of people worldwide (Ball, 2022). To monitor and manage virtual assets in a safe and transparent manner, blockchain technology can help. Blockchain technology, a decentralized ledger, records all transactions in a tamper-proof and transparent manner, and has the potential to transform the way virtual assets are tracked in the Metaverse (Huynh-The et al., 2023).

Accounting for virtual assets in the Metaverse is difficult and time-consuming, as they lack a defined accounting system (Huynh-The et al., 2023). Blockchain technology can provide a secure and easily accessible accounting system for virtual assets in the Metaverse, fostering better trust and collaboration among individuals and enterprises. This opens up new avenues for innovation and growth, as businesses can safely and openly communicate information using blockchain technology (Dwivedi et al., 2022).

However, the rise of blockchain technology as a means of accounting for virtual assets in the Metaverse has its challenges (Saberi, Kouhizadeh, Sarkis, & Shen, 2019). There is no centralized authority to regulate transactions, raising security and fraud issues (Zutshi, Grilo, & Nodehi, 2021). Additionally, the absence of a defined accounting system for virtual assets might cause misunderstandings and disagreements among people and enterprises (Bakarich, Castonguay, & O'Brien, 2020). However, by creating new norms and rules for virtual assets in the Metaverse, individuals and corporations can collaborate to develop a safe and transparent accounting system that fosters trust and collaboration (Fernandez & Hui, 2022).

This research explores the Metaverse's virtual assets and the role of blockchain technology in accounting for them. The research aims to explore the potential benefits and downsides of blockchain technology in managing and tracking virtual assets. Blockchain technology offers a safe, transparent, and efficient solution for managing and tracking virtual assets, making it a promising option for enterprises and the economy. The research aims to inform companies and authorities about the advantages and disadvantages of blockchain technology and provide guidance on proper usage, given the growing importance of virtual assets in the Metaverse.

2. Literature Review

2.1 Metaverse

The Metaverse, a virtual universe created by combining virtual reality, augmented reality, and other cutting-edge technology, is an immersive shared experience accessible to anyone, anywhere, at any time (Mozumder, Sheeraz, Athar, Aich, & Kim, 2022). It allows users to live, work, and play in a virtual world, where they can create and modify avatars, which are virtual representations of themselves (Dwivedi et al., 2022). The Metaverse is expected to significantly influence various industries, including gaming, entertainment, education, and financial services (Dwivedi et al., 2022). It offers a new method of considering how people interact with technology and the nature of reality. The Metaverse is a social, cultural, and technological phenomenon with societal and ethical implications. The accounting industry is embracing the Metaverse, recording, reporting, and analyzing financial information related to Metaverse virtual assets, such as nonfungible tokens (NFTs), cryptocurrencies, and virtual real estate (Belk, Humayun, & Brouard, 2022). Accurate and reliable accounting data is necessary for the transparency, accuracy, and accountability of the new digital ecosystem (Wang, Li, Lu, & Cheng, 2022). The accounting profession must adapt to the new environment and acquire new skills to capitalize on the opportunities and challenges presented by the Metaverse.

2.2 The Rise of Virtual Assets in the Metaverse

The emergence of virtual assets in the Metaverse has led to a new era in the digital economy, offering innovation, growth, and trade opportunities (Dwivedi et al., 2022). Users can trade, purchase, and sell digital assets like cryptocurrencies, NFTs, and virtual properties, enabling them to make tangible funds through virtual activities like gaming and content production (Allam, Sharifi, Bibri, Jones, & Krogstie, 2022). The value of virtual assets is determined by supply and demand, with some surpassing their real-world counterparts (Dwivedi et al., 2022). However, the lack of regulations and standards in the Metaverse raises risks and issues, such as fraud and hacking (Huang, Li, & Cai, 2023). As virtual assets become more popular, there are growing doubts about how current financial institutions will fit into this emerging economy. Some researchers predict that the Metaverse will eventually displace current financial systems and serve as the main medium of trade for virtual assets and money (Belk et al., 2022). However, current financial institutions are expected to adapt and grow to include virtual assets in their services, creating new opportunities for growth and innovation (Zainurin, Haji Masri, Besar, & Anshari, 2023). Despite its early stages, the Metaverse's growth has the potential to upend the current financial system and create fresh opportunities for development and innovation (Wu et al., 2023).

2.3 Importance of Accounting for Virtual Assets in the Metaverse

Accounting for Metaverse virtual assets is essential for accurate financial reporting, tax compliance, and transparency (Huynh-The et al., 2023). Accountants must be able to handle the evaluation and accounting of virtual assets as they become more important in the Metaverse (De Giovanni, 2023). The lack of regulation and standardization in the Metaverse is a significant concern for accounting practices (Huynh-The et al., 2023); nevertheless, it also gives an opportunity for accountants to innovate and develop new accounting methods to meet the needs of this expanding business (Alsalmi, Ullah, & Rafique, 2023). As the Metaverse matures and flourishes, so will the need for accounting for virtual assets, providing new challenges and opportunities for the accounting profession (De Giovanni, 2023).

2.4 Blockchain Technology and Its Role in Accounting for Virtual Assets

Blockchain technology is a decentralized and distributed ledger system that enables safe and transparent peer-to-peer transactions without intermediaries (Esmat, de Vos, Ghiassi-Farrokhfal, Palensky, & Epema, 2021). It is a chain of blocks that is updated with each new transaction, providing numerous benefits in industries like banking, medicine, and logistics (Dutta, Choi, Somani, & Butala, 2020). Blockchain operates on a peer-to-peer basis, with each network participant having a copy of the ledger (Esmat et al., 2021). The system is highly secure and transparent, with no possibility of alteration or deletion (Otte, de Vos, & Pouwelse, 2020). It also offers immutability, making it resistant to fraud and manipulation (Otte et al., 2020).

Blockchain technology uses a consensus approach to ensure consensus among network participants, with popular proof-of-work being the most popular (Handayani, Supriati, & Aisyah, 2020). Alternative mechanisms, such as proof-of-stake and delegated proof-of-stake, have emerged due to potential time and energy requirements (Kaur, Chaturvedi, Sharma, & Kar, 2021). Blockchain technology has the potential to change how we handle and keep data, as traditional databases are vulnerable to hacking and corruption due to a centralized authority (Taş & Tanrıöver, 2020). Blockchain technology also increases the accuracy and integrity of financial reporting, ensuring that financial data is accurate, satisfied, and up-to-date (Huynh-The et al., 2023). This increases investor confidence and encourages transparency, giving the Metaverse an advantage over rivals (Polas et al., 2022). Blockchain technology also makes accounting procedures run more quickly and with less energy, reducing costs and allowing companies to invest in other areas of their operations (Wei, 2022).

Blockchain technology has gained popularity in virtual asset accounting due to its decentralization, security, transparency, and immutability. It has been used in applications like smart contracts, tokenization, supply chain management, decentralized exchanges, and the art industry (Gupta et al., 2020; Hamilton, 2020). Smart contracts enable tamper-proof, transparent ownership of valuable assets, while tokenization facilitates fractional ownership and movement across networks. Decentralized exchanges provide high security and transparency, while unique digital assets enable artists to market their work as digital art (Rehman, e Zainab, Imran, & Bawany, 2021).

3. Challenges and Limitations

Blockchain technology is increasingly being used in the Metaverse to manage virtual assets, but it presents challenges such as privacy protection and security (Bhushan, Sinha, Sagayam, & Andrew, 2021; Rehman et al., 2021). Privacy-focused blockchain protocols aim to provide users with more privacy and anonymity, but they can also pose challenges in identifying and preventing criminal activities like money laundering and terrorism funding (Nelaturu, Du, & Le, 2022). Other approaches to strengthen privacy and security include multi-signature wallets and smart contracts.

Scalability is a critical issue in blockchain-based accounting for virtual assets, as the decentralized nature makes it difficult to manage large numbers of transactions (Wang et al., 2022). Layer two scaling techniques, such as Lightning Network and Plasma, can improve transaction speed and capacity, but raise security risks (Pandey, Fernandez, Bansal, & Tyagi, 2022). State channels and off-chain transactions can also enhance scalability, but they have disadvantages like the need for significant development resources and the possibility of centralization.

Interoperability and standards in blockchain-based accounting for virtual assets are crucial as the Metaverse expands (Murray, Kim, & Combs, 2023). The lack of a standard language and protocol hinders network fragmentation. Industry standards and best practices can ensure consistency, but implementation can be challenging. Legal and regulatory issues, such as ownership, control, intellectual property rights, and monitoring, require collaboration to establish clear frameworks and raise public awareness.

4. Future Implications and Opportunities

Blockchain technology has the potential to revolutionize the way businesses and investors account for virtual assets in the Metaverse. It offers increased efficiency, security, and trust, as well as new opportunities for raising capital, making money, collaborating, and innovating (Centobelli, Cerchione, Del Vecchio, Oropallo, & Secundo, 2022). As the Metaverse evolves, it is crucial for businesses and investors to seize these opportunities and collaborate to build a robust and sustainable economy. Blockchain technology has the potential to disrupt traditional accounting procedures (Secinaro, Dal Mas, Brescia, & Calandra, 2021), boost productivity, reduce transaction costs, improve financial reporting transparency, shift attention from analog to digital accounting methods, and open up new business opportunities for companies and accounting professionals.

Blockchain technology is a catalyst for digital change, enabling organizations to modernize virtual asset accounting, stimulate innovation and cooperation, and redefine how we live and work in the Metaverse. It enables the creation of new goods and services by securely exchanging information, while decentralized autonomous organizations (DAOs) provide a democratic and transparent decision-making framework (Bellavitis, Fisch, & Momtaz, 2023). Additionally, blockchain technology improves digital identity management by giving individuals ownership over their data, enhancing privacy and security, and enabling tailored experiences that build user trust and engagement. The limitless potential for innovation entices enterprises to venture into unknown territory, change sectors, and pave the path for a future where blockchain is an essential component of our digital world.

5. Conclusion

The research explores the role of blockchain technology in managing virtual assets in the Metaverse, revealing potential for transformation in accounting and valuation. The Metaverse offers opportunities for real-world revenue through virtual activities like content production but lacks standards and regulation. Accounting professionals must adapt and adopt creative methods to handle virtual assets, overcoming scalability, legal, and regulatory issues. Interoperability and standardization are crucial, and establishing regulatory and legal frameworks emphasizes responsibility, transparency, and consumer protection. Blockchain technology in conventional accounting practices can improve productivity, reduce transaction costs, and increase financial reporting transparency. Accounting experts, developers, and stakeholders interested in the convergence of blockchain technology and the Metaverse economy will find this chapter useful. Accounting professionals must adopt blockchain technology to stay competitive in the evolving Metaverse and embrace innovation and collaboration in the virtual economy.

Acknowledgment

We acknowledge that this chapter serves as the foundational starting point for a comprehensive literature review chapter.

References

Allam, Z., Sharifi, A., Bibri, S. E., Jones, D. S., & Krogstie, J. (2022). The metaverse as a virtual form of smart cities: Opportunities and challenges for environmental, economic, and social sustainability in urban futures. *Smart Cities*, *5*(3), 771–801. doi:10.3390/smartcities5030040

Alsalmi, N., Ullah, S., & Rafique, M. (2023). Accounting for digital currencies. *Research in International Business and Finance*, *64*, 101897. doi:10.1016/j.ribaf.2023.101897

Bakarich, K. M., Castonguay, J. J., & O'Brien, P. E. (2020). The use of blockchains to enhance sustainability reporting and assurance. *Accounting Perspectives*, *19*(4), 389–412.

Ball, M. (2022). *The metaverse: And how it will revolutionize everything* (1st ed.). New York, NY: Liveright Publishing. ISBN 978-1-324-09203-2

Belk, R., Humayun, M., & Brouard, M. (2022). Money, possessions, and ownership in the Metaverse: NFTs, cryptocurrencies, Web3 and Wild Markets. *Journal of Business Research*, *153*, 198–205.

Bellavitis, C., Fisch, C., & Momtaz, P. P. (2023). The rise of decentralized autonomous organizations (DAOs): A first empirical glimpse. *Venture Capital*, *25*(2), 187–203.

Bhushan, B., Sinha, P., Sagayam, K. M., & Andrew, J. (2021). Untangling blockchain technology: A survey on state of the art, security threats, privacy services, applications and future research directions. *Computers & Electrical Engineering*, *90*, 106897. doi:10.1016/j.compeleceng.2020.106897

Centobelli, P., Cerchione, R., Del Vecchio, P., Oropallo, E., & Secundo, G. (2022). Blockchain technology for bridging trust, traceability and transparency in circular supply chain. *Information & Management*, *59*(7), 103508. doi:10.1016/j.im.2021.103508

De Giovanni, P. (2023). Sustainability of the Metaverse: A Transition to Industry 5.0. *Sustainability*, *15*(7), 6079. doi:10.3390/su15076079

Dutta, P., Choi, T. M., Somani, S., & Butala, R. (2020). Blockchain technology in supply chain operations: Applications, challenges and research opportunities. *Transportation Research Part E: Logistics and Transportation Review*, *142*, 102067. doi:10.1016/j.tre.2020.102067

Dwivedi, Y. K., Hughes, L., Baabdullah, A. M., Ribeiro-Navarrete, S., Giannakis, M., Al-Debei, M. M., … Wamba, S. F. (2022). Metaverse beyond the hype: Multidisciplinary perspectives on emerging challenges, opportunities, and agenda for research, practice and policy. *International Journal of Information Management*, *66*, 102542. doi:10.1016/j.ijinfomgt.2022.102542

Esmat, A., de Vos, M., Ghiassi-Farrokhfal, Y., Palensky, P., & Epema, D. (2021). A novel decentralized platform for peer-to-peer energy trading market with blockchain technology. *Applied Energy*, *282*, 116123. doi:10.1016/j.apenergy.2020.116123

Fernandez, C. B., & Hui, P. (2022, July 10). Life, the metaverse and everything: An overview of privacy, ethics, and governance in metaverse. In *Proceedings of the 2022 IEEE 42nd International Conference on Distributed Computing Systems Workshops (ICDCSW)* (pp. 272–277). Bologna: IEEE.

Gupta, A., Rathod, J., Patel, D., Bothra, J., Shanbhag, S., & Bhalerao, T. (2020). Tokenization of real estate using blockchain technology. In *Applied Cryptography and Network Security Workshops: ACNS 2020 Satellite Workshops, AIBlock, AIHWS, AIoTS, Cloud S&P, SCI, SecMT, and SiMLA,* Rome, Italy, October 19–22, 2020, Proceedings 18 (pp. 77–90). Springer International Publishing.

Hamilton, M. (2020). Blockchain distributed ledger technology: An introduction and focus on smart contracts. *Journal of Corporate Accounting & Finance*, *31*(2), 7–12.

Handayani, I., Supriati, R., & Aisyah, E. S. N. (2020, October). Proof of Blockchain Work on The Security of Academic Certificates. In *2020 8th International Conference on Cyber and IT Service Management (CITSM)* (pp. 1–5). IEEE. doi:10.1109/CITSM50537.2020.9268782

Huang, Y., Li, Y. J., & Cai, Z. (2023). Security and privacy in metaverse: A comprehensive survey. *Big Data Mining and Analytics*, *6*(2), 234–247. doi:10.26599/BDMA.2022.9020047

Huynh-The, T., Pham, Q. V., Pham, X. Q., Nguyen, T. T., Han, Z., & Kim, D. S. (2023). Artificial intelligence for the metaverse: A survey. *Engineering Applications of Artificial Intelligence*, *117*, 105581. doi:10.1016/j.engappai.2022.105581

Kaur, S., Chaturvedi, S., Sharma, A., & Kar, J. (2021). A research survey on applications of consensus protocols in blockchain. *Security and Communication Networks*, *2021*, 1–22.

Mozumder, M. A. I., Sheeraz, M. M., Athar, A., Aich, S., & Kim, H. C. (2022, February 13–16). Overview: Technology roadmap of the future trend of metaverse based on IoT, blockchain, AI technique, and medical domain metaverse activity. In *Proceedings of the 2022 24th International Conference on Advanced Communication Technology (ICACT)* (pp. 256–261). Pyeongchang-gun: IEEE.

Murray, A., Kim, D., & Combs, J. (2023). The promise of a decentralized internet: What is Web3 and how can firms prepare? *Business Horizons*, *66*(2), 191–202.

Nelaturu, K., Du, H., & Le, D. P. (2022). A review of Blockchain in Fintech: Taxonomy, challenges, and future directions. *Cryptography*, *6*(2), 18. doi:10.3390/cryptography6020018

Otte, P., de Vos, M., & Pouwelse, J. (2020). TrustChain: A Sybil-resistant scalable blockchain. *Future Generation Computer Systems*, *107*, 770–780. doi:10.1016/j.future.2017.08.048

Pandey, A. A., Fernandez, T. F., Bansal, R., & Tyagi, A. K. (2022, March). Maintaining scalability in blockchain. In *Intelligent Systems Design and Applications: 21st International Conference on Intelligent Systems Design and Applications (ISDA 2021)* Held During December 13–15, 2021 (pp. 34–45). Cham: Springer International Publishing. doi:10.1007/978-3-030-16657-1_94

Polas, M. R. H., Jahanshahi, A. A., Kabir, A. I., Sohel-Uz-Zaman, A. S. M., Osman, A. R., & Karim, R. (2022). Artificial intelligence, blockchain technology, and risk-taking behavior in the 4.0 IR Metaverse Era: Evidence from Bangladesh-based SMEs. *Journal of Open Innovation: Technology, Market, and Complexity*, *8*(3), 168. doi:10.3390/joitmc8030168

Rehman, W., e Zainab, H., Imran, J., & Bawany, N. Z. (2021, December 21–23). NFTs: Applications and challenges. In *Proceedings of the 2021 22nd International Arab Conference on Information Technology (ACIT)* (pp. 1–7). Muscat: IEEE.

Saberi, S., Kouhizadeh, M., Sarkis, J., & Shen, L. (2019). Blockchain technology and its relationships to sustainable supply chain management. *International Journal of Production Research*, *57*(7), 2117–2135. doi:10.1080/00207543.2018.1533261

Secinaro, S., Dal Mas, F., Brescia, V., & Calandra, D. (2021). Blockchain in the accounting, auditing and accountability fields: A bibliometric and coding analysis. *Accounting, Auditing & Accountability Journal*, *35*(9), 168–203. doi:10.1108/AAAJ-10-2020-4987

Taş, R., & Tanrıöver, Ö. Ö. (2020). A systematic review of challenges and opportunities of blockchain for E-voting. *Symmetry*, *12*(8), 1328. doi:10.3390/sym12081328

Wang, Z., Li, M., Lu, J., & Cheng, X. (2022). Business Innovation based on artificial intelligence and Blockchain technology. *Information Processing & Management*, *59*(1), 102759.

Wei, D. (2022). Gemiverse: The blockchain-based professional certification and tourism platform with its own ecosystem in the metaverse. *International Journal of Geoheritage and Parks*, *10*(2), 322–336.

Wu, J., Lin, K., Lin, D., Zheng, Z., Huang, H., & Zheng, Z. (2023). Financial Crimes in Web3-empowered Metaverse: Taxonomy, Countermeasures, and Opportunities. *IEEE Open Journal of the Computer Society*, *4*, 37–49. doi:10.1109/OJCS.2023.3245801

Zainurin, M. Z. L., Haji Masri, M., Besar, M. H. A., & Anshari, M. (2023). Towards an understanding of metaverse banking: A conceptual paper. *Journal of Financial Reporting & Accounting*, *21*(1), 178–190. doi:10.1108/JFRA-12-2021-0487

Zutshi, A., Grilo, A., & Nodehi, T. (2021). The value proposition of blockchain technologies and its impact on Digital Platforms. *Computers & Industrial Engineering*, *155*, 107187. doi:10.1016/j.cie.2021.107187

Chapter 6

Stakeholders' Perceptions of Sustainability Accounting Education: A Literature Review

Huthaifa Al-Hazaima[a], *Hashem Alshurafat*[a], *Mohannad Obeid Al Shbail*[b] *and Husam Ananzeh*[c]

[a]The Hashemite University, Jordan
[b]Al al-Bayt University, Jordan
[c]Department of Accounting, Irbid National University, Irbid, Jordan

Abstract

To effectively integrate sustainability education into accounting, the needs of stakeholders such as educators, practitioners, regulators, students, and politicians must be considered. While existing literature reflects their separate perceptions, this study considers their influence on the integration process. Sustainability accounting can play a key role in supporting sustainability practices, which businesses need to be accountable for. This study focuses on how sustainability accounting education can improve corporate sustainability practices. However, most existing studies only consider one stakeholder group, and there is a gap in literature on sustainability accounting education in developing countries, particularly in the Middle East. This study informs future researchers about various research gaps in sustainability education.

Keywords: Accounting education; sustainability; accounting curricula; stakeholders; Jordan; universities

1. Introduction

To effectively incorporate sustainability education into the accounting curriculum, it is important to consider the needs of various groups of stakeholders, including industry practitioners, educators, students, regulators, and politicians (Meyer & Bushney, 2008). These groups assert that engaging with a broad range

Technological Innovations for Business, Education and Sustainability, 79–89

Published under exclusive licence by Emerald Publishing Limited
doi:10.1108/978-1-83753-106-620241006

of stakeholders is essential for the successful development of sustainability accounting and other sustainability business courses.

However, the accounting literature does not clearly demonstrate the involvement of key stakeholders in the process of integrating sustainability education into the curriculum (Al-Hazaima, Low, & Sharma, 2021). Rather, it tends to reflect their individual perceptions separately (Al Shbail, Alshurafat, Ananzeh, & Al-Msiedeen, 2021; Alshurafat et al., 2023; Alshurafat, Al Shbail, Masadeh, Dahmash, & Al-Msiedeen, 2021; Mansour, Alzyoud, Abuzaid, & Alshurafat, 2023). For example, some studies focus only on educators' perspectives (Rezaee & Wang, 2022), while others solely examine students' perceptions (Karnalim, Chivers, & Panca, 2022). Few studies consider the views of industry practitioners (Alshurafat, Beattie, Jones, & Sands, 2020). Furthermore, these studies only explore the stakeholders' perspectives without highlighting their impact on the integration process.

It is important to distinguish between stakeholders and salient stakeholders. This study adopts the salient stakeholder perspective, which not only seeks to understand stakeholders' perceptions but also their influence on the integration process in terms of power, legitimacy, and urgency. The following sections discuss the stakeholders' opinions with regard to integrating sustainability education into accounting and business curricula.

2. The Industry's Perception of Sustainability Accounting Practice and Education

Integrating sustainability into traditional accounting and management systems requires substantial changes to the system, as well as new skills and competencies for practitioners, including managers and accountants (Sen, Pattanayak, & Choubey, 2010). Fortes (2002) emphasized this point by suggesting that if organizations decided to address issues such as the full integration of environmental costs into capital budgeting and cost allocations, managers and accountants would need to consider the extent of the necessary accounting changes. Developed countries such as the United States, Japan, and Australia are successful in adopting environmental accounting and reporting practices because they can follow different disclosure guidelines (Frost & English, 2002; Kokubu & Nashioka, 2005, 2008), unlike those in developing countries. Companies in most developing countries only engage in voluntary disclosure and lack comprehensive guidelines for sustainability accounting and reporting (Sen et al., 2010).

Managers and accountants from organizations in developing countries acknowledge their lack of involvement in their organizations' environmental activities and the insignificance of sustainability accounting (Sen et al., 2010). They attribute their weaknesses to the absence of environmental issues in their tertiary education curriculum. For instance, the low level of environmental reporting practices in Indian organizations is due to a lack of knowledge and expertise (Sen et al., 2010).

According to Pahuja and Bansal (2006), managers and accountants of Indian organizations recognize the significance of environmental accounting and support mandatory environmental disclosures. However, Sen et al. (2010) believe that this acknowledgment is insufficient to bring about real change in corporate practices that align with the sustainable development agenda. Therefore, future managers and accountants must be exposed to various sustainability accounting issues. They also believe that one way to achieve this is by integrating sustainability education into the accounting curriculum and other business disciplines' curricula.

Studies exploring the views of industry professionals on sustainability accounting in developing countries are few (Belal, 2008; Belal & Owen, 2007; Collison & Gray, 1997; Jaggi & Zhao, 1996; Lodhia, 2003); however, those that have been conducted have found that sustainability accounting information is significant and relevant. For instance, Pahuja and Bansal (2006) discovered that in India, accountants recognize the importance of disclosing sustainability information and believe that environmental information is crucial for management decision-making. Shareholders and individuals within organizations also view sustainability information as highly relevant in business decision-making (Prasad, 2006), while managers and accountants believe that sustainability reporting can improve an organization's corporate image and status (Malarvizhi, 2007). Corporate sustainability accounting and reporting are required, according to Pramanik, Shil, and Das (2009), who discuss sustainability accounting issues. However, executives in Indian organizations are hesitant to disclose unfavorable sustainability information due to its potential impact on their competitive position (Pradhan & Pattnaik, 2007).

Sen et al. (2010) attempted to determine the opinions of industry practitioners such as financial managers, chartered accountants, and managers in financial services regarding developing a sustainability accounting course for business schools in India. The study asked participants to rank 12 important topics summarized from the literature on a five-point rating scale based on their importance. The purpose of this ranking was to determine the relative importance of each topic and aid in the development of a sustainability accounting course. Sen et al.'s (2010) findings indicate that industry practitioners perceive sustainability accounting and reporting to be essential and that they strongly advocate for a separate sustainability accounting format, implying the need to integrate a course on sustainability accounting into the accounting curriculum. However, Sen et al.'s study neglects social aspects. Society is a vital aspect of sustainability, and the literature suggests that social considerations should be included in any questionnaire developed, and the sustainability accounting course should aim to satisfy social needs and expectations.

3. The University's Perception of Sustainability Accounting Education

Several studies have been conducted to examine the state of sustainability accounting education in British universities. Owen, Humphrey, and Lewis (1994) and Humphrey, Lewis, and Owen (1996) found that sustainability accounting is considered a marginal issue and is not widely taught. However, educators who teach papers on sustainability accounting believe that such courses hold significant pedagogic value. Watt's (1998) findings indicate that academics worldwide support the inclusion of sustainability accounting in both university education and professional training.

Humphrey et al. (1996) also explored the barriers to the development of sustainability accounting two decades ago. Their study revealed that professional accounting bodies' accreditation process has a powerful impact, determining what is core and appropriate in accounting education and serving as a significant obstacle. Universities and academics also face pressures such as funding constraints and pressure on research output.

Mangion (2006) reviewed social and environmental accounting education in Australian universities and replicated the studies of Owen et al. (1994) and Stevenson (2002). Her study found that sustainability accounting was gaining acceptance in undergraduate curricula. Mangion concluded that the most significant reason for teaching sustainability accounting is to increase students' awareness of corporate social and environmental commitments.

Previous studies on students' perceptions of sustainability courses at the tertiary level are positive, with Kagawa (2007) and Von Der Heidt and Lamberton (2011) reporting favorable views. Thomas (2005) investigated students' perception of environmental accounting and its significance for decision-making in organizations. He found that students believe sustainability information is relevant to managerial decision-making. Coulson and Thomson (2006) found that accounting's role in sustainability influences the need to design a sustainability accounting course integrated into specific areas such as management accounting.

A survey conducted on students from Southern Cross University in Australia by Von Der Heidt and Lamberton (2011) found that students strongly believe that courses such as ethics and sustainability and sustainable business management which were provided as part of their syllabus are important and relevant to the accounting discipline. That finding indicates that students may prefer to have more sustainability education within their curriculum. Moreover, a study conducted by Kagawa (2007) on the understanding and perception of students toward sustainable development at the University of Plymouth revealed that over 90% of students had a positive reaction to the idea of sustainability education.

Sharma and Kelly (2012) explore accounting and business students' perception toward sustainability teachings and to explore the students' attitudes toward their sustainability courses. The students were from a regional university in New Zealand. Using a questionnaire survey, the study collected 60 students' opinions. The study found that most students lacked prior knowledge of sustainability, a finding which demonstrates the necessity for higher education to provide students with basic courses on sustainability. The study also found that the majority of students perceive sustainability education positively, and that students who had core papers on sustainability found the papers useful. Many students also felt that it is important to include sustainability papers as compulsory in the curriculum. Sharma and Kelly (2014) argue that students are more influenced by conventional, mandatory accounting courses such as financial and management accounting. Students believe that such courses are more relevant to and practical for their future careers (Hazelton & Haigh, 2010). MacVaugh and Norton (2012) argue that management and business students attempt to obtain only the necessary education that provides the professional skills and knowledge required for their jobs in the future. Sharma and Kelly (2014) believe that this attitude discourages students from studying issues of environmental and global concern.

Carr, Chua, and Perera (2006) investigate the views of 236 accounting graduates in New Zealand on the design of accounting programs. The study also explores the key characteristics of an accounting curriculum that should be considered when designing a program for accounting. Their findings support the view that it is no longer appropriate for higher education providers to adopt a one-size-fits-all approach. The findings also indicate that the social and environmental perspective should have a place in accounting programs along with other perspectives such as global and local perspectives and professionalism. The study finally recognizes the importance of stakeholders in designing accounting programs.

Various options for teaching sustainability accounting have been listed by Mangion (2006), including incorporating it into conventional accounting courses, offering it as a separate module of study, creating specialized curriculum routes, and including it in the general study module on accounting theory. Hazelton and Haigh (2010) and Rusinko (2010) agree with Mangion's list and suggest methods for integrating sustainability into the business and accounting curriculum. The first approach involves incorporating sustainability topics and materials into existing courses, while the second approach involves separating these topics and materials into standalone courses. Standalone courses provide a more detailed explanation of sustainability principles, but they may also result in students perceiving sustainability as a disconnected issue. Therefore, students need to understand different interpretations of sustainability to avoid educational disconnection in business. Bates, Silverblatt, and Kleban (2009) believe that sustainability education should be integrated into all accounting papers, and this notion is also supported by Botes, Low, and Chapman (2014) and Wyness and Dalton (2018). Botes et al. (2014) and Wyness and Dalton (2018) also suggest the need for sustainability education to be embedded in all accounting papers, as they found that sustainability education was inadequate and requires more attention.

A study by Pattanayak, Sen, and Choubey (2011) aimed to evaluate how Indian university management students perceived the integration of environmental accounting into their education. The researchers used a similar method to previous studies conducted by Grinnell and Hunt (2000) and Das, Sen, and Pattanayak (2008). In the study, MBA students were provided with a course on environmental accounting as an intervention. The researchers gathered the students' perceptions before and after the intervention to analyze its impact on them. They used a questionnaire survey to assess the change in the students' perception level and asked them to rank a set of dimensions twice, before and after the intervention. These dimensions were similar to those used in Sen et al.'s (2010) study to assess the perception of industry practitioners. The study found that although the students initially lacked awareness of environmental accounting, the intervention had a positive impact on their perceptions and increased their awareness of the subject. Table 6.1 shows the dimensions and the students' rankings.

In a subsequent study, Choubey and Pattanayak (2014) aimed to assess the perception of various stakeholders, including management students, educators, industry practitioners, and representatives of regulatory bodies, toward the integration of environmental accounting into the curriculum of Indian management education.

In 2014, Choubey and Pattanayak conducted a study to determine the necessary requirements for integrating environmental accounting into management education. The stakeholders were divided into two groups: the first group included students, and the second group included chartered accountants, cost

Table 6.1. Dimensions Prioritized by Students Before and After the Intervention.

S. No	Dimensions	Ranks Before	Ranks After
1	History and basic framework of corporate environmental accounting	6	9
2	Environmental accounting standards and regulations	11	12
3	Environmental cost accounting methods and systems	9	10
4	Environmental accounting information for business reporting	10	7
5	Environmental accounting information for decision-making	12	11
6	Environmental performance measurement systems	5	3
7	Environmental liabilities and contingencies	3	4
8	Environmental tax issues and pollution allowances	8	6
9	Linkage of environmental reporting with CSR and corporate governance	2	2
10	Global environmental issues and reporting practices	7	8
11	Application of environmental accounting in solving real-word corporate environmental problems	4	5
12	Impact of environmental accounting on market reactions and valuations related to environmental variables	1	1

Source: Reproduced from Pattanayak et al. (2011, pp. 31, 35).

accountants, finance managers, educators, and regulatory body representatives. The students were treated as a separate group because they are often overlooked in curriculum development, despite their significant role in shaping course structures. To evaluate the stakeholders' perception of environmental accounting integration, a questionnaire was distributed among 309 participants. This study builds upon previous research by Sen et al. (2010) and Pattanayak et al. (2011), but Choubey and Pattanayak's approach differentiated between various stakeholder groups. The main finding of the study was that all the stakeholders believed that environmental accounting should be included in the curriculum. The study also called for increased awareness among students about environmental accounting's integration into business disciplines, particularly accounting.

Previous research on sustainability education integration into business and accounting curricula has been mixed. Some studies have found little integration, while others have highlighted its importance. However, sustainability accounting education has gained more attention and consideration over time. As a result, standalone courses on sustainability accounting have started to appear in business schools, in addition to sustainability topics within some accounting courses, like management accounting courses.

Several studies indicate that both academics and students have a positive perception toward courses that integrate sustainability accounting into curricula. However, students may be influenced by the traditional accounting curriculum, as they are only interested in acquiring the knowledge and skills necessary to secure a future position. This viewpoint may reflect an unwillingness on the part of employers and professional bodies to incorporate sustainable practices. Few studies have assessed the industry's perception of integrating sustainability accounting into accounting curricula, but those that have indicate that practitioners believe that sustainability accounting practices and education are both essential. Therefore, they support integrating sustainability accounting into accounting and other business disciplines' curricula to improve students' and future practitioners' skills in the business field. The literature gaps are summarized in the Conclusion (Summary of Gaps in the Literature) section.

4. Conclusion (Summary of Gaps in the Literature)

Business organizations have a responsibility to be accountable for their externalities and meet stakeholder expectations for better sustainability practices. Sustainability accounting can play a key role in supporting these practices, but the global environmental consequences of industrialization suggest that sustainability is not taken seriously enough in the business world.

This study focuses on how sustainability accounting education can bridge the gap in weak corporate sustainability practices. Tertiary education is critical in educating future managers to think critically and make decisions that improve sustainability practices. However, current accounting education does not support these practices and needs to be updated.

The literature presents practical studies on stakeholder perceptions of sustainability education in the accounting curriculum, but most studies only consider one stakeholder group (students, educators, or industry practitioners). Few studies investigate different stakeholder groups in one study.

The literature also lacks studies on sustainability accounting education in developing countries, particularly in the Middle East. Most literature focuses on stakeholder perceptions in developed countries, leaving a gap in knowledge about sustainability accounting education in developing countries.

References

Al-Hazaima, H., Low, M., & Sharma, U. (2021). Perceptions of salient stakeholders on the integration of sustainability education into the accounting curriculum: A Jordanian study. *Meditari Accountancy Research*, *29*(2), 371–402.

Alshurafat, H., Al-Msiedeen, J. M., Shbail, A., Obeid, M., Ananzeh, H., Alshbiel, S., & Jaradat, Z. (2023). Forensic accounting education within the Australian universities. In *International Conference on Business and Technology*. doi:10.1007/978-3-031-08954-1_58

Al Shbail, M. O., Alshurafat, H., Ananzeh, H., & Al-Msiedeen, J. M. (2021). Dataset of Factors affecting online cheating by accounting students: The relevance of social factors and the fraud triangle model factors. *Data in Brief*, *40*, 107732.

Alshurafat, H., Al Shbail, M. O., Masadeh, W. M., Dahmash, F., & Al-Msiedeen, J. M. (2021). Factors affecting online accounting education during the COVID-19 pandemic: An integrated perspective of social capital theory, the theory of reasoned action and the technology acceptance model. *Education and Information Technologies*, *26*, 6995–7013. doi:10.1007/s10639-021-10550-y

Alshurafat, H., Beattie, C., Jones, G., & Sands, J. (2020). Perceptions of the usefulness of various teaching methods in forensic accounting education. *Accounting Education*, *29*(2), 177–204.

Bates, C., Silverblatt, R., & Kleban, J. (2009). Creating a new green management course. *The Business Review, Cambridge*, *12*(1), 60–66.

Belal, A. (2008). *Corporate social responsibility reporting in developing countries: The case of Bangladesh*. Farnham: Ashgate Publishing.

Belal, A., & Owen, D. (2007). The views of corporate managers on the current state of, and future prospects for, social reporting in Bangladesh: An engagement-based study. *Accounting, Auditing & Accountability Journal*, *20*(3), 472–494.

Botes, V. L., Low, M., & Chapman, J. (2014). Is accounting education sufficiently sustainable? *Sustainability Accounting, Management and Policy Journal*, *5*(1), 95–124.

Carr, S., Chua, F., & Perera, H. (2006). University accounting curricula: The perceptions of an alumni group. *Accounting Education: An International Journal*, *15*(4), 359–376.

Choubey, B., & Pattanayak, J. (2014). Designing a course curriculum on environmental accounting: Viewpoint of Indian stakeholders. *IUP Journal of Accounting Research & Audit Practices*, *13*(3), 7.

Collison, D., & Gray, R. (1997). Auditors' responses to emerging issues: A UK perspective on the statutory financial auditor and the environment. *International Journal of Auditing*, *1*(2), 135–149.

Coulson, A. B., & Thomson, I. (2006). Accounting and sustainability, encouraging a dialogical approach; integrating learning activities, delivery mechanisms and assessment strategies. *Accounting Education: An International Journal*, *15*(3), 261–273.

Das, N., Sen, M., & Pattanayak, J. (2008). Assessment of students' perception towards developing a course in environmental accounting. *International Journal of Accounting and Information Management*, *16*(2), 122–139.

Fortes, H. (2002). The need for environmental reporting by companies. *Greener Management International*, *40*(1), 77–92.

Frost, G. R., & English, L. (2002). Mandatory corporate environmental reporting in Australia: Contested introduction belies effectiveness of its application. *Australian Review of Public Affairs Digest*, *299*(1). Retrieved from http://www.australianreview.net/digest/2002/11/frost.html

Grinnell, D. J., & Hunt, H. G. (2000). Development of an integrated course in accounting: A focus on environmental issues. *Issues in Accounting Education*, *15*(1), 19–42.

Hazelton, J., & Haigh, M. (2010). Incorporating sustainability into accounting curricula: Lessons learnt from an action research study. *Accounting Education: An International Journal*, *19*(1–2), 159–178.

Humphrey, C., Lewis, L., & Owen, D. (1996). Still too distant voices? Conversations and reflections on the social relevance of accounting education. *Critical Perspectives on Accounting*, *7*(1), 77–99.

Jaggi, B., & Zhao, R. (1996). Environmental performance and reporting: Perceptions of managers and accounting professionals in Hong Kong. *The International Journal of Accounting*, *31*(3), 333–346.

Kagawa, F. (2007). Dissonance in students' perceptions of sustainable development and sustainability: Implications for curriculum change. *International Journal of Sustainability in Higher Education*, *8*(3), 317–338.

Karnalim, O., Chivers, W., & Panca, B. S. (2022). Educating students about programming plagiarism and collusion via formative feedback. *ACM Transactions on Computing Education*, *22*(3), 1–31.

Kokubu, K., & Nashioka, E. (2005). Environmental management accounting practices in Japan. In P. M. Rikhardsson, M. Bennett, J. Bouma, & S. Schaltegger (Eds.), *Implementing environmental management accounting: Status and challenges* (pp. 321–342). Dordrecht: Springer.

Kokubu, K., & Nashioka, E. (2008). Environmental management accounting practices in Japanese manufacturing sites. In S. Schaltegger, M. Bennett, R. L. Burritt, & C. Jasch (Eds.), *Environmental management accounting for cleaner production* (pp. 365–376). Dordrecht, Netherlands: Springer.

Lodhia, S. K. (2003). Accountants' responses to the environmental agenda in a developing nation: An initial and exploratory study on FIJI. *Critical Perspectives on Accounting*, *14*(7), 715–737.

MacVaugh, J., & Norton, M. (2012). Introducing sustainability into business education contexts using active learning. *International Journal of Sustainability in Higher Education*, *13*(1), 72–87.

Malarvizhi, V. (2007). Corporate environmental accounting and reporting: A green framework. *The Accounting World*, 54–59.

Mangion, D. (2006). Undergraduate education in social and environmental accounting in Australian universities. *Accounting Education: An International Journal*, *15*(3), 335–348.

Mansour, E., Alzyoud, S., Abuzaid, R., & Alshurafat, H. (2023). Accounting students perspectives of peer tutoring. In *International Conference on Business and Technology*. doi:10.1007/978-3-031-08954-1_28

Meyer, M., & Bushney, M. (2008). Towards a multi-stakeholder-driven model for excellence in higher education curriculum development. *South African Journal of Higher Education*, *22*(6), 1229–1240.

Owen, D., Humphrey, C., & Lewis, L. (1994). *Social and environmental accounting education in British universities*. London: Certified Accountants Educational Trust London.

Pahuja, S., & Bansal, S. (2006). Corporate environmental reporting in India: The perception of accountants. *The ICFAI Journal of Accounting Research*, *5*(2), 16–37.

Pattanayak, J., Sen, M., & Choubey, B. (2011). Perception of students in designing a course curriculum on environmental accounting: A case study. *IUP Journal of Accounting Research & Audit Practices*, *10*(2), 28.

Pradhan, B., & Pattnaik, S. (2007). Beyond environmental accounting: The triple bottom line approach. *The Accounting World*, *7*(1), 7–15.

Pramanik, A. K., Shil, N. C., & Das, B. (2009). Corporate environmental reporting: An emerging issue in the corporate world. *International Journal of Business and Management*, *3*(12), 146–154.

Prasad, M. (2006). Contents of environmental accounting disclosure: What users require from annual reports? *The ICFAI Journal of Accounting Research*, *5*(3), 35–47.

Rezaee, Z., & Wang, J. (2022). Integration of big data into forensic accounting education and practice: A survey of academics in China and the United States. *Journal of Forensic and Investigative Accounting*, *14*(1).

Rusinko, C. A. (2010). Integrating sustainability in higher education: A generic matrix. *International Journal of Sustainability in Higher Education*, *11*(3), 250–259.

Sen, M., Pattanayak, J., & Choubey, B. (2010). Designing a course curriculum on environmental accounting: Viewpoint of Indian industry practitioners. *Social and Environmental Accountability Journal*, *30*(2), 96–109.

Sharma, U., & Kelly, M. (2012). University accounting and business curricula on sustainability: Perceptions of undergraduate students. In *Paper Presented at the 6th New Zealand Management Accounting Conference*, New Zealand, November 22–23, 2012.

Sharma, U., & Kelly, M. (2014). Students' perceptions of education for sustainable development in the accounting and business curriculum at a business school in New Zealand. *Meditari Accountancy Research*, *22*(2), 130–148.

Stevenson, L. (2002). Social and environmental accounting teaching in UK and Irish universities: A research note on changes between 1993 and 1998. *Accounting Education*, *11*(4), 331–346.

Thomas, I. (2005). Are business students buying it? A theoretical framework for measuring attitudes toward the legitimacy of environmental sustainability. *Business Strategy and the Environment*, *14*(3), 186–197.

Von Der Heidt, T., & Lamberton, G. (2011). Sustainability in the undergraduate and postgraduate business curriculum of a regional university: A critical perspective. *Journal of Management and Organization*, *17*(5), 670–690.

Watt, D. (1998). *A survey of environmental accounting education in Scottish universities*. Working Paper. Glasgow: Caledonian University.

Wyness, L., & Dalton, F. (2018). The value of problem-based learning in learning for sustainability: Undergraduate accounting student perspectives. *Journal of Accounting Education*, *45*, 1–19.

Chapter 7

A Symphony of Insights: Orchestrating Business and Education Research With Google Bard

Omar Arabiat

The Hashemite University, Jordan

Abstract

This study offers an in-depth examination of Google Bard, an advanced artificial intelligence chatbot created by Google, focusing specifically on its potential impact on academic research. This discussion aims to comprehensively explore the features of Google Bard, highlighting its capabilities in data management, facilitating collaborative discussions, and enhancing accessibility to complex research. In addition to the aforementioned positive characteristics, we will also delve into the limitations and ethical considerations associated with this innovative device. The functionality of the system is constrained by the limitations imposed by its pre-established algorithms and training data. In addition, there are significant concerns regarding data privacy, potential biases in its responses stemming from its training data, and the wider societal implications associated with a heavy reliance on machine-generated content. Ensuring responsible and ethical utilization of Bard necessitates Google's provision of transparent communication regarding its development process. In light of the prominent functionalities demonstrated by Google Bard, it is imperative for researchers to engage in a rigorous examination of the information it presents, thereby safeguarding against the inadvertent propagation of misinformation or biased viewpoints. This will lay the groundwork for its effective integration into the academic research methodology.

Keywords: Google Bard; artificial intelligence chatbot; academic research; ethical considerations; training data; data management

Technological Innovations for Business, Education and Sustainability, 91–103

doi:10.1108/978-1-83753-106-620241007

1. Introduction

The advent of artificial intelligence (AI) has had a profound impact on the realm of education, offering significant prospects as well as posing notable obstacles for educators and educational establishments (Guo, 2022). The incorporation of AI technologies within the realm of higher education holds the capacity to fundamentally transform pedagogical approaches, the dissemination of knowledge, and the responsibilities assumed by educators (Alshurafat, Al Shbail, Masadeh, Dahmash, & Al-Msiedeen, 2021; Guo, 2022; Zawacki-Richter, Marín, Bond, & Gouverneur, 2019). AI has the potential to facilitate individualized and self-directed learning encounters, optimize teaching effectiveness, and enhance the precision and relevance of instructional methods (Zhou, 2022). Furthermore, AI has the potential to enhance academic support services, adaptive systems, and intelligent tutoring systems, thereby making a significant contribution to the overall enhancement of education (Zawacki-Richter et al., 2019). Information technology's integration into curriculum can thus be a game changer, not just for specialized fields but for the broader spectrum of educational endeavors (Alshurafat, 2023). As AI progresses, it becomes crucial for educators to cultivate essential competencies, including personalized professional teaching skills and proficiency in modern technology application, in order to adeptly navigate the educational landscape in the AI era (Guo, 2022). The utilization of AI can enhance and customize education to cater to the requirements of learners in the contemporary digital era (Wang, Xie, Wang, Yang, & Hu, 2023).

Chatbots are considered to be a highly utilitarian and extensively employed manifestation of AI in our daily existence. The study and exploration of chatbot development has garnered significant attention and scholarly investigation across multiple fields. The initial efforts in the development of conversational systems, exemplified by Eliza (Weizenbaum, 1983), served as the basis for the subsequent advancement of chatbot development, as discussed by Safi, Abd-Alrazaq, Khalifa, and Househ (2020). Chatbots have been created for a wide range of purposes, such as customer service, medical applications, university information systems, and museums (Atmauswan & Abdullahi, 2022; Følstad, Nordheim, & Bjørkli, 2018; Varitimiadis et al., 2020). The primary objective of chatbot development is to effectively tackle specific challenges by offering users consolidated, authentic, and precise information (Atmauswan & Abdullahi, 2022). The utilization of chatbots in the field of education has garnered significant interest, as it holds promise for various applications such as personalized education, mentoring, and the augmentation of the learning process (Wollny et al., 2021). Nevertheless, the establishment of chatbots necessitates meticulous examination of elements such as user confidence, psychological ramifications, and ethical standards (Følstad et al., 2018; Ho, Hancock, & Miner, 2018; Zhang, Oh, Lange, Yu, & Fukuoka, 2020).

The level of sophistication exhibited by chatbots can exhibit substantial variation, ranging from rudimentary rule-based systems to highly advanced AI-driven models such as ChatGPT developed by OpenAI. These advanced models leverage Natural Language Processing (NLP) techniques and machine learning (ML) algorithms to comprehend and generate responses in a manner that closely resembles human-like behavior (Alshurafat, 2023; Tlili et al., 2023). In recent times, the AI domain has undergone a significant transformation with the emergence of an innovative conversational agent known as "Google Bard." The initial announcement of Bard occurred in March 2023, and it is presently accessible in three languages: English, Japanese, and Korean. The current state of this tool is one of ongoing development, yet its potential as a robust instrument for communication, education, and entertainment is evident. This AI-driven interface, developed by Google's innovative development team, stands out due to its utilization of the Language Model for Dialogue Applications (LaMDA) family of extensive language models. This unique feature enables the interface to generate text, perform language translation, produce various forms of creative content, and provide informative responses to user inquiries. Consequently, this interface offers an unparalleled level of engagement and dynamism in user interaction. Google Bard exemplifies the pinnacle of advancement in the field of AI, as it is designed to effectively interpret, comprehend, and provide responses to human language. The AI system demonstrates the ability to engage in meaningful conversations, provide responses to inquiries, and generate imaginative written works such as poetry or prose, exemplifying a compelling fusion of technological advancements and artistic expression. The introduction of Google Bard highlights a notable transformation within the AI sector, reaffirming the crucial influence of AI in shaping our digital trajectory.

Hence, a comprehensive examination will be conducted on Google Bard, an innovative AI tool developed by Google. This chapter will examine the various ways in which it can provide assistance to researchers. However, it is important to consider not only the advantages but also the limitations of this technology. One notable limitation is its inherent constraint imposed by its programming, which restricts its ability to replicate human thought processes. In the subsequent sections, a comprehensive analysis will be presented to elucidate the capabilities and limitations of Google Bard.

2. Direct Insights From the Google Bard

In our endeavor to delineate the suite of features that Google Bard can offer, we have meticulously crafted a series of exploratory questions, directly posing them to the Google Bard chatbots. This strategy allowed us to glean insights directly from the source, ensuring a high degree of authenticity and relevance in the responses. The ensuing dialogue with Google Bard facilitated a comprehensive understanding of its capabilities, extending beyond mere theoretical assumptions to practical demonstrations of its functionality. For ease of comprehension and clarity, we have collated Google Bard's responses in the subsequent section, thus providing a succinct summary that encapsulates the distinctive features this innovative tool brings to the academic research realm.

2.1 What Specific AI Technologies Does Google Bard Employ to Interact and Engage With Users, and How Do These Technologies Help in Research?

"Google Bard employs a number of AI technologies to interact and engage with users, including:

- NLP: NLP is the ability of a computer to understand and process human language. Bard uses NLP to understand the meaning of user queries and to generate natural-sounding responses.
- ML: ML is the ability of a computer to learn without being explicitly programmed. Bard uses ML to improve its ability to understand and respond to user queries over time.
- Large language models (LLMs): LLMs are a type of neural network that has been trained on a massive dataset of text and code. Bard uses LLMs to generate text, translate languages, write different kinds of creative content, and answer your questions in an informative way.

These AI technologies help in research by enabling Bard to:

- Access and process large amounts of data: Bard can access and process large amounts of data from the real world through Google Search. This allows Bard to stay up-to-date on the latest research and to generate more accurate and informative responses.
- Identify patterns and trends: Bard can identify patterns and trends in data. This allows Bard to generate hypotheses and to suggest new research directions.
- Communicate with researchers: Bard can communicate with researchers in a natural and engaging way. This allows Bard to help researchers to understand their data and to generate new ideas."

2.2 Suggest Some Specific Examples of How Google Bard Can Be Used in Research

- "Bard can be used to help researchers to find information. Bard can access and process large amounts of data from the real world through Google Search. This allows Bard to help researchers to find the information they need quickly and easily.
- Bard can be used to help researchers to summarize data. Bard can identify patterns and trends in data. This allows Bard to help researchers to summarize data in a clear and concise way.
- Bard can be used to help researchers to generate hypotheses. Bard can identify patterns and trends in data. This allows Bard to help researchers to generate hypotheses about the underlying causes of these patterns.
- Bard can be used to help researchers to communicate with each other. Bard can communicate with researchers in a natural and engaging way. This allows Bard

to help researchers to understand each other's work and to collaborate on research projects.

These are just a few examples of how Google Bard can be used in research. As Bard continues to develop, it is likely to become even more useful for research."

2.3 What Role Does Google Bard Play in Data Management, and How Does It Impact Data-Driven Research?

"Google Bard can play a significant role in data management, especially in data-driven research. Here are some of the ways that Google Bard can help with data management:

- Data cleaning: Bard can be used to identify and correct errors in data. This can help to ensure that data is accurate and reliable.
- Data analysis: Bard can be used to analyze data and identify patterns and trends. This can help researchers to gain insights from their data and to make better decisions.
- Data visualization: Bard can be used to visualize data in a way that is easy to understand. This can help researchers to communicate their findings to others.
- Data sharing: Bard can be used to share data with other researchers. This can help to facilitate collaboration and to accelerate the pace of research.

In addition to these specific tasks, Google Bard can also help with data management in a more general sense. For example, Bard can be used to:

- Organize data: Bard can be used to organize data into a structured format. This can make it easier to find and use data.
- Store data: Bard can be used to store data in a secure and accessible location. This can help to protect data and to ensure that it is available when needed.
- Back up data: Bard can be used to back up data in case of a disaster. This can help to prevent data loss.

Overall, Google Bard can be a valuable tool for data management in data-driven research. By automating many of the tasks involved in data management, Bard can free up researchers to focus on more creative and strategic work. This can help to accelerate the pace of research and to improve the quality of research findings.

Here are some additional benefits of using Google Bard for data management:

- Accuracy: Bard is trained on a massive dataset of text and code, which allows it to identify and correct errors in data with a high degree of accuracy.
- Efficiency: Bard can automate many of the tasks involved in data management, which can save researchers a significant amount of time.

- Scalability: Bard can be scaled to handle large datasets, which is important for data-driven research.

Overall, Google Bard is a powerful tool that can significantly improve the efficiency and accuracy of data management in data-driven research."

2.4 How Can Google Bard Facilitate the Collaborative Aspects of Research?

"Google Bard can facilitate the collaborative aspects of research in a number of ways. Here are some examples:

- Real-time collaboration: Bard can be used to facilitate real-time collaboration between researchers. This can be done by allowing researchers to share documents and work on them together in real time.
- Version control: Bard can be used to track changes to documents and to revert to previous versions if necessary. This can help to ensure that research is reproducible and that changes are tracked.
- Commenting: Bard can be used to comment on documents and to provide feedback to other researchers. This can help to improve the quality of research and to ensure that everyone is on the same page.
- Translation: Bard can be used to translate documents into different languages. This can help to facilitate collaboration between researchers from different countries.
- Communication: Bard can be used to communicate with other researchers. This can be done through text, voice, or video chat. This can help to build relationships between researchers and to foster collaboration.

Overall, Google Bard can be a valuable tool for facilitating the collaborative aspects of research. By automating many of the tasks involved in collaboration, Bard can free up researchers to focus on more creative and strategic work. This can help to accelerate the pace of research and to improve the quality of research findings.

Here are some additional benefits of using Google Bard for collaborative research:

- Accuracy: Bard is trained on a massive dataset of text and code, which allows it to generate accurate and informative responses.
- Efficiency: Bard can automate many of the tasks involved in collaboration, which can save researchers a significant amount of time.
- Scalability: Bard can be scaled to handle large teams of researchers, which is important for collaborative research."

2.5 How Does Google Bard Contribute to the Advancement of Knowledge in Various Research Fields?

"Google Bard can contribute to the advancement of knowledge in various research fields in a number of ways. Here are some examples:

- **Data-driven research: Bard can be used to automate many of the tasks involved in data-driven research, such as data cleaning, analysis, and visualization. This can free up researchers to focus on more creative and strategic work, and it can also help to improve the accuracy and efficiency of data-driven research.
- **Literature reviews: Bard can be used to help researchers to conduct comprehensive literature reviews. This can be done by helping researchers to find relevant literature, summarize the literature, and identify key findings. This can help to accelerate the pace of research and to improve the quality of research findings.
- **Collaborative research: Bard can be used to facilitate real-time collaboration between researchers. This can help to improve the efficiency of research, and it can also help to build relationships between researchers.
- **Education: Bard can be used to create educational content, such as tutorials, homework help, and online courses. This can help to make education more accessible and affordable, and it can also help to improve the quality of education.
- **Other research fields: Bard can also be used to contribute to the advancement of knowledge in other research fields, such as medicine, law, and business. For example, Bard can be used to help researchers to develop new treatments, to draft legal documents, and to make business decisions.

Overall, Google Bard is a powerful tool that can contribute to the advancement of knowledge in a variety of research fields. As Bard continues to develop, it is likely to become even more useful for this purpose.

Here are some additional benefits of using Google Bard in research:

- Accuracy: Bard is trained on a massive dataset of text and code, which allows it to generate accurate and informative responses.
- Efficiency: Bard can automate many of the tasks involved in research, which can save researchers a significant amount of time.
- Scalability: Bard can be scaled to handle large datasets and complex research problems.
- Creativity: Bard can generate new ideas and hypotheses, which can help researchers to break new ground."

2.6 What Capabilities Does Google Bard Have That Can Support Researchers in Staying Up-To-Date With the Latest Developments in Their Fields?

"Google Bard has a number of capabilities that can support researchers in staying up-to-date with the latest developments in their fields. These capabilities include:

- Access to a massive dataset of text and code: Bard is trained on a massive dataset of text and code, which includes a wide variety of research papers, articles, and other publications. This allows Bard to stay up-to-date with the latest developments in a variety of fields.

- The ability to understand and summarize large amounts of information: Bard is able to understand and summarize large amounts of information, which allows it to quickly identify the most important developments in a field.
- The ability to generate creative text formats: Bard can generate creative text formats, like poems, code, scripts, musical pieces, email, letters, etc. This allows Bard to communicate research findings in a more engaging and persuasive way.
- The ability to answer questions: Bard can answer questions about research topics, which can help researchers to quickly get the information they need.
- The ability to collaborate with researchers: Bard can collaborate with researchers, which can help to improve the efficiency of research and to build relationships between researchers.

Overall, Google Bard is a powerful tool that can support researchers in staying up-to-date with the latest developments in their fields. As Bard continues to develop, it is likely to become even more useful for this purpose.

Here are some additional ways that Google Bard can help researchers stay up-to-date with the latest developments in their fields:

- Bard can be used to track research trends: Bard can be used to track research trends by monitoring the frequency of keywords and phrases in research publications. This can help researchers to identify new and emerging research areas.
- Bard can be used to identify relevant research: Bard can be used to identify relevant research by searching for keywords and phrases in research publications. This can help researchers to find research that is relevant to their interests.
- Bard can be used to summarize research: Bard can be used to summarize research by extracting the key findings of research publications. This can help researchers to quickly understand the latest research findings.
- Bard can be used to generate alerts: Bard can be used to generate alerts when new research is published that is relevant to a researcher's interests. This can help researchers to stay up-to-date with the latest research developments"

2.7 How Does Google Bard Assist in the Organization, Storage, and Retrieval of Research Materials?

"Google Bard can assist in the organization, storage, and retrieval of research materials in a number of ways. These ways include:

- Automatic tagging: Bard can automatically tag research materials with keywords and phrases, making it easier to find and organize them.
- Abstract generation: Bard can generate abstracts for research materials, providing a quick overview of the content.

- Content summarization: Bard can summarize research materials, providing a more detailed overview of the content.
- Question answering: Bard can answer questions about research materials, providing researchers with the information they need quickly and easily.
- Collaborative editing: Bard can be used for collaborative editing of research materials, making it easier to work with others on research projects.

Overall, Google Bard is a powerful tool that can assist in the organization, storage, and retrieval of research materials. As Bard continues to develop, it is likely to become even more useful for this purpose."

2.8 How Does Google Bard Contribute to Improving the Accessibility and Understanding of Complex Research Topics?

"Google Bard can contribute to improving the accessibility and understanding of complex research topics in a number of ways. These ways include:

- Generating clear and concise summaries: Bard can generate clear and concise summaries of complex research topics, making them easier to understand.
- Answering questions in a comprehensive and informative way: Bard can answer questions about complex research topics in a comprehensive and informative way, even if the questions are open-ended, challenging, or strange.
- Translating research papers into different languages: Bard can translate research papers into different languages, making them accessible to a wider audience.
- Generating different creative text formats: Bard can generate different creative text formats, like poems, code, scripts, musical pieces, email, letters, etc., making research more accessible and engaging.
- Explaining complex concepts in a simple way: Bard can explain complex concepts in a simple way, using plain language and avoiding jargon.
- Providing visual representations of data: Bard can provide visual representations of data, such as charts, graphs, and diagrams, making it easier to understand complex research findings.

Overall, Google Bard is a powerful tool that can help to improve the accessibility and understanding of complex research topics. As Bard continues to develop, it is likely to become even more useful for this purpose.

Here are some additional ways that Google Bard can help improve the accessibility and understanding of complex research topics:

- Bard can be used to create educational content: Bard can be used to create educational content, such as tutorials, homework help, and online courses. This can help to make research more accessible and understandable to a wider audience.

- Bard can be used to communicate with researchers: Bard can be used to communicate with researchers, which can help to build relationships between researchers and to foster collaboration. This can help to improve the quality of research and to make research more accessible to the public.
- Bard can be used to translate research papers: Bard can be translated research papers into different languages, making research accessible to a wider audience. This can help to improve the understanding of research findings and to promote the exchange of ideas between researchers from different cultures."

2.9 What Are the Limitations or Challenges That Researchers Might Face When Using Google Bard?

"Google Bard is a powerful tool that can be used for a variety of research purposes. However, there are some limitations or challenges that researchers might face when using Google Bard. These limitations or challenges include:

- Bias: Google Bard is trained on a massive dataset of text and code, which may contain biases. This means that Bard's responses may reflect these biases, which could lead to inaccurate or misleading results.
- Accuracy: Google Bard is still under development, and its accuracy can vary depending on the task at hand. This means that researchers should be careful about relying on Bard's responses without verifying them independently.
- Creativity: Google Bard is not always able to generate creative text formats, like poems, code, scripts, musical pieces, email, letters, etc. This means that researchers may need to use other tools to generate creative content.
- Interpretation: Google Bard's responses may be difficult to interpret, especially if they are open-ended or challenging. This means that researchers may need to spend time understanding Bard's responses before they can use them.
- Ethics: There are ethical concerns about the use of large language models like Google Bard. For example, some people worry that Bard could be used to generate fake news or to spread misinformation. Researchers should be aware of these ethical concerns and should use Bard responsibly.

Overall, Google Bard is a powerful tool that can be used for a variety of research purposes. However, there are some limitations or challenges that researchers might face when using Google Bard. Researchers should be aware of these limitations or challenges and should use Bard responsibly.

Here are some additional tips for researchers who are using Google Bard:

- Be clear about your goals: Before you start using Bard, be clear about what you want to achieve. This will help you to better understand Bard's responses and to use it more effectively.
- Ask specific questions: Bard is better at answering specific questions than open-ended questions. So, if you want to get the most out of Bard, ask specific questions.

- Verify Bard's responses: Don't rely on Bard's responses without verifying them independently. This is especially important for sensitive or important tasks.
- Use Bard in conjunction with other tools: Bard is not a replacement for other research tools. It's best to use Bard in conjunction with other tools to get the most out of your research"

2.10 How Does Google Bard Ensure Ethical Usage and Data Privacy in the Context of Research?

"Google Bard is committed to ensuring the ethical usage and data privacy of its users, including researchers. Here are some of the ways that Google Bard ensures ethical usage and data privacy in the context of research:

- Transparency: Google Bard is transparent about its capabilities and limitations. This allows researchers to understand how Bard works and to use it responsibly.
- Consent: Google Bard requires researchers to obtain consent from their participants before using Bard to collect or process data. This ensures that participants' privacy is protected.
- Privacy controls: Google Bard provides researchers with privacy controls that allow them to control how their data are collected, used, and shared. This ensures that researchers can protect the privacy of their participants.
- Data security: Google Bard uses industry-standard security measures to protect the data of its users. This ensures that the data of researchers and participants are safe.
- Compliance: Google Bard complies with all applicable privacy laws and regulations. This ensures that the use of Google Bard is in line with the law.

Overall, Google Bard is committed to ensuring the ethical usage and data privacy of its users, including researchers. By following these principles, Google Bard helps to ensure that research is conducted in a responsible and ethical manner.

Here are some additional resources that you may find helpful:

- Google Bard Privacy Policy: https://policies.google.com/privacy
- Google Bard Terms of Service: https://policies.google.com/terms
- Google AI Principles: https://ai.google/principles/

3. Conclusion

To summarize, the purpose of this work is to dive into the complex fabric of Google Bard, identifying its primary characteristics as well as the resulting advantages that have the potential to revolutionize academic research. Google Bard is an AI-powered chatbot that epitomizes a combination of modern technology and language talent. It is a useful tool for data management, content analysis, and collaborative dialogue, among other intriguing uses. Nevertheless, just like any other kind of cutting-edge technology, Google Bard has some restrictions. It is possible that it is not yet able to entirely replace the subtle insights and creative leaps that come from human intelligence and intuition since it functions within the constraints of its algorithms and training data. Despite its ability in language processing and creative ideation, it does so within these boundaries. As we go forward, it is essential to find a balance between maximizing the promise of such a breakthrough technology and responding to these difficulties in a reasonable way. This will ensure that Google Bard becomes a reliable and helpful ally for researchers all across the globe. Moreover, it is crucial to consider the ethical ramifications associated with Google Bard. Like other AI-powered tools, concerns surrounding data privacy, potential biases in responses stemming from training data, and the wider consequences of human dependence on machine-generated content arise. Moreover, there is a potential danger of reinforcing preexisting biases when the system is trained using imbalanced or biased datasets. Researchers must exercise ethical responsibility by maintaining a vigilant approach in critically evaluating the information and guidance offered by the chatbot, thereby ensuring that it does not unintentionally propagate misinformation or biased viewpoints. The establishment of trust and ethical utilization of the technology necessitates Google's provision of comprehensive information regarding Bard's development, training data, and algorithms. Similar to other revolutionary advancements, the difficulty lies not only in effectively utilizing its capabilities but also in guaranteeing responsible and ethical usage, thereby upholding the fundamental principles of research integrity.

References

Alshurafat, H. (2023). *The usefulness and challenges of chatbots for accounting professionals: Application on ChatGPT*. SSRN Scholarly Paper No. 4345921. doi:10.2139/ssrn.4345921

Alshurafat, H., Al Shbail, M. O., Masadeh, W. M., Dahmash, F., & Al-Msiedeen, J. M. (2021). Factors affecting online accounting education during the COVID-19 pandemic: An integrated perspective of social capital theory, the theory of reasoned action and the technology acceptance model. *Education and Information Technologies*, *26*(6), 6995–7013.

Atmauswan, P., & Abdullahi, A. (2022). Intelligent chatbot for university information system using natural language approach. *Albukhary Social Business Journal*, *3*, 6. doi:10.55862/asbjV3I2a007

Følstad, A., Nordheim, C. B., & Bjørkli, C. A. (2018). What makes users trust a chatbot for customer service? An exploratory interview study. In S. S. Bodrunova (Ed.), *Internet science* (pp. 194–208). Springer International Publishing. doi:10.1007/978-3-030-01437-7_16

Guo, C. (2022). Research on improvement of college teachers' teaching abilities in the artificial intelligence era. *International Journal Of Scientific Advances*, *3*(4). doi:10.51542/ijscia.v3i4.19

Ho, A., Hancock, J., & Miner, A. S. (2018). Psychological, relational, and emotional effects of self-disclosure after conversations with a chatbot. *Journal of Communication, 68*(4), 712–733. doi:10.1093/joc/jqy026

Safi, Z., Abd-Alrazaq, A., Khalifa, M., & Househ, M. (2020). Technical aspects of developing chatbots for medical applications: Scoping review. *Journal of Medical Internet Research, 22*(12), e19127. doi:10.2196/19127

Tlili, A., Shehata, B., Adarkwah, M. A., Bozkurt, A., Hickey, D. T., Huang, R., & Agyemang, B. (2023). What if the devil is my guardian angel: ChatGPT as a case study of using chatbots in education. *Smart Learning Environments, 10*(1), 15. doi: 10.1186/s40561-023-00237-x

Varitimiadis, S., Kotis, K., Skamagis, A., Tzortzakakis, A., Tsekouras, G., & Spiliotopoulos, D. (2020). Towards implementing an AI chatbot platform for museums. *International Conference on Cultural Informatics, Communication & Media Studies, 1*(1). Article 1. doi:10.12681/cicms.2732

Wang, C., Xie, H., Wang, S., Yang, S., & Hu, L. (2023). Radiological education in the era of artificial intelligence: A review. *Medicine, 102*(1). doi:10.1097/MD.00000 00000032518

Weizenbaum, J. (1983). ELIZA—A computer program for the study of natural language communication between man and machine. *Communications of the ACM, 26*(1), 23–28. doi:10.1145/357980.357991

Wollny, S., Schneider, J., Di Mitri, D., Weidlich, J., Rittberger, M., & Drachsler, H. (2021). Are we there yet? – A systematic literature review on chatbots in education. *Frontiers in Artificial Intelligence, 4*. Retrieved from https://www.frontiersin.org/articles/10.3389/frai.2021.654924

Zawacki-Richter, O., Marín, V. I., Bond, M., & Gouverneur, F. (2019). Systematic review of research on artificial intelligence applications in higher education – Where are the educators? *International Journal of Educational Technology in Higher Education, 16*(1), 39. doi:10.1186/s41239-019-0171-0

Zhang, J., Oh, Y. J., Lange, P., Yu, Z., & Fukuoka, Y. (2020). Artificial intelligence chatbot behavior change model for designing artificial intelligence chatbots to promote physical activity and a healthy diet: Viewpoint. *Journal of Medical Internet Research, 22*(9), e22845. doi:10.2196/22845

Zhou, Y. (2022). Beliefs and practice evaluation based on artificial intelligence models under the IP environment. *Journal of Environmental and Public Health, 2022*, e1415142. doi:10.1155/2022/1415142

Chapter 8

Interpersonal Competence and Teaching Quality in a Sustainable Public University

Mercedes Huerta-Soto[a], *Karin De la Cruz Inchicaqui*[a], *Hugo Marino Rodríguez-Orellana*[b], *Orlando Leiva-Chauca*[a] *and Hernan Ramirez-Asis*[a]

[a]Universidad Nacional Santiago Antúnez de Mayolo, Perú
[b]Universidad Nacional Mayor de San Marcos, Perú

Abstract

Science and technology are transforming our world in ways that have not been seen in a long time, and we live in a rapidly changing world. Despite these changes, as citizens of today, we must not lose sight of the reality that these changes even cause crises that must be managed in order to place ourselves in a true working environment that allows us to survive as employees despite these changes. The main objective of this research is to find the relationship between interpersonal competences and teacher performance in a sustainable university. The methodology used was the quantitative, nonexperimental approach, as the variables will not be deliberately manipulated. In order to verify whether or not there was a relationship between these variables, 84 teachers from the Universidad Nacional Santiago Antunez de Mayolo were surveyed to evaluate the variables under study. The results obtained show a direct and significant relationship (Spearman's Rho = 0.731) between the two variables. Through this research, it was possible to determine that teachers who have developed interpersonal competences have a better performance, while in the relationships between interpersonal competences and the dimensions of teacher performance, a positive correlation was obtained.

Keywords: Accountability; higher education; interpersonal competence; quality of teaching; mastery; motivation; sustainable

Technological Innovations for Business, Education and Sustainability, 105–115

Published under exclusive licence by Emerald Publishing Limited
doi:10.1108/978-1-83753-106-620241008

1. Introduction

Today, skills, competencies, and above all abilities have become the true value of organizations. This search represents a challenge for organizations, as they need to develop different strategies and methods to reinforce the productivity of their employees in order to make them feel more motivated and perform their work more effectively, leading to the achievement of both organizational and individual goals (Castro & Delgado, 2020). Moreover, human capital is recognized as one of the greatest sources of competitive advantage for large companies (Rivero-Remírez, 2019; Yating et al., 2022). In today's job demand, it is very complicated to find the ideal staff for different activities within the organization, so technical knowledge and especially interpersonal competencies are very important for HR recruiters. Organizations that are in constant search for success require employees with a high degree of motivation and integration and above all who possess the competencies to understand and share in the achievement of objectives.

It is possible to perceive a myriad of positions that become more susceptible and are swept away by changes in technology and automation (Rodríguez-Sánchez, 2020), which is why new professional profiles emerge with high demands for skills and abilities that can help to develop in the labor market that are in constant transformation and development, they become known as interpersonal competencies that are irreplaceable by automation. Each of the skills developed took a proper validity because of the preference of organizations to synergistic and interdisciplinary effort in areas (Armijos, Bermúdez, & Mora, 2019; Pérez & Salcedo, 2022). As a consequence of this recognition, they have also gained prominence. Specifically, they have been singled out as the critical component in determining the outcomes of activities requiring technical expertise.

However, despite the importance of these skills, in Peru, there is no research on the search for interpersonal skills as the main source of recruitment, so there are still difficulties in their development (Guerra-Báez, 2019). In a forum held by Asia-Pacific Economic Cooperation (APEC), it is mentioned that there is a gap in the development of these skills. It is worth mentioning that, little by little, interpersonal skills workshops are being introduced in Peru, whose main ideal is for professionals to grow and be in shape to perform better in their work, and thus achieve an increase in their job opportunities (Rodriguez, 2020). This is why the appropriate structure to measure the expansion of personnel is to conquer organizations that use different means to measure the performance of the collaborator, knowing if they are truly contributing in a significant way to the growth of the organization and the achievement of the objectives (Asís, Figueroa, Quiñones, & Márquez Mázmela, 2022; Fernández-Arias, Antón-Sancho, Vergara, & Barrientos, 2021).

In this sense, interpersonal competences are decisive for employees to be able to perform adequately either in the organization or outside it, thus allowing them to work toward self-fulfillment (Gómez-Gamero, 2019). This type of skills are essential factors for the optimal development of employees when performing a function and especially for those managerial positions, this establishes the job performance of each worker (Cedeño, Veliz, & Mendoza, 2021).

At the National University Santiago Antunez de Mayolo (UNASAM), although university teachers are constantly learning and training, there is a minimum percentage of teachers who are trained in the development of interpersonal skills, which means that for 21st century teachers, it is no longer enough to have disciplinary knowledge and work experience. In addition, they work according to established standards, which is essential for the proper performance of their duties, so that both teachers and students can develop optimally. However, in the current situation, it has been seen that education is changing, which means that university teachers have to be aware of new educational trends, as interpersonal skills have become a requirement in the workplace. According to Villanueva et al. (2021), it is necessary to develop interpersonal skills that help them to have a better job performance and in particular to excel, in addition to the present, they manage to encourage students and thus generate greater interaction, then, the management of these skills is taken into account as an agent of change as it achieves a development and deployment of empathy, active listening, feedback and important thinking, among others, and thus you can get to show and transform the poor education of our country.

A sustainable university teacher considers that nowadays the management of interpersonal skills is very important, especially in education, and either directly or indirectly, it influences his performance as a teacher, since not having this type of skills prevents him from managing the changes that constantly arise, and he will not be able to handle or tolerate frustration, he does not learn from his mistakes and does not know how to work in a team or communicate efficiently with his students, which makes him an unsuitable professional to teach in a university (Casanova, Arias, & Trávezy Ortiz, 2020). On the other hand, Zimmer (2022) mentions that a teacher's work performance is measured by results, i.e., what type of professionals they train in their career, and that one way of doing this is through the way they teach, and this is achieved through the management of skills that allow them to work optimally, and that to obtain a good result, it is essential that teachers develop skills to efficiently manage technology, which is what the current market demands, but also skills that allow them to assertively manage relationships with groups of students (Ramírez, Espinoza, Esquivel, & Naranjo, 2020).

The position that a teacher develops has been in a constant adaptation of strategies that encourage them to optimally enhance teaching, so it has been applying various tools, being essential technology in the various realities where they work, one of them has been the interpersonal skills, whose scenario seeks to integrate a comprehensive training of students (Naranjo, 2019). The optimal performance of interpersonal competences goes hand in hand with the teaching of cognitive skills for an improvement in comprehensive training, where people are capable of performing optimally in different situations efficiently (Rodriguez, Rodríguez, & Fuerte, 2021). Students face a society that requires them to develop competences that allow them to be autonomous, to know how to work in a party and, above all, to solve problems, that is, to be able to develop effective interpersonal competence, and in this way, work optimally in the labor field, as they face a reality that is constantly changing and the development of interpersonal competences is necessary (González, Añez, Burgos, & Hidalgo, 2019). Thus, it is clear that professors must work on their pedagogical skills and develop cognitive competences, and although it is true that there are no programers that promote their development, the effective achievement of these competences would enable university academics to be better prepared for the workplace (González et al., 2019).

The first dimension is called Task Area and refers to those skills that are related to the way in which the subject faces and handles problems and decision-making (Méndez, Asis, García-Figueroa, & Montaño, 2021; Thommandru et al., 2021), together with ways of planning and organizing work and time. The second dimension is the area of the self and includes skills related to the subject's ability to value oneself and to act, even if not asked to do so, as well as the ability to manage and regulate emotions. (Dubovyk, Vashchenko, Moskalenko, Molodychenko, & Molodychenko, 2021). The third dimension is defined as the motivational area and includes skills that are related to the achievement of goals (in this case academic success), to the way individuals make sense of their experience and interpret things that happen to them, as well as aspects related to the ability to interpret things that happen to them, as well as aspects related to the ability to react and resist stressful situations. And the last dimension is that of interpersonal relationships and includes skills related to the relationship with peers and authority figures, together with how the individual manages and organizes their communication and how they deal with conflict situations (Yslado, Ramirez, & Espinoza, 2020).

In job performance, indicators such as teaching skills, responsibilities, secondary needs and recognition, and problem-solving ability will be taken into account (Huang et al., 2021). The assessment relies especially on the teacher's work and the way they perform in teaching. The main dilemma of this chapter is to identify whether interpersonal competences really influence the job performance of teachers at UNASAM, with the purpose of justifying the importance of these skills as a strong indicator in the teaching process (Huang et al., 2021).

2. Methodology

According to its purpose, it is applied, according to its level of depth, it is correlational. Since there will be no planned manipulation of variables, a nonexperimental design was chosen. The research observed the facts as they occur in their natural context and then analyzed them. Also, taking a snapshot in time to describe and analyze variables such as the performance of teachers and their relationship with interpersonal competences. For this study, a total of 84 teachers from different specialties related to economic sciences (administration, accounting, economics, and tourism) were surveyed, these careers with high demand for interpersonal competences, i.e., humanistic and economic. In the study of interpersonal competences, a survey approach was used and its corresponding tool, the questionnaire, proposed by Ricchiardi and Emanuel (2018) was used. It contains four dimensions, task area, motivation area, self-area, and the domain of interpersonal relationships. It consists of 17 items.

On the other hand, in the case of the teaching quality variable, a questionnaire was drawn up based on the main performance indicators of the university itself, student opinion, overall effectiveness, number of publications, and the nature and quantity of administrative work handled. Teachers were asked to rate themselves on the parameters of their overall effectiveness. This self-assessment format was on a Likert scale of 1–5, where 1 represents the lowest rating and 5 the highest. Cronbach's alpha was also used to determine reliability, with indices of 0.869 for the interpersonal competency questionnaire and 0.861 for the teaching quality questionnaire, respectively, reflecting that they are highly reliable. Spearman's Rho was used for both descriptive and inferential statistics to operationalize the data.

3. Results

The results obtained in this study generated by the sample show that interpersonal skills do influence the performance of university teachers, suggesting that the professional profile of teachers is based on the acquisition of skills that enable them to interact with their students and, above all, to perform better when teaching classes. A total of 84 teachers participated in the research, of whom 52.9% were male and 17.1% were female. Of the total sample, different categories were established in terms of belonging to different branches of knowledge; thus, 84.4% have a master's degree, and only 15.6% have obtained a doctorate degree.

This analysis shows in Table 8.1 that 42.9% of the respondents, i.e., 36 UNASAM teachers, have medium-levels of interpersonal competences, while 27.4%, i.e., 23 teachers, have high-levels of interpersonal competence development for the implementation of classes at the sustainable university.

Forty point five percent of the respondents, i.e., 34 UNASAM teachers, have a medium-level of performance, while 25.0%, i.e., 21 teachers, have a high-level of performance, as can be seen in Table 8.2.

Table 8.1. Interpersonal Competences of Teachers.

Levels	**Frequency**	**Percentage**
Low	25	29.8%
Medium	36	42.9%
High	23	27.4%
Total	84	100.00%

Source: Author's original work.

Table 8.2. Levels of Teaching Quality.

Levels	Frequency	Percentage
Low	29	34.5%
Medium	34	40.5%
High	21	25.0%
Total	84	100.00%

Source: Author's original work.

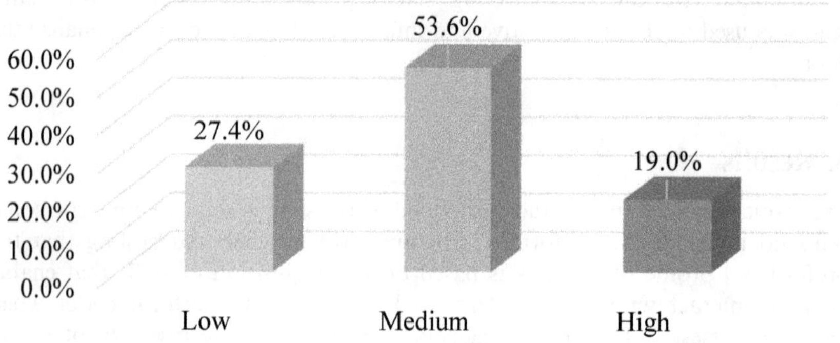

Fig. 8.1. Levels of Responsibility.

Among the main dimensions of the interpersonal competence variable, in this case responsibility, the analysis shows in Fig. 8.1 that 53.6% of the respondents, i.e., 45 UNASAM teachers, have medium-levels of responsibility, while only 19.0%, i.e., 19.0%, have high-levels of responsibility.

Among the main dimensions of the variable university teacher performance, in this case the didactic domain, the analysis shows that 48.96% of the respondents, i.e., 47 UNASAM teachers, have medium-levels in the disciplinary domain, while 22.92%, i.e., 22 teachers, are still working in the disciplinary domain. In addition, Table 8.3 shows that 25.00% of UNASAM teachers have medium-levels of interpersonal skills and teacher performance.

Table 8.3. Quality of Teaching According to Levels of Interpersonal Competences.

	Quality of Teaching			
Interpersonal Competences	**Low**	**Medium**	**High**	**Total**
Low	18.7%	10.43%	2.1%	31.3%
Medium	9.3%	25.0%	4.2%	38.5%
High	2.1%	5.2%	22.9%	30.2%
Total	30.2%	40.6%	29.2%	100.0%

Source: Author's original work.

Table 8.4. Relationship Between Interpersonal Competences and Quality of Teaching.

			Interpersonal Competences	**Quality of Teaching**
Rho de Spearman	Interpersonal competences	Correlation coefficient	1.000	0.731[a]
		Significance (bilateral)		0.000
		N	84	84
	Quality of teaching	Correlation coefficient	0.731[a]	1.000
		Significance (bilateral)	0.000	
		N	94	84

[a]Correlation is significant at the 0.01 level (bilateral).

Table 8.4 shows that the test allowed us to see that the relationship between the two variables is significantly direct and positive on average. Taking into account the results observed in the Correlation Coefficient test $p = 0.000$, it is less than the significance level $\alpha = 0.05$, which indicates that the null hypothesis is rejected. This suggests that there is an influence of interpersonal competences on the performance of teachers at the Universidad Nacional Santiago Antúnez de Mayolo.

4. Discussion

The present study aims to identify the relationship between interpersonal skills and performance of sustainable university teachers, through which it will seek to establish the relationship that interpersonal skills have on the job performance of university teachers; this research reflects the current need that universities have in demanding the improvement of their academic quality, so this study is reasonable because only teachers with a rich knowledge of the subject and work experience are no longer enough (Chura, Huayanca, & Maquera, 2019). The world of work is increasingly changing and urgently needs teachers with interpersonal competences that enable them to achieve success in performance and thus contribute to improving the learning of university students (Vera-Millalén, 2017).

According to the findings of the study, the academic training they received did not equip them with a high-level of professional competence; as a result, in their alternative careers, they only occasionally or hardly ever demonstrate the ability to manage with confidence and independence while carrying out a range of tasks effectively in both every day and unexpected situations related to their field of specialization (Huerta-Soto, Guzmán-Avalos, Flores-Albornoz, & Tomás-Aguilar,

2022). It is important to emphasize that firstly a process was developed in which teachers discussed ideas on how to obtain optimal development of communication, leadership, teamwork, and self-management are some of the "interpersonal competences" mentioned. To achieve this goal, the validated form was used to examine their approaches to learning, which were then related to the development of the interpersonal competences described in this chapter (Fuster, Segura, Guillen, & Ramirez, 2020).

As the Inter-American Development Bank (IDB) explains, the Fourth Industrial Revolution, characterized by the confluence of digital, physical, and biological technology, will revolutionize the world as we know it and force permanent and rapid change on the planet. Moreover, companies now need people who not only understand the new challenges they face but also have the technical and scientific knowledge to solve them (Casanova et al., 2020; Pallathadka et al., 2023). It is also important because it will make it possible to identify the mistakes that may be being made and thus seek more appropriate solutions to prevent them from recurring. In this way, the teaching staff will be able to perform better and thus contribute to the improvement of university education. Furthermore, if we relate interpersonal competences to work performance, we can identify the degree of development of teachers when interacting with their students and thus measure their efficiency (Cedeño et al., 2021; Ramírez et al., 2020).

As stated above, it is paramount to remember that the curriculum is designed with the aim of combining academic knowledge with the responsibility of business organizations and that all learning outcomes and competence requirements are strongly tailored and related to the cultivation of interpersonal competences that support the improvement of employees in response to market needs. It is necessary to focus education with education and training in diverse trades to meet the needs of an increasingly diverse and unstable society (Balladares & Moyano, 2022).

5. Conclusion

In light of the objectives established for this research, the results determined that there is an immediate and significant influence (r = 0.731) between interpersonal skills and teaching quality, which shows that those university teachers who have developed interpersonal skills are likely to have a much better job performance. In addition, it was determined that the communication dimension significantly influences the teachers' performance variable, which indicates that teachers consider that communication can be a relevant thought on their performance, so the relationship coefficient (r = 0.647) was obtained (r = 0.731).

It was determined that the dimension the development of others significantly influences the performance variable of teachers, which shows that teachers are part of the development of their students, was obtained as a relationship coefficient (r = 0.676). In addition, it was determined that the variable interpersonal competencies significantly influences the dimension of disciplinary mastery of UNASAM teachers, which reveals that teachers consider interpersonal competencies as a relevant factor in their disciplinary mastery as teachers, was obtained as a relationship coefficient (r = 0.680).

It was determined that the interpersonal competences variable significantly influences the didactic domain dimension of the teachers, which shows that teachers consider interpersonal competences to be a relevant factor in their didactic domain as teachers, a relationship coefficient (r = 0.673) was obtained.

In summary, although there is a significant relationship between the two variables, it is necessary for UNASAM to promote and evaluate the need for the management of interpersonal skills in all teaching staff, as these skills are related to the professional's ability to be able to manage interpersonal relations, which is directly linked to the behavior he/she has with his/her students when teaching.

The sustainable university should design programer that encourage the management of interpersonal competencies because although it is true that teachers working in this entity are pedagogically prepared, it is still challenging to merge the technical with the soft. To the authorities and public officials focused on the country's education system, seek to promote courses on interpersonal competencies at all levels of education, as these skills are crucial for complete human growth.

References

Armijos, F. B., Bermúdez, A. I., & Mora, N. V. (2019). Gestión de administración de los Recursos Humanos. *Revista Universidad y Sociedad, 11*(4), 163–170. Retrieved from https://rus.ucf.edu.cu/index.php/rus/article/view/1295

Asís, E. H. R., Figueroa, R. P. N., Quiñones, R. E. T., & Márquez Mázmela, P. R. H. (2022). Validation of a cybercrime awareness scale in Peruvian university students. *Revista Científica General José María Córdova, 20*(37), 208–224. doi:10.21830/19006586.791

Balladares, P. E., & Moyano, W. (2022). Estrés laboral en personal de enfermería durante la pandemia por covid-19. *Revista Cientifica Epistemia, 6*(2), 1–16. doi:10.26495/re.v6i2.2292

Casanova, T. A., Arias, E. V., Trávez, J. P., & Ortiz, A. V. (2020). Importancia de estimular las inteligencias múltiples en educación inicial. Habilidades y destrezas. *Revista Boletín Redipe, 9*(10), 168–181. Retrieved from https://revista.redipe.org/index.php/1/article/view/1096/992

Castro, K. O., & Delgado, J. M. (2020). Gestión del talento humano en el desempeño laboral. *Ciencia Latina Revista Científica Multidisciplinar, 4*(2), 684–703. doi:10.37811/cl_rcm.v4i2.107

Cedeño, M. C., Veliz, V. F., & Mendoza, K. L. (2021). Enseñanza: la comprensión para el aprendizaje mediante las inteligencias múltiples o habilidades del pensamiento. *Estudios Del Desarrollo Social: Cuba y América Latina, 9*(Especial 2), 91–103. Retrieved from http://www.revflacso.uh.cu/index.php/EDS/article/view/630/743

Chura, E., Huayanca, P., & Maquera, M. (2019). Bases epistemológicas que sustentan la teoría de las inteligencias múltiples de Howard Gardner en la pedagogía. *Revista Innova Educación, 1*(4), 1–10. doi:10.35622/j.rie.2019.04.012

Dubovyk, S. H., Vashchenko, O. V., Moskalenko, A. M., Molodychenko, V. V., & Molodychenko, N. A. (2021). Features of preparing future teachers for work in an inclusive educational environment. *Journal of Higher Education Theory and Practice*, *21*(14), 41–49. doi:10.33423/jhetp.v21i14

Fernández-Arias, P., Antón-Sancho, Á., Vergara, D., & Barrientos, A. (2021). Soft skills of American university teachers: Self-concept. *Sustainability*, *13*(22), 12397. doi:10.3390/su132212397

Fuster, D. E., Segura, V. R., Guillen, P. E., & Ramirez, E. H. (2020). Teachers empathy in the development of bilingual communication strategies. *International Journal of Early Childhood Special Education (INT-JECSE)*, *12*(1), 542–551. doi: 10.9756/INT-JECSE/V12I1.201036

Gómez-Gamero, M. E. (2019). Las competencias interpersonales competencias para el nuevo milenio. *Divulgare Boletín Científico de la Escuela Superior de Actopan*, *6*(11), 1–5. doi:10.29057/esa.v6i11.3760

González, N. J., Añez, A. P., Burgos, J. G., & Hidalgo, G. (2019). Formación de habilidades interpersonales para la gestión educativa. In V. En Meriño, E. Martinez, & C. Martínez (Eds.), *Gestión del Conocimiento. Perspectiva Multidisciplinaria* (Vol. 16, Pág. 117–132). *Colección unión global.* Santa Bárbara – Zulia – Venezuela: Fondo Editorial Universitario de la Universidad Nacional Experimental del Sur del Lago de Maracaibo Jesús María Semprún.

Guerra-Báez, S. P. (2019). Una revisión panorámica al entrenamiento de las competencias interpersonales en estudiantes universitarios. *Psicologia Escolar e Educacional*, *23*, e186464. doi:10.1590/2175-35392019016464

Huang, X., Cao, J., Zhao, G., Long, Z., Han, G., & Cai, X. (2021). The employability and career development of finance and trade college graduates. *Frontiers in Psychology*, *12*. doi:10.3389/fpsyg.2021.719336

Huerta-Soto, R., Guzmán-Avalos, M., Flores-Albornoz, J., & Tomás-Aguilar, S. (2022). Competencias digitales de los profesores universitarios durante la pandemia por covid-19 en el Perú. *Revista Electrónica Interuniversitaria de Formación del Profesorado*, *25*(1), 49–60. doi:10.6018/reifop.500481

Méndez, R. M. Y., Asis, E. H. R., García-Figueroa, M. E., & Montaño, J. L. A. (2021). Clima laboral y burnout en profesores universitarios. *Revista electrónica interuniversitaria de formación del profesorado*, *24*(3). doi:10.6018/reifop.476651

Naranjo, A. (2019). La importancia de las competencias interpersonales para la docencia universitaria en el contexto actual. *Revista Pensamiento Académico*, *2*(1), 82–100. doi:10.33264/rpa.201901-07

Pallathadka, H., Wenda, A., Ramirez-Asís, E., Asís-López, M., Flores-Albornoz, J., & Phasinam, K. (2023). Classification and prediction of student performance data using various machine learning algorithms. *Materials Today: Proceedings*, *80*, 3782–3785. doi:10.1016/j.matpr.2021.07.382

Pérez, E. L., & Salcedo, I. (2022). Metodología del aprendizaje basado en problemas en la educación de energías renovables. *Revista Cientifica Epistemia*, *6*(2), 64–76. doi:10.26495/re.v6i2.2296

Ramírez, E. H., Espinoza, M. R., Esquivel, S. M., & Naranjo, M. E. (2020). Emotional intelligence, competencies and performance of the university professor: Using the SEM-PLS partial least squares technique. *Revista Electronica Interuniversitaria de Formacion del Profesorado*, *23*(3), 99–114. doi:10.6018/reifop.428261

Ricchiardi, P., & Emanuel, F. (2018). Soft skill assessment in higher education. *Journal of Educational, Cultural and Psychological Studies (ECPS Journal)*, *18*, 21–53. doi:10.7358/ecps-2018-018-ricc

Rivero-Remírez, Y. (2019). Evaluación del desempeño: tendencias actuales. *Revista Archivo Médico de Camagüey*, *23*(2), 159–164. Retrieved from http://www.revistaamc.sld.cu/index.php/amc/article/view/6141/3318

Rodriguez, J. L. (2020). Las competencias interpersonales como base del buen desempeño del docente universitario. *INNOVA Research Journal*, *5*(2), 186–199. doi:10.33890/innova.v5.n2.2020.1321

Rodríguez-Sánchez, J. L. (2020). Acciones necesarias para mejorar la relación causa-efecto entre la inversión en prácticas de gestión de recursos humanos y la motivación en la empresa. *Información tecnológica*, *31*(2), 207–220. doi:10.4067/S0718-07642020000200207

Rodriguez, J. L., Rodríguez, R. E., & Fuerte, L. (2021). Competencias interpersonales y el calidad de la enseñanza en el nivel superior de la educación. *Propósitos y Representaciones*, *9*(1), e1038. doi:10.20511/pyr2021.v9n1.1038

Thommandru, A., Espinoza-Maguiña, M., Ramirez-Asis, E., Ray, S., Naved, M., & Guzman-Avalos, M. (2021). Role of tourism and hospitality business in economic development. *Materials Today: Proceedings*. doi:10.1016/j.matpr.2021.07.059

Vera-Millalén, F. (2017). Infusión de competencias interpersonales en el currículo de la educación superior: clave para el desarrollo de capital humano avanzado. *Revista Akadèmeia*, *15*(1), 53–73. Retrieved from https://revistas.ugm.cl/index.php/rakad/article/view/137

Villanueva, S. V., Campos, S. A. V., Villanueva, C. A. V., Villanueva, L. V., Paredes, H. J. C., & Miguel, J. M. G. (2021). Competencias interpersonales: su importancia para la calidad de la enseñanza. *Paidagogo*, *3*(2), 4–16. doi:10.52936/p.v3i2.63

Yating, Y., Mughal, N., Wen, J., Ngan, T. T., Ramirez-Asis, E., & Maneengam, A. (2022). Economic performance and natural resources commodity prices volatility: Evidence from global data. *Resources Policy*, *78*, 102879. doi:10.1016/j.resourpol.2022.102879

Yslado, R. M. Y., Ramirez, E. H., & Espinoza, M. R. (2020). Burnout, docencia e investigación en profesores universitarios de la Facultad de Ciencias Empresariales de Perú y España. *Educade: revista de educación en contabilidad, finanzas y administración de empresas*, *11*, 3–19. doi:10.12795/EDUCADE.2020.i11.02

Zimmer, J. C. (2022). Problematic social network use: Its antecedents and impact upon classroom performance. *Computers & Education*, *177*, 104368. doi:10.1016/j.compedu.2021.104368

Chapter 9

EdTech Tools for Sustainable Practices: A Green Revolution in Education

Jais V. Thomas, Mallika Sankar, Deepika S. R., Nagarjuna G. and Arjun B. S.

Christ University, India

Abstract

The rapid advancement of Education Technology (EdTech) offers promising opportunities for educational institutions to integrate sustainable business practices into their operations and curriculum. The integration of EdTech into sustainability education has emerged as a powerful tool to promote environmental awareness, foster sustainable behavior, and address the pressing challenges of climate change and resource depletion. This chapter explores the growing significance of EdTech in sustainability education, analyzing its potential to cultivate a generation of environmentally conscious and responsible global citizens. It also aims at identifying and examining the most prominent emerging EdTech tools specifically designed to promote sustainability in educational settings. Furthermore, it aims to comprehend the institutional elements that have successfully incorporated and expanded the utilization of EdTech tools to promote enduring business practices. Additionally, the chapter addresses the challenges and obstacles faced by educational institutions in adopting and implementing these technologies and propose strategies to overcome these barriers.

Keywords: EdTech; education; sustainable education; sustainable development goals; sustainable practices; virtual reality; augmented reality

1. Introduction

Governments and institutions worldwide have been diligently implementing diverse strategies to encourage more responsible environmental behaviors ever

Technological Innovations for Business, Education and Sustainability, 117–129

doi:10.1108/978-1-83753-106-620241009

since the Sustainable Development Summit of 2015 (Carrion-Martinez, Luque-de la Rosa, Fernandez-Cerero, & Montenegro-Rueda, 2020). This resulted in the establishment of 17 Sustainable Development Goals (SDGs) to be achieved by 2030 (Raj & Mallika Sankar, 2022). The 17 SDGs form a comprehensive blueprint for a sustainable and inclusive future. These goals encompass a wide range of interconnected objectives aimed at tackling pressing global challenges. They include eradicating poverty and hunger (SDG 1 and 2), ensuring good health and well-being (SDG 3), promoting quality education (SDG 4), achieving gender equality (SDG 5), ensuring access to clean water and sanitation (SDG 6), and fostering affordable and clean energy (SDG 7). Additionally, the SDGs focus on promoting decent work and economic growth (SDG 8), building resilient infrastructure and fostering innovation (SDG 9), reducing inequalities within and among nations (SDG 10), and creating sustainable cities and communities (SDG 11). The goals also address responsible consumption and production (SDG 12), combating climate change and its impacts (SDG 13), conserving life below water and on land (SDG 14 and 15), promoting peace, justice, and strong institutions (SDG 16), and forging global partnerships for sustainable development (SDG 17). The primary focus of these comprehensive and global objectives is centered on eradicating poverty, safeguarding the planet, and ensuring inclusive and prosperous development for all.

SDG 4 emphasizes the pivotal role of education in creating a fair, inclusive, and high-quality society. It comprises seven specific targets, highlighting the paramount importance of fostering sustainability education through the advancement of theoretical and practical knowledge in support of well-balanced environmental progress (Raj & Mallika Sankar, 2022). Education, as highlighted in SDG 4, intertwines with the attainment of other sustainable development goals and serves as an essential element for the achievement of other goals. For instance, SDG 12 underscores the responsible use of technological resources, while SDG 9 sets forth the urgent need to employ technological resources efficiently, promoting clean and environmentally sound technologies. Additionally, SDG 13 calls for education to play a pivotal role in raising awareness and empowering societies to combat the exacerbation of climate change (Raj & Mallika Sankar, 2022).

The increasing adoption of digital technology has significantly influenced education, reshaping the concept of literacy for individuals in the 21st century. As we consider the environmental impact of these technologies, it becomes crucial to protect our environment and promote sustainable practices. Utilizing information and communication technology (ICT) efficiently, saving energy, extending the lifespan of devices, and establishing communication channels within the educational community for sustainability are essential goals. To achieve this, we must promote the use of ICT while remaining mindful and committed to environmental preservation (Carrion-Martinez et al., 2020).

In recent years, the integration of technology into education has sparked a transformative revolution, particularly focusing on promoting sustainable business practices. The growing global awareness of environmental challenges has led educators, businesses, and policymakers to recognize the urgent need for fostering sustainability-driven mindsets among the future workforce, which is crucial for shaping a greener and more sustainable future. Integrating innovative educational technologies (EdTech) has emerged as a powerful catalyst for promoting sustainable business practices, representing a pivotal moment at the intersection of education and environmental stewardship.

Educators and institutions are now emphasizing the importance of preparing students to face sustainability challenges in the future. Integrating innovative EdTech tools into the curriculum has become essential for facilitating interactive and engaging learning experiences. These tools allow students to directly explore and apply eco-conscious principles to real-world scenarios. By embracing technology in this way to foster sustainable business practices, educational institutions play a vital role in cultivating a generation of environmentally responsible leaders capable of driving positive change in the corporate world. In conclusion, the convergence of education, technology, and sustainability holds immense promise for building a greener and more sustainable future.

As the urgency to address environmental challenges grows, so does the need for transformative educational technologies that foster sustainability in business practices, the emergence of EdTech tools has revolutionized the landscape of education, including business education, by offering innovative solutions that promote environmental stewardship and sustainable practices. In navigating the complex challenges of the 21st century, harnessing the potential of EdTech to instill sustainable business practices is not just a prudent choice but also a moral imperative for shaping a world that values both economic prosperity and ecological well-being. Higher education institutions must actively engage in shaping and leading the SDG 4 agenda instead of remaining passive observers, with the aim of influencing both discussions and actions, especially as the demand for higher education grows worldwide (Ferguson & Roofe, 2020).

2. Research Gap

Digital education represents an innovative integration of modern technology and digital tools to enhance and reinforce teaching and learning endeavors (Carrion-Martinez et al., 2020). As educational institutions strive to foster sustainable business practices, the integration of emerging EdTech tools has become increasingly vital. In the context of today's rapidly evolving world, where the integration of technology and sustainability is becoming increasingly crucial, educational institutions are seeking ways to foster eco-consciousness and sustainable business practices. However, there is a research gap in understanding the specific EdTech tools that effectively promote sustainability in educational settings and their impact on students' learning experiences and attitudes toward environmental responsibility. While various emerging EdTech tools show promise in facilitating experiential and interactive learning experiences centered around sustainability concepts (Tondeur et al., 2012), there is a need to explore the behavioral changes and attitudes of students who have undergone sustainability education through these tools, particularly in terms of their commitment to environmental stewardship (Chen & Jones, 2019). Moreover, there is a paucity of research showcasing successful case studies of educational institutions that have effectively integrated and scaled up the use of EdTech tools to promote sustainable business practices (Kozma, 2008). Understanding how these institutions have overcome challenges and obstacles in adopting and implementing these technologies is essential to formulate effective strategies for broader adoption.

In the context of today's rapidly evolving world, where the integration of technology and sustainability is becoming increasingly crucial, educational institutions are seeking ways to foster eco-consciousness and sustainable business practices (Tondeur et al., 2012). However, there is a research gap in understanding the specific EdTech tools that effectively promote sustainability in educational settings and their impact on students' learning experiences and attitudes toward environmental responsibility. This study aims to address these gaps by conducting a comprehensive investigation into the key EdTech tools fostering sustainable business practices for sustainability education. Additionally, the article will examine successful strategies employed by institutions to integrate these tools into sustainability-focused programs while addressing the challenges and barriers encountered in their adoption and implementation. By shedding light on these areas, this research aims to provide valuable insights and recommendations for educators and stakeholders seeking to enhance sustainability education in academic settings. Hence, the following objectives have been framed:

Objectives:

- To identify and examine the most prominent emerging EdTech tools that have been specifically designed to promote sustainable business practices in educational settings.
- To comprehend the institutional elements that have effectively integrated and scaled up the use of EdTech tools to promote sustainable business practices.
- To highlight the challenges and obstacles faced by educational institutions in adopting and implementing these technologies, and to propose strategies to overcome these barriers.

3. EdTech Tools for Sustainable Practices in Education

Educational technology, often referred to as EdTech, combines ICT and educational practices to facilitate and enhance learning, and companies providing these services are known as EdTech start-ups or EdTech companies. The integration of computers and communication technologies has allowed for enhanced interactions and learning across vast geographic distances, addressing some of the limitations in the education system (Majumdar, 2015; Raj & Mallika Sankar, 2022).

The education system worldwide is undergoing a continuous transformation, driven by "techno-optimism," which has led to the progress of various educational components like "bulletin board systems, smart boards, Massive Open Online Courses (MOOCs) (Raj & Mallika Sankar, 2022), and E-learning" (Weller, 2018, 2020). However, a persistent challenge has been the teacher-student ratio, where individual attention and personalized doubt clarification are often lacking. Modern teaching–learning approaches, such as constructivism, emphasize individual learning, with teachers acting as facilitators rather than dominant figures (Palliyalil & Mukherjee, 2020; Yaduvanshi & Singh, 2015).

Over the past 7 years, the introduction of e-learning applications, interactive videos, and various other hi-tech developments, including personalized content and internet-based live discussions, has been instrumental in the advancement of EdTech. This transformation from a student-centered approach to constructivism has created opportunities for EdTech companies to focus on personalized and experiential learning, catering to the specific needs of individual students. As the urgency to address environmental challenges grows, so does the need for transformative educational technologies that foster sustainability in business practices. In recent years, the emergence of EdTech tools has revolutionized the landscape of education, including business education, by offering innovative solutions that promote environmental stewardship and sustainable practices. EdTech tools possess the potential to cultivate the future generation of environmentally conscious business leaders. Some of the most prominent emerging EdTech tools that have been specifically designed to promote sustainable business practices in educational settings include virtual reality (VR) and augmented reality (AR), gamification, e-learning platforms, blockchain technology, sustainable data analytics for evidence-based decision-making. Many educational institutions that have effectively integrated and scaled up the use of EdTech tools to promote sustainable business practices.

4. VR and AR for Experiential Sustainability Learning

VR and AR technologies have been increasingly adopted in business education to provide immersive learning experiences. For sustainability education, these tools offer unique opportunities to simulate real-world scenarios, allowing students to explore the consequences of their decisions on the environment. For instance, students can use VR to witness the impact of deforestation, pollution, or climate change in a controlled environment, fostering empathy and a deeper understanding of sustainability challenges. The experiences provided by various VR settings can range from passive (i.e., being able to only gaze about) to a more interactive experience in which the user can roam freely and completely interact with the VR world, according to the classification developed by Araiza-Alba, Keane, and Kaufman (2022). Depending on the system and equipment utilized, each type of VR offers a different amount of immersion, control, realism, and interactivity. Depending on the genre being used, participants can explore, experience, interact, and even act while interacting with simulated events. To create a realistic and responsive environment with less interaction, 360-degree, or immersive, VR, for example, mixes 360-degree films and VR headsets (Kim, Kim, & Kim, 2022; Schone, Kisker, Sylvester, Radtke, & Gruber, 2021; Snelson & Hsu, 2020). AR can also be used to overlay sustainable practices onto physical spaces, making sustainable design and resource management tangible and engaging. The hands-on nature of these technologies encourages students to apply sustainable practices in business contexts effectively.

The VR environment allows users to visualize 3D virtual objects and abstract concepts, facilitating interaction with various events and saving time and costs through instantaneous virtual visits to different places (Chen & Jones, 2019; Freina & Ott, 2015; Shu, Huang, Chang, & Chen, 2018). VR also enables safe and repeated experiences of dangerous situations for effective management and teaching methods (Araiza-Alba et al., 2022; Makransky, Terkildsen, & Mayer, 2019). In rehabilitation and health care education, VR offers practice with virtual cases for supporting the disabled, learning essential skills during serious surgery, and providing emotional support (Fang, Wang, Liu, Su, & Yeh, 2014; Jensen & Konradsen, 2018; Parsons & Cobb, 2011). VR can also be used to train firefighters in handling dangerous fire environments (Cha, Han, Lee, & Choi, 2012), leading to positive cognitive, emotional, and behavioral effects on participants. VR provides meaningful knowledge and supports diverse learning styles in an authentic context, enhancing the understanding of theoretical concepts (Hardie et al., 2020). Moreover, VR can alter a user's perspective, fostering inventive thinking and supporting cognitive processes (Kim et al., 2022). It can also impact interest, motivation, emotion, and attitude (Filter, Eckes, Fiebelkorn, & Büssing, 2020; Kim et al., 2022; Scurati & Ferrise, 2020). For instance, VR can create an emotional connection with the environment, instilling a sense of responsibility (Scurati & Ferrise, 2020) and influence emotions through presence (Riva et al., 2007). Furthermore, studies have demonstrated behavioral changes in individuals using VR technology. For instance, immersive VR games can improve cognition and enthusiasm, leading to increased engagement in activities such as water conservation (Hsu, Tseng, & Kang, 2018).

5. Gamification for Sustainable Behavior Change

Gamification involves applying game design elements to nongame contexts to motivate and engage participants actively. In the context of sustainability education, gamification has proven to be a powerful tool for encouraging sustainable behavior change. EdTech platforms use gamification techniques, such as leaderboards, badges, and challenges, to incentivize students to adopt eco-friendly practices. For instance, students might be rewarded for completing sustainability-themed tasks, reducing their carbon footprint, or suggesting innovative green business ideas. This gamified approach nurtures a sense of achievement and competition while instilling sustainability principles into students' daily lives. A digital game designed on significance of SDGs to understand the students' knowledge and attitude toward sustainable development showed a notable enhancement in both cognitive abilities and enthusiasm. Moreover, the participants' comprehension of real-world water consumption and their commitment to water conservation displayed evident growth after engaging in the virtual experience, and it's been found that games based experiential learning proved to be effective in enhancing the knowledge on sustainability among students (Ho, Rajagopalan, Skvortsov, Arulampalam, & Piraveenan, 2022).

6. E-Learning Platforms for Sustainable Business Courses

E-learning platforms have become instrumental in delivering sustainable business education to a global audience. These platforms offer a wide array of courses and resources dedicated to sustainability in business, covering topics such as green marketing, circular economy principles, renewable energy, and sustainable supply chain management. Through interactive modules, webinars, and self-paced learning, students can access relevant and up-to-date information on sustainability practices. The flexibility and accessibility of e-learning enable learners from diverse backgrounds to acquire essential knowledge and skills to drive sustainable initiatives in their future careers. Designers of e-learning platforms conscientiously focus on the potential for acquiring global organizational competencies and skills (NITI Aayog, Government of India, 2021).

E-learning platforms have leveraged the power of the internet and digital platforms to democratize education access and provide personalize learning experiences for individual students. They have made quality educational resources, study materials, and online courses available to students across various geographic locations, including rural areas. This has bridged the gap between urban and rural education and provided equal learning opportunities to students from diverse backgrounds. Adaptive learning algorithms identify the strengths and weaknesses of each student and tailor content accordingly, enabling a more effective learning process. This approach helps students learn at their own pace, boosting engagement and knowledge retention.

The E-learning platforms have not replaced traditional classroom learning but rather complemented it. Teachers now have access to innovative teaching tools, multimedia content, and online assessments that enrich their teaching methods. This blended learning approach has resulted in improved student engagement and academic performance. EdTech solutions have been instrumental in reducing the financial burden of education. By offering online courses and resources, which are often more affordable than traditional education methods, EdTech start-ups have made education accessible to a broader segment of the population and have been instrumental in reducing the financial burden of education. By offering online courses and resources, which are often more affordable than traditional education methods, EdTech start-ups have made education accessible to a broader segment of the population (Blume Ventures, 2021).

7. Blockchain Technology for Transparent Supply Chains

Academics and professionals alike are becoming increasingly interested in sustainable supply chains (Fahimnia, Sarkis, & Davarzani, 2015). In blockchain-enabled technical environment, openness, transparency, neutrality, dependability, and security for all supply chain participants are possible (Abeyratne & Monfared, 2016).

In order to establish standardization and validation of the educational system and its stakeholders to be met to prevent fraud, blockchain in education is vital for students, universities, and entrepreneurs. As a result, it is possible to eliminate translation issues and comparisons between degrees earned in other nations (Sun, Wang, & Wang, 2018). Additionally, it is essential to address internet security issues including authentication, storage, and certification in order to save money and time while enhancing transparency. Credible certification will be provided for degrees, transcripts, student competencies, accomplishments, and professional aptitude.

A comprehensive record is kept by blockchain technology in data blocks that are ordered sequentially by timestamps. The cryptographic approach avoids data tampering and lowers fraud, and the old and new data blocks cannot be removed (Sun et al., 2018). The higher education industry can use blockchain technology for a variety of purposes, including recordkeeping (Jirgensons & Kapenieks, 2018), as it is a time-consuming and expensive task that can be completed with little effort. Personal information (name, identification, address, etc.), information about courses taken and grades, information about degrees and diplomas received, and information about courses attended and marks are all secured in blockchain platforms and trusted/transparent for all counterparties. As a result, it is not necessary to verify them each time.

In order to avoid curriculum vitae (CV) fraud and streamline student transfers between colleges, they will produce a virtual transcript of all academic accomplishments during a person's entire life (Ito & O'Dair, 2019). In order to discourage people from utilizing phoney degrees for employment, institutions may instead provide a URL where the diploma is available rather than issuing a paper diploma. Based on blockchain technology, professors can patent and protect the ideas, inventions, and IP used in their classes. Therefore, the issue of plagiarism is readily resolved. Additionally, the plagiarized study articles will be found quite soon. Professors will stop the online distribution of copyright courses by encrypting them and storing them in a safe chain. Permitted network users will have access to the information (Han et al., 2018).

Blockchain technology, best known for its association with cryptocurrencies, has also found its way into sustainable business education. This decentralized and immutable ledger system offers transparency and traceability, making it a valuable tool for sustainable supply chain management. Students can learn how blockchain enables businesses to verify the origin and sustainability credentials of products, promoting ethical consumerism and responsible sourcing. Moreover, blockchain-based smart contracts can incentivize sustainable practices among suppliers by automating rewards for eco-friendly behavior, fostering a culture of responsibility in the supply chain.

8. Sustainable Data Analytics for Evidence-Based Decision-Making

Sustainable business practices rely heavily on data-driven decision-making. EdTech tools are now integrating sustainable data analytics modules into business education curricula. These tools allow students to analyze environmental performance metrics, carbon footprints, and social impact data to understand the importance of sustainability reporting and benchmarking. By engaging with real-world sustainability data, students develop the ability to make informed decisions that prioritize environmental responsibility, social equity, and long-term profitability.

9. Challenges and Obstacles in Adopting and Implementing EdTech

- Infrastructure and Access: Many educational institutions face challenges related to inadequate infrastructure, such as slow internet connectivity and limited access to devices, which hinders the seamless integration of EdTech tools. Additionally, disparities in access to technology among students can lead to unequal learning opportunities.
- Cost and Budget Constraints: The adoption of EdTech often requires significant financial investments for purchasing licenses, software, hardware, and staff training. Budget constraints may limit the ability of educational institutions, particularly those with limited resources, to implement EdTech on a large scale.
- Faculty Training and Digital Literacy: Faculty members may lack the necessary skills and confidence to effectively use EdTech tools in their teaching. The implementation of EdTech requires substantial training and support to help educators navigate and integrate technology seamlessly into their pedagogical practices.
- Resistance to Change: Some educators and stakeholders may resist the adoption of EdTech due to concerns about the impact on traditional teaching methods and student engagement. Overcoming resistance to change and fostering a culture of innovation is essential for successful EdTech integration.
- Data Privacy and Security: Educational institutions must address concerns about data privacy and security when using EdTech tools. Ensuring compliance with data protection regulations and safeguarding sensitive student information is critical.

10. Strategies to Overcome Barriers

- Build Robust Infrastructure: Invest in upgrading the institution's infrastructure, including high-speed internet connectivity and access to devices, to support the smooth implementation of EdTech tools. Collaborating with technology providers and local governments can help secure funding for infrastructure development.
- Plan for Sustainable Funding: Develop a long-term financial plan that includes budget allocations for EdTech adoption. Seek partnerships with private sector

organizations and foundations interested in supporting educational initiatives to secure sustainable funding.

- Provide Ongoing Professional Development: Offer comprehensive training and support to faculty members to enhance their digital literacy and pedagogical skills. Continuous professional development programs and workshops can empower educators to leverage EdTech effectively in their teaching practices.
- Foster a Culture of Innovation: Encourage open communication and collaboration among faculty, students, and administrators to create a supportive environment for adopting and experimenting with EdTech. Highlight successful case studies and share best practices to inspire others.
- Prioritize Data Privacy and Security: Establish robust data protection policies and protocols to safeguard student information. Collaborate with technology vendors that prioritize data security and comply with relevant regulations.
- Address Digital Inclusion: Implement measures to bridge the digital divide among students by providing access to devices and internet connectivity for underprivileged learners. Partner with community organizations and government initiatives to address digital inclusion challenges.

11. Conclusion

The integration of emerging EdTech tools into sustainable business education represents a transformative leap forward, empowering students with the knowledge and skills to drive a green revolution. Educational institutions can effectively integrate and scale up the use of EdTech tools to promote sustainable business practices. By utilizing virtual simulations, online platforms, AR, VR, MOOCs, and data analytics, these institutions can provide students with experiential and collaborative learning experiences that foster a deep understanding of sustainability concepts. Through the usage of these EdTech tools, students can experience the consequences of their actions on the environment firsthand, while gamification instills a sense of responsibility and achievement. E-learning platforms provide widespread access to sustainability education, and blockchain technology ensures transparent and ethical supply chains. Sustainable data analytics enables evidence-based decision-making for a greener future. As educational institutions continue to embrace these EdTech tools, they pave the way for a new generation of environmentally conscious business leaders who will shape a more sustainable and responsible world.

References

Aayog, N. I. T. I. (2021). *Government of India NITI Aayog Atal Innovation Mission**** 1. Number of Vacancy: 01*. Retrieved from https://policycommons.net/artifacts/2436631/government-of-india-niti-aayog-atal-innovation-mission-1-number-of-vacancy/3458223/

Abeyratne, S. A., & Monfared, R. P. (2016). Blockchain ready manufacturing supply chain using distributed ledger. *International Journal of Research in Engineering and Technology*, *5*(9), 1–10.

Araiza-Alba, P., Keane, T., & Kaufman, J. (2022). Are we ready for virtual reality in K–12 classrooms? *Technology, Pedagogy and Education*, *31*(4), 1–21. doi:10.1080/1475939X.2022. 2033307

Carrion-Martinez, J. J., Luque-de la Rosa, A., Fernandez-Cerero, J., & Montenegro-Rueda, M. (2020). Information and communications technologies (ICTs) in education for sustainable development: A bibliographic review. *Sustainability*, *12*(8), 3288.

Cha, M., Han, S., Lee, J., & Choi, B. (2012). A virtual reality based fire training simulator integrated with fire dynamics data. *Fire Safety Journal*, *50*, 12–24. doi:10.1016/j.firesaf.2012.01.004

Chen, C. Y., & Jones, S. P. (2019). Supporting digital literacy in higher education: A phenomenographic study. *Higher Education Research and Development*, *38*(4), 764–778. doi:10.1080/07294360.2019.1585173

Digital education: India's EdTech opportunity. (2021). Blume Ventures. Retrieved from https://blume.vc/reports/digital-education-indias-edtech-opportunity/

Fahimnia, B., Sarkis, J., & Davarzani, H. (2015). Green supply chain management: A review and bibliometric analysis. *International Journal of Production Economics*, *162*, 101–114.

Fang, T. Y., Wang, P. C., Liu, C. H., Su, M. C., & Yeh, S. C. (2014). Evaluation of a haptics-based virtual reality temporal bone simulator for anatomy and surgery training. *Computer Methods and Programs in Biomedicine*, *113*(2), 674–681. doi:10.1016/j.cmpb.2013.11.005. PMID:24280627

Ferguson, T., & Roofe, C. G. (2020). SDG 4 in higher education: Challenges and opportunities. *International Journal of Sustainability in Higher Education*, *21*(5), 959–975. doi:10.1108/IJSHE-12-2019-0353

Filter, E., Eckes, A., Fiebelkorn, F., & Büssing, A. G. (2020). Virtual reality nature experiences involving wolves on YouTube: Presence, emotions, and attitudes in immersive and nonimmersive settings. *Sustainability*, *12*(9), 3823. doi:10.3390/su12093823

Freina, L., & Ott, M. (2015). A literature review on immersive virtual reality in education: State of the art and perspectives. In *Proceedings of eLearning and software for education (eLSE)*, Bucharest.

Han, M., Li, Z., He, J. S., Wu, D., Xie, Y., & Baba, A. (2018). A novel blockchain-based education, records verification solution. In *Proceedings of the 19th Annual Conference on Information Technology Education (SIGITE'18)*, Fort Lauderdale, FL, USA, 3–6 October 2018 (pp. 178–183). New York, NY: ACM.

Hardie, P., Darley, A., Carroll, L., Redmond, C., Campbell, A., & Jarvis, S. (2020). Nursing & Midwifery students' experience of immersive virtual reality storytelling: An evaluative study. *BMC Nursing*, *19*(1), 1–12. doi:10.1186/s12912-020-00471-5. PMID:32821245.

Ho, E., Rajagopalan, A., Skvortsov, A., Arulampalam, S., & Piraveenan, M. (2022). Game theory in defence applications: A review. *Sensors*, *22*(3), 1032.

Hsu, W. C., Tseng, C. M., & Kang, S. C. (2018). Using exaggerated feedback in a virtual reality environment to enhance behavior intention of water-conservation. *Journal of Educational Technology & Society*, *21*(4), 187–203. Retrieved from https://www.jstor.org/stable/10.2307/26511548

Ito, K., & O'Dair, M. (2019). A critical examination of the application of blockchain technology to intellectual property management. In H. Treiblmaier & R. Beck (Eds.), *Business transformation through blockchain* (pp. 317–335). Cham: Palgrave Macmillan.

Jensen, L., & Konradsen, F. (2018). A review of the use of virtual reality head-mounted displays in education and training. *Education and Information Technologies*, *23*(4), 1515–1529. doi:10.1007/s10639-017-9676-0

Jirgensons, M., & Kapenieks, J. (2018). Blockchain and the future of digital learning credential assessment and management. *Journal of Teacher Education for Sustainability*, *20*, 145–156.

Kim, J., Kim, K., & Kim, W. (2022). Impact of immersive virtual reality content using 360-degree videos in undergraduate education. *IEEE Transactions on Learning Technologies*, *15*(1), 137–149. doi:10.1109/TLT.2022.3157250

Kozma, R. B. (2008). Comparative analysis of policies for ICT in education. In *International handbook of information technology in primary and secondary education* (pp. 1083–1096). New York, NY: Springer.

Majumdar, S. (2015). Emerging trends in ICT for education & training. *General Asia Pacific Region IVETA*, *1*(1), 1–13.

Makransky, G., Terkildsen, T. S., & Mayer, R. E. (2019). Adding immersive virtual reality to a science lab simulation causes more presence but less learning. *Learning and Instruction*, *60*, 225–236. doi:10.1016/j.learninstruc.2017.12.007

Palliyalil, S., & Mukherjee, S. (2020). Byju's the learning app: An Investigative study on the transformation from traditional learning to technology based personalized learning. *International Journal of Scientific & Technology Research*, *9*(3), 5054–5059.

Parsons, S., & Cobb, S. (2011). State-of-the-art of virtual reality technologies for children on the autism spectrum. *European Journal of Special Needs Education*, *26*(3), 355–366. doi:10.1080/08856257.2011.593831

Raj, L., & Mallika Sankar, M. (2022). Exploring the role of social media marketing in the education sector. In *EdTech economy and the transformation of education* (pp. 227–244). Hershey, PA: IGI Global.

Riva, G., Mantovani, F., Capideville, C. S., Preziosa, A., Morganti, F., Villani, D., … Alcañiz, M. (2007). Affective interactions using virtual reality: The link between presence and emotions. *CyberPsychology and Behavior*, *10*(1), 45–56. doi:10.1089/cpb.2006.9993. PMID:17305448.

Schone, B., Kisker, J., Sylvester, R. S., Radtke, E. L., & Gruber, T. (2021). Library for universal virtual reality experiments (luVRe): A standardized immersive 3D/360 picture and video database for VR-based research. *Current Psychology*, 1–19. doi: 10.1007/s12144-021-01841-1

Scurati, G. W., & Ferrise, F. (2020). Looking into a future which hopefully will not become reality: How computer graphics can impact our behavior—A study of the potential of VR. *IEEE Computer Graphics and Applications*, *40*(5), 82–88. doi:10.1109/MCG.2020.3004276. PMID:32833623.

Shu, Y., Huang, Y. Z., Chang, S. H., & Chen, M. Y. (2018). Do virtual reality head-mounted displays make a difference? A comparison of presence and self-efficacy between head-mounted displays and desktop computer-facilitated virtual environments. *Virtual Reality*, 1–10. doi:10.1007/s10055-018-0376-x

Snelson, C., & Hsu, Y. C. (2020). Educational 360-degree videos in virtual reality: A scoping review of the emerging research. *TechTrends*, *64*(3), 404–412. doi:10.1007/s11528-019-00474-3

Sun, H., Wang, X., & Wang, X. (2018). Application of blockchain technology in online education. *International Journal of Emerging Technologies in Learning (IJET)*, *13*, 252–259.

Tondeur, J., Van Braak, J., Sang, G., Voogt, J., Fisser, P., & Ottenbreit-Leftwich, A. (2012). Preparing pre-service teachers to integrate technology in education: A synthesis of qualitative evidence. *Computers & Education*, *59*(1), 134–144. doi:10.1016/j.compedu.2011.10.009

Weller, M. (2018). Twenty years of Ed Tech. *Educause Review Online*, *53*(4), 34–48. Retrieved from https://oro.open.ac.uk/55708/1/ER184101.pdf

Weller, M. (2020). *25 years of Ed Tech.* Athabasca University Press. doi:10.15215/aupress/9781771993050.01

Yaduvanshi, S., & Singh, S. (2015). Constructivist approaches for teaching and learning of science. *International Journal in Management and Social Science*, *3*(12), 164–176.

Chapter 10

Gap Analysis of Employability Attributes Among Job Seekers in Bahrain: Employee Perspective

Nawal Abdulla[a], *Mukthar Al-Hashimi*[a], *Noor Alsayed*[a] *and Hashim Al-Hashimi*[b]

[a]Ahlia University, Bahrain
[b]Riyadh Elm University, Saudi Arabia

Abstract

The study's objective was to address the factors impacting the employability attributes of fresh graduates in the Kingdom of Bahrain while considering the various challenges. This study used a quantitative approach which employed the questionnaire tool, and data were collected by using a convenience sampling method. The study sample comprised $n = 385$ respondents from different industries, including manufacturing, banking and finance, hospitality, healthcare, oil and gas, and real estate sectors of Bahrain. Data gathered from questionnaire were analyzed using Statistical Package for the Social Sciences (SPSS), where descriptive and inferential statistics was used to analyze the data. The results of the study showed for the major Hypothesis 1 that the demographic variables have no significant statistical impact on employment attributes of the new fresh graduates. Moreover, findings suggest that null hypothesis for major Hypothesis 2 has been rejected as applied academic skills and critical thinking skills have no significant impact on employability attribute of fresh graduates in the Kingdom of Bahrain. Null hypothesis for major Hypothesis 3 has been accepted as findings suggest that technology use skills ($\beta_1 = 0.080$), system thinking skills ($\beta_2 = 0.210$), communication skills ($\beta_3 = 0.402$), and information skills ($\beta_4 = -0.100$) which are an antecedent of workplace skills, have significant statistical impact on employability attribute of fresh graduates in Kingdom of Bahrain. Lastly, null hypothesis for major Hypothesis 4 has been accepted as findings suggest that interpersonal skills ($\beta_5 = 0.229$) which are an antecedent of

Technological Innovations for Business, Education and Sustainability, 131–151

doi:10.1108/978-1-83753-106-620241010

effective relationship have significant statistical impact on employability attribute of fresh graduates in the Kingdom of Bahrain.

Keywords: Employability; information skills; critical thinking skills; resource management skills; applied knowledge; workplace skills; effective relationship skills

1. Introduction

Employability refers to one's capacity of moving independently within the market in realizing one's potential through using long-term work. The concept of employability plays a vital role in the development of labor market through guidelines and country standards. The employability is determined through assessing the employee's skills and how they present and use those skills to the employers in their daily work (Adeosun & Owolabi, 2023; Davidescu, Apostu, Paul, & Casuneanu, 2020). Employability is defined as the ability of the employees in achieving the preliminary employment through equipping themselves through necessary key skills and getting in-depth understanding and career advices about the phenomena, real-life concepts, and problems (Harvey, 2001). The fresh jobs seekers require more access to various employment training in the rural communities where employers have to recognize the skill gaps through using their critical thinking ability, which are much necessary in working independently and resolving the issues and obstacles. According to employer's perspective are the communication skill among the student studying in colleges and universities are the major barrier in the employability (Acikgoz, 2019). It has been evident that employers demand skill development and competency from the employee's or jobs seekers in promoting the knowledge-based aspect of the job. The jobs seekers performance in terms of occupation plays a vital role in determining the organizational sustainability and growth, which leads to competitive advantage for the organization in the industry. The growing number of candidates in the colleges and the universities and competitive environment for the job seekers in the companies have provided a gap of skill set in the industry due to the job demand and the employer's requirements. The fresh job seekers are facing several challenges in terms of good employment opportunities after their graduation and postgraduation. Ahmed, Fattani, Ali, and Enam (2022) provided the skills requirement by the employers in terms of the industry engagement and academic which has an essential role in thriving the employability in filling the skill gaps through advancement in the curriculum activities, industrial placement programs, and apprentice and offering real dynamic environment in the industry for the undergraduate students (Ahamad, 2019). Equipping a fresh job seeker with multiple skills is now become a requirement in Bahrain.

The employability skills among the fresh graduates in Bahrain are become essential under the Bahrain Vision 2030, which relying on the three major pillars including the fairness, sustainability, and the competitiveness, which have a significant impact on the human capital through training and education strengthening the private and public sectors. The implementation of Vision 2030 have requirement of commitment and the need assessment in terms of skill development in filling the gap of skills possessed by the young Bahraini graduate through new job entrants in the market. The country's higher qualification and education level is not matching with the candidate's skills and market requirement from the employers.

2. Literature Review

2.1 Employability

The concept of employability plays a vital role in developing labor market guidelines and standards of a country. Employability refers to one's capacity to find and sustain satisfying work. In a broader sense, employability is the capability of moving independently within the labor market to realize one's potential through long-term work. Furthermore, it is determined by an employee's skills and how they use and present those assets to employers and the context (e.g., individual situation) in which they seek work. A study was conducted to investigate the definition and measurement of employability while using policy-driven approaches for the companies where the study's outcomes demonstrated that employability is necessary for understanding the business problem and career growth (Harvey, 2001; McQuaid & Lindsay, 2005).

2.2 Employability Skills

Puad (2015) defines employability as a set of skills, precisely includes communication, analytical, management, and personal skills which subsequently influence employee attractiveness. These capabilities refer to the adaptability of new technologies and organizational goals. Chowdhury (2020) studied the importance of the skill gap in the business graduates of the banking sector in Bangladesh by using a quantitative survey to collect data from the 50 respondents of banking employees. The study's outcome demonstrated that employability skill has a major role in increasing the banking sector employee's competency level.

Employability skills can be categorized into two types, which include (i) general job skills and (ii) soft skills. General job skills include learning new things, dependability, and the ability to get along, whereas the soft employability skills include various skills including (i) communication skills, (ii) team working skills, (iii) problem-solving skills, (iv) organizing skills, and (v) self-management skills (Kemp, Martin, Maier, & Williams, 2015; Misra & Khurana, 2017).

2.3 Factors Influencing Employability of Fresh Graduates

2.3.1 Applied Knowledge

Applied knowledge is defined as learning in various situations and contexts where students use various procedures and analytical tools to formulate and generalize concepts to solve diverse problems and situations. Hawley (2017) states that applied knowledge can be categorized into two types, which include explicit and tactical knowledge where explicit knowledge refers to the formal language of mathematical expression providing technical know-how to individuals, whereas tactical knowledge resembles automatic intuition expressed through belief and perception (Jensen & Webster, 2021; Koloniari & Fassoulis, 2017).

Saeed, Keat, and Tham (2023) investigated the relationship between critical thinking skills and employability with the moderating role of internships. Data was gathered using questionnaire from various HIE in Maldives with sample of 313 respondents which included undergraduate and post graduate students. Findings shows significant statistical relationship between critical thinking skills and employability whereas internship does not moderate the relationship between critical thinking skills and employability.

A research was conducted to investigate employer perception in the Islamic bank of Bahrain for business graduates. The study employed a deductive approach of research to examine the new graduate skills. The findings described that teamwork, decision-making, and risk management skills have a significant impact on the employability of business graduates (Al-Shehab, Mukhtar, Madbouly, Reyad, & Hamdan, 2020).

2.3.2 Workplace Skills

Workplace skills mainly indicate the employees' experience, and it also includes adaptability to the technologies, and creative thinking. It is also helpful to deal with the communities (Ibrahim, Boerhannoeddin, & Kayode, 2017). Metilda and Neena (2016) conducted the gap analysis among entry-level business graduates while employing job theory and survey questionnaires. The study's outcomes explained that problem-solving skills and workplace skills are necessary for student growth in a specific organization.

Furthermore, Garrido, Sullivan, and Gordon (2010) examined the role of technology in improving the employability of low-income groups on 70 private organizations in 30 countries around the globe. The research reported the connection between candidates' skills, nongovernmental organization (NGO) program design, and environmental factors influencing employment. The findings show that ICT skills are important but not enough to secure the desired job.

Yahya, Iskandar, and Sunardi (2017) explored the development and role of employability skills in applying a scientific approach by using a nonexperimental design of survey known as ex post facto. The target population for the study was 523 students, whereas the sample size is 221 students. The research reported that employability is considerably supported by the application of the scientific approach in work.

2.3.3 Effective Relationship

Personal skills are also important to develop employability skills. The employees also have to be specific about their skills. Therefore, it can be said that the main focus of increasing employability skills is to make the business better and profitable. It is also important for the employees to learn about the patterns to solve organizational problems. Personal skills required basics skills and academic knowledge. The most common employability skills are collaboration and teamwork, leadership, problem-solving and critical thinking, professionalism, and communication skills (Abdullah, Ling, Sulaiman, Radzi, & Putri, 2020; Al-Halwachi & Mordi, 2021; Kenayathulla, Ahmad, & Idris, 2019; Kulkarni & Chachadi, 2014).

Mirzaa, Jaffri, and Hashmi (2017) examined the assessment of the job seekers' and employers' perspectives on employability skills with a sample size of 100 industrial employers by using the purposive sampling method for data collection. The study's outcomes showed that the three important skills, including professional skills, communication and business skills, and employability skills, are necessary to grow and provide the leading difference in the students.

Patacsil and Tablatin (2017) measured the importance of IT skills for IT students. The study used purposive sampling of data collection through using a survey questionnaire. The study's outcomes revealed that communication skills and teamwork are important in IT graduates under their soft skills.

2.3.4 Theory of Reasoned Actions

Concerning the theory of reasoned action, it can be concluded that the respective behaviors and traits of every person are determined by their previously made perception about the respective workplace which encourages the person to behave in a certain way and show certain personality attributes and behaviors. Moreover, the theory of reasoned action also suggests that the behavior of a person and the intention or beliefs of that person for that certain behavior are mainly determined by two major aspects, the attitude of the individual toward carrying out that behavior and secondly, subjective norm, which indicates the perception of others about that certain behavior. Similarly, in the context of employability and an individual's ability to show a certain set of behaviors and act in a certain way is influenced by the two aspects: subjective norms and personal attitude toward that behavior. It shows that the behavior reflecting employability skills among job seekers is influenced by one's perception or attitude as well as the perception or belief of peoples (subjective norm) toward certain behavior (Bunce & Birdi, 1998; Hagger, 2019).

2.3.5 Theory of Planned Behavior (TPB)

TPB suggests that behavior is control as well as the perception of the people regarding a certain behavior. TPB suggests that their three factors determine an individual behavior, which includes attitudes, subjective norms, and perceived behavioral control. In the context of the undertaken studies, the theory of planned behavior can be related to the employability skills, including applied knowledge, effective relationships, and workplace skills as employability skills and the behavior exhibited by the job seekers is influenced by subjective norms, attitude toward behavior, and perceived behavior control. Attitude toward behavior represents the overall assessment of the consequences of a particular behavior. Hence the job seekers tend to behave in a certain way that yields positive outcomes and avoid the kind of behavior that fosters negative results and gives rise to unfavorable outcomes (Costantini, Ceschi, & Sartori, 2019; Yang, Choi, & Lee, 2018).

3. Methodology

This study has employed descriptive research design, which refers to the scientific method which involves observing and describing the behavior of a subject without influencing it in any way. However, the rational of choosing the "descriptive research design" is that, descriptive research design provides more understanding of the observation and the behavior of the subjects. This study used quantitative research method for collecting primary data from the respondent through using survey questionnaire. The quantitative research approach is a type of study which began with the collecting of data theory, setting hypothesis, or empirical investigations and then uses statistical techniques to measure and evaluate variables, yielding numerical and quantitative conclusions in a certain manner that gave rise to the generalization of the study outcomes and researches (Kishore, 2023; Kivunja & Kuyini, 2017). The primary quantitative method is used in this study which are based on a questionnaire survey obtained from employers is used in this study. The descriptive design has been chosen in this research as this provides an in-depth view of this study. The target population comprises of employers in Bahrain as questionnaire survey obtained from the companies from various industries including (a) banking and finance, (b) manufacturing, (c) hospitality industry, (d) real estate industry (e) oil and gas (f) healthcare sector, and (g) others. According to Statistica (2018, July 17), more than 85,000 enterprises are registered in Bahrain's Kingdom. Thus, using the Raosoft approach to sampling, where the sample size exceeds 20, the total sample size should be a minimum of $n = 383$ respondents. The sample of the study comprised of $n = 383$ respondents from different industries in Bahrain including the oil and gas, healthcare, hospitality, and the real estate industry. This study has employed convenience sampling method for data collection. In terms of instrumentation of the study, the survey questionnaire consists of 22 questions each. An online survey questionnaire for the researcher is distributed among employers on the web and contains questions about the gaps within the employees which were adapted from the previous studies of Rasul, Abd Rauf, Mansor, and Puvanasvaran (2012), Sarwar and Aftab (2011), and McGarry (2016).

3.1 Hypothesis of the Study

In order to study the relationship between employability attributes, including applied knowledge, workplace skills, and effective relationship with employability.

Major Hypotheses

H1: Demographic variables have significant statistical impact on employability attribute of fresh graduates in Kingdom of Bahrain.

H2: Applied knowledge has significant statistical impact on employability attribute of fresh graduates in Kingdom of Bahrain.

Minor Hypotheses

$H_0 2$: Applied academic skills have significant statistical impact on employability attribute of fresh graduates in Kingdom of Bahrain.

$H_0 3$: Critical thinking skills have significant statistical impact on employability attribute of fresh graduates in Kingdom of Bahrain.

Major Hypotheses

H3: Workplace skills have significant statistical impact on employability attribute of fresh graduates in Kingdom of Bahrain.

Minor Hypotheses

$H_0 4$: Technology skills have significant statistical impact on employability attribute of fresh graduates in Kingdom of Bahrain.

$H_0 5$: System Thinking has significant statistical impact on employability attribute of fresh graduates in Kingdom of Bahrain.

$H_0 6$: Communication skills have significant statistical impact on employability attribute of fresh graduates in Kingdom of Bahrain.

$H_0 7$: Resource management skills have significant statistical impact on employability attribute of fresh graduates in Kingdom of Bahrain.

$H_0 8$: Information use has significant statistical impact on employability attribute of fresh graduates in Kingdom of Bahrain.

Major Hypotheses

H4: Effective relationship has significant statistical impact on employability attribute of fresh graduates in Kingdom of Bahrain.

Minor Hypotheses

$H_0 9$: Interpersonal skills have significant statistical impact on employability attribute of fresh graduates in Kingdom of Bahrain.

$H_0 10$: Personal qualities have significant statistical impact on employability attribute of fresh graduates in Kingdom of Bahrain.

4. Finding and Discussions

4.1 Demographic

Table 10.1 demonstrated the demographics of the study where total n = 385 respondents, 191 (49.6%) were male respondents, and remaining 194 (50.4%) were females 202 (52.5%) of the respondents were Bahraini nationals, whereas remaining 183 (47.5%) of the respondents were non-Bahraini as they were expatriates working on numerous managerial-level positions in their respective organizations. Furthermore, the tables also provided language demographic

Table 10.1. Demographic Table.

Gender		
Male	191	49.60%
Female	194	50.40%
Nationality		
Bahraini	202	52.50%
Non-Bahraini	183	47.50%
Arabic	187	48.60%
Language		
English	143	37.10%
Other language	55	14.30%
Size of Business		
Small	153	39.70%
Medium	147	38.20%
Big enterprises	843	21.60%
Age		
20–25	66	17.10%
26–30	68	17.70%
31–40	100	26%
41–45	30	7.80%
46–55	73	20.30%
56 and above	42	10.90%
Number of Employees		
Below 25	23	6.00%
26–50	46	11.90%
51–75	66	17.10%
76–99	10	2.60%

Table 10.1. *(Continued)*

100–499	66	17.70%
500–999	76	19.70%
1,000–1,499	59	15.30%
5,000	39	10%
Type of Business		
Public limited company	78	20.30%
Limited liability company	69	17.90%
Non-profit organization	60	15.60%
Family owned	30	7.80%
Corporation	18	4.70%
Limited company	67	17.40%
Partnership	45	11.70%
Sole-proprietorship	18	4.70%
Designations		
General manager	41	10.60%
Human resources (HR) manager	19	4.90%
Departmental manager	35	9.10%
Supervisor	55	13.30%
CEO/President	52	13.50%
Senior leadership	28	7.30%
Individual contributor	125	32.50%

Source: Authors' work.

respondents out of n = 385 total respondents, 187 (48.6%) respondents speak only Arabic as the primary language, 143 (37.1%) speak English as their primary language whereas 55 (14.3%) respondent speak other languages as their primary language at workplace. Furthermore, related to size of the business which shows that out of n = 385 respondents, majority of the respondent had affiliation of small medium enterprise or medium size of business with 153 (39.7%), seconded by second majority of small business with 147 (38.2%), and remaining 83 (21.6%) of the respondents reported having affiliation with big enterprises and corporate sector.

4.2 Descriptive Analysis

Table 10.2 shows, Mean value of all the variables is varied, where system thinking skill and information use skill have 3.36 means and 3.35 means have the highest mean value respectively and falls under the strongly agree category while, applied

Table 10.2. Normality Table.

Variable Name	Mean	Std. Deviation
Employability	3.3138	0.86280
Applied academic skill	3.3169	0.98850
Critical thinking skill	3.2338	1.37022
Technology use skill	3.3448	1.13799
System thinking skill	3.3671	0.98264
Communication skill	3.3240	0.86436
Information use skill	3.3597	1.21787
Resource management	3.3058	0.98250
Interpersonal skill	3.2571	0.96666
Personality qualities	3.3117	1.03248

Source: Authors' work.

knowledge, effective relationships, critical thinking skill have a lower mean value of 3.23 in term of employee attributes. System thinking skill has the highest score of the mean of 3.36 and critical thinking skill has the lowest score with an average value of 3.23 means.

4.3 Reliability Analysis

Employability which comprises of five items on a Likert scale reported reliability of $\alpha = 0.89$ which higher than 0.7 which is a lenient cut of value for the threshold which suggests that items reported high internal consistency. Applied knowledge which comprises of five items on a Likert scale reported reliability of $\alpha = 0.77$, which is higher than 0.7, which is a lenient cut of value for the threshold which suggests that items reported high internal consistency. Workplace skills which comprise of five items on a Likert scale reported reliability of $\alpha = 0.83$ which is higher than 0.7 which is a lenient cut of value for the threshold which suggests that items reported high internal consistency. Lastly, effective relationships which comprises of seven items on a Likert scale reported reliability of $\alpha = 0.87$, which is higher than 0.7, which is a lenient cut of value for the threshold which suggests that items reported high internal consistency. In a nutshell, the overall instrument reported the reliability 0.91 which is considered to be highlight reliable (please refer to Table 10.3).

4.4 Correlation

Table 10.4 shows that there is a strong and positive relationship between system thinking skill (IV) and employability (DV) as ($r = -0.719$). This indicates that an increase in system thinking skills (IV) leads to an increase in the chances of

Table 10.3. Reliability Table.

Variable Name	Number of Items	Cronbach's Alpha Value	Interpretation
Employability	5	$\alpha = 0.89$	Highly reliable
Applied knowledge	5	$\alpha = 0.77$	Highly reliable
Workplace skills	5	$\alpha = 0.83$	Highly reliable
Effective relationships	7	$\alpha = 0.87$	Highly reliable
Overall reliability	22	$\alpha = 0.91$	Highly reliable

Source: Authors' work.

employability for fresh job seekers. There is a positive and strong relationship between communication skill (IV) and employability (DV) with value ($R = 0.785$) which indicates that with an increase in the communication skill of employees, employability also increases.

In Table 10.4, it has been shown that there is a strong positive relationship between information use (IV) and employability (DV) with ($r = 0.776$) a significance level of 0.005. This statistics means that with an increase in the information usage of fresh job seekers, employability also increases.

Table 10.4. Correlation Table.

Correlation									
EMPL	1								
AAS	0.7	1							
CTS	0.5	0.508	1						
TUS	0.6	0.568	0.416	1					
STS	0.7	0.621	0.487	0.541	1				
CS	0.785	0.71	0.541	0.617	0.688	1			
IUS	0.479	0.453	0.374	0.443	0.504	0.71	1		
RM	0.739	0.936	0.501	0.575	0.633	0.747	0.469	1	
IS	0.776	0.909	0.527	0.592	0.657	0.766	0.51	0.888	1
PQ	0.688	0.93	0.484	0.534	0.627	0.687	0.477	0.859	0.841

Source: Authors' work.

Furthermore, communication skills (IV) have a weak negative relationship with employability (DV) with (r = −0.293) having a significance level of 0.005. This indicates that with an increase in the communication skill of the job seekers, the employability increases as well.

There is a moderate relationship between critical thinking skill (IV) and employability (DV) (r = 0.533) with a significance level of 0.005 of the fresh job seekers, which explains that with an increase in critical thinking skill of the employee and the employability of fresh job seeker also increases. It has been shown in Table 10.4 that there is a weak positive relationship between the information use skill (IV) and the employability (DV).

4.5 Chi-Square Tests

Chi-Square tests (refer to Table 10.5) were used to analyze the demographic variables. Regarding the results of chi-square tests, the assumption significance values are 0.356 for gender, 0.867 for location, 0.623 for language, 0.923 for size of business, 0.184 for age, 0.649 for number of employees, 0.067 for type of business, 0.585 for employer position, 0.795 for recent academic degree, 0.423 for sector of organization, and 0.795 for recent academic degree. The assumption

Table 10.5. Chi-Square Table.

Variable		Asymp. Sig. (2-Sided)	Significance
Gender	Pearson chi-square	0.356	Insignificant
	Likelihood ratio	0.259	
	Linear-by-linear association	0.839	
Location	Pearson chi-square	0.867	Insignificant
	Likelihood ratio	0.859	
	Linear-by-linear association	0.776	
Language	Pearson chi-square	0.623	Insignificant
	Likelihood ratio	0.561	
	Linear-by-linear association	0.172	
Size of business	Pearson chi-square	0.923	Insignificant
	Likelihood ratio	0.993	
	Linear-by-linear association	0.479	

Table 10.5. *(Continued)*

Variable		Asymp. Sig. (2-Sided)	Significance
Age	Pearson chi-square	0.184	Insignificant
	Likelihood ratio	0.183	
	Linear-by-linear association	0.413	
Number of employees	Pearson chi-square	0.649	Insignificant
	Likelihood ratio	0.586	
	Linear-by-linear association	0.477	
Type of business	Pearson chi-square	0.067	Insignificant
	Likelihood ratio	0.054	
	Linear-by-linear association	0.176	
Employer position	Pearson chi-square	0.585	Insignificant
	Likelihood ratio	0.488	
	Linear-by-linear association	0.353	
Recent academic degree	Pearson chi-square	0.795	Insignificant
	Likelihood ratio	0.676	
	Linear-by-linear association	0.123	
Sector of organization	Pearson chi-square	0.423	Insignificant
	Likelihood ratio	0.616	
	Linear-by-linear association	0.514	
Recent academic degree	Pearson chi-square	0.795	Insignificant
	Likelihood ratio	0.676	
	Linear-by-linear association	0.123	

Source: Authors' work.

significance values of all the demographic variables are all less than the value of 0.05. This means that the null hypothesis is accepted and the alternative one is rejected. Therefore, it can be concluded that demographic variables have no significant statistical impact on employability attribute of fresh graduates in Kingdom of Bahrain.

4.6 Regression

Regression analysis (refer to Table 10.6) revealed that 74.2% of the variance in the dependent variable of employability while taking the group in one model. The percentage shows the dependent variable (employability) explained by the independent variables (applied knowledge, workspace skill, and effective relationship).

Moreover, significant *F* value (refer to Table 10.7) is also reported indicating that model is fit for further analyzation.

In the coefficient Table 10.8, where the *p*-value is given for the basis of testing hypothesis if the significance value is less than 0.05 which is considered as an interval of the remarkable level. The association between the variables can be done if $p= <0.05$ t statistic is $>\pm$ 1.96.

Table 10.8 where *p*-values such as $\beta = 0.080$, *t*-value = 3.042, and $p > 0.05$ demonstrate that there is a positive significant impact of technology use skill on the employability, therefore, the Hypothesis ($H1_A$) is accepted. Furthermore, the path values of system thinking skills ($\beta = 0.210$, *t*-value = 6.129 and $p > 0.05$) demonstrate that there is a significant positive relationship between system thinking skills and employability, therefore, the Hypothesis ($H2_A$) also accepted.

Moreover, the *p*-value such as $\beta = 0.402$, *t*-value = 7.254 and $p > 0.05$ explained that communication skills have a significant positive impact on the employability of the fresh job seekers, therefore, the Hypothesis ($H3_A$) also accepted in this case.

The *p*-values of interpersonal skill where $\beta = -0.100$, *t*-value = −3.708, and $p > 0.05$ indicate that there is a negative significant relationship between the interpersonal skill and the employability of the fresh job seeker, therefore, Hypothesis ($H1_A$) also accepted. Furthermore, the findings also showed that information use skill ($\beta = -0.229$, *t*-value = 3.637 and $p > 0.05$) demonstrates that there is a significant impact of information use skill and employability

Table 10.6. Variance Table.

Model	**R**	**R Square**	**Adjusted R Square**	**Std. The Error of the Estimate**
1	0.861	0.742	0.735	0.44386

Source: Authors' work.

Table 10.7. Analysis of Variance (Anova) Table.

	Sum of Squares	***df***	**Mean Square**	***F***	**Sig.**
Regression	211.978	9	23.553	119.553	0.000
Residual	73.879	375	0.197		
Total	285.857	384			

Source: Authors' work.

Table 10.8. Coefficient Table.

	Unstandardized Coefficients	Standardized Coefficients	*t*	Sig.
(Constant)	0.373		3.933	0
AAS	0.059	0.067	0.585	0.559
CTS	0.033	0.052	1.605	0.109
TUS	0.08	0.106	3.042	0.003
STS	0.21	0.239	6.129	0
CS	0.402	0.403	7.254	0
IUS	0.1	−0.141	−3.708	0
RM	0.007	0.009	0.106	0.916
IS	0.229	0.257	3.637	0
PQ	−0.033	−0.039	−0.533	0.595

Source: Authors' work.

therefore, the Hypothesis ($H4_A$) is also accepted. Other than that, other variables including applied academic skills, critical thinking skills, resource management, and personality qualities have an insignificant impact on the employability of the fresh job seekers.

4.7 Discussion

Null hypothesis for major Hypothesis 1 which includes H_01 and H_02 has been rejected based upon the findings of multiple regression analysis as findings suggest that there is no statistical impact of applied academic skills and critical thinking skills on employability attribute of fresh graduates in the Kingdom of Bahrain. Our findings reject previous studies conducted by Al-Shehab et al. (2020), Pana and Lee (2011), and Tentama and Abdillah (2019) which suggest that applied academic skills and critical thinking skills making applied knowledge have significant statistical impact on employability attribute among fresh graduates.

Hypotheses for *H2* has been accepted. The alternate hypothesis has been accepted as our findings suggest that workplace skills have a significant statistical impact on the employability attribute of fresh graduates in the Kingdom of Bahrain. Findings of the study validate previous studies conducted by Huang, Yuan, and Li (2019), Keshvari, Faraz, Safaie, and Nedjad (2018), Ibarraran, Ripani, Taboada, Villa, and García (2012), Garrido et al. (2010), and Yahya et al. (2017) which highlight that workplace skills is a strong predictor of employability attribute among the fresh graduates. The findings supported the previous study conducted on workplace skills that have a major role in the employability of job seekers.

H3 has been accepted, and the alternate hypothesis has been accepted. Our findings suggest that effectiveness has a significant statistical impact on the employability attribute of fresh graduates in the Kingdom of Bahrain. The findings of the study validate previous studies conducted by Misra and Khurana (2017), Wats and Wats (2009), Al-Mahrooqi and Tuzlukova (2014), and Kulkarni and Chachadi (2014), which highlight that's effective relationships is a strong predictor of employability attribute among the fresh graduates. The previous studies focus on communicative competencies and the effectiveness of communication and skill. But the current study has contributed while addressing the effective relationship of the job seekers' attributes while considering the other important skills in employability in Bahrain (please refer to Table 10.9).

5. Conclusion

The study's primary objectives were to explore the gap analysis of employability attributes among the fresh job seekers in Bahrain in terms of the employer perspectives. The finding demonstrates that under the applied knowledge, applied academic skills and critical thinking skills have no significant impact on the employability among the fresh job seekers in Bahrain. The findings of this study reject previous findings of several researchers in terms of the applied academic skill and the critical thinking skill addressed and analyzed by Pana and Lee (2011), Tentama and Abdullah (2019), and Lowden, Hall, Elliot, and Lewin (2011).

The findings also demonstrated that workplace skills, which are system thinking skills, technology skills, and communication skills, have a significant impact on the employability attributes of fresh graduates in the Kingdom of Bahrain. The findings were also validated by several researcher findings of

Table 10.9. Summary of the Findings.

Hypothesis	Statistics	Findings
H1	Sig. for all demographic variables are >0.05	Not accepted
H_02	Sig = 0.559 > 0.05	Not accepted
H_03	Sig = 0.109 > 0.05	Not accepted
H_04	Sig = 0.003 < 0.05 and Beta value = 0.080	Accepted
H_05	Sig = 0.003 < 0.05 and Beta value = 0.210	Accepted
H_06	Sig = 0.000 < 0.05 and Beta value = 0.402	Accepted
H_07	Sig = 0.916 > 0.05	Not accepted
H_08	Sig = 0.000 < 0.05 and Beta value = 0.100	Accepted
H_09	Sig = 0.000 < 0.05 and Beta value 0.229	Accepted
H_010	Sig = 0.595 > 0.05	Rejected

Source: Authors' work.

previous studies done by Ibarraran et al., 2012, Garrido et al. (2010), and Metilda and Neena (2016), where they had identified that workplace skills have a major role in the employability attributes for the job's seekers and necessary for student growth in a specific organization, these previous findings, supporting the current findings in Bahrain context.

Furthermore, the study's outcomes also explained that under the effective relationship, interpersonal skills have a significant impact on the employability attribute of fresh graduates in the Kingdom of Bahrain. In contrast, personal qualities have an insignificant impact on the employability of job seekers. The study findings are confirmed and validated from the previous studies (Al-Mahrooqi & Tuzlukova, 2014; Kulkarni & Chachadi, 2014; Wats & Wats, 2009) demonstrated that interpersonal skill is a strong predictor of the employee's attributes.

5.1 Recommendations

Concerning this finding, it is recommended that:

- The fresh job seekers have a high school degree to attain and retain jobs in the Kingdom of Bahrain.
- The students and fresh graduates must engage themselves in training and internship programs to effectively learn skills that the employer gives high importance, such as responsible use of ICT, time management, safety awareness, maintain work ethics, personal financial matters innovation, goals setting, math in real life, oral and written communication.
- Moreover, employers usually prefer candidates who possess competent soft skills such as creative problem-solving, quick learning, communication, decision-making, and entrepreneurial thinking. Hence, it is recorded to the fresher to develop soft skills.
- The employers must coordinate closely with the stakeholders to facilitate effective youth employability, productivity, skill enhancement, and acquisition of a talented workforce.
- The employers must have a clear and defined set of criteria and a certain set of skills required for the respective jobs.
- The employer must be willing to teach the employee the job-specific skills required soon after recruitment to teaching several important tasks and operations involved in the job such as use particular computer packages.
- The researchers also found that educational institutes in Bahrain must concentrate on ensuring that the students gain problem-solving, decision-making, learning skills, and enhance skills in all areas of their field.
- The first step Gulf Cooperation Council (GCC) countries should take to produce highly skilled workers is to reform the present education system.
- A shift in the curriculum will consider the relevance of education, quality of subjects, and skills adapted to meet labor market demands.
- Teachers will need to be taught new learning styles and skills and the core topics of math, science, computer science, and different languages.

5.2 Limitation

- The study targets an unlimited number of employers in Bahrain.
- Both academia and industry are responsible for equipping fresh graduates with the necessary competencies. It is one of the crucial aspects which is not explored in the current study.
- Future research must extend its analysis to other countries as well as multiple geographical regions.
- Moreover, the limited time and resources was another significant challenge encountered by the research during the study.

References

Abdullah, Z., Ling, T. Y., Sulaiman, N. S., Radzi, R. A., & Putri, K. Y. (2020). The effects of verbal communication behaviors on communication competence in the pharmaceutical industry. *Journal of Critical Reviews*, *7*(12). doi:10.31838/jcr.07.12.125

Acikgoz, Y. (2019). Employee recruitment and job search: Towards a multi-level integration. *Human Resource Management Review*, *29*(1), 1–13.

Adeosun, O. T., & Owolabi, T. (2023). Owner-manager businesses and youth employee perceptions. *Journal of Business and Socio-economic Development*, *3*(2), 97–117. doi:10.1108/JBSED-03-2021-0032

Ahamad, F. (2019). Impact of word-of-mouth, job attributes and relationship strength on employer attractiveness. *Management Research Review*, *42*(6), 721–739.

Ahmed, F., Fattani, M. T., Ali, S. R., & Enam, R. N. (2022). Strengthening the bridge between academic and the industry through the academia-industry collaboration plan design model. *Frontiers in Psychology*, *13*. doi:10.3389/fpsyg.2022.875940

Al-halwachi, L. F., & Mordi, C. (2021). Gender inequality barriers and solutions to senior management positions: Perspectives on women in Bahraini banking sector. *Journal of Sustainable Finance & Investment*, 1–22. doi:10.1080/20430795.2021.1936441

Al-Mahrooqi, R., & Tuzlukova, V. (2014). English communication skills and employability in GCC. *Social Science and Humanities*, 473–488.

Al-Shehab, N., Mukhtar, A. H., Madbouly, A., Reyad, S., & Hamdan, A. (2020). Do employability skills for business graduates meet the employers' expectations? The case of retail Islamic banks of Bahrain. *Higher Education, Skills and Work-Based Learning*. doi:10.1108/HESWBL-09-2019-0117

Bunce, D., & Birdi, K. S. (1998). The theory of reasoned action and theory of planned behavior and a function of job control. *British Journal of Human Psychology*, 265–275.

Chowdhury, F. (2020). Skills gap of business graduates in the banking sector of Bangladesh employers' expectation versus reality. *International Education Studies*, 48–57.

Costantini, A., Ceschi, A., & Sartori, R. (2019). *The theory of planned behavior as a frame for job crafting: Explaining and enhancing proactive adjustment at work*. New York: Springer International Publisher.

Davidescu, A. A., Apostu, S., Paul, A., & Casuneanu, I. (2020). Work flexibility, job satisfaction, and job performance among Romanian employees—Implications for sustainable human resource management. *Sustainability*, *12*(15), 6086. doi:10.3390/su12156086

Garrido, M., Sullivan, J., & Gordon, A. (2010). Understanding the links between ICT skills training and employability: An analytical framework. In *4th ACM/IEEE International Conference on Information and Communication Technologies and Development*.

Hagger, M. S. (2019). The reasoned action approach and the theories of reasoned action and planned behavior. In D. S. Dunn (Ed.), *Oxford bibliographies in psychology*. New York, NY: Oxford University Press. doi:10.1093/OBO/9780199828340-0240

Harvey, L. (2001). Defining and measuring employability. *Quality in Higher Education*, 97–101.

Huang, W., Yuan, C., & Li, M. (2019). Person–job fit and innovation behavior: Roles of job involvement and career commitment. *Frontiers in Psychology*, *10*. doi:10.3389/fpsyg.2019.01134

Ibarraran, P., Ripani, L., Taboada, B., Villa, J. M., & García, B. (2012). Life skills, employability and training for disadvantaged youth: Evidence from a randomized evaluation design. *SSRN Electronic Journal*. doi:10.2139/ssrn.2085204

Ibrahim, R., Boerhannoeddin, A., & Kayode, B. K. (2017). Organizational culture and development: Testing the structural path of factors affecting employees' work performance in an organization. *Asia Pacific Management Review*, *22*(2), 104–111.

Jensen, P. H., & Webster, E. M. (2021). Knowledge management: Does capture impede creation. *SSRN Electronic Journal*. doi:10.2139/ssrn.3952301

Kemp, S., Martin, F., Maier, P., & Williams, I. (2015). A gap analysis of student employability profiles, employer engagement and work-placements. *Planet*, 16–20.

Kenayathulla, H. B., Ahmad, N. A., & Idris, A. R. (2019). Gaps between competence and importance of employability skills: Evidence from Malaysia. *Higher Education Evaluation and Development*, 97–112.

Keshvari, G. C., Faraz, J. M., Safaie, N., & Nedjad, S. H. (2018). A model for the development of employees' learning (career path) in industrial enterprises. *Engineering, Technology & Applied Science Research*, *8*(1), 2427–2432. Accessed on 2nd June 2021.

Kishore, N. (2023). The impact of marital status on female labour force participation rate – A study on Bangalore City. In J. Aloysius Edward, K. P. Jaheer Mukthar, E. R. Asis, & K. Sivasubramanian (Eds.), *Current trends in economics, business and sustainability. ICEBS 2023 contributions to environmental sciences & innovative business technology*. Singapore: Springer. doi:10.1007/978-981-99-3366-2_5

Kivunja, C., & Kuyini, A. B. (2017). Understanding and applying research paradigms in educational contexts. *International Journal of Higher Education*, *6*(5), 26. doi:10.5430/ijhe.v6n5p26

Koloniari, M., & Fassoulis, K. (2017). Knowledge management perceptions in academic libraries. *The Journal of Academic Librarianship*, *43*(2), 135–142.

Kulkarni, N., & Chachadi, A. H. (2014). Skills for employability: Employers' perspective. *SCMS Journal of Indian Management*. Retrieved from https://www.researchgate.net/publication/325035950_SCMS_Journal_Jul-Sep_2014-64-70-Skills_for_employability

Lowden, K., Hall, S., Elliot, D., & Lewin, J. (2011). *Employers' perceptions of the employability skills*. Glasgow: The SCRE Center, University of Glasgow.

McGarry, K. B. (2016). *An examination of perceived employability skills between employers and college graduates*. Boston, MA: Northeastern University.

McQuaid, R. W., & Lindsay, C. (2005). The concept of employability. *Urban Studies*, 197–219.

Metilda, R. M., & Neena, P. C. (2016). Gap analysis of employability skills of entry level business. *International Journal of Social Science and Management*, *3*, 294–299.

Mirzaa, F. M., Jaffri, A. A., & Hashmi, M. S. (2017). *An assessment of industrial employment skill gaps among university graduates in the Gujrat-Sialkot-Gujranwala*. Washington, D.C.: International Food Policy Research Institute.

Misra, R. K., & Khurana, K. (2017). Employability skills among information technology professionals: A literature review. *Procedia Computer Science*, *122*, 63–70.

Pana, Y.-J., & Lee, L.-S. (2011). Academic performance and perceived employability of graduate students in business and management an analysis of nationwide graduate destination survey. *Procedia – Social and Behavioral Sciences*, 91–103.

Patacsil, F., & Tablatin, C. L. (2017). Exploring the importance of soft and hard skills as perceived by IT internship students and industry: A gap analysis. *Journal of Technology and Science Education*, 347–368.

Puad, M. M. (2015). The role of employability skills training programs in the workforce of Malaysia. *Open Access Dissertation*. Retrieved from https://docs.lib.purdue.edu/open_access_dissertations/52

Rasul, M. S., Abd Rauf, R. A., Mansor, A. N., & Puvanasvaran, A. P. (2012). Employability skills assessment tool development. *International Education Studies*, *5*(5). doi:10.5539/ies.v5n5p43

Saeed, K., Keat, O. B., & Tham, J. (2023). Assessing the relationship between demographic factors and employability among university graduates in the Maldives. *Social Science Journal*, *13*(3).

Sarwar, A., & Aftab, H. (2011). Work stress & family imbalance in service sector of Pakistan. *International Journal of Business and Social Science*, *2*(13). Retrieved from https://www.researchgate.net/publication/320757744_Work_Stress_Family_Imbalance_in_Service_Sector_of_Pakistan

Statistica. (2018, July 17). *Bahrain: Number of enterprises by size 2018*. Statista. Retrieved from https://www.statista.com/statistics/943018/bahrain-number-of-enterprises-by-size/

Tentama, F., & Abdillah, M. H. (2019). Student employability examined from academic achievement and self-concept. *International Journal of Evaluation and Research in Education (IJERE)*, *8*(2), 243. doi:10.11591/ijere.v8i2.18128

Wats, M., & Wats, R. K. (2009). Developing soft skills in students. *International Journal of Learning*. doi:10.18848/1447-9494/CGP/V15I12/46032

Yahya, M., Iskandar, S., & Sunardi, S. (2017). Technical skills and employability skills of vocational high school students in Indonesia. *Journal of Scientific Research and Studies*, *4*(6), 148–155.

Yang, Y., Choi, J. N., & Lee, K. (2018). Theory of planned behavior and different forms of organizational change behavior. *Social Behavior and Personality*, 1657–1672.

Chapter 11

Digital Competencies and Attitude Toward the Use of Information Technologies in Secondary School Teachers in a Peruvian Public Educational Institution

Edwin Ramirez-Asis[a], *Hober Huaranga-Toledo*[b], *Yeni Bullón-Miguel*[c], *Huber Rodriguez-Nomura*[a] *and Hugo Marino Rodríguez-Orellana*[b]

[a]Universidad Señor de Sipán, Peru
[b]Universidad Nacional Mayor de San Marcos, Perú
[c]Universidad Cesar Vallejo, Perú

Abstract

This study analyzes the digital competencies and the attitude toward the use of information and communication technologies (ICT) in secondary school teachers of the Javier Heraud Public Educational Institution, Lima, Peru, according to the technology, pedagogy, and content knowledge (TPACK) model, which focuses on knowledge about technology knowledge (TK), pedagogical content (PK) and content knowledge (CK). This implies that it is important to take these components into account in the development of teaching work, in order to contribute to the quality of student learning, within the framework of the restrictions established due to the global health emergency. The study is based on the quantitative approach, type of correlational research and cross-sectional design, the sample consisted of 106 secondary education teachers, questionnaire was applied which were validated by five experts and its reliability was analyzed by the values obtained for Cronbach's alpha, for the digital competencies variable $\alpha = 0.861$ and for the variable attitude toward the use of ICT $\alpha = 0.854$. It has been shown that there is a relationship between digital competencies and the attitude

Technological Innovations for Business, Education and Sustainability, 153–167

doi:10.1108/978-1-83753-106-620241011

toward the use of information and communication technologies in teachers of a Peruvian Public Educational Institution.

Keywords: Attitude toward school; digital competence; secondary education; information skills; information technology; public educational institution

1. Introduction

Since the beginning of the year 2020, our planet has been going through a sanitary emergency as a consequence of the pandemic, which forced many governments to establish, among other measures, mandatory quarantines in homes, restricting the movement of people. As a result, educational systems worldwide had to opt for distance education, since it was not possible to develop a face-to-face education; this marked a before and after not only in education but also in human interaction, since people have normally lived in society and in contact with others. In this context, the new distance education modality, where students are not in the same physical space with their classmates or with their teachers, means that students in public secondary schools must develop their learning progress from their homes through the use of the internet, radio, or television. This situation constitutes a challenge for teachers in their mastery of the use of technological tools, which are currently insufficient for the challenges they have to face (Vialart, 2020); this new educational scenario requires the use of virtual spaces and methodologies with which both students and teachers are not accustomed (ECLAC, 2020). Distance education brought to light an already existing problem in basic education in public institutions where academic training and teaching skills in the management of digital and virtual interaction tools are deficient because they lack the practice that teachers need for their performance in virtual classrooms (Vólquez & Amador, 2020). It is of transcendental value to recognize, on the part of teachers, the employability of virtual educational resources, cognitive digital competencies, didactic-methodological competencies, and instrumental digital competencies, which are very necessary for this new educational scenario of pandemic and for what will be the postpandemic basic education, which is not a change but an educational evolution (Berrocal, Flores, Montalvo, & Flores, 2021).

In this context, it is also very important to analyze on the attitude of secondary education teachers toward the use of information and Communication Technologies (ICT), i.e. the predisposition (thinking, feeling and acting) of the teacher toward the use of ICT; depending on the teacher's response, this may result in a positive attitude or a negative attitude toward the use of ICT in general, which will influence in one way or another in the learning process (Tapia, 2018).

2. Non-presential Education in Peru

Similar to the measures dictated worldwide, the Peruvian education system proceeded to the development of distance education with a virtual platform in the

work between teachers, for the exchange and coordination between teachers and managers, teachers with parents, teachers with students, using for this purpose virtual classrooms, communication, and organizational tools (Villalobos, 2021). In the absence of a virtual platform, the use of the telephone is considered as a tool for organization and communication, as well as the WhatsApp messaging service, email, cloud storage, which allows the teacher to follow up with students; on this, Hurtado (2020) points out that technological resources could be those that ensure significant learning. In this sense, in distance education it is imperative that teachers have a high level of training and a good level of teaching practice in three scenarios: (i) with connectivity; (ii) with limited connectivity; and (iii) without internet connectivity.

In this line, according to the regulations issued by the Ministry of Education, as part of the health emergency, from 2020, the strategy "I learn at home" was applied, distance education modality, where students received classes from their homes through the internet, television, or radio, with the support of WhatsApp and telephone, for the respective feedback. In addition to this, some public educational institutions, use platforms such as Zoom, Google Meet, or Microsoft Teams, with the purpose of contributing to the strengthening of transversal competencies to all areas, as well as the management of virtual environments in their learning experiences and autonomy in the development of tasks; in these platforms the videoconferences with students are programed; likewise, the management of learning management documents is included such as: elaboration of the auxiliary record, filling out the student attendance record, learning evidence, planning of thematic content, coordination meetings between teachers, coordination between managers, and other activities; this situation has tested the digital capabilities of each of the teachers because as a result of the digital transformation many knowledge and skills are becoming obsolete, and therefore it will be necessary to have new digital skills; at this point it is worth mentioning that it is anticipated that in the future education will be mostly synchronous and asynchronous, assisted, and unassisted nature.

In this article, we analyze the teacher's digital competencies and attitude toward the use of ICT, according to the technology, pedagogy, and content knowledge (TPACK) model, considering distance education, as a result of the health emergency, from the beginning of the year 2020, in order to ensure the quality of learning in schoolchildren.

3. Digital Competencies of the Teacher

UNESCO (2018) defines it as the capabilities that are put in place for the use of computing devices, interaction equipment, and communities to access information and execute a better administration. In that line, it is understood as the digital competencies of the teacher to the knowledge, ability, and attitude for understanding, as well as the execution of digital media and ICTs within their pedagogical practice (Martinez-Garcés & Garcés-Fuenmayor, 2020; Soto, Asis, Figueroa, & Plasencia, 2023). On the other hand, Rodríguez (2021) points out that digital competence can be conceptualized as the teacher's ability to search and transform data, using a diversity of available digital resources and equipment. In scenarios, such as those being developed in the current educational system, digital competence is the ability to effectively use technology in order to improve our daily lives (Grande-de-Prado, Cañón-Rodríguez, García-Martín, & Cantón-Mayo, 2021; Saehu, Diah, Julca-Guerrero, Huerta-Soto, & Valderrama-Plasencia, 2022). In short, digital competence is the digital capacity that allows us to handle technological implements optimally, reflexively, and creatively, with the aim of responding effectively to the demands of work, educational, and entertainment contexts (Moreno-Guerrero, Rodríguez, Ramos, & Rodríguez, 2021; Ramirez et al., 2022). In line with the above, digital competencies have become very necessary in this century, as part of what is called the digital era, to become a key competence of the teacher of this millennium, even more considering the current situation of the non-face-to-face education modality, due to the current health emergency, it is imperative that teachers can have adequate management of digital equipment, in order to promote a better learning process in schoolchildren.

Now, in an attempt to homogenize the terms used in the academic landscape on the diagnosis, measurement or evaluation of teachers' digital competencies, there are several standards, approaches, dimensions, frameworks, or models; according to Jiménez and Cabero (2021), the TPACK model, which will be used in this study.

4. TPACK Model

Shulman (1986) distinguished the pedagogical content knowledge (CK) element, which he called PCK (pedagogical content knowledge), as part of the important characteristics of teachers' professional knowledge. With the passing of time, as part of the conceptual framework of educational technology, Mishra and Koehler (2006) added to this theory the knowledge about technology as the Technological Pedagogical Content Knowledge (TPACK) model, which allows knowing in a general and extensive way the knowledge that the teacher must possess for the insertion of technologies in the teaching practice. According to Koehler and Mishra (2015), this theoretical and teacher training model is based on three main components: technology knowledge (TK), pedagogical knowledge (PK) and CK.

Koehler and Mishra (2015) point out that knowledge about technology allows the person to perform a range of activities handling technological information and interaction equipment; pedagogical content is the knowledge of methodological procedures, techniques, and strategies applied by the teacher in student learning; and CK is the teacher's mastery of the subject he/she teaches; likewise, the interaction of these three basic components results in: (i) PK of the content: is the combination of mastery of knowledge of the discipline and the teacher's management of pedagogical resources for his students; (ii) technological CK: knowledge that contains the skill to develop content using ICT; (iii) TPACK:

didactic knowledge that the teacher possesses to use digital tools in any area of knowledge; and, (iv) technological pedagogical knowledge: application of didactic strategies where technology tools are used. Fig. 11.1 shows the TPACK model with its three basic components and their respective interactions.

5. Teacher's Attitude Toward the Use of ICTs

Attitude is a condition of utmost importance in the performance of every human being; in this regard, Muñoz and Cubo (2014) point out that attitude is the set of intangible behaviors that guide personal decision-making; likewise, they state that attitude organizes the belief, opinion, feelings toward objects or people after evaluation. On the other hand, Cabanillas et al. (2019) state that attitude is a state where the person adopts a positive or negative position toward an observable entity or object; it is by the cognitive, affective, and intentional component. On the other hand, Tapia (2018) points out that attitude is the predisposition of an entity, which can be propitious or detrimental which is projected toward an object, situations, or people as a result of an anticipated appreciation as a result of lived experiences.

Now, the teaching attitude toward ICT comes to be the use that teachers give to technology during their training and in their role as a student counselor in the

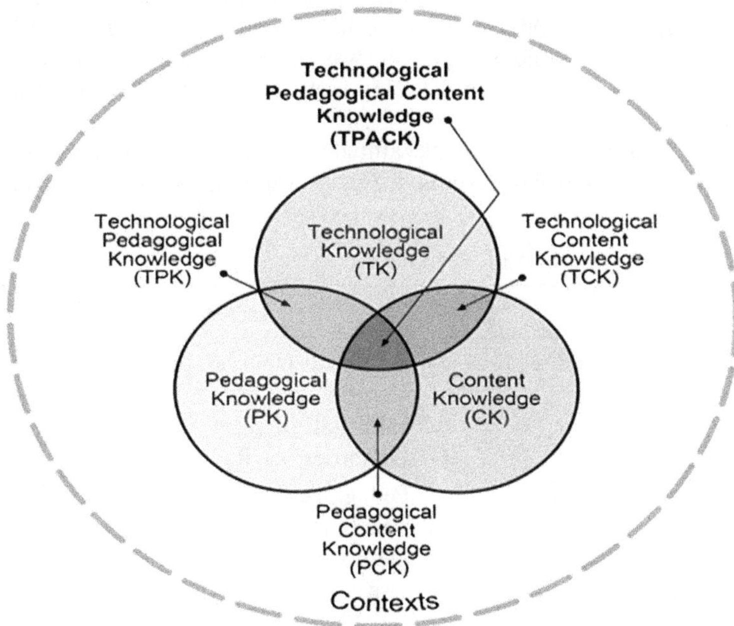

Fig. 11.1. Technology, Pedagogy, And Content Knowledge (TPACK) Model, Own Elaboration.

classroom; these attitudes can be positive as the integration of technologies in the learning processes and the negative attitude as the omission of hardware and software in their teaching practice (Huerta-Soto et al., 2023; Tapia, 2018). Casillas-Martín, Cabezas-González, Ibarra-Saiz, and Rodríguez (2020), on the other hand, point out that the teacher's attitude toward the use of ICTs is the teacher's attitude toward the use of digital tools to perform activities typical of a pedagogical scenario such as performing tasks, solving problems, interacting, creating knowledge, among others. Rudhumbu, Du Plessis, and Du Plessis (2021) point out that the teacher's attitude toward digital technology is how a person responds to the actual use of ICT and that these can be positive or negative; the adoption of a positive attitude is the critical and reflective use oriented to the success of teachers in the classroom.

6. Methodology

The study is based on the quantitative, relational, and cross-sectional approach (Hernández & Mendoza, 2018). The sample consisted of 106 teachers of the curricular areas (mathematics, communication, religion, art, English, physical education, education for work, personal development and citizenship, science, and environment) of the Public Educational Institution Javier Heraud, Lima Sur, Peru. During the collection of information for the present study, the instrument developed by Torres (2014), designed to measure the digital competence of the secondary level teacher, was used; the said questionnaire was adapted and distributed in four sections: (i) TK (20 questions); (ii) PK (15 questions); and, (iii) CK (11 questions), described in Table 11.1.

On the other hand, to measure the attitude toward the use of ICT, the questionnaire proposed by Hernández, Martínez, García, Herrera, and Rodríguez (2012) and

Table 11.1. Distribution of Variable Items.

Dimensions	**Indicators**	**Items**
Technology knowledge (TK)	Technical troubleshooting Communication Information Digital creativity	1–20
Pedagogical content (PK)	Pedagogical management Teaching strategies and/or methodologies Use of technology	21–35
Content knowledge (CK)	Educational innovation projects Continuous improvement	36–46
Attitude toward the use of ICT (AUTIC)	Incorporation of ICT into teaching practice	1–15

Source: Own elaboration.

was adapted with the 15 items. Both questionnaires were validated by five experts, directors of educational institutions and the reliability was analyzed by the values obtained for Cronbach's alpha (Supo & Zacarias, 2020), for the variable digital competencies $\alpha = 0.861$ and as for the variable attitude toward the use of ICT $\alpha = 0.854$, for the application of this questionnaire a form was developed through the Google platform.

7. Results

Regarding the participants of the present study, the largest proportion of teachers, represented by 30% of the respondents, corresponds to the curricular area of Education for Work; this is due to the fact that it is a Public Educational Institution of commercial technical training, which has the specialties of secretarial, accounting, administration, and computer and information technology. In addition, 53.30% of the teachers participating in the study were male and 46.70% were female. On the other hand, 10% of teachers have 1–10 years of service, 20% of teachers have 11–20 years of service, 63% of teachers have 21–30 years of service, and 7% of teachers have more than 31 years of service.

Regarding the results of the basic components of the TPACK model, out of a maximum score of 80 for knowledge of technology, teachers obtained a score of 54, which represents that they have 68% of digital competence for this component. Regarding the pedagogical content component, out of a maximum score of 60, teachers obtained a score of 41, which represents that they have 68% of digital competence for this component. Finally, regarding the CK component, out of a maximum score of 44, teachers obtained 29 points, which represents that they have 66% of digital competence for this component. In this sense, for the components: TK and pedagogical content, respectively, teachers register a shortfall of 32% to reach the ideal digital competence; and, in the case of CK, teachers register a shortfall of 34% to reach the ideal digital competence. As shown in Table 11.2.

Table 11.2. Technology, Pedagogy, And Content Knowledge (TPACK) Model Components.

Components	**Maximum Score to Be Obtained**	**Score Obtained by Teachers**	**% Achieved by Teachers**	**% to Be Achieved by Teachers**
Technology knowledge (TK)	80	54	68%	32%
Pedagogical content (PK)	60	41	68%	32%
Content knowledge (CK)	44	29	66%	34%

Source: Own elaboration.

According to Fig. 11.2, the results of the knowledge of technology component, distributed in the indicators: (a) technical problem-solving; (b) communication; (c) information; and, (d) digital creativity, show that for technical problem-solving teachers reached 70%; for communication they reached 75%; for the information indicator they reached 70%; and for digital creativity 55%. In this sense, for the case of technical problem-solving, teachers register a lack of 30% to reach the ideal digital competence; for the case of communication, teachers register a lack of 25% to reach the ideal digital competence; for the case of the information indicator, teachers register a lack of 30% to reach the ideal digital competence; and a lack of 45% to reach the ideal digital competence, for the case of digital creativity.

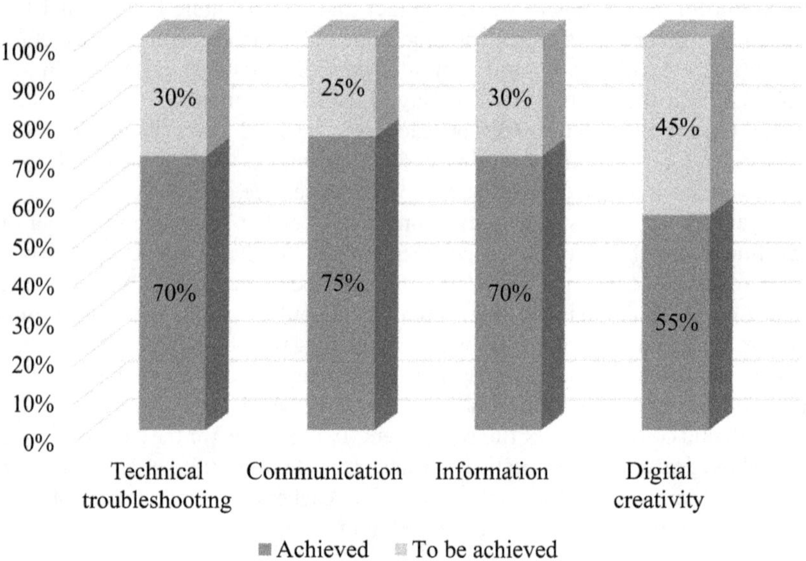

Fig. 11.2. Levels of Digital Competencies.

Fig. 11.3 shows the results of the pedagogical content component, distributed in the indicators: (a) pedagogical management; (b) didactic strategies and/or methodologies; and (c) use of technology; from this, it can be seen that for pedagogical management teachers reached 75%; for didactic strategies and/or methodologies they reached 55%; for the use of technology, they reached 75%. In this sense, for the case of pedagogical management, teachers register a lack of 25% to reach the ideal digital competence; for the case of didactic strategies and/or methodologies, teachers register a lack of 45% to reach the ideal digital competence; and a lack of 25% to reach the ideal digital competence for the case of technology use.

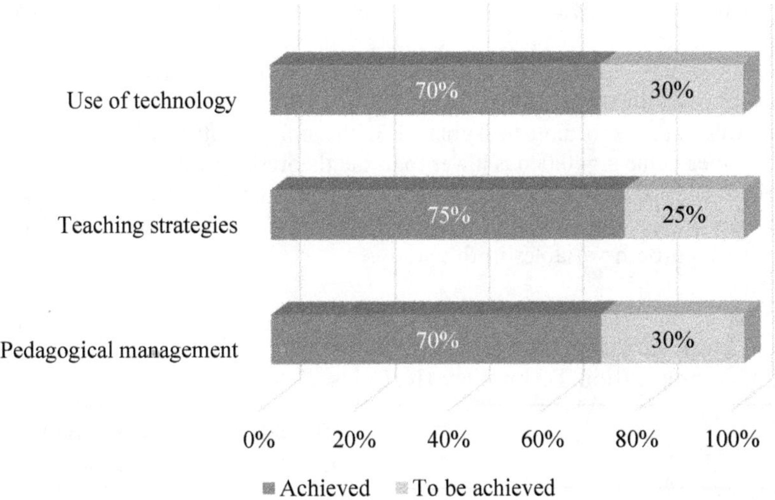

Fig. 11.3. Digital Competencies in the Pedagogical Content Component.

Fig. 11.4 shows the results of the CK component, distributed in the indicators: (a) educational innovation projects; and (b) continuous improvement; from this, it can be seen that for educational innovation projects, teachers reached 57%; and

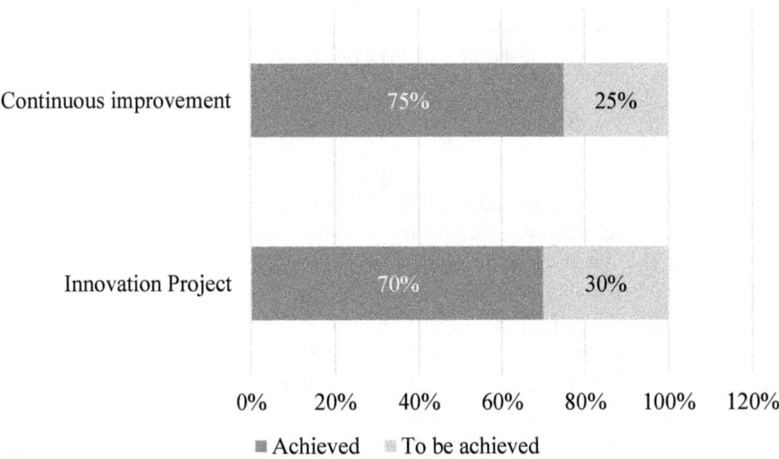

Fig. 11.4. Digital Competencies in the Content Knowledge (CK) Component.

for continuous improvement, teachers reached 81%. In this sense, with regard to educational innovation projects, teachers register a 43% shortfall to reach the ideal competence; and a 19% shortfall to reach the ideal competence, in the case of continuous improvement.

In this case, according to Table 11.3, the null hypothesis is rejected as the significance value $p = 0.000$ is lower than the theoretical value of = 0.05. There is a relationship between digital competences and attitudes toward ICT use in a Peruvian public educational institution; that is, a direct and significant relationship between both variables in this study.

Table 11.3. Correlation of Digital Skills and Attitude Toward Information and Communication Technology (ICT) Use.

		Digital Competencies	**Attitude Toward the Use of ICTs**
Digital competencies	Pearson correlation	1	0.687[a]
	Sig. (bilateral)		0.000
	N	106	106
Attitude toward the use of ICTs	Pearson correlation	0.687[a]	1
	Sig. (bilateral)	0.000	
	N	106	106

[a]The correlation is significant at the 0.01 level (bilateral).

8. Discussion

At the juncture of distance education, due to the health emergency, since the beginning of the year 2020, teachers have discovered that they need to use their digital skills. In this regard, Espino, Hernández, and Pérez (2021) stated that many teachers faced this new modality with little or no skills in the use of technological platforms. It is important to mention that this virtualization scenario brings with it some benefits for the teacher, we can mention the possibility of being promoted in the educational institution where they work, for the evaluation of their teaching performance, among others; since at this juncture the work is developed remotely; being recognized by the students for an adequate use of the various technological tools.

From the results, considering the TPACK model, it is found that in the knowledge about technology, as well as with the pedagogical content, respectively, teachers show a lack of 32% to reach the ideal digital competence; and in the case of CK, teachers show a lack of 34% to reach the ideal digital competence. In a study of a similar nature, developed by Espino (2018), he found a shortfall of 12% to reach the ideal digital competence, regarding knowledge about technology; he also found a shortfall of 13% to reach the ideal digital competence, regarding pedagogical content and CK, respectively. Similarly, Vólquez and Amador (2020) found a shortfall of 32% to reach the ideal digital competence, in terms of knowledge about technology; they also found a shortfall of 57% to reach the ideal digital competence, in terms of pedagogical content; and they evidenced a shortfall of 39% to reach the ideal digital competence, in terms of CK.

The instructors' positive attitude toward ICT, moderate management style, and low level of ICT competence are also worth mentioning. That they are neither digital native or capable of effectively utilizing ICT in the classroom became very obvious (Fuster, Segura, Guillen, & Ramirez, 2020; Napal, Peñalva-Vélez, & Mendióroz, 2018). Research shows that a reasonable degree of digital competence is required for the effective use of technology in the classroom (Mirete, Maquilón, Mirete, & Rodríguez, 2020).

Finally, the acquisition of competence with ICT tools and the ability to determine the best time to use them are two of the difficult decisions facing the skills of the new millennium (Cabezas-González, Casillas-Martín, & García-Peñalvo, 2021). As for the psycho-pedagogical dimension, all psycho-pedagogical processes are permeated by digital competencies, which include the ability to convey the right information (Guillén-Gámez, Mayorga-Fernández, & Álvarez-García, 2020; Huerta-Soto, Guzmán-Avalos, Flores-Albornoz, & Tomás-Aguilar, 2022). For the most part, teachers' attitudes toward new technical tools have changed (Manco-Chavez et al., 2020), but time and practice show that there are significant disparities between teachers' initial engagement with technology and their subsequent use.

9. Conclusion

The digitally competent teacher is one who possesses a set of skills that are acquired during the use of technological tools and applies them in different areas; these skills refer to the competence to solve problems in maintaining their equipment in optimal conditions, digital skills to apply teaching strategies in student learning and digital competence applied at the time of teaching content in the domain area. In this study, it has been evidenced that teachers in non-face-to-face education for COVID-19 reasons have taken charge of secondary level students bringing with them digital competences in a considerable level, according to the results found for each of the components of the TPACK model; it should be noted that in the light of the results, the content knowledge component of the referred model, registers lower values than the other two components, this allows us to suggest that currently the teacher training in the management of virtual environments, is of high priority for good performance in the classroom, pointing out that, to be digitally competent is achieved by running the digital environment; without neglecting, also that within the higher teacher training should be implemented environments with the necessary and appropriate equipment to train teachers to be digitally competent, with content that develops skills in the management, production, preservation, and problem-solving of a technological nature.

It is also important to mention that there is empirical evidence that the age factor plays a very important role in the digital competence of the teacher; that is, the younger the teacher is, the more predisposed he/she is to include the use of technology in the classroom, while older teachers are generally reluctant to be trained and to use technological interaction tools. This is crucial in this new educational scenario in which the use of virtual spaces and methodologies is required, where the academic training and the teacher's ability to handle digital and virtual interaction tools are deficient because they lack the practice that teachers need for their performance in virtuality (Vólquez & Amador, 2020; Yslado et al., 2021).

All this makes it important that the governing bodies of the education system consider blended or hybrid education or blended learning as a necessary alternative to the demand of stakeholders for the return of students to the classroom; given the demand for the return to face-to-face classes, the opinion of students should be taken into account because for some it means that they can continue working without leaving their studies (Ramirez, Espinoza, Esquivel, & Naranjo, 2020). The above indicated could be considered that in the coming years the distance education already implemented takes ground without room for setbacks, which could mean an educational evolution (Berrocal et al., 2021). Teachers at the secondary level of a Peruvian public educational institution should be trained in the use of digital competencies because they have a positive attitude toward the use of ICT.

References

Berrocal, C., Flores, V., Montalvo, W., & Flores, M. (2021). Entornos distribuidos de aprendizaje ubicuo en tiempos de pandemia: una realidad educativa en educación básica. *Revista Dilemas Contemporáneos: Educación, Políticas y Valores*, *13*(3), 1–22. doi:10.46377/dilemas.v8i3.2628

Cabanillas, J., Luengo, R., & Torres, J. (2019). Diferencias de actitud hacia las TIC en la formación profesional en entornos presenciales y virtuales. *Pixel-Bit: Revista de Medios y Educación*, *55*, 37–55. doi:10.12795/pixelbit.2019.i55.03

Cabezas-González, M., Casillas-Martín, S., & García-Peñalvo, F. J. (2021). The digital competence of pre-service educators: The influence of personal variables. *Sustainability*, *13*(4), 2318. doi:10.3390/su13042318

Casillas-Martín, S., Cabezas-González, M., Ibarra-Saiz, M., & Rodríguez, G. (2020). El profesorado universitario en la sociedad del conocimiento: Manejo y actitud hacia las TIC. *Bordon. Revista de Pedagogía*, *72*(3), 45–63. doi:10.13042/Bordon.2020.76746

Espino, J. (2018). *Competencias digitales de los docentes y desempeño pedagógico en el aula*. [Tesis de maestría]. Perú: Universidad San Martin de Porres. Retrieved from https://hdl.handle.net/20.500.12727/4525

Espino, L. E., Hernández, M. A., & Pérez, C. C. (2021). Financial education in the entrepreneurial ecosystem. *Investigación administrativa*, *50*(128), 1–19. doi:10.35426/iav50n128.02

Fuster, D. E., Segura, V. R., Guillen, P. E., & Ramirez, E. H. (2020). Teachers empathy in the development of bilingual communication strategies. *International Journal of Early Childhood Special Education (INT-JECSE)*, *12*(1), 542–551. doi:10.9756/INT-JECSE/V12I1.201036

Grande-de-Prado, M., Cañón-Rodríguez, R., García-Martín, S., & Cantón-Mayo, I. (2021). Competencia digital: docentes en formación y resolución de problemas. *Educar*, *57*(2), 381–396. doi:10.5565/rev/educar.1159

Guillén-Gámez, F. D., Mayorga-Fernández, M., & Álvarez-García, F. J. (2020). A study on the actual use of digital competence in the practicum of education degree. *Technology, Knowledge and Learning*, *25*(3), 667–684. doi:10.1007/s10758-018-9390-z

Hernández, J. P., Martínez, F., García, F. J., Herrera, M. E., & Rodríguez, M. J. (2012). *Escala de actitud hacia el uso de las TIC por parte del profesorado. Estudio de fiabilidad y validez*. En XIV Simposio Internacional de Informática Educativa [en línea]. [Consultado el 25 de abril de 2021]. Retrieved from http://hdl.handle.net/10366/121476

Hernández, R., & Mendoza, C. (2018). *Metodología de la investigación: Las rutas cuantitativa, cualitativa y mixta*. Mexico: Mc Graw Hill.

Huerta-Soto, R., Guzmán-Avalos, M., Flores-Albornoz, J., & Tomás-Aguilar, S. (2022). Competencias digitales de los profesores universitarios durante la pandemia por covid-19 en el Perú. *Revista Electrónica Interuniversitaria de Formación del Profesorado*, *25*(1), 49–60. doi:10.6018/reifop.500481

Huerta-Soto, R., Ramirez-Asis, E., Tarazona-Jiménez, J., Nivin-Vargas, L., Norabuena-Figueroa, R., Guzman-Avalos, M., & Reyes-Reyes, C. (2023). Predictable inventory management within dairy supply chain operations. *International Journal of Retail & Distribution Management*. doi:10.1108/IJRDM-01-2023-0051

Hurtado, F. (2020). La educación en tiempos de pandemia: los desafíos de la escuela del siglo XXI. *Revista arbitrada del Centro de Investigación y Estudios Gerenciales*, *44*, 176–187. Retrieved from https://revista.grupocieg.org/revista/revista-cieg-no-44-julio-agosto-2020/

Jiménez, M., & Cabero, J. (2021). Los conocimientos tecnológicos, pedagógicos y de contenidos del profesorado universitario andaluz sobre las TIC. Análisis desde el modelo TPACK. *Revista Innoeduca. International Journal of Technology and Educational Innovation*, *7*(1), 4–8. doi:10.24310/innoeduca.2021.v7i1.11940

Koehler, M., Mishra, P., & Cain, W. (2015). Que son los Saberes Tecnológicos y Pedagógicos del Contenido (TPACK)? *Virtualidad, Educación y Ciencia*, *6*(10), 9–23. Retrieved from https://revistas.unc.edu.ar/index.php/vesc/article/view/11552

Manco-Chavez, J. A., Uribe-Hernandez, Y. C., Buendia-Aparcana, R., Vertiz-Osores, J. J., Isla Alcoser, S. D., & Rengifo-Lozano, R. A. (2020). Integration of ICTS and digital skills in times of the pandemic COVID-19. *International Journal of Higher Education*, *9*(9), 11–20. doi:10.5430/ijhe.v9n9p11

Martinez-Garcés, J., & Garcés-Fuenmayor, J. (2020). Competencias digitales docentes y el reto de la educación virtual derivado de la covid-19. *Educación y Humanismo*, *22*(39), 1–16. doi:10.17081/eduhum.22.39.4114

Mirete, A. B., Maquilón, J. J., Mirete, L., & Rodríguez, R. A. (2020). Digital competence and university teachers' conceptions about teaching. A structural causal model. *Sustainability*, *12*(12), 4842. doi:10.3390/su12124842

Mishra, P., & Koehler, M. (2006). Technological pedagogical content knowledge: A framework for teacher knowledge. *Teachers College Record*, *108*(6), 1017–1054. Retrieved from https://www.tcrecord.org/content.asp?contentid=12516

Moreno-Guerrero, A., Rodríguez, A., Ramos, M., & Rodríguez, C. (2021). Competencia digital docente y el uso de la realidad aumentada en la enseñanza de ciencias en Educación Secundaria Obligatoria. *Revista Fuentes*, *23*(1), 108–124. doi:10.12795/revistafuentes.2021.v23.i1.12050

Muñoz, E., & Cubo, S. (2014). Competencia digital, formación y actitud del profesorado de educación especial hacia las tecnologías de la información y la comunicación (TIC). Profesorado. *Revista de currículum y formación del profesorado*, *23*(1), 209–241. doi:10.30827/profesorado.v23i1.9151

Napal, M., Peñalva-Vélez, A., & Mendióroz, A. M. (2018). Development of digital competence in secondary education teachers' training. *Education Sciences*, *8*(3), 104. doi:10.3390/educsci8030104

Ramirez, E. H., Espinoza, M. R., Esquivel, S. M., & Naranjo, M. E. (2020). Inteligencia emocional, competencias y desempeño del docente universitario: Aplicando la técnica mínimos cuadrados parciales SEM-PLS. *Revista Electrónica Interuniversitaria de Formación del Profesorado*, *23*(3), 99–114. doi:10.6018/reifop.428261

Ramirez, E. H., Rosario, H. S., Laura, N. V., Hober, H. T., Julio, V. A., & Victor, F. L. (2022). Distribution of public service and individual job performance in Peruvian municipality. *20*(10), 11–17. doi:10.15722/jds.20.10.202210.11

Rodríguez, A. (2021). Competencias digitales docentes y su estado en el contexto virtual. *Revista Peruana de Investigación e Innovación Educativa*, *1*(2), 1–9. doi:10.15381/rpiiedu.v1i2.21038

Rudhumbu, N., Du Plessis, E., & Du Plessis, P. (2021). Predictors of behavioural intentions of teachers to adopt and use information and communication technologies in secondary schools in Zimbabwe. *International Journal of Learning, Teaching and Educational Research*, *20*(11), 366–386. doi:10.26803/ijlter.20.11.20

Saehu, M. S., Diah, A. M., Julca-Guerrero, F., Huerta-Soto, R., & Valderrama-Plasencia, L. (2022). Environmental awareness and environmental management practices: Mediating effect of environmental data distribution. *Journal of Environmental Management & Tourism*, *13*(5), 1339–1352. doi:10.14505/jemt.v13.5(61).11

Shulman, L. (1986). Those who understand: Knowledge growth in teaching. *American Educational Researcher Association*, *15*(2), 4–14. doi:10.2307/1175860

Soto, R. H., Asis, E. H., Figueroa, R. P., & Plasencia, L. (2023). Autoeficacia emprendedora y desempeño de micro y pequeñas empresas peruanas. *Revista Venezolana de Gerencia: RVG*, *28*(102), 751–768. doi:10.52080/rvgluz.28.102.19

Supo, J. A., & Zacarias, H. R. (2020). *Metodología de la investigación Científica: Para las Ciencias de la Salud y las Ciencias Sociales*. Lima: Sociedad Hispana de Investigadores Cientificos, Sincie.

Tapia, H. (2018). Actitud hacia las TIC y hacia su integración didáctica en la formación inicial docente. *Revista Actualidades Investigativas en Educación*, *18*(03), 702–731. doi:10.15517/aie.v18i3.34437

Torres, T. (2014). *Competencia digital del profesorado de educación secundaria: un instrumento de evaluación*. Retrieved from https://digitum.um.es/digitum/handle/10201/40351

Vialart, M. (2020). Estrategias didácticas para la virtualización del proceso enseñanza aprendizaje en tiempos de COVID-19. *Educación Médica Superior*, *34*(3). Retrieved from http://www.ems.sld.cu/index.php/ems/article/view/2594/1103

Villalobos, K. (2021). ¿Cómo es el trabajo de los profesores de educación básica en tiempos de pandemia? modalidades de aprendizaje y percepción del profesorado chileno sobre la educación a distancia. *Perspectiva Educacional*, *60*(1), 107–138. doi:10.4151/07189729-vol.60-iss.1-art.1177

Vólquez, J., & Amador, C. (2020). Competencias digitales de docentes de nivel secundario de Santo Domingo: un estudio de caso. *RIDE. Revista Iberoamericana para la investigación y el desarrollo educativo*, *11*(21). doi:10.23913/ride.v11i21.702

Yslado, R. M., Ramirez, E. H., García, M. E., & Arquero, J. L. (2021). Clima laboral y burnout en profesores universitarios. *Revista Electrónica Interuniversitaria de Formación del Profesorado*, *24*(3), 101–114. doi:10.6018/reifop.476651

Chapter 12

Effect of Business Intelligence Applications on the Contribution of Accounting Departments at Jordanian Universities in Developing University Accounting Education and Its Quality Assurance

Walid Zakaria Siam and Hashem Alshurafat

The Hashemite University, Jordan

Abstract

This study aimed to determine the impact of Business Intelligence (BI) applications on accounting department contributions to the development and quality assurance of university accounting education in Jordan. A questionnaire was given to accounting faculty members in 25 universities, and the results showed that BI applications had a significant effect on the development and quality assurance of university accounting education. Private universities had a greater impact than public universities. Recommendations of this study include improving awareness of BI applications, focusing on decision support systems in private universities and risk analysis in public universities, and promoting cooperation between public and private universities to achieve excellence in an increasingly competitive global environment.

Keywords: Business intelligence applications; decision support systems; knowledge management; risks analysis; accounting education; Jordanian universities

Technological Innovations for Business, Education and Sustainability, 169–180

Published under exclusive licence by Emerald Publishing Limited
doi:10.1108/978-1-83753-106-620241012

1. Introduction

In today's world, university education is a top priority for many thinkers and decision-makers (Saleh, Jawabreh, Al-Amro, & Saleh, 2023). The sector plays a crucial role in human development, encompassing technology, telecommunications, industry, trade, agriculture, health, and other areas (Morshed, 2022). Over the past decade, university education has undergone significant development in terms of content, learning, and teaching patterns. This development aims to serve universal human development and has become a priority for many governments in the next stage (Carvalho & Almeida, 2022).

As modern technologies and communications continue to advance, new statements have emerged in the business field, such as e-commerce, e-transactions, e-learning, knowledge economy, and Business Intelligence (BI) applications (Akbulaev, Mammadov, & Shahbazli, 2021; Alshurafat, Al Shbail, Masadeh, Dahmash, & Al-Msiedeen, 2021). Jordanian universities and accounting departments are not immune to these developments. In fact, they are required to interact with these statements to achieve development and respond to the rapid spread of communication tools (Akbulaev et al., 2021; Al-Hazaima, Low, & Sharma, 2021).

Recently, there has been a lot of discussion about the need to use intelligence applications to enhance the contribution of scientific departments in the teaching process and ensure its quality (Jaradat, Al-Dmour, Alshurafat, Al-Hazaima, & Al Shbail, 2022; Mertens, 2023). The use of these applications in Jordanian universities, particularly in accounting departments, is varied and includes speed of completion of tasks, accuracy, good management of activities, efficiency in planning and implementation of the educational process, success in development of education, and quality assurance and improvement of outputs.

Both public and private Jordanian universities aim to develop university education services and graduate qualified practitioners to work in various fields of marketplace. Therefore, this study aims to identify the effect of BI applications on the contribution of accounting departments to the development of university accounting education and quality assurance in Jordanian universities. This study is based on the fact that universities are better able to lead in BI techniques and applications (Qasim & Kharbat, 2020).

As technology and modern communication continue to advance and global competition intensifies, universities are increasingly focused on improving the quality of their education and ensuring their competitiveness (Akbulaev et al., 2021; Al-Hazaima, Al Shbail, Alshurafat, Ananzeh, & Al Shbeil, 2022). To achieve this, scientific departments in highly-reputed universities must adopt contemporary methods and enhance their performance. The aim is to equip graduates with the skills and knowledge needed to meet future challenges, moving away from traditional methods of education.

This study aims to investigate the impact of BI applications on accounting departments in Jordanian universities. Specifically, the study seeks to answer the following questions:

- Do decision support systems, one of the BI applications, affect the contribution of accounting departments to the development and quality assurance of university education?
- Does knowledge management, another BI application, affect the contribution of accounting departments to the development and quality assurance of university education?
- Do risk analysis applications, a third BI application, affect the contribution of accounting departments to the development and quality assurance of university education?
- Are there significant statistical differences in the effect of BI applications on the contribution of accounting departments to the development and quality assurance of university accounting education between public and private universities in Jordan?

2. Theoretical Framework and Previous Studies

The term "Business Intelligence" (BI) was first introduced by IBM researcher Hans Luhn in 1958. Luhn emphasized the importance of understanding how different pieces of information relate to each other in order to achieve specific goals, such as increasing market share or improving customer satisfaction. BI is more than just a technological term, like Data Warehouses or Business Analysis; it requires a deep understanding of an organization's various aspects (Jaradat et al., 2022).

It's worth noting that "intelligence" is not the same as "knowledge." While two individuals may have access to the same set of facts and rules, their ability to learn and use that knowledge will differ. This difference represents their level of intelligence (Mertens, 2023). However, it's challenging to study intelligence because people's knowledge levels are often vastly different, making it difficult to distinguish between intelligence and knowledge. For example, an accountant may be better at remembering numbers, but is this due to their intelligence or their experience and knowledge of numbers? This overlap makes studying intelligence challenging (Siam, 2012).

Researchers have different opinions on what "Business Intelligence" means. Some see it as a decision support system, while others view it as a system for knowledge generation and management (Mertens, 2023). Still, others believe it's about avoiding surprises, reducing risk exposure, and sending early warning signals about potential risks. With advances in technology, the definition of BI is becoming clearer, and its applications are better understood (Jaradat et al., 2022).

Decision support is the process of analyzing data to help decision-making units gain a better understanding of an organization's operations and make better decisions. Decision support systems use high-tech information technologies, which give organizations a competitive advantage over those who don't use these systems (Siam, 2013).

Knowledge management is another important aspect of BI. It involves transforming data and information into knowledge through a continuous dynamic process of identifying, finding, distributing, using, preserving, and retrieving knowledge (Despres & Chauvel, 1999). Knowledge management is an investment in the skills and experiences of individuals working in an organization through teamwork and brainstorming sessions to achieve the organization's objectives and competitive advantage (de Bem Machado, Secinaro, Calandra, & Lanzalonga, 2022). Finally, analysis techniques are crucial in BI applications. These techniques help reshape and present information in different ways to add value to the information.

3. As a Brief Overview of the Higher Education Sector and Public and Private Jordanian Universities

In Jordan, the higher education sector plays a crucial role in promoting comprehensive development across various fields. Over the past decade, there has been notable progress in terms of curriculum diversity, teaching methods, and expansion of higher education institutions. Despite limited resources, the Kingdom considers higher education a top priority due to its significant impact on improving citizens' economic, social, and cognitive well-being. The sector has witnessed remarkable growth, with an increase in the number of institutions, registered students, faculty members, and government support (Siam, 2013). There are 10 public universities, 17 private universities, 51 intermediate community colleges, and the World Islamic Sciences and Education University (Al-Hazaima et al., 2022; Saleh et al., 2023).

The number of students enrolled in public and private universities for various programs and degrees is estimated at 236,000, including 28,000 from Arab and foreign countries (Siam, 2018). Jordan's education system is highly regarded in the region, attracting about 28,000 international students. Graduates of Jordanian universities have excellent employment prospects in public and private institutions and public departments (Alshurafat et al., 2021). The Ministry of Higher Education and Scientific Research's vision is to achieve internationally distinguished higher education, with a mission to support and follow-up on the implementation of policies and strategies for higher education, promote accountability, justice, and transparency, and foster creativity and leadership in partnership with the private sector (Siam, 2012).

4. Study Model

The model of the study, and the link between its variables, can be formulated in Fig. 12.1.

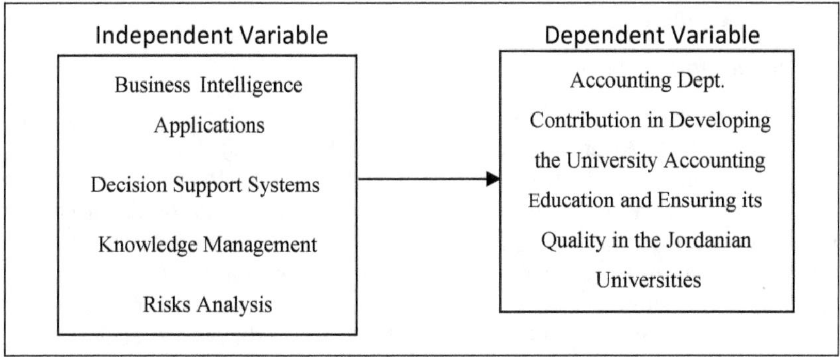

Fig. 12.1. Research Model. *Source:* Authors' own creation.

5. Study Hypotheses

In order to achieve the objectives of the study and answer its questions, and based on the findings of previous studies, the hypotheses of the study were formulated as follows:

First Major Hypothesis:

H01: BI applications do not affect the contribution of accounting departments in Jordanian universities to the development of university accounting education and its quality assurance.

From the above, the following three sub-hypotheses are suggested:

Second Major Hypothesis:

H011: Decision Support Systems – as one of BI applications – do not affect the contribution of accounting departments in the Jordanian universities to the development of university accounting education and quality assurance.

H012: Knowledge Management – as one of BI applications – does not affect the contribution of the accounting departments in the Jordanian universities to the development of university accounting education and quality assurance.

H013: Risks Analysis Applications – as one of BI applications – do not affect the contribution of accounting departments in the Jordanian universities to the development of university accounting education and quality assurance.

H02: There are no statistically significant differences at $\alpha \leq (0.05)$ level in the impact of BI applications on the contribution of the accounting departments in the development of university accounting education and its quality assurance among the public and private universities of Jordan.

6. Methodology

6.1 Population and Sample

This study focuses on the Jordanian universities that teach accounting, which includes a total of 25 universities (9 public and 16 private), as reported by the Jordanian Ministry of Higher Education and Scientific Research in 2022 (see Table 12.1). The study conducted a comprehensive survey of the accounting faculty members, including department heads, from these universities. A total of 200 questionnaires were distributed, with 8 questionnaires per university. Of these, 182 questionnaires were recovered (67 from public universities and 115 from private universities), indicating a high level of data completeness and suitability for statistical analysis. Therefore, 182 questionnaires were approved for statistical analysis, representing 91% of the distributed questionnaires. Table 12.1 displays the distribution of questionnaires between public and private universities.

Based on the data presented in Table 12.1, 36.8% of questionnaire respondents were from public universities and 63.2% were from private universities. This distribution aligns with the overall proportion of universities in each sector, which is due to the greater number of private universities. The study focuses on accounting departments in Jordanian universities due to the lack of existing literature and research in this area despite its important role at both national and regional levels.

7. Data Collection Methods

In this study, the researcher created a questionnaire using a theoretical framework and past research. Table 12.2 provides an overview of the questionnaire sections and specific questions used to measure each variable.

To ensure that the findings of the questionnaire were reliable and that the questions were linked, we presented them to a group of colleagues, including university professors in accounting departments, specialists in education development (from the Faculty of Educational Sciences), and colleagues who work in quality control in Jordanian universities. They reviewed the questionnaire and expressed their views on the integrity of the formulation and interdependence of paragraphs. Additionally, we used the reliability analysis to calculate the correlation coefficients of Cronbach's Alphaα. The result was approximately 82.3%, which exceeds the acceptable percentage (70%) (Sekaran & Bougie, 2015). This means that the findings of the questionnaire are credible and can be relied upon to achieve the objectives of the study.

8. Methods of Data Analysis

For the purposes of achieving the objectives of the study and testing hypotheses, descriptive statistics and *T*-test were used for one sample to test the hypotheses of the study.

Table 12.1. Number of Questionnaires Distributed According to the Sectors of the Jordanian Universities.

Sectors of the Jordanian Universities	No. of Universities	No. of Distributed Questionnaires	No. of Questionnaires Recovered and Valid for Analysis	Percentage of Questionnaires Recovered and Valid for Analysis	Percentage of Questionnaires Recovered per Each Sector of the Total Recovered Ones
Government	9	72	67	93.1%	36.8%
Private	16	128	115	89.8%	63.2%
Total	25	200	182	91%	100%

Source: Authors' own creation.

Table 12.2. Questionnaire Sections and the Questions That Measure Each of the Study's Variables.

Questionnaire Sections	Variable	The Questions Which Measure the Variable
Section I: Demographic data	Academic ranking	A
	No. of experience years in the field of accounting education	B
Section II: Effect of business intelligence applications on the contribution of accounting departments at Jordanian universities in developing university accounting education and its quality assurance	The effect of decision support systems	(1–12)
	The effect of knowledge management	(13–24)
	The effect of risks analysis applications	(25–35)

Source: Authors' own creation.

9. Results

To test this hypothesis, a (*T*-test) was used for a single sample using a reference value representing the average score of the Likert Scale of (3). Table 12.3 shows the findings of the test of this hypothesis.

Based on the findings presented in the previous table, the calculated value of t (19.03) is higher than its tabular value, and the level of α is less than 0.05. This means rejecting the null hypothesis and accepting the alternative hypothesis. This means that decision support systems have an effect on the contribution of accounting departments in Jordanian universities to the development of university accounting education and quality assurance.

Based on the findings presented in the previous table, the calculated value of t (23.22) is higher than its tabular value, and the level of α is less than 0.05. This means rejecting the null hypothesis and accepting the alternative hypothesis. This means that knowledge management has an effect on the contribution of accounting departments in Jordanian universities to the development of university accounting education and quality assurance.

Based on the findings presented in the previous table, the calculated value of t (13.88) is higher than its tabular value and the level of α is less than 0.05. This means rejecting the null hypothesis and accepting the alternative hypothesis. This means that risks analysis has an effect on the contribution of accounting

Table 12.3. Result of the "*t*" Test for One Sample.

Hypothesis	Arithmetic Mean	Standard Deviation	Calculated t	*t* Tabular Value	Degrees of Freedom	Level of Significance	Hypothesis Result
First sub-hypothesis	3.86	0.61	19.03	1.96	181	0.000	Rejection
Second sub-hypothesis	3.98	0.57	23.22	1.96	181	0.000	Rejection
Third sub-hypothesis	3.69	0.67	13.88	1.96	181	0.000	Rejection
The first major hypothesis	3.84	0.64	17.72	1.96	181	0.000	Rejection

Source: Authors' own creation.

departments in Jordanian universities to the development of university accounting education and quality assurance.

Based on the findings presented in the previous table, the calculated value of t (17.72) is higher than its tabular value and the level of α is less than 0.05. This means rejecting the null hypothesis and accepting the alternative hypothesis. This means that BI applications have an effect of the contribution of accounting departments in Jordanian universities to the development of university accounting education and quality assurance.

Table 12.4 presents a summary of the arithmetical means and standard deviations that measure the effect of each BI application area on the arithmetic means and the standard deviations that measure the effect of BI applications in their respective fields in the public and private Jordanian universities separately.

Based on the findings presented in the previous table, the arithmetic means for each field of BI applications in private universities are higher than in public universities. In general, the arithmetic mean of the total statements related to measuring the effect of BI applications on the contribution of accounting departments in private Jordanian universities (4.07) is higher than in public Jordanian universities (3.46), which indicates the effect of their application in private universities to a high degree and in the public universities to a medium degree. This means rejecting the null hypothesis and accepting the alternative hypothesis, i.e., there are statistical indicative differences at the level of $\alpha \leq (0.05)$ in the effect of BI applications on the contribution of the accounting departments in the development of university education and its quality assurance among the public and private universities in Jordan. This variation is in favor of private universities.

Table 12.4. Arithmetic Means and Standard Deviations of the Effect of Business Intelligence Applications on the Contributions of the Accounting Departments in the Development of University Accounting Education and Its Quality Assurance Among the Government and Private Universities of Jordan.

		Government Universities Sector		**Private Universities Sector**	
No.	**Scope**	**Arithmetic Mean**	**Standard Deviation**	**Arithmetic Mean**	**Standard Deviation**
1	Decision support systems	3.66	0.77	3.98	0.71
2	Knowledge management	3.57	0.81	4.22	0.55
3	Risks analysis	3.14	0.92	4.01	0.61
Effect of BIA		3.46	0.84	4.07	0.67

Source: Authors' own creation.

10. Conclusion

Based on the analysis of data and testing of hypotheses, the following conclusions were drawn. The use of BI applications in accounting departments of Jordanian universities has a significant impact on the development of university accounting education and quality assurance. The combined effect of these applications is particularly high, with an arithmetic mean of 3.84.

Among the different areas of BI applications, knowledge management has the highest impact on the contribution of accounting departments to the development of university accounting education, followed by decision support systems and risks analysis. Furthermore, there are significant differences in the impact of BI applications on accounting departments between Jordanian public and private universities, with private universities showing a more favorable effect.

In light of these findings, it is recommended that awareness of the benefits of BI applications be increased among university administrators and owners. Private universities should focus on decision support systems, while public universities should prioritize risks analysis. Additionally, co-operation between accounting departments in public and private universities should be enhanced to maximize the positive effects of BI applications on university accounting education and quality assurance. This will help universities to remain competitive and achieve excellence in an increasingly globalized world.

References

Akbulaev, N., Mammadov, I., & Shahbazli, S. (2021). Accounting education in the universities and structuring according to the expectations of the business world. *Universal Journal of Accounting and Finance*, *9*.

Al-Hazaima, H., Al Shbail, M. O., Alshurafat, H., Ananzeh, H., & Al Shbeil, S. O. (2022). Dataset for integration of sustainability education into the accounting curricula of tertiary education institutions in Jordan. *Data in Brief*, *42*, 108224.

Al-Hazaima, H., Low, M., & Sharma, U. (2021). Perceptions of salient stakeholders on the integration of sustainability education into the accounting curriculum: A Jordanian study. *Meditari Accountancy Research*, *29*, 371–402.

Alshurafat, H., Al Shbail, M. O., Masadeh, W. M., Dahmash, F., & Al-Msiedeen, J. M. (2021). Factors affecting online accounting education during the COVID-19 pandemic: An integrated perspective of social capital theory, the theory of reasoned action and the technology acceptance model. *Education and Information Technologies*, *26*, 6995–7013.

Carvalho, C., & Almeida, A. C. (2022). The adequacy of accounting education in the development of transversal skills needed to meet market demands. *Sustainability*, *14*, 5755.

de Bem Machado, A., Secinaro, S., Calandra, D., & Lanzalonga, F. (2022). Knowledge management and digital transformation for Industry 4.0: A structured literature review. *Knowledge Management Research & Practice*, *20*, 320–338.

Despres, C., & Chauvel, D. (1999). Knowledge management(s). *Journal of Knowledge Management*, *3*, 110–123.

Jaradat, Z., Al-Dmour, A., Alshurafat, H., Al-Hazaima, H., & Al Shbail, M. O. (2022). Factors influencing business intelligence adoption: Evidence from Jordan. *Journal of Decision Systems*, 1–21.

Mertens, F. (2023, January 27). The use of artificial intelligence in corporate decision-making at board level: A preliminary legal analysis. Financial Law Institute Working Paper Series 2023-01. SSRN. https://ssrn.com/abstract=4339413 or http://doi.org/10.2139/ssrn.4339413

Morshed, A. (2022). Evaluation of practical accounting education in Jordan. *Higher Education Evaluation and Development*, *16*, 47–62.

Qasim, A., & Kharbat, F. F. (2020). Blockchain technology, business data analytics, and artificial intelligence: Use in the accounting profession and ideas for inclusion into the accounting curriculum. *Journal of Emerging Technologies in Accounting*, *17*, 107–117.

Saleh, M. M. A., Jawabreh, O. A., Al-Amro, S. A. H., & Saleh, H. M. I. (2023). Requirements for enhancing the standard of accounting education and its alignment with labor market requirements a case study hospitality and industrial sector in Jordan. *Journal of Sustainable Finance & Investment*, *13*, 176–193.

Sekaran, U., & Bougie, R. (2015). *Research methods for business: A skill building approach*. John Wiley & Sons.

Siam, W. Z. (2012). The extent of the contribution of business intelligence applications to the development of accounting information systems in Jordanian commercial banks. In *A Research Presented to the 11th Annual International Scientific Conference (Business Intelligence and Knowledge Economy)*. Amman: Faculty of Economics and Administrative Sciences, Al-Zaytoonah University.

Siam, W. Z. (2013). The extent of e-learning contribution to quality assurance of higher education: A case study of accounting education in Jordanian universities. *Arab Journal for Quality Assurance of Higher Education*, *6*(14), 81–100.

Siam, W. Z. (2018). The extent of contribution in the application of international accounting standards in quality assurance of higher education: A case study of the accounting programs in Jordanian universities. In *A Research Presented at the Eighth Arab International Conference for Quality Assurance of Higher Education (IACQA' 2018)*. Bekaa Branch: International Lebanese University.

Part III

Digital Technologies, Economic Diversification, Entrepreneurial Capacities, and Sustainability

Chapter 13

Building Productive Capacity for Economic Diversification in the Gulf Region

Amer Al-Roubaie and Bashar Matoog

Ahlia University, Bahrain

Abstract

This chapter aims to discuss the challenges facing these countries building productive capacity for development. This chapter makes use of data published by international organizations as indicators for measuring the state of development in the Arab region. Several indicators are presented to compare Arab countries with other world regions. The use of data identifies some of the gaps that countries in the Arab region need to close to strengthen capacity building for development and fostering economic growth. The findings from the data presented reveal that the productive structure in most Arab countries remains weak to generate production linkages and provide incentives for investment in nonenergy sectors. The failure of the export-led growth model to diversify output and promote development in energy producing countries has increased the dependence of these countries on global trade. Fluctuations in commodity prices and uncertainty about global demand for energy have influenced the ability of the state to construct strategies for rapid transformation. Except for the energy sector, the productivity of nonoil sectors remains low reflecting inadequate incentives and ineffective entrepreneurial capabilities. The study examines the challenges for building productive capacity in the Arab world. It illustrates the failure of the led-export model and its inability to prompted economic diversification, especially in the Gulf countries. The study contributes to the literature on capacity building in the Arab world so that to encourage researchers and students of development conducting studies concerning the main development challenges facing these countries.

Keywords: Productive capacity; economic diversification; diasporas; linkages; capabilities; Gulf region

Technological Innovations for Business, Education and Sustainability, 183–201

doi:10.1108/978-1-83753-106-620241013

1. Introduction

Building productive capacity for development is critical for economic diversification and productivity growth. For several decades, the economies of most developing countries, including the Gulf Cooperation Council (GCC), have been shaped by production and export of a limited number of commodities, raw materials, and primary products. Revenues from these exports provided the financial means for public expenditures and other government support programs. The share of these revenues accounts for a large percentage of both export earnings and gross domestic product (GDP), making the economies of these countries vulnerable to global financial instability (IMF, 2018; Ulrichsen, 2017). No serious initiatives taken to strengthen the productive capacity and diversify output outside the leading export sector. This, in turn, has weakened production linkages and reduced incentives for investment in the domestic economy. Not only production linkages stimulate growth across sectors of the economy but also provide local enterprises new opportunities to diversify output and compete in new markets.

GCC countries need to switch to a new model of development that promotes inclusiveness, lifelong learning, equity, and economic diversification. The model must encourage all actors to participate in development as well as to provide support for knowledge absorption, technology transfer, and innovation diffusion. For several decades, oil-led growth model has hindered socioeconomic development in the Arab world by creating duality within the productive system. Thus, rethinking development becomes essential to restructure the productive systems and increase value added of various sectors of the economy (Aubert & Reiffers, 2003). In this regard, it is essential that investment takes place to increase entrepreneurial capabilities and strengthen the fundamentals for building productive capacity.

The aim of this chapter is to examine the state of economic diversification in GCC countries and discuss the challenges facing these countries building productive capacity for development. This chapter focuses on productivity growth in nonoil sectors to reduce economic vulnerability and sustain growth. A key feature of growth in the 21st century has been the rise of the Fourth Industrial Revolution, driven by digital technologies. A successful development model must incorporate digitization to strengthen the productive capacity and accelerate the process of transformation. Digital technologies allow countries to tap global knowledge and attract more foreign direct investment (FDI). This chapter highlights some of the challenges facing these countries building productive capacity for economic diversification and reducing the risk of high dependency on international trade.

2. Literature Review

There is a substantial amount of published literature dealing with the importance of productive capacity and its impact on economic growth (Osakwe, 2020a,

2020b; United Nations, 2013; UNCTAD, 2006). The literature comprises different analytical methods and depends on data published by national and international institutions. It is understandable that these published studies are not always consistent in their conclusions. Among nations, the factors that participate in the construction of productive capacities differ reflecting the gaps in entrepreneurial capabilities, productive resources, and production linkages (UNCTAD, 2006). These capabilities empower domestic enterprises to create new knowledge, develop new technologies, and diffuse innovation that are essential for structural transformation. The existing of various knowledge, digital, and technological gaps hinders the ability of the economy to stimulate growth and strengthen capabilities for capacity building. For example, counties in Africa, Latin America, and Asia are still lacking to some of the basic capabilities for building productive capacity. Not only low capabilities weaken investment in the domestic market but also discourage inflows of FDI. In 2019, for example, the share of Africa in total global FDI accounted for 2.9% compared to 29% and 31% for North America and Europe, respectively. FDI enables local enterprises to acquire skills, absorb knowledge and communicate information, and therefore, speed up the process of capacity building. As pointed out by Kadri without internally generated technological learning, modern industry will remain locked in low-tech type activity (Kadri, 2015).

Creating appropriate business environment that encourages entrepreneurship and stimulates investment is another important feature for rapid structural transformation (Lejárrage & Walkenhorst, 2013). Stable business environment increases confidence in the marketplace and encourages investments by small and medium enterprises. Also, dynamic business environment motivates banks and other financial institutions to increase lending for business enterprises. Access to finance is critical not only for start-up by newcomers but also for participation in the global value chains and gain access to global markets.

Building productive capacity requires sound digital infrastructure to enhance connectivity and increase contacts between local and foreign firms. Digital technologies enable local enterprises developing new technologies and diffusing innovation by providing greater access to knowledge, skills, and information (UNCTAD, 2019). In the new economy, the internet and computer technologies facilitate knowledge sharing and increase collaboration with foreign universities and research institutions which help domestic firms finding solutions to domestic problems. To this end, effective state institutions play significant role in how well building productive capacity succeed in diversifying productivity and promoting economic growth (Digital Mckinsey, 2016). Countries that do not build capacity for information and communication technology (ICT) will not be able to benefit from the new digital age by foregoing many of the opportunities to acquire knowledge and foster innovation. In the case of the Arab region, institutional weakness has been responsible for the causes of socioeconomic and political exclusion (Al-Roubaie, 2010; United Nations, 2011).

3. Productive Capacity

Economic development is a process of structural transformation that requires strengthening the productive capacity of the economy to produce goods and services. The inclusive nature of development enables the society to harness the economic potential of its citizens and diversify output. Economic development is a product of two interconnected processes of productive capacity building and structural transformation (UNCTAD, 2020a, 2020b, 2020c). In other words, how much the economy can produce and develop will depend on the ability of the productive capacity to generate production linkages and strengthen entrepreneurial capabilities. Productive capacity is defined as the "productive resources, entrepreneurial capabilities and production linkages which together determine the capacity of a country to produce goods and services and enable it to grow and develop" (UNCTAD, 2006, p. 61).

Building productive capacity for development rests on three essential elements including productive resources, entrepreneurial capabilities, and production linkages (UNCTAD, 2006). In support of these pillars, there is a need for an educational system not only to ensure continuous learning and promote creativity but also to provide the basic skills and core knowledge that enable firms adapt and upgrade new technologies to local markets. The flexibility of the educational system makes the productive capacity more relevant to the global environment which encourages local firms to integrate into the global markets. Linkages between local and foreign firms provide domestic enterprises greater access to core capabilities. In this regard, weak global linkages hinder the ability of the economy to participate in global trade and benefit from globalization. The challenge facing developing countries is to overcome the impediments that hinder the development of productive resources and increase the productivity of resources to high-productivity economic activities. To develop productive resources, these countries must implement three processes: (i) capital or resource accumulation; (ii) technological learning and innovation; and (iii) deepening of division of labor and increasing specialization of sectors, firms, and farms (UNCTAD, 2020a, 2020b, 2020c).

Entrepreneurial capabilities play a key role in building productive capacity and strengthening the ability of the economy to produce more goods and services. Capabilities include such "attributes of economic agents" as knowledge, skills, competences, investment, technological, strategic marketing, financial, linkage, and innovation capabilities. They represent several types of "productive, organizational, technological and innovation capabilities embedded in organizations, institutions and infrastructures whose integration determines the capacity of a country to produce goods and services in a competitive global market" (UNCTAD, 2020c, p. 29). Also, called firm capabilities, serve as enablers for upgrading technologies, developing new products, and creating new knowledge. For example, production linkages are enablers of knowledge sharing, information flows, exchange of goods and services, and mobility of productive resources. They stimulate business activities, including participation in global value chains, outsourcing, subcontracting, collaboration, and partnership among businesses worldwide so that to increase competitiveness in both local and global markets.

In the new economy, investment in people is critical for building capacity for development. Not only knowledge and skills empower the economy to produce goods and services but also enhance firm's capabilities to participate in the global value chains. In recent decades, globalization has been offering new opportunities for developing countries to gain access to global markets and acquire skills, absorb knowledge, and transfer technology. Countries with inadequate financial, natural, and managerial resources can improve domestic capabilities through collaboration and cooperation with global partners. Integration in the global chains provides domestic enterprises greater access to technical and managerial skills to enhance technological learning and upgrade technologies for domestic use.

In addition to investment in physical infrastructure, investment in human capital increases the ability of the economy to absorb and adapt global knowledge and technology. Countries that fail to take advantage of the opportunities offered by globalization and use global knowledge are likely to remain behind. "The challenge for developing countries is to reinforce their capabilities – both human and institutional-so that all sectors, firms, and individuals can acquire, adapt, and use knowledge effectively" (World Bank, 1998, p. 26). Not only adapting global knowledge to local conditions encourages entrepreneurship and attracts foreign investment but also enhances production linkages and stimulates innovation. Technical education, training, and research and development are considered as knowledge ingredients used by firms to build productive capacity and improve entrepreneurial capabilities. In this age of globalization, business enterprises are given greater opportunities to choose among alternatives and select quality of capabilities that enable firms to generate production linkages and increase competitiveness. In doing so, firms will be able to improve the process of technological learning and increase the stock of knowledge and skills for capacity building (Al-Roubaie, 2013).

Productive capacity increases market opportunities for collaboration and cooperation between domestic and foreign firms to work together in a joint venture and invest in various sectors of the economy. Such partnership will enhance local capabilities to acquire skills, talent, and technical knowledge which are essential for building capacity for development. This increases the demand for goods and services providing local entrepreneurs new opportunities for investment not only to meet local demand but also to produce for foreign markets. Access to global markets allows countries to participate in global value chains and improve competitiveness. Partnership with foreign firms introduces new products, new techniques, new industries, and new managerial skills necessary for upgrading domestic capabilities and enhancing technological learning. In addition, technological capabilities, which is defined as "the knowledge, experience and skills needed to introduce new products, new production processes and forms of organizing production, or to improve old ones" (UNCTAD, 2006, p. 68), represent important components of the productive capacity. Enhanced access to foreign knowledge and technology can boost local capabilities and increase their contribution to economic diversification.

Building productive capacity will require government support and incentives to encourage local firms to cooperate and collaborate with foreign firms so that to strengthen global linkages and improve entrepreneurial capabilities in the domestic market. The system of rules, including incentives, financing, market regulations, and protections, are influenced by the institutional framework of the state, and therefore, the state can have considerable impact on the process of capacity building. Enforcing the rules increases confidence in market activities and encourages entrepreneurs, both local and foreign, to invest in the economy. In this regard, governments need to create suitable business environment to make it attractive for FDI and multinational corporations investing in the domestic economy so as to facilitate knowledge absorption and technology transfer. Public investments in physical infrastructure, the internet, human capital, and research and development empower local capabilities with the means to participate in market activities and compete in the global markets. Government intervention in the market could also increase the economy's choices to select projects with high production linkages that are more applicable to the domestic environment. Opportunities for entrepreneurship through the internet could increase the economy's capabilities to produce goods and services.

In addition, government spending on research and development could increase the potential for innovation and knowledge creation to support local entrepreneurs' participation in market activities and compete in global markets. To this end, private–public partnership should be encouraged to allocate resources and cultivate the economic potential of domestic capabilities. Improving participation of small and medium-sized enterprises enhances entrepreneurial capabilities to build productive capacity and diversify output.

The state institutions, including the financial, educational, managerial, and the social systems, are critical for development capabilities and productivity growth. The quality of education and skill requirements are among the top priorities that an economy requires to adapt to the new technologies. The development of indigenous knowledge to embrace the local environment is important for building capacity for economic diversification. By creating and adopting environmentally friendly technologies, there be greater potential for the economy to strengthen linkages creation, disseminate innovation, and boost entrepreneurship (Al-Roubaie & Al Zayer, 2007).

Building productive capacity and fostering economic growth rises from increasing production within and among sectors of the domestic economy. A major source of economic growth in developing countries lies in the ability of these countries to imitate and adapt technologies already existing in other countries. However, realizing such adaptability will require technological capabilities, mainly related to the quality of the educational system to produce graduates equipped with skills and knowledge relevant to the need for structural change and sustainable growth. "Arab countries have not attained a level of development that would enable them to adapt the technologies they have imported at different times" (Abdel Majid, Abu-Khalid, Al-Amin, Al-Azmeh, & Al-Banna, 2003, p. 99).

Absorptive capacity of an economy is determined by the ability of domestic entrepreneurs, firms, and institutions to recognize the contribution of novel knowledge and technology and to acquire and assimilate it into production of goods and services. It is the capacity that "determines if and to what extent a firm, an industry or, indeed, an economy, can use existing and new knowledge to compete" (UNCTAD, 2014, p. 23) Transfer of Technology and Knowledge Sharing for Development). Thus, expanding the economy's ability to absorb knowledge and acquire technology will foster growth and speed up the process of building productive capacity. Arab countries should be able to allocate oil revenues toward building digital infrastructure and establishing social networks to allow local firms communicate and collaborate with global knowledge systems to enable them harness the benefit of the existing knowledge in the rest of the world. For countries with inadequate domestic knowledge system, priority should be given to the readily available knowledge elsewhere. Production of knowledge at home could be very costly and beyond the resources available to the country.

An important feature representing global business today is the global value chains. Developing countries must consider participating in these chains to build productive capacity and increase the share of manufacturing production in total output. Integration into the global value chains could have a positive impact on productive capacity and structural transformation. Participation in a value chains helps the economy to acquire new capabilities that can be utilized for promoting technological learning and providing new opportunities for local firms to integrate in the global economy. Global linkages could increase the share of manufacturing production in total output by encouraging local enterprises to compete in global markets. "A country's position in a chain and its ability to upgrade its participation determines success, as do adequate services and governance, innovative entrepreneurs, and the requirements specific to the chain" (African Development Bank Group, p. 126) (https://www.ids.trade/files/africa_economic_outlook.pdf). Not only global value chains can strengthen the fundamentals for building productive capacity but also have the potential to speed up the process of structural transformation and boost employment. They require an appropriate business environment that is attractive for investment and to enable firms and entrepreneurs acquire skills and knowledge for identifying potential and enhancing the economy's productive capabilities. Participation in the global value chains increases productive linkages in the domestic economy which create new opportunities for capacity building and development sustainability (Pandey & Panchal, 2023).

Globalization has empowered developing countries to tap global knowledge and participate in the global value chains so that to increase manufacturing production and promote productive capacity. Over the last few decades, countries in Southeast Asia, including China, have been able to benefit from globalization and build capacity for development. They have been able to transform their economies from a low productivity structure to high productive activities generating in the process high linkages, creating more jobs, diversifying output, and fostering economic growth. For several decades, governments in the Gulf region have been making efforts to reduce dependence on export-led growth sector and diversify output; however, very little success has been accomplished so far to balance development and sustain growth. A new model is required aiming at integrating the economies of the region into the international trading system to strengthen linkages creation and facilitate knowledge absorption.

4. Contribution of Diasporas to Productive Capabilities

Highly skilled immigrants and other members of diaspora can significantly contribute to building productive capacity in the home country (United Nations, 2004). Diaspora refers to a "community of expatriates who are spread or dispersed around the world, outside their homeland" (UNCTAD, 2012, p. 106). These migrants consist of people with all kinds of educational background including scientific, technical, and managerial skills. Working abroad, migrants can acquire different skills and experiences which can be transferred and shared with individuals and firms in the home country. In particular, the developing countries have a substantial number of their citizens working in various educational, technical, managerial, and scientific fields in a large number of Western countries. Making use of diaspora services could have important impact on development, especially in countries lacking to scientific and technical skills (Al-Roubaie, 2005). Recent decades have witnessed brain-gain movements representing people from countries such as China and India going back to their native countries. Most of these individuals are highly skilled and well-trained to work in various fields of ICT and in manufacturing.

Creating adequate working conditions and providing incentives for workers to return home, the developing countries will be able to harness the knowledge, know-how, experience, and skills of the knowledge workers to build productive capacity for development. Diasporas can serve as "brain banks abroad: when properly organized, they can become a source of knowledge sharing and technology transfer with their home country" (UNCTAD, 2012). Knowledge embodied in people has a positive impact on development, and therefore, migrants not only represent a loss of knowledge to the native country but also hinder the ability of the economy to diversify output and foster economic growth. The adverse effects of the migration of workers on the home economy depend on the educational background of migrants and the knowledge and skills they possess. Highly skilled migrants could have negative impact on development by reducing the stock of human capital and disrupting market demand for labor. For example, the loss of medical doctors and other health workers at the time of COVID-19 could have an important impact on productivity growth in home countries. The cost to the home country from migrants of highly skilled people is the loss of creativity and innovation that the country needs to build productive capacity. However, keeping connection with the home country has the potential to increase flows of knowledge, investments, goods, and services. Not only family members can benefit from remittances of migrants but also the country balance of payments by having money received in foreign currencies.

Diaspora contributes to capacity building by enhancing the economy capabilities to absorb knowledge, diffuse innovation, and facilitate technology transfer. Migrants working in developed countries are usually equipped with up-to-date skills, knowledge, and know-how which can be used to increase local capabilities and diversify output. Migrant workers can invest the skills and apply the experience they acquired in the host country to build productive capacity in the home country. These workers are highly specialized, and they can increase the stock of knowledge which is essential for the global knowledge economy and society. "Brain drain can have an adverse effect on local science and knowledge systems, impairing the economy's capacity to produce and implement innovation" (UNCATD, 2012, pp. 98–99). In other words, higher rate of migration could reduce the ability of the economy to absorb knowledge and acquire skills for promoting technological learning and improving productive capacity.

Digital technologies have made it possible to establish social networks and create channels that facilitate the flow of knowledge and information to home countries. Building adequate ICT infrastructure becomes essential for connecting diasporas with home countries to participate in structural transformation and enhance local capabilities taking part in the digital economy. Also, diaspora can establish communication networks and provide digital services for bridging the knowledge gap, facilitating business creation, promoting trade transactions, and transferring technology between home and host countries. Such digital networks help the home country acquire finance, expertise, know-how as well as provide access to global value chains. Not only digital technologies reduce transaction costs but also create new opportunities for individuals and enterprises to obtain knowledge and information about markets and prices. Digital services empower local firms to improve local capabilities and compete in international markets.

Diaspora encourages international tourism and stimulates export of services which foster linkages creation and generate new job opportunities. There are wide range of linkages attributed to tourism including at micro, macro, and global levels. Thus, building capacity for tourism will contribute positively to productive capacity by increasing demand for goods and services which in turn encourages local firms to invest and benefit from expenditures by tourists. "Opening up the country through programs and services to attract foreign tourist provides new opportunities, especially for youth, women, the poor, and the unemployed. In regions where government services are not adequately provided, tourism encourages economic diversification and stimulates linkages" (Al-Roubaie, 2019, p. 98). In short, high-skilled diaspora members increase the country capabilities to diversify output and sustain growth.

There are more than 20 million diasporas of Arab origin representing about 5% of its total Arab population. "Diaspora communities can provide not just remittances but also knowledge transfer or 'brain gain', direct investment, and contacts". Unfortunately, most Arab countries are doing very little to harness the economic and knowledge benefits that their diasporas possess. Migrants are well-equipped with knowledge, technical and managerial skills, languages, and information that can be used as valuable inputs in building capacity for development. This will make it more attractive for foreign firms to join venture and increase invest in the local economy (Malouche, Plaza, & Salsac, 2016).

5. Economic Diversification

For several decades, the productive structure of most Arab countries has been shaped by the performance of the energy industries impacting public expenditures, unemployment, and economic growth. Despite efforts to reduce the share of the oil export sector in total output and diversify the economy, so far very little success has been achieved. The economies of these countries continued to suffer from financial instability due to fluctuations in commodity prices and demand for energy in the global markets. "A high rate of dependence on oil and gas revenues reinforces patterns of volatile government revenues, whose level and stability remains outside producing countries control" (United Nations, 2012, p. 54). Most investment expenditure by the public sector was directed toward building physical infrastructure and providing consumer services to support high living standards. This diversion from productive market activities has weakened the productive capacity of the economy and discouraged domestic production, especially manufactured goods, from taking place. High dependence on global trade generated very little stimulus to support domestic industries and encourage entrepreneurship. In other words, opportunities for developing capabilities and improving production linkages were limited to support rapid structural transformation and foster productivity growth. Instead "Oil-led economic growth has led to premature de-industrialization and reinforced the subordinate position of the Arab region in the global hierarchy of production. The process has been market by unbalanced development within and between Arab countries that has hindered manufacturing and agricultural sectors and led to anemic growth of outlying areas" (United Nations, 2011, p. 2).

Countries in the Gulf region suffer from low level of economic diversification to minimize the risk of external shocks and sustain growth (Callen, Cherif, Hasanov, Hegazy, & Khandelwal, 2014; Hvidt, 2013). This means placing high priority on policymakers to adapt strategies aiming at increasing the economy's entrepreneurial capabilities and creating new job opportunities for its citizens. It will require measures that bring about an important upgrading of the productive capacity for adapting policies to increase knowledge creation and effective allocation of productive resources (Hesse, 2009). Economic diversification empowers the economy to produce goods and services as well as to enhance the country's productive capabilities. "Economic diversification is considered a key element of economic development in which a country moves to a less concentrated, more varied production and trade structure. Lack of economic diversification is associated with increased economic vulnerability such that external shocks can undermine the development process" (WTD, OECD, 2019, p. 30). Not only diversification encourages domestic enterprises to invest and increase production linkages but also to improve local firms capabilities to compete in the global markets.

Access to global markets facilitates knowledge absorption and technology transfer to improve entrepreneurial capabilities and support economic diversification. Integration in the global economy promotes inclusiveness and creates new opportunities for employment of productive resources. The productive capacity of the domestic economy rises from increasing production within and among sectors. Furthermore, growth in productivity and the speed at which the economy grows will be influenced by entrepreneurial capabilities and the ability of local firms to compete in the global markets. Thus, global linkages empower domestic enterprises with new opportunities to participate in international trade and harness the benefits of global business.

The emergence of digital technologies is providing local firms with greater access to knowledge and information to build production capabilities and support diversification. Trade enables local firms to obtain resources that are not available in the domestic market. Not only digital technologies contribute to capacity building by reducing the cost but also contribute to the development of domestic capabilities. Such constraints as low levels of skills and training, inadequate manufacturing capacity, limited access to finance, and poor competitiveness can be eased by using e-services. As an "engine of growth," international trade creates enabling environment in which both local and foreign firms collaborate in research and development, knowledge sharing, and innovation diffusion. The rise of digitization has increased opportunities for enterprises worldwide to communicate and discuss issues of common interest. Developing countries can take advantage of the new digital economy to find solutions for productivity growth and structural transformation.

Building productive capacity and fostering economic growth rises from increasing production within and among sectors of the domestic economy. A major source of economic growth in developing countries lies in their ability to imitate and adapt technologies already existing in other countries. Realizing such adaptability, however, will require technological capabilities, mainly related to the quality of the educational system to produce graduates equipped with skills and knowledge relevant to the need for structural change and sustainable growth. The development of indigenous knowledge to embrace the local environment is important for building capacity for economic diversification. There will be greater potential for the economy to strengthen production linkages, disseminate innovation, and boost entrepreneurship through the creation and adopting environmentally friendly technologies (Al-Roubaie, 2018).

In the Arab world, building productive capacity can be achieved through the allocation of greater share of oil revenues for investment in nonenergy sectors of the economy. Fiscal linkages expand the productive capacity of the economy by promoting both vertical and horizontal diversification. The involvement of small and medium enterprises in productive activities contributes to economic diversification through innovation and knowledge creation. Collaboration with global firms enables local firms to transfer technology and improve entrepreneurial capabilities across sectors of the economy. Trade, licensing, and FDI are among the important channels through which nations can obtain foreign technology for capacity building. The challenge for developing countries, however, is to encourage diaspora students and scientists to return home and participate in training local entrepreneurs how to adapt foreign technologies to local conditions (Maskus, 2003).

Building capacity for knowledge absorption and technology diffusion is determined by the ability of domestic entrepreneurs, firms, and institutions to recognize the contribution of creativity and innovation, creation of new knowledge and technology, and to acquire and assimilate it into production of goods and services. It is the capacity that "determines if and to what extent a firm, an industry or, indeed, an economy, can use existing and new knowledge to compete" (See UNCTAD, 2014, p. 23). Hence, the tendency of the economy to absorb knowledge and acquire technology will foster growth and speed up the process of building productive capacity. In this regard, building infrastructure and establishing social networks could play an important role in helping local firms to communicate and collaborate with the global knowledge system and benefit from the existing knowledge in the rest of the world. Countries that are lacking to adequate knowledge system, they can use the knowledge available elsewhere to enhance their capabilities and build knowledge capacity for development. Not only it is costly to produce knowledge in the early stages of development, but also the existing of market imperfections and shortage of resources could hinder the ability of local firms to produce goods and service and compete in the global markets. Thus, to build their knowledge base, the developing countries should explore all means of tapping the global stock of knowledge (World Bank, 1998, p. 39).

The global value chains are among the important features representing global business today. Joining these chains will strengthen the fundamentals for capacity building and increase the share of manufacturing production in total output. The chains help the economy to acquire new capabilities that can be utilized for promoting technological learning and providing new opportunities for local firms to integrate in the global economy. "A country's position in a chain and its ability to upgrade its participation determines success, as do adequate services and governance, innovative entrepreneurs, and the requirements specific to the chain" (African Development Bank Group, p. 126). To this end, not only global value chains can strengthen the fundamentals for building productive capacity but also have the potential to speed up the process of structural transformation and boost employment. It is important, therefore, that the developing countries create appropriate business environment that is attractive for investment and for enabling firms and entrepreneurs acquire skills and knowledge for identifying potential and enhancing the economy's productive capabilities. Integration into the global value chain increases production linkages and enhances entrepreneurial capabilities, which create new opportunities for building productive capacity and diversifying output (Okunlola, Sani, & Ayetigbo, 2023).

The Arab countries should take advantage of the digital revolution and build digital infrastructure to enhance the economy's productive capabilities and diversify productivity. Investment in digital technologies enables these countries to participate in Global Value Chains (GVCs) and gain access to global business. Not only digital technologies reduce the cost of doing business and encourage entrepreneurship but also provide the economy with new opportunities to engage in international trade and acquire knowledge and skills for empowering local capabilities. Closing the digital gap is essential for participation in the global markets and promoting competitiveness. The Arab countries need to translate Vision 2030s into inclusive development driven by high-quality productive capabilities that contribute to productivity growth and economic transformation. They need to rethink development and embrace strategy to induce economic diversification and reduce dependence on limited number of commodities. Global trade enables countries to choose among alternatives and deploy technologies that are more applicable for building productive capacity and speeding up the process of structural transformation.

Column 1 in Table 13.1 represents the productive capacity index which measures the gap in productive capacities among nations. It identifies the economy limitations that hinder efforts to foster productive capacities and promote development. Also, the index serves as a policy tool which helps decision-makers formulate strategies for achieving progress and sustaining economic growth. There are 193 countries involved in the construction of the index with the United States ranked the highest economy scoring 50.51, whereas Chad ranked the lowest scoring 17.14 in the index. As about the Arab economies, except for a few in the Gulf region, the rest of the economies scored low values reflecting the weakness of the productive capacities and their inability to promote rapid transformation. In other words, the Arab economies are characterized by low production linkages and weak entrepreneurial capabilities that are essential for building productive capacity and encouraging economic diversification. To expand the productive capacity, policymakers in Arab countries need to invest in such entrepreneurial capabilities as human capital, technological learning, knowledge creation, and innovation. Investment in human capital is vital not only to speed up the process of capacity building but also to encourage local enterprises participating in global value chains and foster economic diversification.

The economic complexity index highlights more serious weaknesses of the productive capacities in Arab countries. The index measures the knowledge and skills of a country as expressed in the products it produces and exports. As shown in Table 13.1, the knowledge contents in the production and exports of most Arab countries are very low to give these countries comparative advantage and compete in the global markets. The ubiquitous nature of the products exported by Arab countries underline the inadequacy of the knowledge and innovative systems to produce unique products for export markets. Also, this reflects the inability of the economic system to generate sufficient spillover effects to support entrepreneurial capabilities and diversify output. The economic complexity index postulates that diversification is linked to sophistication. It is the ability to competitively produce unique goods and services that induce diversification. The more diversified the economy, the higher its productivity growth.

Diversification and concentration indices are indicators representing the linkages between the trade sector and the capacity of the economy to produce goods and services. It shows how exports and imports of countries are dependent on few products. In countries where the productive capacity is dominated by production and export of one sector, the value of the diversification index is closer to one,

Table 13.1. Development Indicators for Selected Countries.

Country	1 Productive Capacity Index 2020	2 Economic Complexity Index 2017	3 Concentration Index 2019	4 Diversification Index 2019	5 Global Competitiveness Index 2019	6 Competitive Industrial Index 2020
The United States	50.51	1.76	0.101	0.227	83.7	0.345
Netherlands	48.22	1.30	0.085	0.311	82.4	0.252
Japan	45.39	2.31	0.142	0.393	82.3	0.344
Algeria	27.76	−0.81	0.471	0.817	56.3	0.014
Bahrain	39.03	NA	0.296	0.676	82.3	0.058
Egypt	29.39	−0.32	0.142	0.585	65.4	0.037
Iraq	22.92	NA	0.916	0.874	NA	0.001
Jordan	31.01	−0.15	0.169	0.620	60.9	0.028
Kuwait	33.98	0.12	0.669	0.795	65.1	0.052
Lebanon	33.68	0.08	0.190	0.643	56.3	0.016
Morocco	30.51	−0.89	0.181	0.655	60.0	0.041
Oman	34.60	−0.06	0.413	0.682	63.6	0.067
Qatar	40.81	0.40	0.484	0.794	72.9	0.063
Saudi Arabia	34.73	0.75	0.590	0.766	70.0	0.084

Sudan	22.01	−1.46	0.397	0.847	NA	NA
Syria	24.67	−0.74	0.223	0.647	NA	0.008
Tunisia	33.24	−0.29	0.141	0.526	56.4	0.035
UAE	42.30	0.13	0.264	0.556	75.0	0.089
Yemen	23.28	−0.97	0.422	0.776	35.5	0.014

Sources: Data in Table 13.1 are obtained from the sources below: (1) Productive Capacity Index from UNCTAD, UNCTAD Capacities Index 2020. (2) https://oec.world/en/rankings/country/eci/ (3) https://unctadstat.unctad.org/wds/ReportFolders/reportFolders.aspx?IF_ActivePath=P,15912&sCS_ChosenLang=en (4) https://unctadstat.unctad.org/wds/ReportFolders/reportFolders.aspx?IF_ActivePath=P,15912&sCS_ChosenLang=en (5) http://www3.weforum.org/docs/WEF_TheGlobalCompetitivenessReport2019.pdf (6) https://www.unido.org/news/unidos-competitive-industrial-performance-index-2020-country-profiles-published

whereas a highly diversified economy is expected to have value closer to zero. Table 13.1 illustrates that the value of the diversification index of most countries in the Gulf region is closer to one reflecting the dominance of a limited number of commodities, mainly the energy sector, in total export trade. Such dominance of a leading export sector underlines the inability of the economy to expand the productive capacity and improve productive capabilities so that to increase production linkages and diversify output. Development in these countries seems to have locked in low productivity type of market activities with little internally generated production linkages to stimulate economic diversification (Sattar, 2014).

The global competitiveness index in Table 13.1 provides a comparative overview of the productivity potential in different countries. Most Arab countries shown in the table are not highly competitive in global markets to take advantage of participating in global trade and gain access to modern technologies. Low competitiveness index hinders the ability of these countries to develop entrepreneurial capabilities and promote strong production linkages that enhance economic diversification. Not being able to compete in the global markets weakens the ability of the country to strengthen the fundamentals for building productive capacity. Engagement in international trade allows the economy to acquire knowledge and information that can be used to enhance local capabilities and support productive capacity.

The competitive Industrial Performance Index measures the competitiveness of national industries. It illustrates low economic diversification and weak capabilities to initiate rapid structural transformation. In other words, it measures global comparison of industrial productivity and the contribution of the manufacturing sector to the national economy. As shown in the index, industrialization in the Arab world remains below the world average of 0.067. Manufacturing production represents an important measure of an economy's productive capacity. It enhances entrepreneurial capabilities and increases production linkages that empower the ability of the economy to produce goods and services. Low economic diversification in the Arab world is linked to low industrial productivity as well as to the failure of economic policies to promote industrialization and reduce the economy dependence on a few commodities.

6. Conclusion

The main focus in this chapter has been the state of economic development in the Arab world with specific reference to the Gulf region. For decades, economic development in the region has been dominated by the energy industry, mainly oil and gas production and exports. Earnings from the oil export sector provided the financial means for public expenditures on development infrastructure and welfare support programs. Despite efforts to reduce dependency on oil revenues and diversify output, very little success has been achieved. The failure of the oil-led development model to address the development challenges and strengthen the productive capacity to produce goods and services has hindered the ability of the state to diversify output and foster economic growth. The share of manufacturing production in total output remained low to stimulate production linkages and encourage entrepreneurship. Furthermore, the dominance of the public sector in the economy has weakened the participation of private enterprises in market activities and benefit from entrepreneurial capabilities.

Building productive capacity for development promotes economic diversification and reduces the risk of global shocks. Countries in the region need to formulate strategies capable of improving productive capabilities, increase production linkages, and deepen integration in the global economy. Such strategies will enable the economy to build productive capacity capable of broadening the productive structure and diversify output. Economic development is a process of structural transformation that requires harnessing the productive capabilities and supporting inclusiveness. Implementation of Visions 2030 underscores the importance of investment in human capital resources and technological learning to strengthen the economy productive capabilities and enhance competitiveness.

Access to global markets increases the country ability to absorb knowledge and acquire skills that empower local firms and support economic diversification. In most Arab countries, economic diversification remains insufficient to generate strong production linkages and encourage investment in nonenergy sectors. There is a need for immediate action to rethink development and adapt new model driven by digital technologies and social networks so that to speed up the process of transformation and reduce the risk of economic and financial vulnerability. The new model needs to respond to the new challenges brought by the Fourth Industrial Revolution. It is imperative that these countries take advantage of the vast global knowledge and make use of it to build productive capacity for development. Similarly, diasporas can contribute to the knowledge economy through the establishment of trade relations, social networks, and knowledge sharing.

The failure of developing countries to improve productivity and diversify output is linked to the inability of the economy to produce linkages and foster economic growth. Heavy dependence of these countries on production and export of primary products has led to the creation of dual economy driven by an export leading sector with little or no linkages with the nonexport sectors. Over time, such duality has weakened the productive capacity of the nonexports sectors to produce goods and services not only to satisfy local demand but also from actively participating in the global markets. Recent studies focus on economic diversification to reduce the economy's dependence on production and export of limited number of commodities.

References

Abdel Majid, L., Abu-Khalid, F. A., Al-Amin, M. H., Al-Azmeh, A., & Al-Banna, S. (2003). *Arab Human Development Report 2003. Building a knowledge society United Nations Development Programme, Regional Bureau for Arab States (RBAS)* (p. 10017). New York, NY.

Al-Roubaie, A. (2005). Labour movement in the Middle East: A regional perspective. In *JCAS Symposium Series* (No. 17, pp. 53–88).

Al-Roubaie, A. (2013). Building knowledge capacity for development in the Arab World. *International Journal of Innovation and Knowledge Management in the Middle East & North Africa*, *2*(1), 7–20.

Al-Roubaie, A. (2018). Linkages creation and economic diversification: The case of Muslim countries. *SHS Web of Conferences*, *56*, 01001. ICLM 2018. doi:10.1051/shsconf/20185601001

Al-Roubaie, A., & Al Zayer, J. (2007). Knowledge creation and global readiness in GCC countries. In A. Ahmed (Ed.), *Science, technology and sustainability in the Middle East and North Africa*. London: Inderscience.

Al-Roubaie, A. (2010). Building indigenous knowledge capacity for development. *World Journal of Science, Technology and Sustainable Development*, *7*(2), 113–128.

Aubert, J. E., & Reiffers, J. L. (2003). *Knowledge economies in the Middle East and North Africa: Toward new development strategies*. Washington, DC: The World Bank.

Callen, M. T., Cherif, R., Hasanov, F., Hegazy, M. A., & Khandelwal, P. (2014). *Economic diversification in the GCC: Past, present, and future*. New York, NY: International Monetary Fund.

Digital Mckinsey. (2016). *Digital Middle East: Transforming the region into a leading digital economy*. Retrieved from https://www.mckinsey.com/business-functions/digital-mckinsey/how-we-help-clients

Hesse, H. (2009). Export diversification and economic growth. In R. Newfarmer, W. Shaw, & P. Walkenhorst (Eds.), *Breaking into new markets: Emerging lessons for export diversification* (pp. 55–80). Washington, D.C.: The World Bank.

Hvidt, M. (2013). *Economic diversification in Gulf Cooperation Council (GCC) countries: Past record and future trends* (Vol. 27, pp. 1–49). London: London School of Economics and Political Science. Kuwait Programme on Development, Governance and Globalisation in the Gulf States.

International Monetary Fund (IMF). (2018). *Trade and foreign investment – Keys to diversification and growth in the GCC*. Washington, DC. Retrieved from pp120618gcc-trade-and-foreign-investment (5).pdf

Kadri, A. (2015). Productivity decline in the Arab world. *Real-World Economics Review*, *70*, 140–160.

Lejárraga, I., & Walkenhorst, P. (2013). Economic policy, tourism trade and productive diversification. *International Economics*, *135*, 1–12.

Malouche, M., Plaza, S., & Salsac, F. (2016). *Mobilizing the Middle East and North Africa diaspora for economic integration and entrepreneurship*. World Bank. Retrieved from http://documents1.worldbank.org/curated/en/251661484064811210/pdf/111806-REVISED-PULIC-4530-MENADiasporaPaper-March29-5pm.pdf

Maskus, K. (2003). Transfer of technology and technological capacity building, ICTSD-UNCTAD.

Okunlola, O. C., Sani, I. U., & Ayetigbo, O. A. (2023). Socio-economic governance and economic growth in Nigeria. *Journal of Business and Socio-economic Development*. doi:10.1108/JBSED-03-2023-0019

Osakwe, P. (2020a). *Developing productive capacities to industrialize and diversify African economies and achieve SDGs*. UNCTAD/ALDC/MISC 2020-2.

Osakwe, P. (2020b). *Building productive capacities and transforming economies to achieve sustained and inclusive development in Africa*. Geneva: UNCTAD. Retrieved from https://www.un.org/development/desa/dspd/wp-content/uploads/sites/22/2020/03/Osakwe_DESAmeeting_Rome2020.pdf

Pandey, P., & Panchal, M. (2023). Food sustainability in India – A challenge. In J. Aloysius Edward, K. P. Jaheer Mukthar, E. R. Asis, & K. Sivasubramanian (Eds.), *Current trends in economics, business and sustainability. ICEBS 2023. Contributions to environmental sciences & innovative business technology*. Singapore: Springer. doi:10.1007/978-981-99-3366-2_17

Sattar, Z. (2014, June). Challenges of export-led growth. In *Bangladesh Economists' Forum Conference*, Dhaka.

Ulrichsen, K. C. (2017). *Economic diversification in Gulf Cooperation Council (GCC) states*. Center of Energy Studies, Rice University.

UNCTAD. (2006). *The Least Developed Countries Report 2006: Developing productive capacities*. New York, NY: United Nations.

UNCTAD. (2012). *The Least Developed Countries Report 2012. Harnessing remittances and diaspora knowledge to build productive capacities*. Retrieved from https://unctad.org/system/files/official-document/ldc2012_en.pdf

UNCTAD. (2014). *Transfer of technology and knowledge sharing for development*. Retrieved from https://unctad.org/system/files/official-document/dtlstict2013d8_en.pdf

UNCTAD. (2019). *Digital Economy Report 2019*. United Nations. Retrieved from https://unctad.org/webflyer/digital-economy-report-2019

UNCTAD. (2020a). *Productive capacities index*. Retrieved from https://unctadstat.unctad.org/EN/Pci.html

UNCTAD. (2020b). *The Least Developed Countries Report 2020*. Geneva: United Nations. Retrieved from https://unctad.org/webflyer/least-developed-countries-report-2020

UNCTAD. (2020c). *Building and utilizing productive capacities in Africa and the least developed countries*. Retrieved from https://unctad.org/system/files/official-document/aldcinf2020d1_en.pdf

UNIDO. (2016). *Industrial Development Report. The Role of Technology and Innovation in Inclusive and Sustainable Industrial Development*.

United Nations. (2004). *World Economic and Social Survey 2004*. New York, NY: United Nations.

United Nations. (2011). *Arab Development Challenges Report 2011*. Cairo: UNDP. Retrieved from https://www.undp.org/content/undp/en/home/librarypage/hdr/arab-development-challenges-report-2011

United Nations. (2012). *Arab Human Development Report. Energy and Arab Economic Development*.

United Nations. (2013). *Building productive capacities to enhance structural transformation in landlocked developing countries (LLDCS)*. Retrieved from http://unohrlls.org/custom-content/uploads/2013/09/Structural-Transformation.pdf

World Bank. (1998). *World Development Report 1998/1999: Knowledge for Development*. The World Bank.

WTO, OECD. (2019). *Aid for Trade at a Glance 2019: Economic Diversification and Empowerment*. Retrieved from https://www.oecd.org/dac/aft/aid-for-trade-at-a-glance-22234411.htm

Chapter 14

Assessing the Sustainability of GCC Economic Growth: A Proposed Theoretical Framework

Fahad K. Alkhaldi and Mohamed Sayed Abou Elseoud

University of Bahrain, Bahrain

Abstract

The current chapter proposes a theoretical framework to assess the sustainability of economic growth in the Gulf Cooperation Council (GCC) States. The authors integrate insights from endogenous growth models and consider the unique socioeconomic characteristics of the GCC region to provide a comprehensive and tailored approach to understanding the determinants of economic growth and formulating effective policy measures to foster sustainable development and growth. This chapter highlights the environmental challenges faced by GCC; based on this, the authors suggested indicators to construct a theoretical framework (Economic Growth, Climatic Indicators, Energy Indicators, Social Indicators, and Economic Resources Indicators). The authors propose that policymakers and researchers in GCC States should take these factors into account when devising policies or conducting research aimed at fostering sustainable economic growth. Overall, this chapter presents significant insights for policymakers, researchers, and stakeholders involved in promoting the sustainable economic advancement of the GCC States.

Keywords: Gulf cooperation council (GCC) states; economic growth; endogenous growth; environmental challenges; economic challenges; sustainability

Technological Innovations for Business, Education and Sustainability, 203–221

Published under exclusive licence by Emerald Publishing Limited
doi:10.1108/978-1-83753-106-620241014

1. Introduction

Since the mid-1980s, many proposals have explained the differences between the growth rates of production and the level of per capita income among different countries. Based on the so-called new or modern Endogenous theory of growth, there has been a recognized failure to achieve the convergence of individual incomes between different world countries, encompassing both developing and developed nations, as postulated by the neoclassical theory.

Thus, the neoclassical model of growth has been criticized several times and has proved limited in explaining some of the economic growth situations of some countries; this is what later was the cornerstone of building a new economic orientation of growth theories known as models of domestic growth (McCombie & Thirlwall, 2016, Economic Growth and the Balance-of-Payments Constraint). Moreover, the limited performance of neoclassical theories in interpreting sources of long-term economic growth has failed to give an acceptable explanation of the historical growth of economies around the world (Sredojević, Cvetanović, & Bošković, 2016).

The New Growth Theory, the Endogenous Growth Model, emerged in the late 1980s and early 1990s (Stimson & Stough, 2016), in response to criticism of Solow's Growth Model, as it tries to explain the factors that determine gross national product (GNP) size and rate of growth, which has not been interpreted and determined outside the Solow Residual growth equation (McCombie, 2000). The long-term technological change rate depends on the model's basic parameters, such as the investment rates in material and human capital and the population growth rate (Leimbach, Kriegler, Roming, & Schwanitz, 2017).

This theory has focused on long-term economic growth due to the continuing development gap between developed and developing countries. It, therefore, reinforces the role of government policies to increase investments in human capital formation and encourage foreign private investment in knowledge-intensive industries (Dellink, Chateau, Lanzi, & Magné, 2017). It is noted that the models of endogenous growth are similar somehow in the form of the structure to neoclassical models (Schilirò, 2019), emphasizing the importance of saving and investing in human capital for rapid growth in the developing world but significantly different from those in assumptions and conclusions as the endogenous growth (Cvetanović, Mitrović, & Jurakić, 2019).

The endogenous theory has dropped the assumption of neoclassical yields and that there is an increase in labor and capital. Consequently, investment in physical and human capital can create external savings and productivity improvements (Sredojević et al., 2016). However, it cannot be said that this theory has wholly ruled out long-term economic growth being determined by external factors and has focused on the importance and accumulation of human capital in achieving growth (Teixeira & Queirós, 2016).

Perhaps the most prominent models of endogenous growth are by Paul Romer (Popa, 2016). This model began with Paul Romer's studies in 1986 and 1990, where he discovered the conditions or the cases in which economic growth was stable when there were no external increases in production (Akcigit, 2017).

Romer's motivation in doing so was influenced by two important observations: the first is that the growth rate in the developed world showed no signs of decline or decrease. The second is that stable growth is possible only when there is no contradiction in returns on capital accumulation (Arnold, 2000).

While various theories of economic growth have been extensively studied in economic thought, the increasing development gap between developed and developing countries has prompted a shift toward exploring alternative frameworks to explain and assess long-term economic growth. The emergence of the New Growth Theory, particularly the Endogenous Growth Model, in the late 1980s and early 1990s has opened new avenues of inquiry, challenging the limitations of neoclassical models in elucidating growth dynamics in diverse economic settings. In this context, this chapter proposes a novel theoretical framework that addresses the complexities of sustaining economic growth specifically within the Gulf Cooperation Council (GCC) States. By integrating the insights from endogenous growth models and considering the unique socioeconomic characteristics of the GCC region, this framework seeks to provide a comprehensive and tailored approach to understanding the determinants of economic growth and formulating effective policy measures to foster sustainable development. The contribution of this chapter lies in its novel synthesis of established growth theories with region-specific considerations, thus offering valuable insights for policymakers, researchers, and stakeholders concerned with the sustainable economic progress of the GCC States.

2. The Economic Growth Theory

2.1 The Concept of Economic Growth

Economic growth has received wide attention in economic thought and is considered an ancient phenomenon, as it is the main feature of a developed economy. It has, therefore, taken an important and prominent place in the economic policies of most world nations (Friedman, 2010). The concept of economic growth is quantitative, reflecting increased production in the long run, and economic growth is defined as the long-term increase in a country's production (Dellink et al., 2017; Kuznets, 1973).

The history of economic thought has shown that most economists such as Adam Smith, Roy Harrod and Evsey Domar, Joseph Schumpeter, Karl Marx, and David Ricardo sought to show the determinants of economic growth and its sustainability conditions (Button, 2011; Muzhani, 2014; Piętak, 2014). According to them, the accumulation of material and human capital was an essential determinant of economic growth, and the principle of division of labor allowed for increased production and, thus, economic development and growth. During the mid-19th century, Robert Solow proposed a new determinant of the growth model by technical progress, which gave great importance to stimulating economic growth as an encouraging factor for national income growth (Zhao, 2019). However, in the late 1980s, endogenous growth theories emerged with Robert Lucas, Robert Barro, and Paul Romer. Based on untraditional factors driving economic growth, such as human capital, innovations, technology, and public spending, it helped to highlight that internal or subjective factors could contribute significantly to economic growth (Popa, 2016).

2.2 The Elements of Economic Growth

2.2.1 Capital Accumulations

Most economists point out the importance of capital consolidation in achieving rates of economic growth, and this process requires the availability of an appropriate amount of actual savings so that resources are provided for investment purposes rather than directed toward areas of consumption (McKinnon, 2010). In order to add to the backlog of capital goods, society must refrain from consuming part of the current production to convert part for investment purposes (Van Duijn, 2013).

Moreover, financing these investments requires the presence of financing agencies capable of mobilizing savings from individuals and various entities, and then providing them to investors. Additionally, there is a need to streamline the investment process to ensure that savings, both accurate and in cash form, are effectively utilized for creating investments, as this process is instrumental in providing financial resources (Lewis & Messy, 2012).

2.2.2 Natural Resources

The resources of a particular economy and its economic growth depend on the quantity and quality of its natural resources: Land, water, solar, wind, soil fertility, mines availability, water, forests, and fossil fuel (Kanazawa, 2021). However, some economists believe that there are no such things as natural resources, as the resources that nature has provided us are worthless to society unless humans can use them to achieve society's economic and social goals and objectives (Davis, 2017). Therefore, the country will likely be rich in natural resources, but its material level or economic growth rate will not be affected at all if these resources remain untapped (Rees, 2019). Therefore, countries must balance supply and demand for scarce natural resources to avoid depleting them (Van der Ploeg, 2011). Therefore, demand conditions and costs must encourage a particular resource's transformation from its natural state.

2.2.3 Labor and Human Capital

The importance of labor has been proven historically as the sum of force and intellectual capacity that can be employed to produce the goods and services necessary to meet its needs, as it is an essential element in increasing production efficiency in a society (Breton, 2017). After that, investment in human resources significantly impacts the productive process.

Furthermore, population growth and, thus, the final increase in the labor force is a traditional positive factor to stimulate economic growth. Increasing the labor force means a more significant increase in the number of productive workers (Bowen & Finegan, 2015). However, despite that, there is disagreement as to whether increased population growth has a positive or negative impact on economic growth (Begum, Sohag, Abdulla, & Jaafar, 2015), for example, in China, such as a labor-surplus country, where the impact of population growth depends on the ability of the economic system to absorb and employ additional workforce. Thus, the labor market's capacity depends mainly on the accumulation rate and type of competencies and the availability of associated factors such as management and organization skills (Cai & Wang, 2010).

2.2.4 Technological Change and Progress

Mughal et al. (2022) argue that technological progress considers to be the most essential element of the process of economic growth. Moreover, Hanushek (2013) considered technology the essential element of economic growth resulting from increased investment in human capital.

Technology progress is classified into three categories: neutral technology, technological progress, and work-saving technology and capital-saving technology (Yemelyanov, Symak, Petrushka, Lesyk, & Lesyk, 2018). Although neutral technological progress occurs at high production levels with the same number of inputs to the elements of production, these simple effects arising from the division of labor can result in high production levels and more consumption for all individuals (Acikgoz & Mert, 2014).

On the other hand, capital-saving technological advance is a rarer phenomenon because most global practical and technological research is carried out by developing countries, which look to provide work rather than capital (Yi, Wang, Sheng, Sharp, & Zhang, 2020). To be noted, enhanced technological advance occurs when the quality, skill, and workforce are upgraded, and similarly, capital-enhancing technological advance is achieved when existing capital goods are used with a productive impact (Szalavetz, 2019).

2.3 The Growth Indicators

2.3.1 Gross National Product (GNP)

It is one of several measures of the well-being of such an economy. It is estimated that the total outcome of productive activity (products and services) is achieved in a country and presented in that country's currency (Brezina, 2011). However, the problem with considering GNP as an economic growth measurement is that each country has its national currency, and therefore, the growth achieved in different countries cannot be compared by this measure. Therefore, a single international currency is often used to assess different countries' national products/outputs, making it easier to compare their growth rates.

2.3.2 Gross Domestic Product (GDP)

One of the most common and significant indicators used to measure economic growth. Thus, GDP can be defined as the total value of all goods and services produced within the local economy (Thakur, 2021; Zeng, 2022). Moreover, Hernández-Ramírez, del Castillo-Mussot, and Hernández-Casildo (2021) explain that the GDP of any national economy is more frequently used as a value of individuals' living standard in the country or purchasing power as well as an economic growth indicator.

2.3.3 Gross National Income (GNI)

Contains the sum of the goods and services produced within a particular country and the income obtained from another (Delhey & Kroll, 2013). Though, this measure has not been met in economic circles by acceptance because increased income – or lack of it – may not lead to positive or negative results.

3. GCC Environment Challenges

The GCC countries have oil-based economies, where oil revenues represent the highest percentage of the government incomes that are considered the trigger for economic growth. Lately, it was noticed that there is a boosted attention toward the challenges associated with oil price fluctuation, and how it impacts the economic growth in oil-based countries (Al-Khouri & Dhade, 2014).

Furthermore, for an extended period of time, there were constant exchange rates in the oil market within the GCC oil-based countries, which referred to the successful coordination of these countries' policies of economy, which in turn assisted in removing and avoiding the currency shocks (El-Sakka & Amin, 2016).

Exploring how oil prices impact stock markets in the GCC countries is a significant field for studying, as the GCC countries are characterized by their substantial primary energy provision to the world and have a vulnerable stock market to oil price fluctuation. As well as these markets are affected by any political change in the area. However, the GCC countries are futural auspicious countries with diversification economic sources (Arouri & Rault, 2012).

Thus, decision-makers are recently facing significant issues regarding the risks of climate change and requirements for securing energy. Addressing these challenges depends on the versatile initiatives that boost the steam of environmental governance efforts.

Though, such challenges develop an impasse for the GCC countries. However, climate change will have a substantial impact on the GCC countries and therefore needs the contribution of these countries in the efforts of mitigation procedures. Nevertheless, the repairs against climate change depend on reducing fossil fuels, particularly oil production and consumption, which is the primary source of economy for the GCC countries (Sever, Tok, & Alessandro, 2019). Several studies have addressed the situations and procedures the GCC countries have conducted regarding climate change and environmental issues. However, environmental concerns in this area are due to the high dependence on gas and oil in these countries, in addition to its massive consumption of energy (Al-Maamary, Kazem, & Chaichan, 2016).

As a result, the countries of the GCC are now the top energy consumers at the world level. This leads to the fact that the environment in GCC countries is in real danger, and actions toward mitigating the consequences of climate change must be taken seriously. In addition, the area has witnessed several natural hazards that have risen recently, and possibilities for more acute crises are expected. However, these natural disasters greatly impacted the GCC countries' competitiveness (Al-Maamary et al., 2016).

A leading example of the willingness of the Gulf countries in the protection of the environment is the Kingdom of Saudi Arabia; this country has lately revised its laws to be harmonious with environmental protection, and this country signed the Protocol of Kyoto in 2005. In addition, though, reports have shown the importance of the GCC countries acting toward a sustainable development strategy soon (D'Souza & Taghian, 2018).

On the other hand, the world is focusing on risk management techniques, becoming famous for preventing and mitigating risks and hazards resulting from climate change and environmental issues. However, this technique is still underrepresented in the GCC countries (Zaidan, Al-Saidi, & Hammad, 2019).

Moreover, the loss from natural events (rainstorms and floods) significantly affected the ecosystems. Mainly, the damage was evident in the agriculture discipline, where food security was unstable in the GCC area (Zaidan et al., 2019). Subsequently, the discussion turns to some of the key environmental challenges faced by GCC states:

3.1 Climate Change

The GCC States face a significant threat from climate change, particularly from the adverse effects of high temperatures. As a result, the GCC economies risk extensive damage, with temperatures projected to rise by up to 4 degrees by the end of the 21st century (Asi, 2021; Howarth, Galeotti, Lanza, & Dubey, 2017). As temperatures increase, climate patterns change, leading to severe weather events such as droughts, floods, wildfires, heat waves, and storms (Clarke, Otto, Stuart-Smith, & Harrington, 2022; Duchenne-Moutien & Neetoo, 2021). For example, heat waves have recently caused significant concern in the GCC countries (Sever, 2019). Other consequences of climate change, such as increased water scarcity, a warmer and less predictable climate, and reduced rainfall, also affect the region (Odhiambo, 2017). These effects of global warming will ultimately reduce the region's biodiversity, aquatic management, and farming, having a significant economic impact. In addition, the economies of the GCC States are heavily reliant on nonrenewable energy sources such as petroleum and gas, with a significant proportion of their GDP coming from fossil fuels (Griffiths, 2017).

This dependence means that these nations are both contributors to and targets of climate change. As a result of the consequences of climate change, including the shift toward renewable energy sources such as solar and wind power, economies worldwide, including the GCC States, are transitioning away from nonrenewable energy sources (Al-Sarihi, 2019; Howarth et al., 2017). This transition will likely harm the GCC States' GDP due to the reduction in oil demand. Therefore, several oil-based GCC economies focus on diversifying their economies by shifting from oil-based to service sectors (Fatima, Mentel, Doğan, Hashim, & Shahzad, 2021).

3.2 Desertification

Desertification is a significant environmental concern worldwide, and arid areas are the most vulnerable to desertification. Human activities are deemed the primary cause of environmental degradation, including desertification (Alam & Azalie, 2023). The agricultural sector is a significant employer and source of income for most households in GCC countries, and a decrease in arable land due to desertification may pose a severe economic threat to the GCC States' economy (Akkas & Altiparmak, 2023). In the Gulf States and the Arabian Peninsula, most of the area in the region is regarded as wastelands or complete deserts with no value. Millions of hectares of land in this region are permanent pastures and have traditionally been the primary foundation for livestock production and growth (Hassen & El Bilali, 2019).

3.3 Biodiversity Loss

Biodiversity loss is a pressing environmental concern for the Gulf countries, as a decline in biodiversity may lead to an irreversible tipping point, causing an ongoing environmental crisis. The GCC countries' terrestrial, coastal, and marine ecosystems are home to various biodiversity, boasting over 5000 endemic plant species and several wild progenitors or relatives of crucial crops, cereals, oil-fiber-yielding crops, vegetables, and fruits. It is impressive how these species adapt to the harsh environment of the GCC States; however, the rates of biodiversity loss in the region due to environmental challenges are alarming. Moreover, biodiversity loss in the GCC countries poses a significant threat to economic growth in the region, as agriculture, forestry, fishery products, and other vital ecosystem activities rely on biodiversity (Bálint et al., 2011). For example, food production depends on biodiversity for various crop vegetation, cross-pollination, nutrient provision, and inherent diversity.

Moreover, medicinal plants and manufactured pharmaceuticals also rely on biodiversity. Biodiversity is also essential for promoting outdoor tourism, as beautiful sceneries, wildlife, and landscapes depend on it for food, clean water, and other ecosystem services. Therefore, decreased biodiversity can lead to reduced food production, increased disease transmission, healthcare costs, and reduced income for the tourism industry due to the destruction of beautiful sceneries and the death of wild and aquatic animals. All these activities are vital for the economic growth of the GCC States (Zhang, Zhou, & Luo, 2023).

3.4 Pollution and Carbon Footprint

The GCC countries are among the top 25 economies contributing to global CO_2 emissions. This is because the GCC economies rely heavily on fossil fuels for economic growth, emitting approximately 45%–50% of the total carbon emissions in the Arab countries (Baydoun & Aga, 2021). Furthermore, the rate of CO_2 emissions in the GCC countries exceeds the global emission rates. For instance, the carbon emissions rate in the United Arab Emirates, Bahrain, Kuwait, and Qatar is approximately 13, 8, 9, and 7, respectively, more than the world average (Bader & Ganguli, 2019; Dkhili & Dhiab, 2019). The high economic growth rate in the GCC economies is linked to increased economic and industrial activities, inevitably leading to increased CO_2 emissions.

Consequently, various research findings by scholars indicate that the significant increase in carbon emissions and pollution in the GCC economies is accompanied by high GDP. In other words, a positive correlation exists between high GDP and an increase in CO_2 emissions. Mining, quarrying, and fuel sectors are undeniably the highest pollutants in the GCC economies. Additionally, the electricity and gas sectors, heavily reliant on fossil fuels, are the third sector emitting CO_2 into the atmosphere (Zaidan et al., 2019).

3.5 Sea Level Rise

Scholars argue that by 2050, more than 800 million people residing in coastal cities will be susceptible to displacement due to the rapid rise in the sea level globally. Consequently, sea levels could increase by more than half a meter in many coastal regions. Being a coastal region, several GCC States are considered at high risk of sea level rise (Al-Maamary, Kazem, & Chaichan, 2017). For example, the Intergovernmental Panel on Climate Change (IPCC) predicts that if the sea level rises by 1.5 meters, Bahrain could lose up to 27% of its coastal land (Malik & Abdalla, 2016). Kuwait is also susceptible to rising sea levels, especially the islands. Warba and most of the Boubyan Islands occasionally flood due to high tides. The United Arab Emirates is already experiencing the adverse effects of climate change, as high sea levels are continuously reshaping the coastlines of Abu Dhabi (Al-Maamary et al., 2017). Several GCC States are also experiencing the adverse effects of high sea levels, such as flooding and displacement. High sea levels in Saudi Arabia are causing flooding in most cities (Dano et al., 2022). The escalation of sea levels could result in catastrophic consequences for GCC countries' coastal settlements and infrastructure. The impact of sea level rise in the GCC States is not restricted to the strain on individuals' infrastructure but extends to coastal ecosystems. This, in turn, could contaminate freshwater aquifers with saltwater intrusion, many of which support agricultural water supplies and natural ecosystems. The resulting water scarcity and reduced food production could have devastating implications for individuals and marine habitats. As a result, the economic growth rate of several GCC economies could decline due to the dependence on agriculture for growth, such as in the case of Saudi Arabia.

Moreover, several GCC economies are shifting from oil-based industries to service sectors like tourism. However, the adverse effects of global warming, including increased temperatures, could negatively impact the service industry and agricultural farming, thereby reducing the sources of income for numerous households in the GCC States. Consequently, this could reduce economic growth (Al-Maamary et al., 2017).

3.6 Waste Generation

Solid waste constitutes a significant ecological concern and a primary source of environmental pollution in the GCC States (Al.Ansari, 2012). This waste contaminates the air, soil, and water, adversely affecting human health (Sarker, Sarker, Islam, & Sharmin, 2013). Waste refers to unwanted or unused materials that are either discarded or anticipated to be disposed of or are mandated to be disposed of (Alajmi, 2016). The management of waste has become a subject of concern for many economies around the globe. Several researchers have established a positive and causal correlation between the amount of substance waste and GDP (Bader & Ganguli, 2019). The GCC waste management market is categorized by waste type, including industrial waste, municipal waste, hazardous waste, plastic waste, and biomedical waste. These wastes are disposed of through collection, landfills, incineration, and recycling. The population growth rate is one of the significant factors and indicators that predict the amount of waste generated in a given country (Thabit, Nassour, & Nelles, 2022). In the GCC countries, around 120 million tons of waste are produced annually (Ouda et al., 2018). Most landfills in the country are on the verge of collapse, and without proper disposal mechanisms, waste products will eventually contaminate the soil, water, and air, leading to environmental and health problems. Therefore, the lack of proper waste management among the GCC States can result in economic and health effects (El Bilali & Ben Hassen, 2020).

4. Suggested Theoretical Framework

This section seeks to establish a comprehensive theoretical framework by incorporating the findings of an extensive range of previous studies, theories, and research gaps. Given the global nature of climate change, the construction of this study's theoretical framework was not confined solely to examining scholarly works focusing on the GCC States. Recognizing that climate change is a global phenomenon, transcending regional and national boundaries, the researcher broadened the scope of the literature review to encompass global articles and studies. This approach ensures a comprehensive understanding of the complex interplay between economic growth, climate indicators, energy indicators, social indicators, and economic resources and their respective impacts across various geographic contexts. Therefore, this chapter has explored the various interactions between economic growth and climate change within different contexts, including but not limited to the GCC States. This approach allows us to distill insights and understand patterns contributing to the complex discourse around economic growth and climate change by encompassing a broad spectrum of international studies. To illustrate, let us consider a range of noteworthy findings from this vast body of research.

In the United States, while actual output was linked to environmental improvements, GDP increases were associated with higher gas emissions. This finding contradicts the Environmental Kuznets Curve (EKC) hypochapter (Dogan & Türkekul, 2015). On the contrary, China found that per capita GDP and energy consumption per unit of GDP correlated with shutting down capacity (Zhang, Zhu, & Bo, 2016). Building upon this, such economic growth is unsustainable due to environmental degradation caused by energy consumption used in production and consumption (Ginez & Tabag, 2023).

Subsequent research has explored these dynamics in greater detail. For instance, financial markets' monetary policy should adjust GDP to charges to compensate for CO_2 emissions in their various sectors (Sane, Hájek, Phiri, Babangida, & Nwaogu, 2022). Furthermore, the study of Zhang, Chen, Wang, and Dong (2022) investigated the nexus of CO_2 emissions, tourism, fossil fuels, and GDP growth in China. This line of inquiry was further extended by Ali, Razman, and Awang (2020), who examined the nexus of population, GDP growth, electricity generation, electricity consumption, and carbon emissions output using time series data (Ali et al., 2020; Zhang et al., 2022).

On the one hand, the significant environmental impact of CO_2 emissions in Bangladesh and India has been underscored (Roy & Halder, 2022), while a reliable causality has been found between energy consumption and economic growth in Kuwait and other single-source, oil-producing countries, such as the GCC states (Al-Zuhair & AL-Bazali, 2022).

Building on these findings, other studies have delved into the issue of CO_2 emissions and its relationship with other economic variables. For example, a causal relationship has been identified between annual CO_2 territorial emissions, crude oil price, energy consumption, and GDP in Ecuador (Nwani, 2017). In contrast, urban CO_2 emissions have been highlighted as a significant problem in China (Wang, Liu, & Shi, 2019).

Furthermore, crude oil production is linked with the rapid increase in US oil production, which has implications for economic growth (Brandt et al., 2016). This line of inquiry was also followed by a decoupling relationship between energy consumption, electricity production, value-added industries, population, and CO_2 emissions by GDP in China (Khan, 2021).

The implications of economic growth on environmental degradation were examined and concluded that economic growth leads to higher CO_2 emissions (Sharif, Hussain, & Qubtia, 2023). Moreover, electricity generation is a significant source of CO_2 emissions in the ASEAN Member States (Triani, 2023). Moreover, population, GDP, nonrenewable energy consumption, and renewable energy consumption impact CO_2 emissions in G-20 Member Countries (Islami, Prasetyanto, & Kurniasari, 2022).

Accordingly, the theoretical framework of this study draws on a wide range of research exploring the complex relationships between economic growth, environmental indicators, energy consumption, and social factors. By integrating these findings, the study seeks to provide a nuanced understanding of these dynamics within the context of the GCC States, ultimately offering valuable insights for policymaking geared toward sustainable development.

Therefore, to better understand these interactions, the author constructs a theoretical framework, as shown in Fig. 14.1, according to the Endogenous Growth theory, the most applicable for this study, which suggests that economic growth is driven by factors within the system (endogenous factors), rather than outside forces (exogenous factors), following the elements of the theoretical framework:

- *Climatic Indicators*: This could be seen as a proxy industrial activity often resulting in increased greenhouse gas emissions, contributing to climate change. The adverse effects of climate change, such as desertification or extreme weather events, can hamper sectors like agriculture and tourism, thus impacting the overall economic growth within the GCC States.
- *Energy Indicators*: Endogenous Growth theory underscores the role of capital accumulation and technological change. For the GCC States, harnessing technologies to improve energy efficiency and renewable energy sources can drive economic growth while mitigating environmental impacts.
- *Social Indicator*: This is another critical factor in the Endogenous Growth Theory; high population density in GCC countries can fuel demand for goods and services, propelling GDP growth. However, unchecked growth could lead to resource depletion and social inequality. On the other hand, a highly educated populace may also drive innovation, contributing to economic growth.
- *Economic Resources Indicator*: This aspect is part of the capital and can also be seen as evidence of how the GCC's wealth in hydrocarbon resources plays a vital role in their economies. Advancements in technologies for oil extraction can increase productivity and boost GDP, but may also escalate environmental challenges if not counter-balanced with sustainability measures.

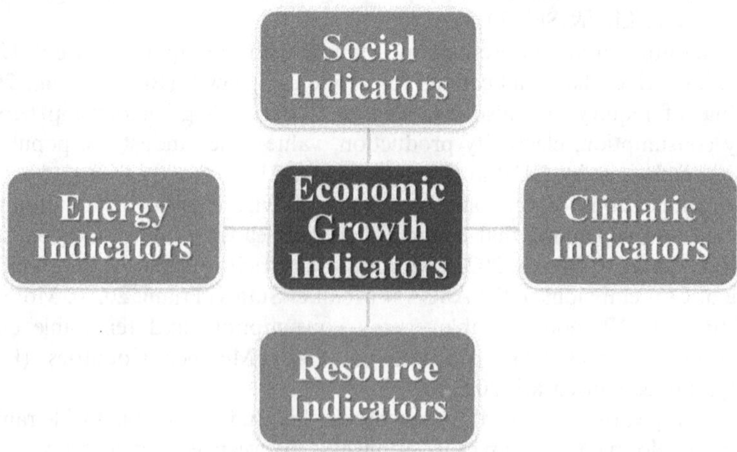

Fig. 14.1. Theoretical Framework. *Source:* Authors.

The theoretical framework can be developed by examining the interplay between these variables and the potential feedback loops that may exist. For example, economic growth may lead to increased energy consumption, contributing to higher CO_2 emissions and climate change. Climate change impacts, such as changes in temperature and precipitation patterns, can then affect economic growth by influencing factors like agricultural productivity and energy demand. Simultaneously, population density can influence the demand for resources and the capacity of the GCC States to adapt to climate change, while the reliance on oil production as an economic resource can exacerbate environmental challenges.

Therefore, a comprehensive theoretical framework should consider the complex interactions between economic growth, climate indicators, energy indicators, social indicators, and economic resources. Understanding these interactions can provide valuable insights for policymakers in the GCC States as they seek to promote sustainable development, mitigate climate change impacts, and ensure long-term economic growth.

5. Conclusion

In conclusion, this comprehensive study has provided a nuanced exploration of the intricate relationship between economic growth, environmental indicators, energy consumption, and social factors within the context of the GCC States. This chapter has successfully integrated a wide range of research findings to construct a theoretical framework based on the Endogenous Growth theory, which posits that economic growth is driven by internal factors rather than external forces.

The study has underscored the critical role of climatic indicators, energy indicators, and social indicators in shaping the economic trajectory of the GCC States. It has highlighted how industrial activity, often associated with increased greenhouse gas emissions, can contribute to climate change, thereby impacting sectors like agriculture and tourism and, consequently, the overall economic growth within the GCC States.

Moreover, this chapter has emphasized the potential of technological advancements in energy efficiency and renewable energy sources to drive economic growth while mitigating environmental impacts. It has also shed light on the social dynamics within the GCC States, noting how high population density can fuel demand for goods and services, propelling GDP growth. However, unchecked growth could lead to resource depletion and social inequality, underscoring the need for sustainable development strategies.

This chapter has also delved into the economic and environmental challenges faced by the GCC States, providing a detailed analysis of the impact of oil prices on their economies and the need for economic diversification. It has highlighted the significant environmental challenges, including climate change and desertification, and the need for the GCC States to adopt mitigation strategies.

In light of these findings, the study underscores the need for the GCC States to balance economic growth with environmental sustainability. It calls for a shift toward more sustainable practices, harnessing technological advancements, and implementing policies that promote social equity.

The insights gleaned from this study have significant implications for policymakers in the GCC States and beyond, offering a roadmap toward sustainable economic growth. Future research could further explore the practical implementation of the strategies discussed in this chapter and evaluate their effectiveness in promoting economic growth while mitigating environmental impacts.

In summary, this chapter provides a valuable contribution to the literature on economic growth and sustainability, particularly within the context of the GCC States. It offers a robust theoretical framework and insightful analysis that can guide future research and policymaking in this critical area.

References

Acikgoz, S., & Mert, M. (2014). Sources of growth revisited: The importance of the nature of technological progress. *Journal of Applied Economics*, *17*(1), 31–62. doi:10.1016/S1514-0326(14)60002-7

Akcigit, A. (2017). Economic growth: The past, the present, and the future. *Journal of Political Economy*, *125*(6), 1736–1747. doi:10.1086/694617

Akkas, E., & Altiparmak, S. O. (2023). Innovation, technology transfer, and endogenous growth in the GCC countries. In *Social change in the Gulf region: Multidisciplinary perspectives* (pp. 397–413). Singapore: Springer Nature.

Al.Ansari, M. S. (2012). Improving solid waste management in Gulf co-operation council states: Developing integrated plans to achieve reduction in greenhouse gases. *Modern Applied Science*. doi:10.5539/mas.v6n2p60

Al-Khouri, R., & Dhade, A. (2014). The role of savings in reducing the effect of oil price volatility for sustainable economic growth in oil based economies: The case of GCC countries. *International Journal of Economics and Finance*, *6*, 172. doi:10.5539/ijef.v6n4p172

Al-Maamary, H., Kazem, H., & Chaichan, M. (2016). Changing the energy profile of the GCC states: A review. *International Journal of Applied Engineering Research*, *11*, 1980–1988.

Al-Maamary, H. M., Kazem, H. A., & Chaichan, M. T. (2017). Climate change: The game changer in the Gulf cooperation council region. *Renewable and Sustainable Energy Reviews*, *76*, 555–576.

Al-Sarihi, A. (2019). Climate change and economic diversification in Saudi Arabia: Integrity, challenges, and opportunities. *Policy Chapter*, *1*, 11–12.

Al-Zuhair, M., & AL-Bazali, T. (2022). Causality between energy consumption and economic growth: The case of Kuwait. *International Journal of Energy Economics and Policy*. doi:10.32479/ijeep.13477

Alajmi, R. G. (2016). The relationship between economic growth and municipal solid waste & testing the EKC hypochapter: Analysis for Saudi Arabia. *Journal of International Business Research and Marketing*, *1*, 20–25.

Alam, M., & Azalie, I. A. (2023). Greening the desert: Sustainability challenges and environmental initiatives in the GCC states. In *Social change in the Gulf region: Multidisciplinary perspectives* (pp. 493–510). Singapore: Springer Nature.

Ali, S. S., Razman, M. R., & Awang, A. (2020). The Nexus of population, GDP growth, electricity generation, electricity consumption and carbon emissions output in Malaysia. *International Journal of Energy Economics and Policy*. doi:10.32479/ijeep.8987

Arnold, L. G. (2000). Endogenous technological change: A note on stability. *Economic Theory*, *16*(1), 219–226.

Arouri, M., & Rault, C. (2012). Oil prices and stock markets in GCC countries: Empirical evidence from panel analysis. *International Journal of Finance and Economics*, *17*, 242–253. doi:10.1002/ijfe.443

Asi, Y. M. (2021). *Climate change in the Arab World: An existential threat in an unstable region*. Washington, D.C.: Arab Center.

Bader, Y., & Ganguli, S. (2019). Analysis of the association between economic growth, environmental quality and health standards in the Gulf Cooperation Council during 1980–2012. *Management of Environmental Quality: An International Journal*. doi:10.1108/meq-03-2018-0061

Bálint, M., Domisch, S., Engelhardt, C., Haase, P., Lehrian, S., Sauer, J., . . . Nowak, C. (2011). Cryptic biodiversity loss linked to global climate change. *Nature Climate Change*, 313–318.

Baydoun, H., & Aga, M. (2021). The effect of energy consumption and economic growth on environmental sustainability in the GCC countries: Does financial development matter? *Energies*. doi:10.3390/en14185897

Begum, R., Sohag, K., Abdulla, S., & Jaafar, M. (2015). CO2 emissions, energy consumption, economic and population growth in Malaysia. *Renewable and Sustainable Energy Reviews*, *41*, 594–601. doi:10.1016/j.rser.2014.07.205

Bowen, W., & Finegan, T. (2015). *The economics of labor force participation*. Princeton, NJ: Princeton University Press.

Brandt, A. R., Yeskoo, T., McNally, M. S., Vafi, K., Yeh, S., Cai, H., & Wang, M. (2016). Energy intensity and greenhouse gas emissions from tight oil production in the Bakken formation. *Energy & Fuels*. doi:10.1021/acs.energyfuels.6b01907

Breton, A. (2017). *The economic theory of representative government*. New York, NY: Routledge.

Brezina, C. (2011). *Understanding the gross domestic product and the gross national product*. New York, NY: The Rosen Publishing Group, Inc.

Button, K. (2011). The economist's perspective on regional endogenous development. In R. Stimson, R. Stough, & P. Nijkamp (Eds.), *Endogenous regional development: Perspectives, measurement and empirical investigation (New Horizons in regional science series)* (pp. 20–39). Cheltenham: Edward Elgar Publishing.

Cai, F., & Wang, M. (2010). Growth and structural changes in employment in transition China. *Journal of Comparative Economics*, *38*(1), 71–81. doi:10.1016/j.jce.2009.10.006

Clarke, B., Otto, F. E., Stuart-Smith, R., & Harrington, L. J. (2022). Extreme weather impacts of climate change: An attribution perspective. *Environmental Research Climate*. doi:10.1088/2752-5295/ac6e7d

Cvetanović, S., Mitrović, U., & Jurakić, M. (2019). Institutions as the driver of economic growth in classic, neoclasic and endogenous theory. *Economic Themes*, *57*(1), 111–125.

Dano, U. L., Abubakar, I. R., AlShihri, F. S., Ahmed, S. M., Alrawaf, T. I., & Alshammari, M. S. (2022). A multi-criteria assessment of climate change impacts on urban sustainability in Dammam Metropolitan Area, Saudi Arabia. *Ain Shams Engineering Journal*, 102062.

Davis, K. (2017). The case for and against business assumption of social responsibilities. *Academy of Management Journal*, *16*(2).

Delhey, J., & Kroll, C. (2013). A "Happiness Test" for the new measures of national well-being: How much better than GDP are they? In *Human happiness and the pursuit of maximization* (pp. 191–210). Singapore: Springer. doi:10.1007/978-94-007-6609-9_14

Dellink, R., Chateau, J., Lanzi, E., & Magné, B. (2017). Long-term economic growth projections in the shared socioeconomic pathways. *Global Environmental Change*, 200–214. doi:10.1016/j.gloenvcha.2015.06

Dkhili, H., & Dhiab, L. B. (2019). Management of environmental performance and impact of the carbon dioxide emissions (CO2) on the economic growth in the GCC countries. *Marketing and Management of Innovations*. doi:10.21272/mmi.2019.4-20

Dogan, E., & Türkekul, B. (2015). CO2 emissions, real output, energy consumption, trade, urbanization and financial development: Testing the EKC hypochapter for the USA. *Environmental Science and Pollution Research*. doi:10.1007/s11356-015-5323-8

D'Souza, C., & Taghian, M. (2018). Small and medium size firm's marketing competitive advantage and environmental initiatives in the Middle East. *Journal of Strategic Marketing*, *26*, 568–582.

Duchenne-Moutien, R. A., & Neetoo, H. (2021). Climate change and emerging food safety issues: A review. *Journal of Food Protection*. doi:10.4315/jfp-21-141

El Bilali, H., & Ben Hassen, T. (2020). Food waste in the countries of the gulf cooperation council: A systematic review. *Foods*, *9*, 463.

El-Sakka, M., & Amin, Z. (2016). Determining real exchange rate fluctuations in the oil-based GCC economies. *Asian Economic and Financial Review*, *6*, 374–389. doi: 10.18488/journal.aefr/2016.6.7/102.7.374.389

Fatima, T., Mentel, G., Doğan, B., Hashim, Z., & Shahzad, U. (2021). Investigating the role of export product diversification for renewable, and non-renewable energy consumption in GCC (Gulf Cooperation Council) countries: Does the Kuznets hypochapter exist? *Environment, Development and Sustainability*. doi:10.1007/s10668-021-01789-z

Friedman, B. M. (2010). *The moral consequences of economic growth*. New York, NY: Vintage Books.

Ginez, E. K., & Tabag, E. J. (2023). Eco-efficiency and sustainability: An analysis for the Philippines. *Journal of Economics Finance and Accounting Studies*. doi:10.32996/jefas.2023.5.1.4

Griffiths, S. (2017). Renewable energy policy trends and recommendations for GCC countries. *Energy Transitions*, 1–15.

Hanushek, E. (2013). Economic growth in developing countries: The role of human capital. *Economics of Education Review*, 204–2012. doi:10.1016/j.econedurev.2013.04.005

Hassen, T. B., & El Bilali, H. (2019). Food security in the gulf cooperation council countries: Challenges and prospects. *Journal of Food Security*, 159–169.

Hernández-Ramírez, E., del Castillo-Mussot, M., & Hernández-Casildo, J. (2021). World per capita gross domestic product measured nominally and across countries with purchasing power parity: Stretched exponential or Boltzmann–Gibbs distribution? *Physica A: Statistical Mechanics and Its Applications*, *568*, 125690. doi:10.1016/j.physa.2020.125690

Howarth, N., Galeotti, M., Lanza, A., & Dubey, K. (2017). Economic development and energy consumption in the GCC: An international sectoral analysis. *Energy Transitions*. doi:10.1007/s41825-017-0006-3

Islami, F. S., Prasetyanto, P. K., & Kurniasari, F. (2022). The effect of population, GDP, non-renewable energy consumption and renewable energy consumption on carbon dioxide emissions in G-20 member countries. *International Journal of Energy Economics and Policy*. doi:10.32479/ijeep.12548

Kanazawa, M. (2021). *Natural resources and the environment: Economics, law, politics, and institutions*. New York, NY: Routledge.

Khan, R. (2021). Beta decoupling relationship between CO2 emissions by GDP, energy consumption, electricity production, value-added industries, and population in China. *PLoS One*. doi:10.1371/journal.pone.0249444

Kuznets, S. (1973). Modern economic growth: Findings and reflections. *The American Economic Review*, *63*(3), 247–258.

Leimbach, M., Kriegler, E., Roming, N., & Schwanitz, J. (2017). Future growth patterns of world regions – A GDP scenario approach. *Global Environmental Change*, *42*, 215–225. doi:10.1016/j.gloenvcha.2015.02.005

Lewis, S., & Messy, F. (2012). Financial education, savings and investments: An overview. *OECD Working Chapters on Finance, Insurance and Private Pensions*, *22*. doi:10.1787/5k94gxrw760v-en

Malik, A., & Abdalla, R. (2016). Geospatial modeling of the impact of sea level rise on coastal communities: Application of Richmond, British Columbia, Canada. *Modeling Earth Systems and Environment*, 1–17.

McCombie, J. (2000). The Solow residual, technical change, and aggregate production functions. *Journal of Post Keynesian Economics*, *23*(2), 267–297. doi:10.1080/01603477.2000.11490280

McCombie, J., & Thirlwall, A. (2016). *Economic growth and the balance-of-payments constraint*. London: Palgrave Macmillan.

McKinnon, R. I. (2010). *Money and capital in economic development*. Washington, D. C.: Brookings Institution Press.

Mughal, N., Arif, A., Jain, V., Chupradit, S., Shabbir, M., Ramos-Meza, C., & Zhanbayev, R. (2022). The role of technological innovation in environmental pollution, energy consumption and sustainable economic growth: Evidence from South Asian economies. *Energy Strategy Reviews*, *39*, 100745. doi:10.1016/j.esr.2021.100745

Muzhani, M. (2014). *Mainstream growth economists and capital theorists: A survey*. Montreal: McGill-Queen's University Press.

Nwani, C. (2017). Causal relationship between crude oil price, energy consumption and carbon dioxide emissions in ecuador. *Opec Energy Review*. doi:10.1111/opec.12102

Odhiambo, G. O. (2017). Water scarcity in the Arabian Peninsula and socio-economic implications. *Applied Water Science*, 2479–2492.

Ouda, O. K., Peterson, H. P., Rehan, M., Sadef, Y., Alghazo, J. M., & Nizami, A. S. (2018). A case study of sustainable construction waste management in Saudi Arabia. *Waste and Biomass Valorization*, 2541–2555.

Piętak, Ł. (2014). Review of theories and models of economic growth. *Comparative Economic Research*, *17*(1), 45–60.

Popa, F. (2016). Aspects concerning endogenous growth in the macroeconomic theories. *Economics, Management, and Financial Markets*, 231–243.

Rees, J. (2019). *Natural resources: Allocation, economics and policy*. New York, NY: Routledge.

Roy, T. K., & Halder, N. (2022). Factors impact on population and environment in Bangladesh and India. *Man Environment and Society*. doi:10.47509/mes.2022.v03i01.03

Sane, M., Hájek, M., Phiri, J., Babangida, J. S., & Nwaogu, C. (2022). Application of decoupling approach to evaluate electricity consumption, agriculture, GDP, crude oil production, and CO2 emission nexus in support of economic instrument in Nigeria. *Sustainability*. doi:10.3390/su14063226

Sarker, B. C., Sarker, S. K., Islam, M. S., & Sharmin, S. (2013). Public awareness about disposal of solid waste and its impact: A study in Tangail Pourashava, Tangail. *Journal of Environmental Science and Natural Resources*. doi:10.3329/jesnr.v5i2.14821

Schilirò, D. (2019). The growth conundrum: Paul Romer's endogenous growth. *International Business Research*, *12*(10).

Sever, S. D. (2019). Agenda-setting, progress and challenges for environmental policy transfer in the Gulf Cooperation Council. *Brazilian Journal of Policy and Development*, 61–85.

Sever, S., Tok, M., & Alessandro, C. (2019). Global environmental governance and the GCC: Setting the agenda for climate change and energy security. In *Global governance and Muslim organizations* (pp. 197–227). Singapore: Springer.

Sharif, F., Hussain, I., & Qubtia, M. (2023). Energy consumption, carbon emission and economic growth at aggregate and disaggregate level: A panel analysis of the top polluted countries. *Sustainability*. doi:10.3390/su15042935

Sredojević, D., Cvetanović, S., & Bošković, G. (2016). Echnological changes in economic growth theory: Neoclassical, endogenous, and evolutionary-institutional approach. *Economic Themes*, *54*(2), 177–194.

Stimson, R., & Stough, R. (2016). Regional economic development methods and analysis: Linking theory to practice. In J. Rowe (Ed.), *Theories of local economic development* (pp. 191–214). London: Routledge.

Szalavetz, A. (2019). Digitalisation, automation and upgrading in global value chains – Factory economy actors versus lead companies. *Post-Communist Economies*, *31*(5), 646–670. doi:10.1080/14631377.2019.1578584

Teixeira, A., & Queirós, A. (2016). Economic growth, human capital and structural change: A dynamic panel data analysis. *Research Policy*, *45*(8), 1636–1648. doi:10.1016/j.respol.2016.04.006

Thabit, Q., Nassour, A., & Nelles, M. (2022, November). Facts and figures on aspects of waste management in Middle East and North Africa region. *Waste*, *1*, 52–80.

Thakur, S. (2021). Regional sustainable development and natural resource decision-making in India: Methods and implications. In B. Thakur, R. Thakur, S. Chattopadhyay, & R. Abhay (Eds.), *Resource management, sustainable development and governance. sustainable development goals series* (pp. 105–131). Singapore: Springer. doi:10.1007/978-3-030-85839-1_7

Triani, M. (2023). Prediction of carbon dioxide emission from electricity generation in Asean. *Indonesian Journal of Urban and Environmental Technology*. doi:10.25105/urbanenvirotech.v6i1.14810

Van Duijn, J. J. (2013). *The long wave in economic life*. London: Routledge.

Van der Ploeg, F. (2011). Natural resources: Curse or blessing? *Journal of Economic Literature*, 366–420.

Wang, H., Liu, G., & Shi, K. (2019). What are the driving forces of urban CO2 emissions in China? A refined scale analysis between national and urban agglomeration levels. *International Journal of Environmental Research and Public Health*. doi:10.3390/ijerph16193692

Yemelyanov, O., Symak, A., Petrushka, T., Lesyk, R., & Lesyk, L. (2018). Assessment of the technological changes impact on the sustainability of state security system of Ukraine. *Sustainability*, *10*(40), 1–24. doi:10.3390/su10041186

Yi, M., Wang, Y., Sheng, M., Sharp, B., & Zhang, Y. (2020). Effects of heterogeneous technological progress on haze pollution: Evidence from China. *Ecological Economics*, *169*(106533), 1–11. doi:10.1016/j.ecolecon.2019.106533

Zaidan, E., Al-Saidi, M., & Hammad, S. H. (2019). Sustainable development in the Arab World – Is the Gulf Cooperation Council (GCC) region fit for the challenge? *Development in Practice*, *29*, 670–681. doi:10.1080/09614524.2019.1628922

Zeng, W. (2022). Research on the quality of China's GDP data. In *A study of quality management of official statistics in China. Research series on the Chinese dream and China's development path* (pp. 97–126). Singapore: Springer. doi:10.1007/978-981-33-6602-2_6

Zhang, M., Chen, M., Wang, X., & Dong, Y. (2022). A nexus of CO2, tourism industry, GDP growth, and fossil fuels. *Frontiers in Environmental Science*. doi:10.3389/fenvs.2022.912252

Zhang, Y., Zhou, W., & Luo, D. (2023). The relationship research between biodiversity conservation and economic growth: From multi-level attempts to key development. *Sustainability*, *15*, 3107.

Zhang, W., Zhu, Y., & Bo, W. (2016). Empirical analysis on the factors influencing China's sulfur dioxide emissions based on IPAT. doi:10.14257/astl.2016.121.18

Zhao, R. (2019). Technology and economic growth: From Robert Solow to Paul Romer. *Human Behavior and Emerging Technologies*, 62–65. doi:10.1002/hbe2.116

Chapter 15

Emotional Intelligence, Job Satisfaction, and Work Engagement at a Public University

Martha Esther Guerra Muñoz[a], *Rober Trinidad Romero Ramirez*[a] *and Freddy David Zuluaga Guerrra*[b]

[a]Universidad Popular del Cesar, Colombia
[b]Universidad Industrial de Santander, Colombia

Abstract

This chapter provides a literature review on the topic of emotional intelligence (EI) in the workplace. Quantitative methods were used, with surveys sent to a predetermined sample and processed with the SPSS statistical package. The overall aim of the study was to investigate the effect of EI based on self-awareness, self-management, empathy, and relationship management on work engagement in a public university. One hundred eight professors at the public university. The data for this study were collected by means of a questionnaire. In total, there are 23 questions on a Likert scale. Cronbach's alpha showed that the reliability of the instrument was higher than 0.763. In light of the data, it has been shown that there is correlation between self-awareness, self-management, relationship management, empathy with both work engagement and job satisfaction. Furthermore, the results show that EI is significantly related to both university loyalty and job happiness. Only a conditional link was created between professors' achievements and the success of the public university.

Keywords: Engagement emotional intelligence; empathy; self-management; self-awareness; job satisfaction; work engagement

Technological Innovations for Business, Education and Sustainability, 223–234

doi:10.1108/978-1-83753-106-620241015

1. Introduction

Emotional intelligence (EI) has the potential to bring enormous real-world benefits to the education sector. Improved interpersonal connections at work and increased efficiency and output are just some of them. This means more success and happiness for the person concerned. Increased morale and participation are two positive outcomes for the institution. Having happy professors who work harder, care about their work, and contribute to first-class results is another advantage (Soto-Rubio, Giménez-Espert, & Prado-Gascó, 2020). Because of the influence universities have on global culture, the policies they implement will have an impact on all faculty and the communities they are charged with representing. As technology advances and universities expand, a human-centered approach is more important than ever. According to Domingo and Díaz (2022), in these times of transition, we need a new direction, an emotional compass, to guide and channel our actions for the good of our own and those around us.

This anchor should help strengthen the quality of emotional self-awareness. In theory, greater EI will provide a more level playing field in business and business planning. However, the conventional business perspective puts profit before ethics and human rights. Therefore, until there is sufficient reason for companies and businesses to integrate EI into a plan, verifiable economic and profitability advantages must be established. In universities, the value of a teacher is constantly measured in terms of the products or services they provide. This will force universities to choose profit over teacher welfare. However, the individual will share in the success of the university as a whole, both in terms of their coworkers and the customers they serve. According to Sudibjo and Sutarji (2020), studies have shown the benefits of IT for many different industries, but the link between individual success and performance has only been shown indirectly.

2. The Connection Between EI and Job Success

According to Pérez-Correa, Pedraza-Álvarez, y Viloria-Escobar (2022), one of the most important functions of EI is how information is interpreted and processed. EI, as he describes it, is the ability to recognize and respond appropriately to one's own emotions. Taking constructive action to recognize these feelings are two of the three most important factors he elucidated in relation to the development of a teacher's EI.

Fuster, Segura, Guillen, and Ramirez (2020) argued against the idea that a person needs a single capacity for self-awareness, impulse control, internal motivation, knowledge of self and others, and attention to interactions, feelings and the application of this knowledge to one's own and others' strategies. According to Huaranga-Toledo, Ruiz, Vergara, and Rodríguez (2023), a university's EI improves the project manager's ability to understand his own emotions and those of his team members. It recognizes negative emotions and helps professors to deal with them for the benefit of the university.

The rate of progress is more reliable in people with compelling social talents and more meaningful occupations (Coronado-Guzmán, Valdivia-Velasco,

Aguilera-Dávila, & Alvarado-Carrillo, 2020; Ramírez, Colichón, & Barrutia, 2020), and the same is true for increased work efficiency and university management. Team members with high EI are more analytically capable and more likely to achieve their goals. EI, interpersonal success, and management styles have been found to have a strong relationship according to studies on the subject.

3. Teacher Performance, Emotional Intelligence, and Job Engagement

Having a job is indicative of a more ambitious, rewarding, committed, and dedicated mindset (Extremera, Mérida-López, Sánchez-Álvarez, Quintana-Orts, & Rey, 2019). Teacher engagement has been linked to better performance in a number of areas, such as external presentation, university goals, and operational procedures (Bonilla-Yucailla, Balseca-Acosta, Cárdenas-Pérez, & Moya-Ramírez, 2022). People who work hard at work tend to be more successful in life and make greater contributions to their universities (Tortosa et al., 2020). Professors' engagement to the success of the university is the hallmark of a job well done (Huerta-Soto, Vergara, Brito, & Tinoco, 2023). Dedicated professors will put in extra hours to develop their capacity to adapt. The success of any university is directly proportional to the level of engagement of its professors. The regulation of how individuals operate and perform their activities is predictable, which makes teacher engagement in the workplace beneficial to the individual and to the university as a whole (Rojas-Vega, Brito, Medrano, & Leiva, 2023).

Engagement of professor is also crucial (Coronado-Guzmán et al., 2020). A strong, focused, and dedicated work ethics are manifestations of the right mindset (Castillo, Fernández, Camones, & Guerra, 2022). Many people involved in their work find inspiration in their level of dedication. Instead of having a negative effect on burnout, specialists should prioritize productive communities by emphasizing contact. Integration in the workplace decreases the potential for burnout and increases competence at work (Gong, Wu, Huang, Yan, & Luo, 2020). Professor who has access to important personal assets are an asset to any university (Fernandez-Martinez et al., 2019). For starters, because they are better able to handle constructive criticism, administrators and students are more likely to solicit feedback from professors who exude confidence in themselves and their abilities (self-assets) (Alsughayir, 2021). Professors need feedback to help them become more effective on their own (individual development). Traditional methods of achieving goals often involve the use of EI. In addition to comprehensive personality assessments and conscientious behavior, meaningful intervention takes place (Ahad, Mustafa, Mohamad, Abdullah, & Nordin, 2021).

Positive acts involving EI and productivity are indicative of a teacher who is committed to their work. The extent to which EI is used is a reliable indicator of professional success. Dedication to work can help professors find a healthy balance between their professional and personal lives (Moreno-Fernandez et al., 2020). An adequate amount of personal assets is important for professors' effort and success in the workplace. Professors are more motivated when they have access to a positive social environment at work (Milhem, Muda, & Ahmed, 2019):

- Self-awareness is directly related to the work engagement of professors at a public university.
- Self-management is directly related to the work engagement of professors at a public university.
- Relationship management is directly related to the work engagement of professors at a public university.
- Empathy is directly related to the work engagement of professors at a public university.

4. Methodology

The sample size is 108 professors from the public university. The data for this study were collected by means of a questionnaire. In total, there are 23 questions on a Likert scale. Cronbach's alpha showed that the reliability of the instrument was higher than 0.763, which indicates that the content of the questionnaires used in this study has been verified by three experts. SPSS (V26) was used to handle and analyze the data, also, multiple regression analysis was performed. The *R*-value represents the strength of the correlation between the dependent and independent variables, and the direction of the sign indicates whether the correlation is negative or positive. The *R*-squared value is often used to indicate the "goodness of fit" of a regression model. Differences between 0 and 1 are possible. It exemplifies how the independent variable characterizes changes in the equation. A higher *R*-squared indicates that the model describes the observed data of the dependent variable well.

The *p*-value of the test is commonly referred to as the significance. Acknowledging the possibility of different hypotheses is indicative of the level of confidence one has. If the significance is below the 5% or 10% threshold, then the null hypothesis cannot be rejected. However, a multiple regression with a standard error of 5% was used to analyze the connection between the dependent and independent variables.

5. Results

Males made up 58% of those preferring the above outcomes, while females accounted for 42%. Seventeen percent were aged 23–33, 36% were aged 34–44, 34% were aged 45–55, and 13% were aged 56 and over.

Below are the results of the regression study, in which the dependent variable was job satisfaction, as can be seen in Tables 15.1 and 15.2. We will then analyze the relationship between job satisfaction and the other factors. But this is how we know that the theories are correct: $Y_1 = A + BX_1 + BX_2 + BX_3 + BX_4 + BX_5$.

Table 15.1. Regression Analysis in Job Satisfaction.

Model	***R***	***R* Square**	**Adjusted *R* Square**	**Standard Error of the Estimate**
1	0.681[a]	0.563	0.542	0.023201

[a]Predictors: (Constant), work engagement, empathy, self-management, self-awareness, relationship management.

Table 15.2. Job Satisfaction Contrast.

	Unstandardized Coefficients		**Standardized Coefficients**		
Model	***B***	**Standard Error**	**Beta**	***t***	**Significance**
(Constant)	0.014	0.007		1.902	0.479
Self-awareness	0.196	0.082	0.174	2.392	0.022
Self-management	−0.191	0.088	−0.001	−2.17	0.031
Relationship management	0.197	0.079	0.105	2.493	0.027
Work engagement	0.533	0.068	0.586	7.877	0.019
Empathy	−0.438	0.106	−0.026	−4.132	0.018

Professor satisfaction = 0.479 + 0.022 Self-awareness + 0.031 Self-management + 0.027 Relationship management + 0.019 Work engagement + 0.018 Empathy management.

However, the results of another regression study in which work engagement was the dependent variable are presented below: Since only a single dependent variable can be sampled at a time, we will construct a second regression instead. This is followed by an analysis of the relationship between work engagement and the other factors. But this is how we know the theories are correct:

H1: There is a relation between self-awareness and job satisfaction.

H2: There is a relation between self-management and job satisfaction.

H3: There is statistical data showing a relation between relationship management and job satisfaction.

H4: There is statistical data between empathy management and job satisfaction.

H5: There is statistical data showing a relation between job engagement and job satisfaction.

The regression analysis above was used to examine the connection between the dependent and independent variables using a 5% confidence interval. All variables had a margin of error of less than 5%, indicating a significant association and leading to the rejection of *H0* and acceptance of *H1*, as can be seen in Tables 15.3 and 15.4. However, to verify the conclusions of the analysis, the following regression equation will be used: $Y_2 = A + BX_1 + BX_2 + BX_3 + BX_4 + BX_5$.

A teacher's engagement to the university is calculated as follows:

Work engagement = 0.031 + 0.021 self-awareness + 0.019 self-management + 0.032 relationship management + 0.034 job satisfaction + 0.026 empathy management.

Therefore, an increase in self-awareness usually has a multiplier effect on work engagement of 1.5 percentage points.

Engagement usually increases by 2% for every 1% increase in self-management.

Engagement typically increases by 2.7% for every 1% improvement in relationship management.

Engagement typically changes by 2.3% for every 1% improvement in job satisfaction.

Table 15.3. Regression Analysis of Job Engagement.

Model	***R***	***R* Square**	**Adjusted *R* Square**	**Standard Error of the Estimate**
1	0.533[a]	0.368	0.357	0.496

[a]Predictors: (Constant), self-awareness self-management-relationship management, empathy, job satisfaction.

Table 15.4. Work Engagement Contrast.

Model	**Unstandardized Coefficients**		**Standardized Coefficients**		
	B	**Standard Error**	**Beta**	***t***	**Significance**
(Constant)	0.748	0.324		2.304	0.031
Self-awareness	0.385	0.078	0.107	4.935	0.021
Self-management	0.389	0.076	0.408	5.125	0.019
Relationship management	−0.23	0.059	−0.039	−3.898	0.032
Empathy	−0.22	0.094	−0.017	−2.34	0.026
Job satisfaction	0.173	0.075	0.189	2.3	0.034

H1: A one percentage point increase in empathy is relation with a 3.5% change in teacher engagement.

H2: In view of the data, we accept the null hypothesis that there is a relation between self-awareness and job satisfaction.

H3: There is statistical data showing a relation between self-management and job satisfaction.

H4: There is statistical data between empathy and job satisfaction.

H5: There is statistical data showing a relation between organizational loyalty and job satisfaction.

6. Discussion

This study has revealed numerous problems in interactions between managers and professors. Managers can exert authority over subordinates, instill confidence in their staff and steer the university in the desired direction, according to a review of the literature on the subject. Managers can foster a welcoming workplace culture to show how the two are at odds, or they can create an unwelcoming and stressful culture. Managers may have no empathy for university professors.

Managers may be demanding and difficult to deal with, while professors' efforts may be ignored or rewarded. The job satisfaction and engagement of the study participants were analyzed, along with the impact that the EI sessions had on these parameters. The results demonstrated the importance of these factors for principal–teacher interaction, which is often overlooked. Good managers are cooperative, tolerant, responsible, empathetic, and appreciative, but often neglect these traits because they are too focused on achieving university goals (Castro, Castillo, Camones, & Cochachin, 2022). These characteristics, which are vital for managerial skills, were discovered by the research.

Professors value their relationship with their managers and expect their supervisors to maintain a close working relationship with them. According to the data, professors care about the regularity of their interactions with their managers. They care about their managers and need common ground, encouragement, sympathy, and easy access to function as a cohesive unit.

Professors pay attention to the personality and quirks of their managers, and the computer skills of their supervisors can have a significant impact on morale and productivity. Professors' motivation levels may change depending on their estimates of their supervisors' EI skills. Participants noted that their bosses are not good leaders, and some even used words such as "dictators" and "tyrants" to describe them. However, others reported feeling inspired and emotionally attached to their superiors. There is at least one study that suggests that EI skills are more important for leadership success than IQ. This is consistent with findings in the published literature (Soto, Avalos, Albornoz, & Aguilar, 2022). EQ competences are valued similarly to IQ and are considered a crucial connection between EQ and EQ competences.

According to the literature reviewed, many professors learn to suppress their feelings at work. This hinders their ability to manage their superiors. According to the data collected here, the manager's EI skills are only put into practice in one context: that of the individual. This supervisor does not recognize the critical need to deploy EI skills everywhere. This important finding may not resonate with some managers, but EI has a significant influence on management, motivation, and leadership. Experts agreed that management did not use EI when discussing difficult issues such as performance reviews with staff.

The results of the study reaffirmed the importance of participants' EI skills. Their development reflects the daily interactions they have with their supervisors and the influence these managers have on their own pay, job happiness, and performance. This finding lends credence to the argument made in the literature that managers' EI skills are crucial to inspiring their staff, boosting morale and productivity in the workplace. Without the ability to develop and use EI skills, managers may have less of a sense of collaboration with their professors, which could have a negative impact on morale, job satisfaction, and productivity. Due to a lack of EI skills, managers lacked confidence in themselves and their abilities, and felt dissatisfied with their work and their career in general (Saehu, Diah, Julca-Guerrero, Huerta-Soto, & Valderrama-Plasencia, 2022). Some respondents said they were motivated to do their best for the people they worked with, while others said they knew that their increased job satisfaction was due to their EI skills.

Managers thought they were emotionally intelligent because they could identify with professors' feelings and respond to their wants and needs in the workplace. These individuals spoke highly of their managers because their managers inspired them to work harder, made them feel prouder of their profession, and brought the team closer together. The high degree of EI shown by their supportive and encouraging bosses may explain why so few participants disliked their work and did not continue to strive to achieve the goals set by the university. It seems that the boss felt harassed by the participant because of his unfavorable attitude toward the teacher and his antagonistic behavior toward another professor.

The researcher did not turn a blind eye to the boss's harmful behavior, as she understood how things appeared to be when the boss was away. This fits with literature suggesting that people react negatively to an aggressive and hostile environment because of the emotional experiences and memories they have stored in their brains as a result of their interactions with others. Several respondents reacted negatively to managers' lack of empathy compared to managers with higher levels of EI (Ramirez et al., 2022). This is consistent with findings from the literature on how individuals should relate to each other. When there is a lack of empathy, people learn to repress their emotions and not show their true feelings. Some have blamed the low self-esteem of managers for professors' lack of EI skills. Participants had the opportunity to share their ideas and opinions through open-ended questions. Participants' views on EI skills and the motivation of their bosses were the focus of the first research. The majority of respondents believed that they had found evidence of EI skills and motivation from the participants' bosses. Some professors claimed that their supervisors boosted their morale with their EI skills, while others admitted that their bosses' lack of EI skills had the opposite effect (Soto et al., 2023). Some claimed to be intrinsically motivated, while others admitted that their superiors' lack of EI skills was a factor.

Overall, the participants agreed that there is a relationship between how they rate their bosses' EI and how happy they are in their job. Professors' satisfaction with their managers has increased, according to some surveys. EI managers were not very happy with their work because of their lack of knowledge. 61% of the respondents said that their success was linked to how well they regarded their bosses in the EI. The majority of respondents said they had become better at using their EI in managerial positions.

One of the most important modern resources for teaching and developing EI skills is the EI model. Finally, most survey participants recognized the importance of managers being aware of and valuing their emotional and professional strengths. The research literature supports these findings. All participants agreed that the EI skills of their supervisors had a significant impact on their motivation, job satisfaction, and productivity. According to the results, professors' motivation, sense of work, and overall performance are affected by the EI skills of their supervisors.

Since creative universities can only judge themselves by their profits, managers who are in charge of specific professor need EI to do their jobs well. Learning the mechanics of shared concepts can help them connect on an emotional level. Each specialist in their respective disciplines has their own profile of strengths and limitations, and so does each university.

7. Conclusion

In light of the data, it has been shown that there is a correlation between self-awareness, self-management, relationship management empathy with both work engagement and job satisfaction. This strengthens that EI is considered a crucial area of study in advanced societies. It has a significant impact on the behavior of a university's teaching staff, as well as on their ability to make decisions and cope with possible crisis situations. It is also vital to focus on the internal and external factors that impact on professors' behavior and EI. Sectoral research can also be conducted to assess the EI of stakeholders with a view to improving the economic fortunes of the country by cultivating human capital. More research needs to be done on how different aspects of a university's culture and structure affect the impact of professors' EI on their ability to communicate.

The improved connection between managers and professors that can result from these findings could have far-reaching social effects. The research will be useful for philanthropists, educators, social activists, and public policy reformers because it will address challenges and suggest solutions that can help administrators, HR professionals, and university authorities to better connect with their professors.

To better manage IT, previous literature highlighted the need for EI. The results of the study showed that professors who work closely with their managers have a more positive and professional impression of those interactions. The literature review does not include these details. When managers and leaders understand the importance of this connection, it can help set a path for all parties to be significantly friendlier at work.

Human resource experts can take full advantage of this research by improving their ability to recruit, attract, and develop competent managers. One way to find ways to increase productivity, reduce turnover, and attract the best talent is to learn more about the teacher–teacher partnership and the positive outcomes that can result from it.

References

Ahad, R., Mustafa, M. Z., Mohamad, S., Abdullah, N. H. S., & Nordin, M. N. (2021). Work attitude, work engagement and emotional intelligence of Malaysian vocational college professor. *Journal of Technical Education and Training*, *13*(1), 15–21. Retrieved from https://publisher.uthm.edu.my/ojs/index.php/JTET/article/view/7898

Alsughayir, A. (2021). The effect of emotional intelligence on work engagement: Understanding the mediating role of job satisfaction. *Management Science Letters*, *11*(4), 1309–1316. doi:10.5267/j.msl.2020.11.008

Bonilla-Yucailla, D., Balseca-Acosta, A., Cárdenas-Pérez, M. J., & Moya-Ramírez, D. (2022). Inteligencia emocional, compromiso y autoeficacia académica. Análisis de mediación en universitarios ecuatorianos. *Interdisciplinaria*, *39*(2), 249–264. doi:10.16888/interd.2022.39.2.16

Castillo, A., Fernández, C. E., Camones, O. G., & Guerra, M. E. (2022). Digitalización de la cadena de suministro y la competitividad de las empresas peruanas del sector minorista. *Revista Científica Epistemia*, *6*(2), 77–95. doi:10.26495/re.v6i2.2297

Castro, J. A., Castillo, A., Camones, O. G., & Cochachin, L. F. (2022). Mejoramiento del servicio al cliente y ampliación de las oportunidades de venta mediante el uso de tecnología de punta en el comercio textil peruano. *Revista Científica Epistemia*, *6*(2), 35–49. doi:10.26495/re.v6i2.2294

Coronado-Guzmán, G., Valdivia-Velasco, M., Aguilera-Dávila, A., & Alvarado-Carrillo, A. (2020). Compromiso organizacional: antecedentes y consecuencias. *Conciencia tecnológica*, *60*. Retrieved from https://www.redalyc.org/articulo.oa?id=94465715006

Domingo, B. G., & Díaz, J. Q. (2022). Inteligencia Emocional como Predictor de Satisfacción en Docentes de Infantil y Primaria. REICE: Revista Iberoamericana sobre Calidad. *Eficacia y Cambio en Educación*, *20*(4), 51–68. Retrieved from https://portalcientifico.uned.es/documentos/6334f9d5a91e865f2fdd031e

Extremera, N., Mérida-López, S., Sánchez-Álvarez, N., Quintana-Orts, C., & Rey, L. (2019). Un amigo es un tesoro: inteligencia emocional, apoyo social organizacional y engagement docente. *Praxis & Saber*, *10*(24), 69–92. doi:10.19053/22160159.v10.n25.2019.10003

Fernandez-Martinez, E., López-Alonso, A. I., Marques-Sanchez, P., Martínez-Fernández, M. C., Sanchez-Valdeon, L., & Liebana-Presa, C. (2019). Emotional intelligence, sense of coherence, engagement and coping: A cross-sectional study of university students' health. *Sustainability*, *11*(24), 6953. doi:10.3390/su11246953

Fuster, D. E., Segura, V. R., Guillen, P. E., & Ramirez, E. H. (2020). Professor empathy in the development of bilingual communication strategies. *International Journal of Early Childhood Special Education (INT-JECSE)*, *12*(1), 542–551. doi: 10.9756/INT-JECSE/V12I1.201036

Gong, Y., Wu, Y., Huang, P., Yan, X., & Luo, Z. (2020). Psychological empowerment and work engagement as mediating roles between trait emotional intelligence and job satisfaction. *Frontiers in Psychology*, *11*, 232. doi:10.3389/fpsyg.2020.00232

Huaranga-Toledo, H. L., Ruiz, J. R., Vergara, C. S., & Rodríguez, J. L. (2023). Cultura organizativa y el crecimiento empresarial de la medianas empresa de la ciudad de Huaraz, Perú. *Revista Científica Epistemia*, *7*(1), 01–13. doi:10.26495/re.v7i1.2426

Huerta-Soto, C. E., Vergara, C. S., Brito, C., & Tinoco, L. F. (2023). Desarrollo del ecosistema digital en los países de sudamérica durante la pandemia por COVID-19. *Revista Científica Epistemia*, *7*(1), 14–37. doi:10.26495/re.v7i1.2431

Milhem, M., Muda, H., & Ahmed, K. (2019). The effect of perceived transformational leadership style on employee engagement: The mediating effect of leader's emotional intelligence. *Foundations of Management*, *11*(1), 33–42. doi:10.2478/fman-2019-0003

Moreno-Fernandez, J., Ochoa, J. J., Lopez-Aliaga, I., Alferez, M. J. M., Gomez-Guzman, M., Lopez-Ortega, S., & Diaz-Castro, J. (2020). Lockdown, emotional intelligence, academic engagement and burnout in pharmacy students during the quarantine. *Pharmacy*, *8*(4), 194. doi:10.3390/pharmacy8040194

Pérez-Correa, K., Pedraza-Álvarez, L., & Viloria-Escobar, J. (2022). Inteligencia emocional y compromiso laboral. *Revista Venezolana de Gerencia*, *27*(99), 1140–1150. doi:10.52080/rvgluz.27.99.18

Ramírez, E. H., Colichón, M. E., & Barrutia, I. (2020). Rendimiento académico como predictor de la remuneración de egresados en Administración, Perú. *Revista Lasallista de Investigación*, *17*(2), 88–97. doi:10.22507/rli.v17n2a7

Ramirez, E. H., Rosario, H. S., Laura, N. V., Hober, H. T., Julio, V. A., & Victor, F. L. (2022). Distribution of public service and individual job performance in Peruvian municipality, *20*(10), 11–17. doi:10.15722/jds.20.10.202210.11

Rojas-Vega, J. A., Brito, E., Medrano, W., & Leiva, O. C. (2023). Relación de la responsabilidad empresarial en los conflictos medioambientales y sociales en una unidad minera de la Región Ancash. *Revista Científica Epistemia*, *7*(1), 69–82. doi: 10.26495/re.v7i1.2436

Saehu, M. S., Diah, A. M., Julca-Guerrero, F., Huerta-Soto, R., & Valderrama-Plasencia, L. (2022). Environmental awareness and environmental management practices: Mediating effect of environmental data distribution. *Journal of Environmental Management & Tourism*, *13*(5), 1339–1352. doi:10.14505/jemt.v13.5(61).11

Soto-Rubio, A., Giménez-Espert, M. D. C., & Prado-Gascó, V. (2020). Effect of emotional intelligence and psychosocial risks on burnout, job satisfaction, and nurses' health during the COVID-19 pandemic. *International Journal of Environmental Research and Public Health*, *17*(21), 7998. doi:10.3390/ijerph17217998

Soto, R. H., Asis, E. H., Figueroa, R. P., & Plasencia, L. (2023). Autoeficacia emprendedora y desempeño de micro y pequeñas empresas peruanas. *Revista Venezolana de Gerencia: RVG*, *28*(102), 751–768. doi:10.52080/rvgluz.28.102.19

Soto, R. M., Avalos, M., Albornoz, J. I., & Aguilar, S. J. (2022). Competencias digitales de los profesores universitarios durante la pandemia por COVID-19 en el Perú. *Revista electrónica interuniversitaria de formación del profesorado*, *25*(1), 49–60. doi:10.6018/reifop.500481

Sudibjo, N., & Sutarji, T. (2020). The roles of job satisfaction, well-being, and emotional intelligence in enhancing the professor' employee engagements. *Management Science Letters*, *10*(11), 2477–2482. doi:10.5267/j.msl.2020.4.002

Tortosa, B. M., del Carmen Pérez-Fuentes, M., del Mar Molero, M., Soriano, J. G., Oropesa, N. F., del Mar Simón, M., ... Gázquez, J. J. (2020). Engagement académico e Inteligencia Emocional en adolescentes. *European Journal of Child Development, Education and Psychopathology*, *8*(1), 111–122. doi:10.30552/ejpad.v8i1.136

Chapter 16

Entrepreneurial Capabilities and Survival of Microentrepreneurs in Rural Peru

Edwin Hernan Ramirez Asis

Universidad Nacional Santiago Antunez de Mayolo, Peru

Abstract

Microenterprises (MEs) are vital to the growth and prosperity of economies around the world. All levels of society, from universities to national governments, have collaborated to improve the chances of survival and future growth of these businesses. The threat to life is serious, and unless concerted action is taken, the situation will spiral out of control. Policymakers and business leaders must work together to address the sustainability crisis. The study, therefore, set out to determine how various entrepreneurial skills (such as creativity, collaboration, networking, and risk-taking) affect the long-term viability of MEs. The overall objective of the study was to determine the importance of innovative problem-solving, collaboration, networking, and willingness to take calculated risks of microentrepreneurs for the long-term success of their businesses. A total of 274 microentrepreneurs in rural areas of the Ancash region of Peru were surveyed in the grocery, hardware, clothing, and food service sectors. The survival of the MEs was tested on four dimensions: innovation, leadership, networking, and risk-taking. According to the results, MEs managers can increase their longevity by cultivating creative skills, strengthening leadership as a key to business sustainability and survival, maximizing the use of networks to gain a market advantage and expand their customer base, and employing calculated risk-taking.

Keywords: Innovation; risk-taking; networking; entrepreneurship; leadership; sustainability; survival of microentrepreneurs; rural areas

Technological Innovations for Business, Education and Sustainability, 235–248

doi:10.1108/978-1-83753-106-620241016

1. Introduction

Almost all national economies rely heavily on microenterprises (MEs) as the main engines of growth. Since Schumpeter's early work, researchers have believed that MSEs and invention are intimately and favorably associated (Ramírez-Torres, 2022).

There is an alarming failure rate among MEs in their first three years of operation. Academics, politicians, and governments are also notable for their efforts to improve the viability and subsequent establishment of MEs. Many MEs struggle to be profitable in the long term. According to Zuluaga-Arango, Useche Rincón, and Rojas Berrio (2023), in today's competitive and rapidly changing organizational contexts, MEs need to strengthen their entrepreneurial skills. They believe that entrepreneurial expertise is crucial for the long-term health and prosperity of an enterprise. MEs include corporations, partnerships, and even family businesses that sell their products to the public. In the modern business landscape, MEs can be found in a wide variety of shapes and sizes and can form close links with large corporations. It can be difficult, if not impossible, to distinguish between a small enterprise and a large one when both are associated. Economists often classify MEs using standard quantitative measures and then add descriptive adjectives to describe their size. The number of employees is often used as a proxy for the size of a firm (Ynzunza & Izar, 2021).

The regulatory definition of a small or medium-sized enterprise takes into account factors such as number of employees and sales. The European Commission has identified this as a primary need (Manzaneque, Merino, & Sánchez, 2021). In Peru, MEs are defined as those with between one and nine employees, while small enterprises have between 10 and 99 employees. In this context, "work" does not automatically correspond to the actual number of workers employed, whether fully or partially paid (Acosta-Véliz & Jiménez-Cercado, 2020). Firms with more than 10 employees are excluded from this study.

2. Literature Review

A theory attempts to account for, predict, and analyze outliers as well as validate or extend accepted knowledge within certain parameters (Acosta-Véliz & Jiménez-Cercado, 2020). A strategy based on theoretical analysis can help to sustain or continue the research. The research is presented in a theoretical framework that explains how and when the topic of study arose. Current ideas should be provided in a theoretical context, including their terms, interpretations, and references to appropriate scientific literature. The theoretical framework demonstrates an awareness of the relevance of these principles for related research.

Galicia-Gopar, Mendoza-Ramírez, and Espinosa-Trujillo (2020) stress the importance of the researcher's personal philosophy and awareness of the relevance of the study and the researcher's role in conducting the research and applying its results. The value and meaning of the analysis lose its clarity without a theoretical framework. The researcher's theoretical framework includes the theory used for the analysis of the topic as well as the underlying assumptions, interpretations, and conclusions of this theory.

3. Innovation Theory or Schumpeterian Innovation Theory

Plans are believed to be effective, but coming up with new options is challenging (Hinojo-Lucena, Aznar Díaz, & Romero Rodríguez, 2020). If you are stuck in your business, it is worth reflecting deeply on the problem. Although it is not a simple procedure, it is clear that good ideas would be implemented. However, building the whole structure on such a weak foundation would be a poor choice, given the difficulty of the task (Boza-Valle, Narcisa, & Yolanda, 2020, pp. 1–23). It is crucial that the core concept of the enterprise makes sense (Hinojo-Lucena et al., 2020). Whether or not a company is able to successfully manage competition or compete for viability and existence determines the adaptability of the product that is produced and spread.

There are emerging financial transactions, new types of sustainable value creation, and profit erosion. Changes in this area should be seen as disruptive rather than a gradual process of "creative destruction". Developers are inspired by disruptive ideas to go beyond the status quo. Companies are blamed for job losses due to wage stagnation (Khalid, Raza, Sawangchai, Allauca, & Huerta, 2021; Zhang, Raza, Khalid, Parveen, & Ramírez-Asís, 2021). Revenues increase and new fields of development practice develop. When marketing or manufacturing new products or services, companies can look inward for inspiration. They can revitalize themselves by innovating and adapting their own methods, systems, or capabilities. They can play a defining and adaptive role of many kinds in the established market strategy. To meet the high standards of innovation, it is necessary to draw on a pool of expertise and practical experience in a particular subject or business.

4. Teoría del Liderazgo por Objetivos

Según Huaranga-Toledo, Ruiz, Vergara, and Rodríguez (2023), el liderazgo es la capacidad de ejercer influencia sobre subconjuntos de los miembros de un grupo. La capacidad de examinar, valorar y acordar lo que se puede hacer y cómo hacerlo es esencial. Para alcanzar un objetivo compartido, Pinzón (2021) describió la gestión como un proceso que influye en muchos individuos. El liderazgo es un proceso, el liderazgo implica influir en los demás, el liderazgo se produce en un grupo, el liderazgo consiste en alcanzar un objetivo, y los participantes y seguidores luchan por cuál debe ser ese objetivo. El liderazgo se considera un proceso y no un atributo otorgado a unos pocos individuos selectos desde su nacimiento. El intercambio entre los líderes y sus representantes es el núcleo del proceso de liderazgo. El liderazgo es una estrategia que asegura la motivación de sus seguidores, ya sea favorable o adversa. Según Arias-Vargas, Ribes-Giner, Botero-Arango, and Garces (2021), la gestión no es un proceso lineal, sino más bien un esfuerzo cooperativo entre un líder y sus subordinados; en este arreglo, el líder ejerce autoridad sobre sus seguidores y no al revés. Cualquiera puede participar; no se limita a quienes tienen dotes naturales de liderazgo. Para ser más específicos, los grupos formales poderosos no tienen por qué tener un único líder (Loyaga, Ballena, Arboleda, & Lama, 2021; Raza, Wisetsri, Chansongpol, Somtawinpongsai, & Ramírez, 2020).

¿Hacia qué? Según Bote-López (2021), el estilo proporciona un marco para los subordinados en forma de lista de control, una exigencia de participación y un conjunto de directrices orientadas al logro. En consonancia con los requisitos previos para el éxito y las estructuras existentes, dilucida las prioridades y ofrece sugerencias específicas para alcanzar los objetivos requeridos. Un líder que se preocupa por sus empleados responde a sus necesidades y fomenta un entorno en el que los empleados sienten que su trabajo importa. Sin embargo, el líder tiene la última palabra sobre los procedimientos de compromiso, como consultar a los empleados antes de tomar una decisión. Los directivos orientados a los resultados exigen mucho a sus empleados, insisten en que rindan al máximo, les empujan a mejorar la productividad en cada oportunidad que se les presenta y les aseguran que tendrán que rendir cuentas de sus acciones y que se les apoyará cuando trabajen para lograr objetivos importantes (Huerta-Soto, Vergara, Brito, & Tinoco, 2023).

5. Innovative Capacity and the Prosperity of MEs

Antonizzi and Smuts (2020) argue that MEs that fail to leverage technical talents in a complex and competitive marketplace are doomed to fail. Declining market share related to adoption is making MEs that continuously innovate more likely to survive. To thrive, you have to use your imagination (Ali, Kan, & Sarstedt, 2016). According to conventional wisdom, there is a direct correlation between organizational creativity and performance (Manzaneque et al., 2021).

According to Ali, Sirkova, and Ferencova (2015), innovation increases profits. The implementation of an innovation strategy can be beneficial for MEsS in many situations, as it allows entrepreneurs to obtain rents through temporary monopolistic development. Monopoly rents can be granted for longer periods of time to smaller firms than to larger ones, as the former will be in operation earlier. To differentiate themselves from their rivals, MEs need to develop novel technologies, techniques, or market models targeted at appropriate niches (Tenemesa, Macías, Quijije, & Coya, 2021). Since consumers value uniqueness in innovation, MEs benefit from high brand loyalty and low-price responsiveness in the industry. Due to their size and flexibility, MEs play a crucial role in meeting the demand for desirable creative goods (Tenemesa et al., 2021).

However, no research has shown that innovation threatens the viability of firms (Rodríguez, Choez, & González, 2022). Organizations' efforts to pursue more resource-intensive innovations, both monetary and technological, are the main focus of this effect (Figueroa-Soledispa, Parrales-Reyes, & katiuska Peña-Ponce, 2022; Ramirez, Mukthar, Norabuena, Yslado, & Guerra, 2021). While further analysis suggests that the favorable benefits of innovation on survival may be significant, it also suggests that the firm has not benefited from innovation in recent years. Despite mounting evidence supporting a causal relationship between innovation and development, no link between invention and continued existence has been demonstrated. There is also a need for an in-depth analysis of the impact of research efforts on the long-term viability of an organization (Rodríguez et al., 2022).

6. Leadership Skills and MEs Prosperity

According to research by Ali et al. (2015), Effective management is viewed as a competitive advantage and a means to increase operational efficiency. To ensure that employees are motivated to perform their work effectively, MEs can reap the rewards of transactional leadership (Demuner-Flores, 2021). By using metaphorical concepts and their application, forming a point of view based on first-hand experience, and establishing a commitment to the goal, visionary leaders develop an optimistic picture of a future world (López-Lemus & Garza Carranza, 2019). Harmony, participation, trust, motivation, and development can be outcomes of visionary leadership in today's organizations.

Their fate is determined solely by the quality of their leadership. However, previous research has shown that managers must act on initiatives that seek a change in the direction or experience of the company, providing the necessary advice (Correia-Caetano, 2022). Cárdenas, Ramos, Beltrán, and Pazos (2019) assert that confidence, imagination, charisma, passion, sense of humor, and vision are characteristics of "reasonable" leaders. The challenge for today's leaders is to balance the ideals, aspirations, and expectations of many stakeholders in an ever-changing and often self-inflicted world. Management, according to Ramirez, Mora, Silva, and Amaral (2019), is essential for business success. As companies expand, so do their cravings for formidable leadership and success. Those who possess the skill of management are highly sought after and financially rewarded. Leadership is said to have a significant impact on the success of MEs (Arango-Benjumea, 2022).

7. Networking and the Achievements of MEs

Networking facilitates the marketing efforts of small enterprises by opening up communication channels with numerous target audiences and improving the interconnectedness of social capital (Cárdenas et al., 2019). When it comes to improving productivity, networking is crucial for MEs. Small business owners and managers can improve their marketing skills by participating in networking events. Accordingly, Ramirez et al. (2021) argue that MEs use networking in the form of clusters, strategic alliances, and business arrangements as a competitive weapon. According to Tenemesa et al. (2021), there seems to be a connection between networking and MEs in both formal and informal settings.

A cohesive network is made up of people who are all or almost all involved. According to Díaz, Andrade, and Ramírez (2019), firms can gain confidence to take calculated risks by participating in informal networking events. Businesses can also develop networks for the purpose of gathering data, ideas, and expert opinions. In particular, micro business owners can gain access to research and development services often reserved for large firms. They could also form R&D joint ventures.

Firms will have to compete with similar assets owned by other economic actors, work with fewer resources, and sell parts of the supply chain. As economic activities become embedded in wider networks of organizations, internal contacts are crucial for the development and exploration of market potential (Aragón-Falomir & Cárdenas, 2020). Martínez-Peña and Delgado-Vélez (2020) state that when launching a new venture, it is critical to leverage existing networks to identify weaknesses, potential sources of innovation, and applicable talents. Potential partners are hesitant to put themselves at risk publicly or risk losing their equity, reputation, or savings. Launch is facilitated through deep-rooted partnerships with partners, which are reinforced by mutual trust and investment (Cárdenas et al., 2019). Networks provide access to information, making it less difficult to identify an equity firm (Muñoz, Matabanchoy, & Guevara, 2020).

8. Risk-Taking and the Prosperity of MES

According to the World Economic Forum, fundamental financial issues, rising prices, rapidly expanding supply chains, and ongoing development contribute to a more volatile global business climate. Despite methodological concerns, the last decade has seen good financial circumstances for global economic progress and wealth. The initial official role of the industry was risk management. Risk-taking style, also known as risk perception and management of environmental hazards, is often an essential part of an entrepreneur's personality (Alvarado-Lagunas, Morales Ramírez, & Ortiz Rodríguez, 2020).

Despite cultural differences in risk-taking, several researchers have shown that small business managers, CEOs, and corporations around the world perceive themselves to be in a relatively similar situation when faced with potentially disastrous decisions. Entrepreneurs take calculated risks with the present moment very much in mind. Within a functional risk assessment paradigm, prudent decision-making is required (Hameed & Irfan, 2019). Since entrepreneurship is intrinsically linked to a variety of unknowns, experts advise aspiring entrepreneurs to be bold and accessible. Workers prefer to take risks even when they have some agency and financial reward, as found by García-Leonard and Sorhegui-Rodríguez (2020). They concluded that entrepreneurs do not become inventive or take risks because they "should", but rather because they need to.

9. Methodology

The main consideration for determining the sample size was the population of MEs in the highlands of the Ancash region. It is considered an infinite population, so there is a sample of 385 microentrepreneurs. Only 274 of the 385 microentrepreneurs filled in the survey. In this study, information was collected through a questionnaire. A questionnaire designed to obtain the specified data is an example of a data collection instrument. It consists of 25 questions on a Likert scale. The content of the questionnaires used in this study was validated by three experts, and Cronbach's alpha proved the reliability of the instrument with a value greater than 0.758.

The data collection procedure shows how to interact with respondents to collect information. Stratified random sampling was used to better understand the opinions of the traders. Initially, each respondent was categorized according to the category (grocery, hardware, food, and clothing). Respondents were given frame surveys and asked to complete them immediately, but if they could not concentrate or were otherwise distracted, they were given the option to leave the questions and return to them at a later time.

Using a linear regression model with a significance level of 0.05, which was drawn from the *p*-value of the variable, we compared each participant's independent variables (innovation, communication skills, networking ability, and risk-taking ability) with the dependent variable (microenterprise survival [MES]). When deciding whether or not to reject the null hypothesis, we used a multi-tailed test with a significance level of 0.05 for both the total variable and the dependent variable. When the *p*-value was less than or equal to half the defined sum (*p*-value/2), the empirical hypotheses were eliminated as unclear. The researcher struggled to find evidence that contradicted the null studies (or ideas that there was a relationship between the variables examined) in order to reach this conclusion.

10. Multiple Regression Analysis

MES was tested against four dimensions: innovation, risk, leadership, and networking. The theoretical basis was used to develop the research model. A diagram illustrating the interaction of these factors is presented below:

- $Ys = \beta 0 + \beta\, 1 \times 1 + \beta\, 2 \times 2 + \beta\, 3 \times 3 + \beta\, 4 \times 4$, where
- Ys = survival of SMEs
- $\beta 0$ = constant (coefficient of intercept)
- $X1$ = innovation
- $X2$ = risk
- $X3$ = leadership
- $X4$ = networking
- 1 ... $\beta 4$ = regression coefficient of the four variables.

The overall significance of the model was examined by analysis of variance (ANOVA) with a significance threshold of 0.05.

11. Regression Analysis

Table 16.1 shows the results of a regression analysis performed on the dependent and independent variables, with a significance level of 5%. *H0* would be rejected and *H1* accepted, respectively, if the significance threshold was below 5%. A statistically significant correlation was observed between all independent variables at the 5% level or lower. The coefficients of innovation (0.039), risk (0.041), leadership (0.030), and networking (0.031) point in the direction of MES. Using the data in Table 16.2, the following calculation could be made:

Survival = 0.026 + 0.038 (Innovations) + 0.043 (Risk) + 0.032 (leadership) + 0.034 (Networking).

It was shown that:

- MES will be affected by 3.9% for each unit increase in innovation and by 4.1% for each unit increase in risk.
- MES improves by 3% for each unit increase in leadership.
- The survival of MEs will be affected by 3.1% for each unit increase in networking.

Table 16.1. Regression Analysis.

Model Summary				
Model	R	R^2	Adjusted R^2	Std Error of the Estimate
1	0.588[a]	0.546	0.517	0.00214

Source: Author's original work.

[a]Predictors: (Constant), networking, risk, innovations, leadership.

Table 16.2. Analysis of Variance Test.

ANOVA[a]						
Model		**Sum of Squares**	**df**	**Mean Square**	F	**Sig.**
1	Regression	0.023	3	0.007	12.047	0.000[b]
	Residual	0.054	271	0.001		
	Total	0.082	274			

Source: Author's original work.

[a]Dependent variable: Survival.

[b]Predictors: (Constant), networking, risk, innovations, leadership.

Table 16.3. Model Testing.

	Coefficients					
		Unstandardized Coeff.		Standardized Coeff.		
Model		*B*	Std. Error	Beta	*T*	Sig.
1	(Constant)	0.027	0.011		2.429	0.026
	Innovations	0.287	0.121	0.081	2.388	0.038
	Risk	0.283	0.128	0.198	2.031	0.043
	Leadership	0.271	0.105	0.080	2.609	0.032
	Networking	0.342	0.091	0.377	3.738	0.034

Source: Author's original work.

Therefore, according to Table 16.3, the following hypotheses can be examined:

- Statistics support an association between innovation and MES.
- MEs benefit from leadership to promote the survival of their businesses.
- The ability to network effectively is correlated with the survival of MEs.
- Accepted statistical theory relates risk-taking ability to MES.

12. Discussion

This article aims to do just that: to analyze how innovation helps Ukrainian MEs to expand. In most cases, respondents report coming up with new ideas twice a year. Most of those who participated in the survey used mobile banking applications to integrate their businesses with other digital tools. Internet marketing, short message service (SMS) banking, and robotic process automation are just some of the technological advances made by MEs (López-Lemus & Garza Carranza, 2019). Many firms have already promoted themselves once despite efforts to rebrand. The inferential statistics in this chapter show strong correlations between creative capacity and MEs success. In the past, people used to agree that coming up with new products, processes, and markets was essential for the growth and prosperity of a company.

The secondary objective of the study was to examine how entrepreneurial leadership affects the development of MEs. The authors of the study attribute this to the leaders of MEs. The research also revealed that many institutions are equipped with the electronic means of communication of their choice, such as telephones and emails. Most of the participating employers made at least one payment to employees for good performance.

In addition, the majority of respondents stated that routing, role modeling, and final control and order were beneficial to business success. According to the results, the leaders of these MEs had a significant impact on business success. These results are in line with those found by Arango-Benjumea (2022), who argues that effective corporate leadership enables more creative and collaborative problem-solving by staff and higher overall productivity.

The third study sought to investigate how effective networking influences the long-term viability of MEs. The data showed that several participants provided services to other joint providers, called on former clients, and listed several revenue streams in order to expand their professional network. The results show that a large number of respondents were involved in at least three social factors. While some participants used their free time to relax, the vast majority focused on preparing for leadership positions. In addition, the results showed that most participants engaged in conferences, seminars, exhibitions, and discussion groups as significant social networking activities. On the social networking platform chosen for the research, the use of WhatsApp has increased. Overall, the inferential statistics of this study imply that networking skills have a significant and positive effect on the long-term viability of small businesses. Consumer success in the digital realm is linked to the effectiveness with which new connections can be made and new possibilities created (Rojas-Vega, Brito, Medrano, & Leiva, 2023).

The secondary objective of the study was to determine the impact of risks on the long-term viability of MEs in the EU. The vast majority of the surveyed entrepreneurs did not take significant risks to improve their business situation (Martínez-Peña & Delgado-Vélez, 2020). In addition, the vast majority of respondents have conducted a risk assessment of their business. According to the data collected, the vast majority of participants thought that the longevity of companies was influenced by factors such as correct risk analysis, proper risk assessment, and calculated measures.

Inferential statistics show that risk-taking skills contribute significantly to the long-term viability of small businesses. Based on these results, we can state that calculated risk-taking is essential for small firms expanding into novel markets and product categories.

13. Conclusion

The long-term viability and success of MEs were the driving forces of this study. Enterprises of various sizes were included in the analysis, although the focus was on those with fewer than 274 microentrepreneurs. It would be interesting to conduct a similar study in a rural area and compare the results.

Creativity, co-operation, networking, and the ability to take calculated risks are the four pillars of successful entrepreneurs. The effects of many other types of entrepreneurial qualities, such as experience and management skills, can also be investigated. The main concern of this study is how microenterprises can improve their chances of survival. Entrepreneurship is crucial for MEs, so similar studies could investigate its effects on leadership and production.

The findings of this study suggest that the success of an enterprise depends to a large extent on the knowledge and experience of its management team. Other elements that can improve the long-term viability of microenterprises could be examined, such as government policy interventions, financing flexibility, location flexibility, recordkeeping, marketing expertise, and economic conditions.

References

Acosta-Véliz, M. M., & Jiménez-Cercado, M. E. (2020). Modelo de gestión empresarial del Ecuador. Revista Científica FIPCAEC (Fomento de la investigación y publicación científico-técnica multidisciplinaria). *Polo de Capacitación, Investigación y Publicación (POCAIP)*, *5*(5), 115–131. ISSN: 2588-090X. doi:10.23857/fipcaec.v5i5.218

Ali, M., Kan, K. A. S., & Sarstedt, M. (2016). Direct and configurational paths of absorptive capacity and organizational innovation to successful organizational performance. *Journal of Business Research*, *69*(11), 5317–5323. doi:10.1016/j.jbusres.2016.04.131

Ali, V., Sirkova, M., & Ferencova, M. (2015). The impact of organizational culture on creativity and innovation. *Polish Journal of Management Studies*, *14*(1), 7–17. doi:10.17512/pjms.2016.14.1.01

Alvarado-Lagunas, E., Morales Ramírez, D., & Ortiz Rodríguez, J. (2020). Determinantes de la probabilidad de robo a micronegocios en el área metropolitana de Monterrey. *Revista de economía*, *37*(94), 57–80. doi:10.33937/reveco.2020.129

Antonizzi, J., & Smuts, H. (2020). The characteristics of digital entrepreneurship and digital transformation: A systematic literature review. In M. Hattingh, M. Matthee, H. Smuts, I. Pappas, Y. Dwivedi, & M. Mäntymäki (Eds.), *Responsible design, implementation and use of information and communication technology. I3E 2020. Lecture Notes in Computer Science* (Vol. 12066). Cham: Springer. doi:10.1007/978-3-030-44999-5_20

Aragón-Falomir, J., & Cárdenas, J. (2020). Análisis de redes empresariales y puertas giratorias en México: Cartografía de una clase dominante público-privada. *Temas y debates*, *39*, 81–103. doi:10.35305/tyd.v0i39.458

Arango-Benjumea, J. J. (2022). Factores determinantes de la consolidación empresarial: un enfoque integrador desde el emprendedor, la empresa y el entorno. *Contaduría y administración*, *67*(2), 5. doi:10.22201/fca.24488410e.2022.2981

Arias-Vargas, F. J., Ribes-Giner, G., Botero-Arango, D., & Garces, L. F. (2021). Factores sociodemográficos que inciden en el emprendimiento rural de jóvenes en Antioquia, Colombia. *Revista Venezolana de Gerencia*, *26*(96), 1219–1240. doi:10.52080/rvgluz.26.96.14

Bote-López, S. (2021). Redes sociales y el desarrollo empresarial, en el contexto del COVID-19. *Revista Científica Arbitrada de Investigación en Comunicación, Marketing y Empresa REICOMUNICAR*, *4*(7 Ed. esp.), 8–20. ISSN 2737-6354. doi:10.46296/rc.v4i7.edespjun.0027

Boza-Valle, J. A., Narcisa, M. F., & Yolanda, M. V. (2020). Emprendimiento sostenible en comunidades rurales de la Provincia de los Ríos. *Dilemas contemporáneos: Educación, Política y Valores*. *VII*(Esp), 1–23. doi:10.46377/dilemas.v35i1.2254

Cárdenas, F. X. H., Ramos, C. R. F., Beltrán, Á. R. P., & Pazos, P. E. L. (2019). Sostenibilidad empresarial en relación a los objetivos del desarrollo sostenible en el Ecuador. *RECIAMUC*, *3*(1), 670–699. doi:10.26820/reciamuc/3.(1).enero.2019.670-699

Correia-Caetano, D. M. (2022). Incubadoras de Empresas Regionais e Universitárias em Portugal: Similitudes e Diferenças no Acesso a Redes e Acompanhamento Pós-Incubação. *Brazilian Journal of Business*, *4*(1), 476–491. doi:10.34140/bjbv4n1-028

Demuner-Flores, M. D. R. (2021). Capacidad de innovación en empresas mexicanas: mediación en la relación orientación al aprendizaje-rendimiento empresarial. *Acta universitaria*, *31*, 1–19. doi:10.15174/au.2021.3185

Díaz, Y. C., Andrade, J. M., & Ramírez, E. (2019). Liderazgo transformacional y responsabilidad social en asociaciones de mujeres cafeteras en el sur de Colombia. *Información tecnológica*, *30*(5), 121–130. doi:10.4067/S0718-07642019000500121

Figueroa-Soledispa, M. L., Parrales-Reyes, J. E., & katiuska Peña-Ponce, D. (2022). Micro Empresas en la gestión de Innovación. Revista Científica FIPCAEC (Fomento de la investigación y publicación científico-técnica multidisciplinaria). *Polo de Capacitación, Investigación y Publicación (POCAIP)*, *7*(1), 697–710. ISSN: 2588-090X. Retrieved from https://www.fipcaec.com/index.php/fipcaec/article/view/544

Galicia-Gopar, M. A., Mendoza-Ramírez, L., & Espinosa-Trujillo, M. A. (2020). Estrategias de supervivencia y desempeño de mipymes en un ambiente de incertidumbre. Ciencias Administrativas. *Teoría y Praxis*, *16*(2), 31–47. doi:10.46443/catyp.v16i2.260

García-Leonard, Y., & Sorhegui-Rodríguez, R. A. (2020). La teoría de los recursos y capacidades como fundamento metodológico para el estudio de la gestión de la innovación empresarial. *Revista Científica Ecociencia*, *7*, 1–15. doi:10.21855/ecociencia.70.304

Hameed, I., & Irfan, Z. (2019). Entrepreneurship education: A review of challenges, characteristics and opportunities. *Entrepreneurship Education*, *2*, 135–148. doi:10.1007/s41959-019-00018-z

Hinojo-Lucena, F. J., Aznar Díaz, I., & Romero Rodríguez, J. M. (2020). Factor humano en la productividad empresarial: un enfoque desde el análisis de las competencias transversales. *Innovar*, *30*(76), 51–62. doi:10.15446/innovar.v30n76.85194

Huaranga-Toledo, H. L., Ruiz, J. R., Vergara, C. S., & Rodríguez, J. L. (2023). Cultura organizativa y el crecimiento empresarial de la medianas empresa de la ciudad de Huaraz, Perú. *Revista Científica Epistemia*, *7*(1), 01–13. doi:10.26495/re.v7i1.2426

Huerta-Soto, C. E., Vergara, C. S., Brito, C., & Tinoco, L. F. (2023). Desarrollo del ecosistema digital en los países de sudamérica durante la pandemia por COVID-19. *Revista Científica Epistemia*, *7*(1), 14–37. doi:10.26495/re.v7i1.2431

Khalid, R., Raza, M., Sawangchai, A., Allauca, W. J., & Huerta, R. M. (2021). Women entrepreneurial innovative behavior: The role of lean start-up and business coaching. *Studies of Applied Economics*, *39*(8), 1–19. doi:10.25115/eea.v39i8.5132

López-Lemus, J. A., & Garza Carranza, M. T. D. L. (2019). Las prácticas de gestión empresarial, innovación y emprendimiento: factores influyentes en el rendimiento de las firmas emprendedoras. *Nova scientia*, *11*(22), 357–383. doi:10.21640/ns.v11i22.1795

Loyaga, W. F. D., Ballena, J. A. A., Arboleda, P. A. P., & Lama, J. A. H. (2021). Competencias de emprendimiento en estudiantes universitarios en Perú: metodología para su desarrollo. *Revista Venezolana de Gerencia: RVG*, *26*(96), 1172–1188. doi:10.52080/rvgluz.26.96.11

Manzaneque, M., Merino, E., & Sánchez, J. A. (2021). Survival of financially distressed SMEs and out-of-court versus in-court reorganization: Explanatory internal factors. *Revista de Contabilidad – Spanish Accounting Review*, *24*(1), 116–134. doi:10.6018/rcsar.349891

Martínez-Peña, B. I., & Delgado-Vélez, L. D. (2020). La Asociatividad Empresarial. *Escenarios: empresa y territorio*, *9*(14), 47–62. Retrieved from http://esumer.edu.co/revistas/index.php/escenarios/article/view/199

Muñoz, D. F., Matabanchoy, S. M., & Guevara, N. T. (2020). Empresas familiares: Definiciones, características y contribuciones. *Tendencias*, *21*(1), 197–220. doi:10.22267/rtend.202101.133

Pinzón, L. R. P. (2021). Políticas educativas para el emprendimiento rural en Colombia. *Reflexión política*, *23*(47), 60–71. doi:10.7440/res64.2018.03

Ramírez-Torres, W. E. (2022). Gestión del capital humano por competencias laborales en el contexto empresarial: una revisión de literatura. *Lúmina*, *23*(1), E0019. doi:10.30554/lumina.v23.n1.4081.2022

Ramirez, C. P., Mora, B. A. A., Silva, S. S. D., & Amaral, M. G. D. (2019). Incubadoras de negocios en red: capital intelectual de incubadoras de negocios de Latinoamérica y la relación con su éxito. *REAd. Revista Eletrônica de Administração (Porto Alegre)*, *25*, 96–118. doi:10.1590/1413-2311.245.90041

Ramirez, E. H., Mukthar, K. P. J., Norabuena, R. P., Yslado, R. M., & Guerra, M. E. (2021). Lessons from COVID-19 pandemic and its reflection on global public policy formulation. *Journal of Management Information and Decision Sciences*, *24*(S1), 1–9. Retrieved from https://www.abacademies.org/abstract/lessons-from-covid19-pandemic-and-its-reflection-on-global-public-policy-formulation-12569.html

Raza, M., Wisetsri, W., Chansongpol, T., Somtawinpongsai, C., & Ramírez, E. H. (2020). Fostering workplace belongingness among employees. *Polish Journal of Management Studies*, *22*(2), 428–442. doi:10.17512/pjms.2020.22.2.28

Rodríguez, X. E. S., Choez, J. M. P., & González, M. C. S. (2022). La gestión administrativa, factor clave para la productividad y competitividad de las microempresas. *Dominio de las Ciencias*, *8*(1), 280–294. doi:10.23857/dc.v8i1.2571

Rojas-Vega, J. A., Brito, E., Medrano, W., & Leiva, O. C. (2023). Relación de la responsabilidad empresarial en los conflictos medioambientales y sociales en una unidad minera de la Región Ancash. *Revista Científica Epistemia*, *7*(1), 69–82. doi:10.26495/re.v7i1.2436

Tenemesa, D. D. C., Macías, K. A. S., Quijije, W. V. Z., & Coya, J. Y. C. (2021). Innovación tecnológica y su impacto en el desarrollo de las microempresas por COVID-19. *Ciencia Latina Revista Científica Multidisciplinar*, *5*(4), 4576–4590. doi:10.37811/cl_rcm.v5i4.641

Ynzunza, C. B., & Izar, J. M. (2021). Las motivaciones, competencias y factores de éxito para el emprendimiento y su impacto en el desempeño empresarial. Un análisis en las MIPyMES en el estado de Querétaro, México. *Contaduría y administración*, *66*(1). doi:10.22201/fca.24488410e.2021.2327

Zhang, J., Raza, M., Khalid, R., Parveen, R., & Ramírez-Asís, E. H. (2021). Impact of team knowledge management, problem solving competence, interpersonal conflicts, organizational trust on project performance, a mediating role of psychological capital. *Annals of Operations Research*, 1–21. doi:10.1007/s10479-021-04334-3

Zuluaga-Arango, P., Useche Rincón, D., & Rojas Berrio, S. P. (2023). Relevancia, evolución y tendencias de la supervivencia empresarial. Una revisión de literatura en finanzas. *Tendencias*, *24*(1), 252–278. doi:10.22267/rtend.222302.223

Chapter 17

Socioeconomic Factors and Financial Inclusion in the Department of Ancash, Peru, 2015 and 2021

Hernan Ramirez-Asis, Jorge Castillo-Picon, Jenny Villacorta Miranda, José Rodríguez Herrera and Walter Medrano Acuña

Universidad Nacional Santiago Antunez de Mayolo, Peru

Abstract

Financial inclusion in Peru has been addressed through coverage, quality of financial services, movement of transactions, and service points. The purpose of this chapter is to evaluate for the department of Ancash, Peru, the link between financial inclusion and its socioeconomic factors. Socioeconomic variables and financial inclusion of the Ancash department of the National Household Survey are taken as indicators, later contrasted through the logit model, with the financial inclusion variable being the explained variable.

There is evidence of positive and negative relationships between financial inclusion and socioeconomic variables; these are important components for planning financial inclusion. Raising the levels of formal employment, the educational level and considering the area of residence would be a strategy to generate a dynamic of inclusion in the department of Ancash.

Keywords: Formal employment; socioeconomic indicators; financial inclusion; income; educational attainment; cash transfers

1. Introduction

Economic literature states that financial inclusion refers to the access of individuals and firms to financial services that meet their needs and are provided in a responsible manner (World Bank, 2019). In recent years, financial inclusion has

Technological Innovations for Business, Education and Sustainability, 249–264

Published under exclusive licence by Emerald Publishing Limited
doi:10.1108/978-1-83753-106-620241017

gained relevance in developing countries because their population that has some financial service improves its capacity to generate income, makes its consumption sustainable, finances physical assets, human capital, and can face adverse events (Acosta-Palomeque, 2019; Peprah, Kwesi Ofori, & Asomani, 2019). In addressing the theory of financial inclusion, research seeks consensus on its definition; some of them address the contribution of financial inclusion to the economic development of low-income people (Datta & Singh, 2019; Peprah et al., 2019); others study access to and use of financial services (Anser et al., 2021; Collins & Urban, 2021; Demir, Pesqué-Cela, Altunbas, & Murinde, 2022); and a third group studies the factors that both enable and constrain financial inclusion (Asis, Palma, Lázaro, & Soto, 2021; Goyal & Kumar, 2021; Wang & Fu, 2022).

It is also relevant to establish whether financial inclusion is inherent to the culture and socioeconomic characteristics of the low-income population or whether these characteristics hinder access to financial inclusion and to take into account macroeconomic and microeconomic factors that could influence financial inclusion. Financial inclusion has been approached from a variety of perspectives, for example: From the influence of macroeconomic variables and financial deepening (Antonio-Anderson, Peña Càrdenas, & López Saldaña, 2020); through the measurement of government policies on access to the financial system (Vargas-Garcia, 2021); from the socioeconomic factors that influence the decision to use financial services (Tuesta, Sorensen, Haring, & Cámara, 2015); measuring the effect of income on access to financial services (Huerta-Soto et al., 2022); assessing the effects of having a bank account on people's social, labor, and economic vulnerability (Demir et al., 2022; Ramirez et al., 2022).

In Peru, the development of financial inclusion has been assumed by the state, and its goal is to expand the coverage and responsible use of financial services, for which it has established a regulatory environment based on three pillars: use, access, and quality of financial services, as outlined in the National Strategy for Financial Inclusion, with the goal that by 2021, 75% of the population will use a mobile or savings account. Despite the efforts made, a large part of the Peruvian population does not have access to financial services because they have a different profile to that required by financial institutions, a large part of the Peruvian population lives in rural areas, has low income, no internet access, a low average level of education, a high level of labor informality and no collateral assets, aspects that do not match the requirements of the financial system and limit their financial inclusion. The department of Ancash is located in the highlands of Peru, and its economic activities are mining, fishing, and agriculture. According to the Ministry of Inclusion and Social Development, in 2020, its poverty rate was 28.9%, extreme poverty reached 4.2%, 45.2% of the population is vulnerable to poverty, 91.1% of farmers are engaged in subsistence agriculture, 89.7% of the population has access to electricity, 76% has access to public water, 76.9% has access to telephony (MIDIS, 2020). According to the Superintendence of Banking and Insurance (SBS, 2018), there are 503 banking points per 100,000 inhabitants; the number of districts with banking services is 57.2%. Given the socioeconomic characteristics of the Department of Ancash, financial inclusion is still scarce, especially in the highland districts.

Existing national studies measure access to financial services through coverage, quality of financial services, and movement of transactions: Collins and Urban (2021) note that having access to financial inclusion is synonymous with having financial education, financial services, and consumer protection. Priale (2018) states that there are quantitative and qualitative indicators that measure access to financial services. The World Bank (2019) states that in Peru, during 2017, 51% of men and 34% of women had access to the financial system; 47% of those over 25 years of age had access to the financial system; 53% of those with secondary education or more had access to the financial system; 45% of those with secondary education or more had access to the financial system. The Superintendencia de Banca *y* Seguro (SBS, 2018) notes that between 2008 and 2017, the share of deposits in relation to gross domestic product (GDP) has increased from 28% to 36%; this indicator measures financial penetration, and that there were 106 banking channels for every 1,000 km^2 of land area, 21 branches of financial offices per 10,000 people, 109 ATMs per 10,000 adults, 42 people with savings accounts per 1,000 people, 109 debtors per 1,000 people, the depositor/GDP ratio is equal to 0.18, and the debt/GDP ratio is equal to 0.95.

At a theoretical level, one of the arguments relates poverty and exclusion as a limiting factor for financial inclusion. Saehu, Diah, Julca-Guerrero, Huerta-Soto, and Valderrama-Plasencia (2022) state that the symptoms of poverty are low household income and insufficient consumption of goods and services. Soto, Avalos, Albornoz, and Aguilar (2022) state that there are three perspectives from the income side, to measure poverty: (a) the income perspective whereby a person is poor only when their income level is below the poverty line, (b) the basic needs perspective when a person is deprived in terms of food, health, education, employment, and social participation, and (c) the capability perspective when poverty represents the absence of certain basic capabilities such as being nourished, being clothed, having an education. Regarding exclusion, Juárez-Ramírez, Villalobos, Sauceda-Valenzuela, and Nigenda (2021) state that it is a complex social process, and that it presents different stages ranging from total integration to complete exclusion, it is a matter of degrees rather than absolutes, and it is evident that a person can be marginal in some sense or with respect to certain spheres of life or institutions while being highly integrated in others. Not having access to financial inclusion is clearly a case of exclusion.

With regard to poverty reduction, the United Nations Development Programme (UNDP) states that poverty reduction strategies should encompass all aspects of national life, social cohesion, and environmental health (Juárez-Ramírez et al., 2021). It proposes eight strategies: Basic social services, land reform, credit for all, employment, participation, social security, economic growth, and sustainability. Credit for all is a financial inclusion strategy that enables economic growth and individual well-being.

In relation to financial inclusion, Lusardi (2019) underlines that the concept of financial inclusion has achieved significant relevance in the world because of the potential benefits derived from it; however, it is still under construction. Góngora, Banda, and Vivanco (2023) mention that "financial inclusion is a state in which all people can use and have access to a full set of quality financial services, delivered at affordable prices, in a convenient manner and with dignity for customers." The World Bank (2019) states that efficient financial systems offer savings, payment, credit and risk management tools to individuals and firms, and inclusive systems are those that have a high percentage of individuals and firms with access to financial services. Córdova (2021) points out that financial inclusion contributes to reducing poverty and drives economic growth; its expansion influences technological progress; limiting access is negative for expanding the assets of individuals and companies, which would affect growth and poverty reduction.

Martínez-Licerio, Marroquín-Arreola, and Ríos-Bolívar (2019) indicate that in some countries the dominant elite design institutions to enrich themselves at the expense of the majority. In Peru, this situation translates into banking concentration, making financial inclusion difficult due to the requirements that banks ask for in order to access financial services. Sánchez-Carballo, Ruiz Sánchez, and Barrera Rojas (2020) indicate that the cultural differences of the different social groups, together with uneven development, have contributed to the existence of a group of Peruvians with greater purchasing power that allows for greater financial inclusion to the detriment of the other group that lives in subsistence. Sotomayor, Talledo, and Wong (2018) state that the use of financial services is also influenced by the customs of the community. Likewise, in Peru, education, income level, living in rural areas or in an informal environment may or may not contribute to financial inclusion (Martínez, Guercio, Orazi, & Vigier, 2022; Orazi, Martinez, & Vigier, 2019; Soto, Asis, Figueroa, & Plasencia, 2023). Ladman (2021) explains that greater financial development reduces information asymmetries and allows more people to have access to financial products under better conditions.

Regarding the determinants of financial inclusion, the literature relates it to the excluded population. Demir et al. (2022) indicate four causes of involuntary exclusion from financial services: (1) insufficient income or high risk, (2) discriminatory policies, (3) deficient contractual or information frameworks, and (4) price configuration. They also identify three barriers to access among them (1) geography or physical access, (2) request for documents needed to open an account, and (3) high fees to maintain an account. On the other hand, they point out that information infrastructure influences financial inclusion in low-income countries, and in high-income countries, it is consumer protection. González-Núñez (2019) states that financial inclusion coexists with socioeconomic barriers, macroeconomic, microeconomic, and institutional aspects of each country. At the socioeconomic level, there are variables such as the income level of users, gender, age, type of occupation, confidence in the financial system, informality, cultural barriers, costs; at the macroeconomic level, they point to the variables of wealth, institutional framework, stability of the financial system, variables that influence financial inclusion.

Datta and Singh (2019) point out that the history of financial activities is a barrier to financial inclusion for those who do not have it and acts relatively for those who do, and that information asymmetry is a constraint to financial inclusion. Kern and Amri (2021) indicate that the legal framework is a factor that hinders financial inclusion, limiting transactions between financial intermediaries and borrowers within the financial system.

Very little analysis has been done at the regional level on the determinants of access to the financial system, which could be related to demand, supply, financial market development, and socioeconomic characteristics of the population. The department of Ancash is generally characterized by a rural population living in areas far from urban areas, a low income level, a low financial culture, a mostly young population, and a high level of informal employment and self-employment; these factors could affect the access of its population over 18 years of age to the financial services offered.

In this context, the research analyzes the probabilistic relationship that exists between the socioeconomic characteristics of the population of the department of Ancash and their access to financial inclusion, the probability of being financially included if the socioeconomic variables of the person are known (Huerta-Soto et al., 2023). The subject of the study was the person over 18 years of age, and the socioeconomic variables were: income, occupation, education, age, sex, marital status, head of household, own home, place of residence, and whether or not he/she is financially included. Statistical data from the National Household Survey (ENAHO) were used, and the econometric logit model was employed. By addressing the problem, the aim is to increase the empirical evidence on financial inclusion related to the socioeconomic characteristics of the population, which are scarce at the regional level.

2. Methodology

In order to analyze the relationship between financial inclusion and the socioeconomic factors that characterize the population of the department of Ancash, the years 2015 and 2021 were analyzed using data from the "Encuesta Nacional de Hogares" (ENAHO) of the "Instituto Nacional de Estadística e Informática de Perú" (INEI). The target population in the ENAHO are private households in urban and rural areas of the country (INEI, 2019); members of the armed forces living in barracks, camps, ships, and others are not included; likewise, people living in collective dwellings are not included; the sample is 1,454 households belonging to 206 clusters; the variables used were: sex, age, marital status, work last week, have a permanent job, have a business, employer, self-employed, employee, worker, domestic worker, main occupation paid, total income, employed Economically active population (EAP) indicator, openly unemployed EAP indicator, hidden unemployed EAP indicator, informal main occupation. In order to establish the relationship between financial inclusion and socioeconomic factors, the econometric logit model was used because this model allows us to answer the question "how?" And it allows us to relate in terms of probabilities the influence of each of the variables considered, obtaining a coefficient for each variable.

2.1 Mathematical Model

$$Y_{ij} = (X_{ij})$$

Where:

Y_{ij}: Financial inclusion: access to financial service, Yes (1) and No (0).
X_{ij}: is a vector of variables that explain or do not explain financial inclusion.

2.2 Econometric Model

Is the logit model,

$$p_i = \frac{1}{1 + e\,(-\beta_1 + \beta_2\text{ed} + \beta_3\text{sx} + \beta_4\text{il} + \beta_5\text{ne} + \beta_6\text{ec} + \beta_7\text{mh} + \beta_8\text{ar} + \beta_9\text{tr} + \beta_8\text{rn} + \beta_8\text{tp})}$$

Where:

β_i: parameters.
ed: age
sx: sex: male (1) and female (0)
il: liquid income: less than 500 (1), 501 and 1,000 (2), 1,001 to 1,500 (3), 1,501 to S/2000 (4), and more than S/2000 (5)
ne: level of education: Primary (1), Secondary (2), Higher (3), and Post-graduate (4)
ec: marital status: married (1), widowed (2), divorced (3), separated (4), and single (5)
mh: household members: between 2 and 3 (1), between 4 and 5 (2), and 6 or more (3)
ar: area of residence: urban (1) and rural (0)
tr: transfers: if received (1) and not received (0)
rn: natural region coast (1) and highland (0)
tp: type of payment: salary (1), wages (2), commission (3), piecework (4), fees (5), and in kind (6)
ef: permanent job: yes (1) and no (0)
to: type of occupation: employer (1), Trab. Self-employed (2), Employee (3), Worker (4), Unpaid Fam. Unpaid family worker (5), Household worker (6), and Other (7)
in: informality: formal employment (1) and informal employment (0)

The first step consisted of downloading the statistical data from the ENAHO modules: 687 module 1, 687 module 2, and 687 module 5. The data were converted to dichotomous variables except for the scale variables in order to adapt to the requirements of the Logit model, the results of the model were analyzed following the protocol of the Logit model, and the results were then interpreted and discussed.

3. Results

The variables that influence financial inclusion are: age, education, income, urban area of residence, transfers, type of payment, permanent employment, type of occupation, and formal employment. Odds ratios of variables less than one indicate a negative relationship and those greater than one a positive relationship; the value of some odds ratios between 2015 and 2021 shows positive or negative variations, as shown in Table 17.1.

Table 17.1. Odds Ratio 2015 y 2021 Logit Model.

Inclusion	Odds Ratio 2015	Odds Ratio 2021	$P >$ (z) 2015	$P >$ (z) 2021	$\frac{1}{\text{Odds Ratio}}$ 2015	$\frac{1}{\text{Odds Ratio}}$ 2021
Age						
Between 18 and 22	0.889	0.766	0.004	0.004	1.124	1.305
Between 23 and 27	0.292	1.475	0.000	0.000	3.424	–
Between 53 and 57	1.52	1.198	0.000	0.000	–	–
Between 58 and 62	0.118	0.751	0.000	0.000	8.474	1.331
63+	1	1				
Education						
Secondary	1.870	1.407	0.000	0.000	–	–
Higher	4.218	3.144	0.000	0.000	–	–
Postgraduate	3.212	1	0.000	0.000	–	–
Household Members						
Between 2 and 3	0.492	0.548	0.000	0.000	2.032	1.824
Between 4 and 5	0.840	0.582	0.000	0.000	1.190	1.718
6+	0.345	0.705	0.000	0.000	2.898	1.418
Liquid Income						
Between 501 and 1,000	2.993	1.364	0.000	0.000	–	–
Between 1,001 and 1,500	5.966	1.961	0.000	0.000	–	–

(Continued)

Table 17.1. *(Continued)*

Inclusion	Odds Ratio 2015	Odds Ratio 2021	$P >$ (z) 2015	$P >$ (z) 2021	$\frac{1}{\text{Odds Ratio}}$ 2015	$\frac{1}{\text{Odds Ratio}}$ 2021
Between 1,501 and 2,000	3.708	8.519	0.000	0.000	–	–
2,001+	15.89	3.577	0.000	0.000	–	–
Area of Residence						
Urban	1.097	1.480	0.000	0.000	–	–
Transfers						
If received	6.565	5.032	0.000	0.000	–	–
Type of Payment						
Salary	3.106	2.991	0.000	0.000	–	–
Salary	1.040	0.742	0.000	0.000	–	1.34
Unpaid	2.424	1	0.000	0.000	–	–
Permanent Employment						
Yes	8.308	0.611	0.000	0.000	–	1.63
Occupation						
Worker	1.257	0.951	0.000	0.000	–	1.05
Domestic worker	1.197	0.127	0.000	0.000	–	7.87
Activity						
Formal employment	15.19	21.56	0.000	0.000	–	–
Constant	0.183	0.533	0.000	0.000	–	–

Source: ENAHO (2015, 2021).

In Table 17.2, the positive values (financially included) and the negative values (not financially included) are shown; in 2015, the prediction value of the model is 82.88% correct, and in 2021, the prediction accuracy is 77.15%.

The area under the curve and the diagonal for 2015 is 0.90 and 0.86 in 2021, showing in both cases a high accuracy and validating the predictability of the model, as can be seen in Figs. 17.1 and 17.2.

The results of Table 17.1 show that the variables that are positively related to financial inclusion in the department of Ancash in 2015 and 2021 are age between 53 and 57 years; education: secondary, higher, and postgraduate, liquid income, area of urban residence, receiving transfers; type of payment: salary, wage and piecework, permanent employment, occupation worker and household worker, and formal employment; and show a negative relationship with the variables: age between 18 and 23 years, 58 and 62 years and number of members in the

Table 17.2. Ranking Matrix 2015 and 2021.

		2015	
Classified	*D*	˜*D*	Total
+	321	66	387
–	84	405	489
Total	405	471	876
Correctly classified			82.88%
		2021	
	D	˜*D*	Total
+	408	87	495
–	88	183	271
Total	496	270	766
Correctly classified			77.15%

Source: ENAHO (2015, 2021).

household. Odds ratios are used in logistic regression and represent a standardized measure that allows us to compare the level of influence of the independent variables on the dependent variable. The odds ratio value for age 53–57 years is

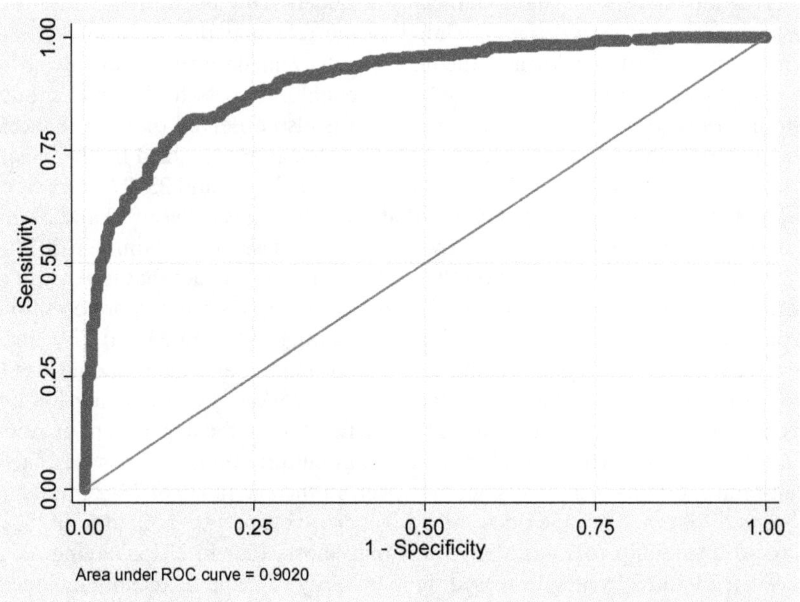

Fig. 17.1. Receiver Operating Characteristic (ROC) Curve, 2015.

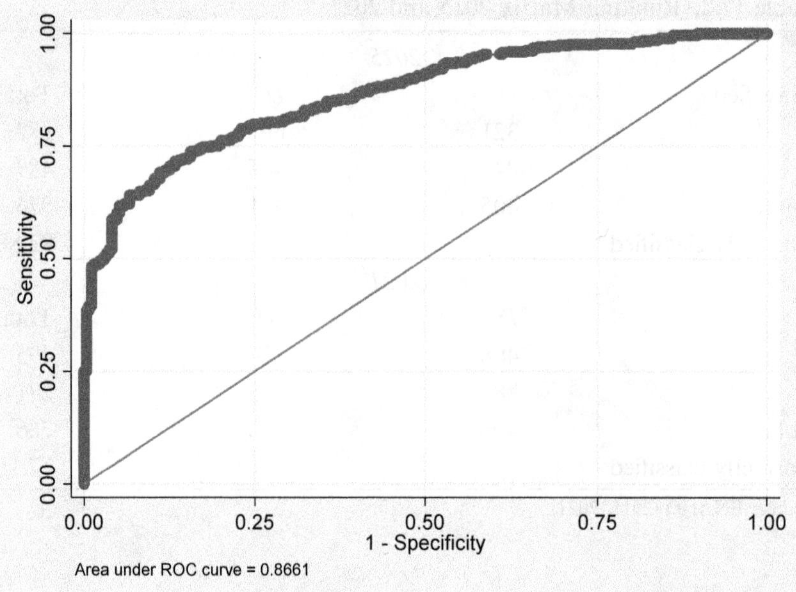

Fig. 17.2. Receiver Operating Characteristic (ROC) Curve, 2021.

equal to 1.52 for 2015 and 1.19 for 2021, indicating that as age increases in this interval the chances of being financially included grow by 1.52 and 1.19 times, respectively, a situation that is related to the fact that this age range possibly represents, in Peru and Ancash, the highest achievement of the person at the level of dependent and independent work, thus enabling access to financial products and not only to having a savings account, it is also observed that the chances of being financially included decreased in 2021, an aspect explained by the negative influence of COVID-19 on the economy; between 18–22 and 23–27 years of age, the relationship is negative indicating that if the person is between 18 and 22 years old, their chances of being financially included decrease by 1. 12 times in 2015 and by 1. 30 times in 2021, a situation that is explained by the fact that in Ancash and Peru people still in that age range (18 and 22) are not yet incorporated into the economically active population and in the age range between 23 and 27 years old generally the person is just starting in the labor market and their income was low as a dependent worker and as an independent worker is experiencing the management of their business, in addition to the fact that in the department of Ancash a large part of the activities are related to agriculture, trade and services, factors that limit their financial inclusion. However, in the age range of 23–27 years, it is observed that in 2015, the odds ratio was negative equal to 3.42, and in 2021, it was positive equal to 1.47, a situation that shows that in 2015, having an age between 23 and 27 years decreased the possibility of being financially included in 3.42 times, and in 2021, having the same age range meant increasing the possibility of being financially included by 1.47 times, a situation that can be explained by the fact that between 2015 and 2021, economic activities such as mining, commerce, and services were consolidated in the department of Ancash, which made possible the financial inclusion of people from the point of view of improving their income.

4. Discussion

Education has a positive relationship with financial inclusion; secondary education in 2015 and 2021 increased the chances of being financially included by 1.87 and 1.40 times, respectively, for each additional year; however, these chances decreased in 2021 even though educational coverage at the secondary level increased; if secondary education is related to the possibilities of labor income and income, it is observed that it does not prepare for the labor market, and it is added that entry to the labor market with secondary education is limited, one can understand the decrease in the chances of being financially included in 2021. Higher education in 2015 and 2021 increased the possibility of being financially included by 4.21 and 3.14 times; it is observed that this possibility in 2021 decreased to 3. This situation has to be related to the increase of professionals that are not in accordance with the demand for them, finding a group of professionals that far exceeds the social offer of the same, generating underemployment and nondecent work and consequently lower possibilities of obtaining employment and high income, the same that would be decreasing financial inclusion; it must also be taken into account that the number of people accessing higher education is limited and does not exceed 30% of the population.

The number of members in the household has a negative relationship with financial inclusion in 2015; having between 2 and 3 members in the household decreased the chances of being financially included by 2.03 times, between 4 and 5 by 1.19 times and having more than 6 members in the household by 2.89 times; in 2021, these reached the values of 1.82, 1.71, and 1. 41 for 2 and 3 members, 4 and 5 members, and more than 6 members, respectively, a situation that evidently shows that the higher the family burden the lower the possibilities of being financially included; in the department of Ancash, the intercensal population growth rate 2007–2017 was 1.9% so that on average, households have between 4 and 5 members; this situation is reversing as the intercensal growth rate decreased by 0.2% in relation to the previous census period.

Income has a positive relationship with financial inclusion, the higher the income, the greater the chances of being financially included. Undoubtedly, the level of income is an indicator of guarantee to repay loans, if we consider that for small amounts it is a guarantee, and taking into account that a large majority of people in Ancash earn minimum wages, its influence is positive. Earning more than 2001 soles increases the chances of being included financially by 15.89 times, as the higher the income, the higher the chances increase. This group includes public employees and workers in large and medium-sized companies, which have boosted loans by agreement in Ancash for a single signature.

Earning a wage or salary increased the possibilities of financial inclusion in Ancash. Salary increased the chances of financial inclusion by 3.10 and 2.99 times in 2015 and 2021 and wage by 1.04 in 2015, but in 2021, it decreased the chance of financial inclusion by 1.34 times. The higher the salary, the greater the chances of being financially included; however, we must take into account the evolution of salaries and wages in order to relate it to financial inclusion. Since the effects of the pandemic, Peru has been experiencing price increases that have reduced the purchasing power of salaries; in 2019, 2020, and 2021, inflation was 1.90%, 1.97%, and 6.97%, respectively and at a disaggregated level in various economic sectors, they exceeded their long-term average; together with the monetary policy measures aimed at reducing bank delinquency, they reduced the possibilities of financial inclusion, as observed in 2021.

If a person resides in urban areas, their chances of being financially included increase 1.09 times in 2015 and 1.48 times in 2021, explained by the fact that in urban areas, there are greater possibilities of finding a financial institution, internet banking, and greater access to banking applications, a situation that in rural areas is limited, acting as a brake on financial inclusion.

Cash transfers drive financial inclusion by 6 times; cash transfers are related to social programs, transfers within the country and transfers from abroad; during the last few years, transfers by social programs have increased and are made through the nation's bank system. These transfers have increased financial inclusion because it is mandatory to have a savings account; however, they do not give access to other financial products.

Permanent employment has a positive relationship with financial inclusion, so having permanent employment increased the chances of being financially included in 2015 by 8.30 times, but in 2021, the relationship was negative, equal to 1.63 times, that is, having permanent employment decreased the chances of financial inclusion by 1.63 times, a situation that is explained by the drop in economic growth and employment during the pandemic, considering that the reactivation of the economy of Ancash is associated with the export of minerals and agriculture, sectors that were affected by the pandemic, and the effects of the climate. However, permanent employment still constitutes a guarantee for financial inclusion and access to financial products. It should be noted that financial inclusion in Ancash occurs at various levels: at the level of banks, rural savings banks, cooperatives, and development entities for small and micro enterprises.

Being a worker increased the possibilities of being financially included in 2015 by 1.25 times, but in 2021, these possibilities were negative, equal to 1.05 times, given the conditions of macroeconomic stability in which Peru found itself, being a worker constituted a guarantee for being financially included, but in 2021, the relationship between being a worker and financial inclusion became negative, taking a value of 1.05 times; however, this value is close to 1, so its incidence is neutral. The issue of being a worker is linked to the issue of employment and what it means in terms of income generation; the issue of the effects of the pandemic explains the negative relationship between these two variables, as jobs decreased during this period. Having a formal occupation increases the possibilities of being financially included by 15.19 and 21.56 times in 2015 and 2021, respectively, if we consider that in the department of Ancash and in Peru, business informality represents 75%, having a formal job constitutes a characteristic of great impact in order to be financially included.

The results show that, in the department of Ancash, there are socioeconomic variables that increase or decrease the possibilities for a person to be financially included, an aspect that is consistent with the theory that studies access to financial services analyzed by (Demir et al., 2022; World Bank, 2019); and consistent with the factors that enable and constrain financial inclusion (Asis et al., 2021; Goyal & Kumar, 2021; Wang & Fu, 2022). The results are also consistent with the thesis of Demir et al. (2022) who note that there are involuntary causes for being excluded from financial services such as insufficient income and geographic access; the research found that as income increases and living in urban areas, the likelihood of financial inclusion increases. The results are also supported by the thesis of Collins and Urban (2021) who state that financial inclusion coexists with socioeconomic barriers inherent to each country such as income level, age, type of occupation, trust in the financial system, informality, cultural barriers, costs. This is in line with the results of Sánchez-Carballo et al. (2020), who state that Peru's uneven economic development has influenced the existence of social groups with different purchasing power levels, which does not allow for equal financial inclusion. Likewise, income level, education level, place of residence, and the informal labor and business environment may or may not contribute to financial inclusion (Arbulú & Heras, 2019; Martínez et al., 2022).

The research, having been conducted for one region, cannot be generalized because in Peru, geographical regions are not homogeneous in terms of natural resources, access to development infrastructure, human capital, technology, demographics, economic growth; some regions concentrate many of these factors and others do not; however, the study serves to understand financial inclusion in Ancash and possible applications to similar regions. The research did not analyze issues such as financial history, information infrastructure, asymmetries, consumer protection, financial culture, influence of the country's economic model, supply-side factors, access to financial products other than savings accounts.

5. Conclusion

The relationship between financial inclusion and socioeconomic factors of people living in the department of Ancash, Peru, in 2015 and 2021 was analyzed. The 2015 estimates indicate that there are positive and negative relationships with socioeconomic factors, with variables such as age, education, income, area of residence, cash transfer, type of payment, permanent employment, type of occupation, and formal employment driving financial inclusion, but the variable number of household members showing a negative relationship. In the year 2021, the estimates for the same variables show variations in the direction of the relationship, the age range between 23 and 27 years became positive, salary shows a negative relationship; fixed employment and type of occupation showed a negative relationship, and the variables show statistically significant results. In addition, variables such as formal employment, higher education, monetary transfers, salary, and urban residence have a strong impact on financial inclusion, as their odds ratios are 21.56, 3.14, 5.03, 2.99, and 1.48, respectively.

The results suggest that in addition to government involvement in designing public policies that foster financial inclusion and promoting changes in financial literacy, socioeconomic factors are key components in increasing financial inclusion. Boosting higher education, formal employment, and expanding geographic financial access would be a positive strategy related to financial inclusion. It is also necessary to pursue a specific research agenda on the relationship between financial inclusion and socioeconomic factors at the national or regional level, including other variables and considering qualitative research approaches.

References

Acosta-Palomeque, G. R. (2019). Responsabilidad social empresarial: inclusión financiera en el sistema bancario privado ecuatoriano. *Visión de futuro*, *23*(1), 1–11. Retrieved from https://visiondefuturo.fce.unam.edu.ar/index.php/visiondefuturo/article/view/302/252

Anser, M. K., Khan, M. A., Zaman, K., Nassani, A. A., Askar, S. E., Abro, M. M. Q., & Kabbani, A. (2021). Financial development during COVID-19 pandemic: The role of coronavirus testing and functional labs. *Financial Innovation*, *7*, 1–13. doi:10.1186/s40854-021-00226-4

Antonio-Anderson, C., Peña Càrdenas, M. C., & López Saldaña, C. D. P. (2020). Determinantes de la alfabetización financiera. *Investigación administrativa*, *49*(125). doi:10.35426/iav49n125.05

Arbulú, F., & Heras, S. (2019). *Género e inclusión financiera*. Lima: Superintendencia de Banca, Seguros y. Retrieved from https://www.sbs.gob.pe/boletin/detalleboletin/idbulletin/1189. Accessed on September 22, 2020.

Asis, E. H. R., Palma, M. E. M., Lázaro, R. J. C., & Soto, R. M. H. (2021). Microcrédito y desarrollo de las microempresas en las zonas rurales de Ancash, Perú. CIENCIA ergo-sum. *Revista Científica Multidisciplinaria de Prospectiva*, *28*(1). doi:10.30878/ces.v28n1a3

Collins, J. M., & Urban, C. (2021). Measuring financial well-being over the lifecourse. In *Financial literacy and responsible finance in the FinTech era* (pp. 45–63). Routledge. Retrieved from https://www.routledge.com/Financial-Literacy-and-Responsible-Finance-in-the-FinTech-Era-Capabilities/Wilson-Panos-Adcock/p/book/9781003169192

Córdova, G. A. (2021). *Determinantes del acceso y uso de la inclusion financiera en el area urbana de paises de la comunidad andina 2005–2018*. Tesis pregrado, Universidad de Lima, Peru. Retrieved from https://hdl.handle.net/20.500.12724/12781

Datta, S. K., & Singh, K. (2019). Variation and determinants of financial inclusion and their association with human development: A cross-country analysis. *IIMB Management Review*, *31*(4), 336–349. doi:10.1016/j.iimb.2019.07.013

Demir, A., Pesqué-Cela, V., Altunbas, Y., & Murinde, V. (2022). Fintech, financial inclusion and income inequality: A quantile regression approach. *The European Journal of Finance*, *28*(1), 86–107. doi:10.1080/1351847X.2020.1772335

ENAHO. (2015). National household survey. National Institute of Statistics and Informatics. Living conditions in Peru: October-November-December 2015. https://m.inei.gob.pe/media/MenuRecursivo/boletines/informe-tecnico-n02_condiciones-vida_octnovdic15.pdf

ENAHO. (2021). National household survey. National Institute of Statistics and Informatics. Living conditions in Peru: October-November-December 2021. https://m.inei.gob.pe/media/MenuRecursivo/boletines/01-informe-tecnico-condiciones-de-vida-oct-nov-dic-2021.pdf

Góngora, S. R., Banda, H. B., & Vivanco, M. (2023). Impacto de la inclusión financiera en el crecimiento económico en México por Entidad Federativa 2013–2021. *Revista Mexicana de Economía y Finanzas Nueva Época REMEF*, *18*(3), 891. doi:10.21919/remef.v18i3.891

González-Núñez, J. C. (2019). Los determinantes de la conducta financiera para no tener una cuenta de ahorro formal: aplicación de un modelo logístico multinomial. *Revista de economía*, *36*(93), 90–117. doi:10.33937/reveco.2019.110

Goyal, K., & Kumar, S. (2021). Financial literacy: A systematic review and bibliometric analysis. *International Journal of Consumer Studies*, *45*(1), 80–105. doi:10.1111/ijcs.12605

Huerta-Soto, R., Ramirez-Asis, H., Mukthar, K. J., Rurush-Asencio, R., Villanueva-Calderón, J., & Zarzosa-Marquez, E. (2022). Purchase intention based on the brand value of pharmacies in a locality of the Peruvian Highlands. In *International Conference on Business and Technology* (pp. 67–78). Cham: Springer International Publishing. doi:10.1007/978-3-031-26956-1_7

Huerta-Soto, R., Ramirez-Asis, E., Tarazona-Jiménez, J., Nivin-Vargas, L., Norabuena-Figueroa, R., Guzman-Avalos, M., & Reyes-Reyes, C. (2023). Predictable inventory management within dairy supply chain operations. *International Journal of Retail & Distribution Management*. doi:10.1108/IJRDM-01-2023-0051

INEI. (2019). *Ficha Técnica. ENAHO 2019*. Retrieved from http://iinei.inei.gob.pe/microdatos/

Juárez-Ramírez, C., Villalobos, A., Sauceda-Valenzuela, A. L., & Nigenda, G. (2021). Barreras en mujeres indígenas para acceder a servicios obstétricos en el marco de redes integradas de servicios de salud. *Gaceta Sanitaria*, *34*, 546–552. doi:10.1016/j.gaceta.2019.05.015

Kern, A., & Amri, P. (2021). Political credit cycles. *Economics & Politics*, *33*(1), 76–108. doi:10.1111/ecpo.12158

Ladman, J. R. (2021). Loan-transactions costs, credit rationing, and market structure: The case of Bolivia. In *Undermining rural development with cheap credit* (pp. 104–119). Routledge. Retrieved from https://www.routledge.com/Undermining-Rural-Development-With-Cheap-Credit/Adams/p/book/9780429270178

Lusardi, A. (2019). Financial literacy and the need for financial education: Evidence and implications. *Swiss Journal of Economics and Statistics*, *155*(1), 1–8. doi:10.1186/s41937-019-0027-5

Martínez-Licerio, K. A., Marroquín-Arreola, J., & Ríos-Bolívar, H. (2019). Precarización laboral y pobreza en México. *Análisis Económico*, *34*(86), 113–131. Retrieved from https://www.redalyc.org/articulo.oa?id=41360954006

Martínez, L. B., Guercio, M. B., Orazi, S., & Vigier, H. P. (2022). Instrumentos financieros claves para la inclusión financiera en América Latina. *Revista Finanzas y Política Económica*, *14*(1), 17–47. doi:10.14718/revfinanzpolitecon.v14.n1.2022.2

MIDIS. (2020). *Reporte Regional de Indicadores Sociales del Departamento de Ancash 2020*. MIDIS.

Orazi, S., Martinez, L. B., & Vigier, H. P. (2019). La inclusión financiera en América Latina y Europa. *Ensayos de Economía*, *29*(55), 181–204. doi:10.15446/ede.v29n55.79425

Peprah, J. A., Kwesi Ofori, I., & Asomani, A. N. (2019). Financial development, remittances and economic growth: A threshold analysis. *Cogent Economics & Finance*, *7*(1), 1625107. doi:10.1080/23322039.2019.1625107

Priale, R. G. (2018). *Inclusión financiera en el Perú. Analisis de los principales determinantes*. Tesis doctoral, Pontificia Universidad Javeriana, Colombia. doi:10.11144/Javeriana.10554.43017

Ramirez, E. H., Rosario, H. S., Laura, N. V., Hober, H. T., Julio, V. A., & Victor, F. L. (2022). Distribution of public service and individual job performance in Peruvian Municipality. 유통과학연구, *20*(10), 11–17. doi:10.15722/jds.20.10.202210.11

Saehu, M. S., Diah, A. M., Julca-Guerrero, F., Huerta-Soto, R., & Valderrama-Plasencia, L. (2022). Environmental awareness and environmental management practices: Mediating effect of environmental data distribution. *Journal of Environmental Management & Tourism*, *13*(5), 1339–1352. doi:10.14505/jemt.v13.5(61).11

Sánchez-Carballo, A., Ruiz Sánchez, J., & Barrera Rojas, M. Á. (2020). La transformación del concepto de pobreza: Un desafío para las ciencias sociales. *Intersticios Sociales*, (19), 39–65. doi:10.55555/IS.19.255

SBS. (2018). *Carpeta de cuadros estadísticos*. Lima: SBS.

Soto, R. H., Asis, E. H., Figueroa, R. P., & Plasencia, L. (2023). Autoeficacia emprendedora y desempeño de micro y pequeñas empresas peruanas. *Revista Venezolana de Gerencia: RVG*, *28*(102), 751–768. doi:10.52080/rvgluz.28.102.19

Soto, R. M., Avalos, M., Albornoz, J. I., & Aguilar, S. J. (2022). Competencias digitales de los profesores universitarios durante la pandemia por covid-19 en el Perú. *Revista Electrónica Interuniversitaria de Formación del Profesorado*, *25*(1), 49–60. doi:10.6018/reifop.500481

Sotomayor, N., Talledo, J., & Wong, S. (2018). *Determinantes de la inclusión financiera en el Perú: Evidencia Reciente*. Documento de Trabajo. Superintendencia de Banca, Seguros y Administradoras Privadas de Fondos de Pensiones, (SBS). Retrieved from https://www.sbs.gob.pe/inclusion-financiera/Publicaciones/Estudios-e-investigaciones

Tuesta, D., Sorensen, A., Haring, A., & Cámara, N. (2015). *Inclusión financiera y sus determinantes: el caso argentino*. Madrid: BBVA. Retrieved from https://www.bbvaresearch.com/publicaciones/inclusion-financiera-y-sus-determinantes-el-caso-argentino/

Vargas-Garcia, A. H. (2021). La banca digital: Innovación tecnológica en la inclusión financiera en el Perú. *Industrial Data*, *24*(2), 99–120. doi:10.15381/idata.v24i2.20351

Wang, X., & Fu, Y. (2022). Digital financial inclusion and vulnerability to poverty: Evidence from Chinese rural households. *China Agricultural Economic Review*, *14*(1), 64–83. doi:10.1108/CAER-08-2020-0189

World Bank. (2019). *Global financial development report 2019/2020: Bank regulation and supervision a decade after the global financial crisis*. The World Bank. doi:10.1596/978-1-4648-1447-1

Chapter 18

Board Structure and Financial Performance: A Survey to Directors' Perception

Fadi Shehab Shiyyab, Abdallah Bader Alzoubi and Leena Abdelsalam Almajaly

The Hashemite University, Jordan

Abstract

Corporate governance research suggests that board structure can impact organizational outcomes such as financial performance and executive remuneration. Agency theory posits that a board composed of independent directors and chaired by an independent chairperson can provide effective control over agency costs, while stewardship theory suggests that effective decision-making is facilitated when the board is chaired by the CEO and majority of directors are from the executive team. Empirical research into the association between board structure and performance in Jordan has provided mixed results, with no consensus supporting either theory. This study takes a different approach to researching the assumed association between board structure and performance by surveying directors' perspectives on such assumed relationship between financial performance and four of boards' characteristics (i.e., board independence, CEO duality, board size, and female ratio on board). Findings of this research indicate that Jordanian directors perceive a medium to strong association between financial performance and each of board independence, independent chair of board, and female ratio on board. However, directors of Jordanian boards perceive no association between financial performance and board size.

Keywords: Corporate governance; agency theory; stewardship theory; board of directors; board structure; Jordan

Technological Innovations for Business, Education and Sustainability, 265–282

doi:10.1108/978-1-83753-106-620241018

1. Introduction

Corporate governance research (Aslam, Haron, & Tahir, 2019; Bansal, Lopez-Perez, & Rodriguez-Ariza, 2018; Nguyen, Elmagrhi, Ntim, & Wu, 2021) has related different organizational outputs (e.g., financial performance, executives' remuneration and disclosure) to boards' characteristics (e.g., independence, board size, and boards' meetings); such research was conceptualized in accordance with normative theories that perceive superiority of some certain board composition configurations (Dalton, Daily, Ellstrand, & Johnson, 1998).

In general, corporate governance theories suggest that board structure may shape corporate outcomes. Agency theory (Fama & Jensen, 1983), as the dominant theory of researching boards and governance, posits that enhanced decision-making, and hence financial performance, is associated with boards controlling decision-making, whereby the composition of the board plays a crucial role in the decision control process. Thus, in agency theory logic, a board that is comprised of majority of independent directors and chaired by an independent chairperson would provide effective control over agency costs (e.g., shirking, managerial opportunism). On the other hand, stewardship theory (Donaldson, 1990; Donaldson & Davis, 1994) posits that effective decision-making is facilitated where board is chaired by the CEO and majority of those directors from the executive team (i.e., unity in command).

In Jordan, large-scale empirical research (e.g., Al-Msiedeen, Rashid, & Shams, 2018; Alshirah et al., 2022; Amedi & Mustafa, 2020; Kanakriyah, 2021; Makhlouf, Laili, Ramli, & Basah, 2017; Mohammad, Abdullatif, & Zakzouk, 2018; Saidat, Silva, & Seaman, 2018) into the association between board characteristics (e.g., board independence, board size, and board leadership structure) and financial performance has provided mixed results with no consensus that provide support to either agency theory or stewardship theory. Thus, it has not been yet clear how board characteristics may relate to financial performance. Moreover, prior research has mostly employed regression to investigate archival data of firms to reach at a conclusion for board structure-performance association.

This research is taking a different approach to test the presumed relationship in an attempt to provide another insight to the topic; this research is surveying directors' perspective to the association between board structure and financial performance. This research is an attempt to answer the following overarching question:

How directors of Jordanian companies perceive the association between board characteristics and financial performance?

This research specifically investigates directors' view to the association between firm financial performance and four of the board characteristics (i.e., board independence, CEO duality, board size, and gender diversity on boards).

Prior research on Jordanian corporate environment has provided mixed results for the presumed association of these four characteristics and financial performance. Some studies have provided evidence for a positive association between board independence and performance (Amedi & Mustafa, 2020; Kanakriyah, 2021; Saidat et al., 2018), while other studies have provided evidence for a negative association between board independence and performance (Al-Msiedeen et al., 2018; Alshirah et al., 2022; Makhlouf et al., 2017), leading to the first question:

RQ1. How directors of Jordanian companies perceive the association between board independence and financial performance?

In the same pattern of inconsistency in findings, some studies have provided evidence for a positive association between CEO duality and performance (Al-Msiedeen et al., 2018; Alshirah et al., 2022; Kanakriyah, 2021), while other studies have provided evidence for a negative association between CEO duality and performance (Makhlouf et al., 2017; Qadorah & Fadzil, 2018; Saidat et al., 2018), leading to the second question:

RQ2. How directors of Jordanian companies perceive the association between CEO duality and financial performance?

Board size also has been one aspect that is investigated in regard to its association with financial performance, whereby some studies have provided evidence for a positive association between board size and performance (Alshirah et al., 2022; Makhlouf et al., 2017; Qadorah & Fadzil, 2018), while other studies have provided evidence for a negative association between board size and performance (Alshirah et al., 2022; Jaafar & El-Shawa, 2009), leading to the third question:

RQ3. How directors of Jordanian companies perceive the association between board size and financial performance?

Gender diversity on boards is a new aspect that has been investigated with regard to its association to performance; some studies have provided evidence for a positive association between gender diversity and performance (Al-Msiedeen et al., 2018; Amedi & Mustafa, 2020; Alshirah et al., 2022), while (Mohammad et al., 2018) a study has provided evidence for a negative association between gender diversity and performance, leading to the fourth question:

RQ4. How directors of Jordanian companies perceive the association between gender diversity on boards and financial performance?

2. Research Objectives and Importance

The main objective of this study is to examine directors' view for the relationship between four key board composition elements (board independence, CEO duality, board size, and female ratio on board) and financial performance in the Jordanian context. The aim is to provide insights into the ongoing emphasis on board characteristics and draw implications for future research on boards of directors. The study acknowledges that using board composition variables in corporate governance settings presents significant challenges in measurement and functionality. The study generates hypotheses based on the theoretical logic prevalent in the literature and proposes ways researchers can address these challenges.

The findings from this research are expected to provide different implications to Jordanian corporate environment as corporate governance guidelines (Instructions of Corporate Governance for Shareholding Listed Companies, 2017) in Jordan emphasizing a specific prescribed configuration of board composition (e.g., independence of the board, independence of the chair and board committees, separate roles of chairperson and CEO). Moreover, the findings from this research may provide reconsideration to the methods employed by researchers who wish to continue investigating board characteristics-performance links.

3. Literature Review

Most studies investigating the connection between board composition and financial performance have relied on data from the United States, but there are noteworthy differences between the United States and other nations, like Jordan, in terms of regulatory frameworks, market characteristics, and cultural factors that may impede the applicability of these findings. For instance, it is argued that in Jordan, institutional regulatory bodies are not effective in enforcing corporate governance principles and standards (Al-Msiedeen et al., 2018) unlike in the United States, which follows a more strict legalistic approach. In Jordan, the board practices are similar to those in Anglo-American countries, with CEO duality and a one-tier system, but the mechanisms for controlling firms are mostly internally focused (Zheng, Moudud-Ul-Huq, Rahman, & Ashraf, 2017). The idea of board independence is not common in Jordan, and the board chairman and CEO are typically the same person, with no supervisory role for the board in relation to management, unlike in Anglo-American countries where outside directors play a vital role in overseeing management (Al-Msiedeen et al., 2018; Shanikat & Abbadi, 2011). In developing countries like Jordan, the board size has a weaker controlling role compared to firms in developed countries, and any negative impact of a large board of directors is likely due to the board's advisory role not functioning correctly (Almashhadani, 2021). While international studies have demonstrated a positive relationship between gender diversity in boards of directors and a firm's financial performance, the number of female board members in Jordan's listed companies is low (Alshirah et al., 2022; IFC, 2012). These differences in board composition practices between countries suggest the need for research specifically focused on the Jordanian context.

Indeed, it is important to take into account the specific characteristics of the Jordanian corporate governance system when studying the relationship between board characteristics and financial performance. The principles-based approach to board composition in Jordan as well as the lower proportion of outside directors and separation of CEO and Chair roles are important factors to consider. Additionally, the smaller size of Jordanian boards and the gender diversity may also play a role in the relationship between board characteristics and financial performance. Therefore, it is necessary to conduct separate investigations in the Jordanian context to gain a better understanding of these relationships.

4. Board Independence and Firm Performance

The modern corporation is characterized by a separation of ownership and control, which can result in conflicts of interest between shareholders and managers (Berle & Means, 1932). According to agency theory, this separation can be managed by implementing mechanisms that align the interests of shareholders and managers or by monitoring managers to ensure that they act in the best interests of shareholders (Fama, 1980; Jensen & Meckling, 1976).

The board of directors is considered to be the primary internal mechanism for monitoring shareholders' interests (Fama & Jensen, 1983). The directors who are independent of management are believed to provide objective oversight of shareholders' interests (Dalton, Hitt, Certo, & Dalton, 2007) as they are not subject to the potential conflicts of interest that inside directors may have. Outside directors are also thought to enhance corporate performance by offering important services or advice. As they are perceived to have a different knowledge base and network of contacts compared to insiders (Hillman, Withers, & Collins, 2009), they can offer novel advice as well as access additional resources to manage external relationships (Pfeffer, 1972).

Stewardship theory, in contrast to agency theory, focuses on the positive motivations of managers and their desire to act as good stewards of the organization and its resources (Donaldson, 1990; Donaldson & Davis, 1991). This theory draws on insights from psychology and sociology, such as the work of McGregor (1960) and Herzberg (1966), to emphasize the importance of intrinsic motivation in decision-making. According to stewardship theory, managers are not solely driven by self-interest but are committed to achieving organizational goals and acting in the best interests of shareholders.

This argument aligns with the stewardship theory which suggests that managers are motivated to act in the best interest of shareholders because doing so is congruent with their own self-interest (Davis, Schoorman, & Donaldson, 1997). As a result, managers are inclined to use their discretion to enhance firm performance. Proponents of this theory argue that because executive directors have greater knowledge and expertise about the company, they are best placed to make decisions and should have more control over the company's affairs (Baysinger & Hoskisson, 1990). Given the ambivalent direction of relationship, we hypothesize that:

H1. Directors of Jordanian firms perceive no statistically significant correlation between board independence and firm performance.

5. CEO Duality and Firm Performance

Additionally, some studies suggest that CEO duality is associated with lower levels of firm performance (Daily & Dalton, 1994; Dalton et al., 1998; Villalonga & Amit, 2006; Yermack, 1996). However, others argue that CEO duality can have positive effects, such as better coordination and communication between the CEO and board (Dalton et al., 2007). Given these conflicting views, the relationship between CEO duality and firm performance remains a topic of ongoing research and debate.

If the principles of stewardship theory are accurate, a unitary leadership structure is expected to result in improved performance by providing clear decision-making authority and a unified leadership at the top of the organization, which can send positive signals to stakeholders and employees (Finkelstein & D'aveni, 1994, p. 1080).

Globally, there is no substantial or consistent evidence of a relationship between board leadership structure and financial performance, according to Dalton et al. (2007). However, it is worth noting that the prevalence of CEO duality is lower in Australian companies compared to other Anglo systems, particularly during the time period examined in the US meta-analyses, as stated by Rhoades, Rechner, and Sundaramurthy (2001). Various studies conducted in the Jordanian context show conflicting results for the relationship between board leadership structure and firm performance. Given the dichotomous correlation direction, we hypothesize that:

H2. Directors of Jordanian firms perceive no statistically significant correlation between CEO duality and firm performance.

6. Board Size and Firm Performance

There are differing viewpoints on the relationship between board size and firm performance, similar to the constructs of board independence and leadership. One perspective is that increasing the size of the board will enhance firm performance, as suggested by research that positions the board as a source of human capital. According to this perspective, a larger board is needed to establish effective external linkages, which includes both accessing resources and the knowledge base required for a director's advisory role to the CEO (Lorsch & MacIver, 1989, p. 64; Salancik & Pfeffer, 1978, p. 172).

Alternatively, some scholars propose that larger boards may be less effective and easier for CEOs to control. This view is based on the dynamics of group decision-making, with smaller boards fostering greater focus, participation, and genuine interaction and debate. As board size increases, coordination and group processing problems may arise, leading to ineffective monitoring and control (Firstenberg & Malkiel, 1994, p. 34; Jensen, 1993, p. 865).

The available evidence regarding the connection between the size of a company's board and its performance is inconclusive. Yermack (1996) emphasized that there is a negative association between board size and firm performance, and this finding has been confirmed by other studies (Chintrakarn, Jiraporn, Tong, & Proctor, 2017). Nevertheless, a comprehensive review of the evidence indicated a moderate positive correlation (Dalton, Daily, Johnson, & Ellstrand, 1999).

One of the key considerations taken into account for this study was that the national institutional characteristics could potentially impact the overall relationship between board size and firm performance (Guest, 2009). For example, boards in Jordan tend to be smaller than those in the United States. While numerous studies on US data have found a negative correlation, research conducted in different regions tends to show a positive correlation. For instance, data from the United Kingdom (Guest, 2009), South Africa (Ntim, Opong, & Danbolt, 2015), and the banking industry in Indonesia (Tulung & Ramdani, 2018) all demonstrate a positive association. Considering the conflicting theoretical reasoning and empirical findings, we suggest that:

H3. Directors of Jordanian firms perceive no statistically significant correlation between board size and firm performance.

7. Gender Diversity on Board and Firm Performance

Board gender diversity has gained significant attention in both research and regulatory circles since the beginning of the 21st century and is currently considered one of the most important board structural variables (Terjesen, Sealy, & Singh, 2009). What distinguishes this area of board structural research is the broad range of research encompassing the precursors and outcomes of board gender diversity (Kirsch, 2018).

While some argue for increasing board gender diversity based on individual and social justice reasons (Kumar & Zattoni, 2016), our focus is on the proposed business case for increasing the number of women on boards. The business case suggests that women serving on boards are significantly different from men, and this difference would bring a range of benefits to the board decision-making process. Firstly, extensive psychological research has demonstrated that men and women differ significantly at the population level in terms of attributes such as risk profile and values (Adams, 2016). Secondly, it is expected that differing life experiences would bring diverse perspectives and alternative problem-solving approaches (Anderson, Reeb, Upadhyay, & Zhao, 2011). Finally, due to the low representation of women on boards, those who are appointed are thought to be less likely to be insiders, potentially increasing board independence (Hillman, 2015; Kumar & Zattoni, 2016).

Reviews of the literature on gender diversity, such as Kirsch (2018) and Velte (2017), generally conclude that the relationship between women on boards and firm performance across studies "remains inconclusive, with different studies finding positive, negative, or no effects" (Kirsch, 2018, p. 353). Three significant meta-analyses report either no effect or a practically insignificant effect that varies with the performance measure (Hoobler, Masterson, Nkomo, & Michel, 2018; Pletzer, Nikolova, Kedzior, & Voelpel, 2015; Post & Byron, 2015).

One important aspect that distinguishes the gender diversity literature is the potential variation in national-level effects. Some studies, such as Post and Byron (2015), have found that the relationship between gender diversity and performance can differ depending on the national context. As there have been various regulatory interventions aimed at increasing the representation of women on boards, there has been a significant amount of research focused on the national effects of such interventions. For instance, in Norway, where a 40% women quota was implemented, some studies report a negative effect (Ahern & Dittmar, 2012). Similarly, gender quotas in Belgium, France, and Spain have been associated with either a negative or no effect (Comi, Grasseni, Origo, & Pagani, 2017). However, other studies have reported a positive effect of gender quotas in Spain (Reguera-Alvarado, de Fuentes, & Laffarga, 2017) and Italy (Gordini & Rancati, 2017). Therefore, we suggest that:

H4. Directors of Jordanian firms perceive no statistically significant correlation between female ratio on board and firm performance.

8. Method

Given the difficulty in attracting busy directors to an in-depth face to face interview setting (Leblanc & Schwartz, 2007), this study employs an online survey sent to directors through different social media platforms. The survey was formatted using "Microsoft Forms, Surveys, Polls and Quizzes/Microsoft 365." The survey's instrument is composed of an instructional paragraph and four questions. After greeting the respondent, the instructional paragraph indicates that the survey is only conducted for scientific research and that the response is confidentially treated. In addition, the purpose of the study is highlighted in the instructional paragraph followed by the instructions to respond.

This study employs "Pearson correlation" in measuring the degree to which directors of Jordanian listed firms view the assumed relationship between board characteristics and financial performance. In accordance to Cohen (1992) measures of correlation strength, the scale employed for this study recognizes five measures of correlation: first, no correlation at all (r= zero) and secondly, four correlational strengths: (1) small correlation ("$r < 0.10$" or "$r < -0.10$"), (2) medium correlation ("$r = 0.10$ to $r = 0.30$" or "$r = -0.10$ to $r = -0.30$"), (3) strong correlation ("$r > 0.30$ to $r = 0.5$" or "$r > -0.30$ to $r = -0.50$"), and (4) very strong correlation ("$r > 0.50$" or "$r > -0.50$").

As the strength of "Pearson correlation" may be evident negatively and positively, the scale recognizes the four nonzero measures of correlational strength on both direction of the relationship. Hence, including the zero correlation case, the scale is composed of nine measures of correlation so that a respondent is asked to indicate on the nine-scaled measure their view to the degree to which financial performance is related to the four board characteristics (i.e., board independence, CEO duality, board size, and female representation on boards) as per the four questions. For example, in the first question of the four questions of the survey, the respondent is asked the following "I believe that the strength of correlation between financial performance and board independence is:" So that the choices are as follow:

- positive correlation that is $r > 0.50$, coded one for statistical analysis;
- positive correlation that ranges from $r > 0.30$ to $r = 0.50$, coded two for statistical analysis;
- positive correlation that ranges from $r = 0.10$ to $r = 0.30$, coded three for statistical analysis;
- positive correlation that is $r < 0.10$, coded four for statistical analysis;
- no correlation $r = 0$, coded five for statistical analysis;
- negative correlation that is $r < -0.10$, coded six for statistical analysis;
- negative correlation that ranges from $r = -0.10$ to $r = -0.30$, coded seven for statistical analysis;
- negative correlation that ranges from $r > -0.30$ to $r = -0.50$, coded eight for statistical analysis;
- negative correlation that is $r > -0.5$, coded nine for statistical analysis.

The other three questions are presented to respondents using the same scale.

For each of the four questions of the survey, the "Mean" of the answers will be calculated as per the codes given to respondents' answers. For instance, a "Mean" that equals four or a value that is close to four will be interpreted that directors of Jordanian listed companies view no correlation for an assumed given relationship. The standard deviation around a given "Mean" will be used as a measure of confidence in that "Mean."

9. Population and Sample of the Study

The population of the study includes all directors of all Jordanian firms listed on Amman Stock Exchange (ASE); as of the day of identifying the population, there was 170 firms listed on ASE. A random sample of 70 companies was chosen for this study. After reviewing the annual reports of these 70 companies, and based on directors' names, the search for directors' profiles on social media platforms (i.e., LinkedIn, Facebook messenger, and Twitter) was conducted for a random sample of 350 directors (five directors from each company). Randomization was facilitated using an "Excel sheet/'The RAND function' and 'custom sorting'." For each identified profile, a link to the research instrument (the survey) was sent. Where a director's profile could not be found, a randomly chosen director was replaced. In total, 64 usable replies were received for analysis.

10. Results

10.1 Descriptive Statistics

The responses from directors were analyzed using the Statistical Package for Social Sciences (SPSS) so that "Mean" and "Standard Deviation" for the correlation strength between financial performance and each of the four board characteristics were obtained. Table 18.1 presents a summary of the results obtained from directors. Moreover, SPSS was also used to obtain "Frequency" and "Percentage" for the nine-scaled provided answers for each of the four questions of the survey. Details of the responses are presented in four sections as per the four investigated characteristics of boards.

10.2 Board Independence and Firm Performance

For the relationship between financial performance and board independence, the results indicated that 41% of the sample indicated that there is a strong positive correlation between board independence and financial performance/"positive correlation that ranges from $r > 0.30$ to $r = 0.50$" (coded two). About 38% of the sample indicated that there is a medium positive correlation between board independence and financial performance/"positive correlation that ranges from $r = 0.10$ to $r = 0.30$" (coded three). So that, these two answers compose what is nearly 80% of the sample's view to the assumed relationship. Moreover, when referring to Table 18.1, we can see that the mean of answers is "$M = 2.7$," which is between the code "two" (strong positive correlation) and the code "three" (medium positive correlation). In addition, the standard deviation for this mean is "SD= 1.27," which is less than half

Table 18.1. Descriptive Statistics of Our Samples of Jordanian Firms.

Table 5–1 Descriptive Statistics

Variable	*N*	Mean	Std. Deviation
Board independence	64	2.70313	1.268416
CEO duality	64	2.73437	1.237537
Board size	64	4.5	2.085475
Female representation	64	3.29687	1.443977
Valid *N* (list wise)	64	–	–

Source: Authors' own creation.

of the mean; that is, there is a strong confidence in the mean value obtained (Pallant, 2013). Table 18.2 presents respondents' answers to the first question of the survey.

Taking respondents' answers together, we may conclude that the respondents in the sample believe that the association between board independence and financial performance could be expressed as strong to medium positive correlation.

Table 18.2. Results for Directors' View to the Relationship Between Financial Performance and Board Independence.

I Believe That the Strength of Correlation Between Financial Performance and Board Independence Is

The Choices	Coded	Frequency	Percentage
Positive correlation that is $r > 0.50$	1	6	9%
Positive correlation that ranges from $r > 0.30$ to $r = 0.50$	2	26	41%
Positive correlation that ranges from $r = 0.10$ to $r = 0.30$	3	24	38%
Positive correlation that is $r < 0.10$	4	3	5%
No correlation $r = 0$	5	1	2%
Negative correlation that is $r < -0.10$	6	2	3%
Negative correlation that ranges from $r = -0.10$ to $r = -0.30$	7	2	3%
Negative correlation that ranges from $r > -0.30$ to $r = -0.50$	8	0	0%
Negative correlation that is $r > -0.50$	9	0	0%
Total	–	64	100%

Source: Authors' own creation.

Based on such results, the null hypothesis that there is no correlation between board independence and firm financial performance may be rejected.

10.3 CEO Duality and Firm Performance

For the relationship between financial performance and CEO duality, the results indicated that 95% of the sample believes that there is a positive correlation between CEO duality and financial performance, only one respondent out of the 64 respondents believes that there is a strong negative correlation between the two variables/"Negative correlation that ranges from $r > -0.30$ to $r = -0.50$" (coded eight). Three percentage of the sample (two respondents) indicated that there is no correlation between the two variables/"No correlation $r = 0$" (coded five). Moreover, when referring to Table 18.1, we can see that the mean of answers is "$M = 2.73$" which is between the code "two" (strong positive correlation) and the code "three" (medium positive correlation). In addition, the standard deviation for this mean is "SD= 1.24," which is less than half of the mean; that is, there is a strong confidence in the mean value obtained (Pallant, 2013). Table 18.3 presents respondents' answers to the second question of the survey.

Table 18.3. Results for Directors' View to the Relationship Between Financial Performance and CEO Duality.

I Believe That the Strength of Correlation Between Financial Performance and CEO Duality Is

The Choices	Coded	Frequency	Percentage
Positive correlation that is $r > 0.50$	1	9	14%
Positive correlation that ranges from $r > 0.30$ to $r = 0.50$	2	20	31%
Positive correlation that ranges from $r = 0.10$ to $r = 0.30$	3	20	31%
Positive correlation that is $r < 0.10$	4	12	19%
No correlation $r = 0$	5	2	3%
Negative correlation that is $r < -0.10$	6	0	0%
Negative correlation that ranges from $r = -0.10$ to $r = -0.30$	7	0	0%
Negative correlation that ranges from $r > -0.30$ to $r = -0.50$	8	1	2%
Negative correlation that is $r > -0.50$	9	0	0%
Total	–	64	100%

Source: Authors' own creation.

Taking respondents' answers together, we may conclude that the respondents in the sample believe that the association between CEO duality and financial performance could be expressed as strong to medium positive correlation.

Based on such results, the null hypothesis that there is no correlation between CEO duality and firm financial performance may be rejected.

10.4 Board Size and Firm Performance

For the relationship between financial performance and board size, the results were inconclusive. Although 36% of the sample indicated a medium positive correlation between board size and financial performance/"positive correlation that ranges from $r = 0.10$ to $r = 0.30$" (coded three), it is also noticed that 19% of the sample indicated the there is no correlation at all between the two variables/ "No correlation $r = 0$" (coded five). The rest of the answers were scattered at the different given answers. Importantly, when referring to Table 18.1, we can see that the mean of answers is "$M = 4.50$," which is between the code "four" (small positive correlation) and the code "five" (no correlation). In addition, the standard deviation for this mean is "SD= 2.09," which is less than half of the mean; that is, there is a strong confidence in the mean value obtained (Pallant, 2013). Table 18.4 presents respondents' answers to the third question of the survey.

Table 18.4. Results for Directors' View to the Relationship Between Financial Performance and Board Size.

I Believe That the Strength of Correlation Between Financial Performance and Board Size Is			
The Choices	Coded	Frequency	Percentage
Positive correlation that is $r > 0.50$	1	0	0%
Positive correlation that ranges from $r > 0.30$ to $r = 0.50$	2	7	11%
Positive correlation that ranges from $r = 0.10$ to $r = 0.30$	3	23	36%
Positive correlation that is $r < 0.10$	4	7	11%
No correlation $r = 0$	5	12	19%
Negative correlation that is $r < -0.10$	6	0	0%
Negative correlation that ranges from $r = -0.10$ to $r = -0.30$	7	7	11%
Negative correlation that ranges from $r > -0.30$ to $r = -0.50$	8	4	6%
Negative correlation that is $r > -0.50$	9	4	6%
Total	–	64	100%

Source: Authors' own creation.

Taking respondents' answers together, we may conclude that the respondents in the sample believe that the association between board size and financial performance could be expressed as a small positive correlation to no correlation.

Based on such results, the null hypothesis that there is no correlation between board size and firm financial performance may not be rejected.

10.5 Gender Diversity and Firm Performance

For the relationship between financial performance and gender diversity, the results indicated that 86% of the sample believe that there is a positive correlation between gender diversity and financial performance, whereby 33% of the sample indicated that there is a medium positive correlation between the two variables/ "positive correlation that ranges from $r = 0.10$ to $r = 0.30$" (coded three). Moreover, when referring to Table 18.1, we can see that the mean of answers is "$M = 3.30$," which is between the code "three" (medium positive correlation) and the code "four" (small positive correlation). In addition, the standard deviation for this mean is "SD= 1.44," which is less than half of the mean; that is, there is a strong confidence in the mean value obtained (Pallant, 2013). Table 18.5 presents respondents' answers to the second question of the survey.

Table 18.5. Results for Directors' View to the Relationship Between Financial Performance and Female Ratio on Board.

I Believe That the Strength of Correlation Between Financial Performance and Female Ratio on Board Is

The Choices	Coded	Frequency	Percentage
Positive correlation that is $r > 0.50$	1	7	11%
Positive correlation that ranges from $r > 0.30$ to $r = 0.50$	2	10	16%
Positive correlation that ranges from $r = 0.10$ to $r = 0.30$	3	21	33%
Positive correlation that is $r < 0.10$	4	17	27%
No correlation $r = 0$	5	4	6%
Negative correlation that is $r < -0.10$	6	2	3%
Negative correlation that ranges from $r = -0.10$ to $r = -0.30$	7	3	5%
Negative correlation that ranges from $r > -0.30$ to $r = -0.50$	8	0	0%
Negative correlation that is $r > -0.50$	9	0	0%
Total	–	64	100%

Source: Authors' own creation.

Taking respondents' answers together, we may conclude that the respondents in the sample believe that the association between gender diversity and financial performance could be expressed as medium to small positive correlation.

Based on such results, the null hypothesis that there is no correlation between gender diversity and firm financial performance may be rejected.

10.6 Summary of Results

This research intended to investigate the directors' perceptions to the association between board characteristics (board independence, CEO duality, board size, gender diversity on boards) and financial performance. The results suggest in general that there is a positive association between financial performance and three of the investigated characteristics (board independence, CEO duality, and gender diversity on boards). The results obtained for board size, however, failed to detect any association between board size and financial performance.

The first hypothesis (*H1*) proposed that there is no relationship between board independence and financial performance. The findings according to directors' perceptions revealed that there is strong to medium positive correlation between board independence and financial performance. The second hypothesis (*H2*) proposed that there is no relationship between CEO duality and financial performance. Thus, first and second hypotheses were rejected. Therefore, it may be concluded that the results obtained are in the line with the agency theory's perspective, which holds that a board composed of a majority of independent directors and chaired by an independent director is more efficient in controlling the management and the CEO (Fama & Jensen, 1983).

The third hypothesis (*H3*) proposed that there is no relationship between board size and financial performance. The findings according to directors' perceptions revealed that we may not be able to reject the third hypothesis. These results rival a number of studies which indicated that large boards are positively associated with financial performance (Dalton et al., 1999; Qadorah & Fadzil, 2018).

And finally, the fourth hypothesis (*H4*) proposed that there is no relationship between gender diversity and financial performance. The findings according to directors' perceptions revealed that we may be able to reject the fourth hypothesis. The positive result is in a line with a number of studies which indicated that the relationship between female ratio on board and firm performance has a positive relationship (Gordini & Rancati, 2017; Pletzer et al., 2015; Reguera-Alvarado et al., 2017).

11. Conclusion

This study aimed at providing directors' views on the association between board characteristics and financial performance. Specifically, this study answered four questions in this matter. For the first research question, whether there is any correlation between board independence and financial performance of the Jordanian firms, the findings of this study indicated that there is a strong to medium positive correlation between board independence and financial performance Similarly, for the second research question, whether there is any correlation between CEO duality and financial performance of the Jordanian firms, the findings of this study indicated that there is a strong to medium positive correlation between CEO duality and financial performance. For the third research question, whether there is any correlation between board size and financial performance of the Jordanian firms, the findings of this study indicated that there is a small to no correlation between board size and financial performance. For the fourth research question, whether there is any correlation between gender diversity and financial performance of the Jordanian firms, the findings of this study indicated that there is a medium to small correlation between female ratio on board and financial performance.

References

Adams, R. B. (2016). Women on boards: The superheroes of tomorrow? *The Leadership Quarterly*, *27*(3), 371–386.

Ahern, K. R., & Dittmar, A. K. (2012). The changing of the boards: The impact on firm valuation of mandated female board representation. *Quarterly Journal of Economics*, *127*(1), 137–197.

Almashhadani, M. (2021). A brief review of corporate governance structure and corporate profitability in developed and developing economy: A review. *International Journal of Business and Management Invention*, *10*(11), 42–46.

Al-Msiedeen, J. M., Rashid, A., & Shams, S. (2018). Board independence and firm performance: Evidence from Jordan. In *Proceedings of Sydney International Business Research Conference 2018*, Novotel Sydney Central, Sydney, Australia, 25–26 March 2018.

Alshirah, M. H., Alfawareh, F. S., Alshira'h, A. F., Al-Eitan, G., Bani-Khalid, T., & Alsqour, M. D. (2022). Do corporate governance and gender diversity matter in firm performance (ROE)? Empirical evidence from Jordan. *Economies*, *10*(4), 84.

Amedi, A. M. R., & Mustafa, A. S. (2020). Board characteristics and firm performance: Evidence from manufacture sector of Jordan. *Accounting Analysis Journal*, *9*(3), 146–151.

Anderson, R. C., Reeb, D. M., Upadhyay, A., & Zhao, W. (2011). The economics of director heterogeneity. *Financial Management*, *40*(1), 5–38.

Aslam, E., Haron, R., & Tahir, M. N. (2019). How director remuneration impacts firm performance: An empirical analysis of executive director remuneration in Pakistan. *Borsa Istanbul Review*, *19*(2), 186–196.

Bansal, S., Lopez-Perez, M. V., & Rodriguez-Ariza, L. (2018). Board independence and corporate social responsibility disclosure: The mediating role of the presence of family ownership. *Administrative Sciences*, *8*(3), 33.

Baysinger, B. D., & Hoskisson, R. E. (1990). The composition of boards of directors and strategic control: Effects on corporate strategy. *Academy of Management Review*, *15*(1), 72–87.

Berle, A. A., & Means, G. C. (1932). *The modern corporation and private property*. New York, NY: Commerce Clearing House.

Chintrakarn, P., Jiraporn, P., Tong, P. S., & Proctor, R. M. (2017). Using demographic identification to estimate the effects of board size on corporate performance. *Applied Economics Letters*, *24*(11), 766–770.

Cohen, J. (1992). Statistical power analysis. *Current Directions in Psychological Science*, *1*(3), 98–101. doi:10.1111/1467-8721.ep10768783

Comi, S., Grasseni, M., Origo, F., & Pagani, L. (2017). *Where women make the difference the effects of corporate board gender quotas on firms' performance across Europe University of Milan Bicocca Department of Economics*. Management and Statistics Working Paper No 367. Retrieved from https://ssrn.com/abstract=3001255

Daily, C. M., & Dalton, D. R. (1994). Bankruptcy and corporate governance: The impact of board composition and structure. *Academy of Management Journal*, *37*(6), 1603–1617.

Dalton, D. R., Daily, C. M., Ellstrand, A. E., & Johnson, J. L. (1998). Meta-analytic reviews of board composition, leadership structure, and financial performance. *Strategic Management Journal*, *19*(3), 269–290. doi:10.1002/(SICI)1097-0266(199803)19:33.0.CO;2-K

Dalton, D. R., Daily, C. M., Johnson, J. L., & Ellstrand, A. E. (1999). Number of directors and financial performance: A meta-analysis. *Academy of Management Journal*, *42*(6), 674–686.

Dalton, D. R., Hitt, M. A., Certo, S. T., & Dalton, C. M. (2007). 1 The fundamental agency problem and its mitigation: Independence, equity, and the market for corporate control. *The Academy of Management Annals*, *1*(1), 1–64.

Davis, J. H., Schoorman, F. D., & Donaldson, L. (1997). Toward a stewardship theory of management. *Academy of Management Review*, *22*(1), 20–47.

Donaldson, L. (1990). The ethereal hand: Organizational economics and management theory. *Academy of Management Review*, *15*(3), 369–381.

Donaldson, L., & Davis, J. (1991). Stewardship theory or agency theory: CEO governance and shareholder returns. *Australian Journal of Management*, *16*(1), 49–64. doi:10.1177/031289629101600103

Donaldson, L., & Davis, J. H. (1994). Boards and company performance-research challenges the conventional wisdom. *Corporate Governance: An International Review*, *2*(3), 151–160.

Fama, E. F. (1980). Agency problems and the theory of the firm. *Journal of Political Economy*, *88*(2), 288–307. doi:10.1086/260866

Fama, E. F., & Jensen, M. C. (1983). Separation of ownership and control. *The Journal of Law and Economics*, *26*(2), 301–325. doi:10.1086/467037

Finkelstein, S., & D'aveni, R. A. (1994). CEO duality as a double-edged sword: How boards of directors balance entrenchment avoidance and unity of command. *Academy of Management Journal*, *37*(5), 1079–1108.

Firstenberg, P. B., & Malkiel, B. G. (1994). The twenty-first century boardroom: Who will be in charge? *MIT Sloan Management Review*, *36*(1), 27.

Gordini, N., & Rancati, E. (2017). Gender diversity in the Italian boardroom and firm financial performance. *Management Research Review*, *40*(1), 75–94.

Guest, P. M. (2009). The impact of board size on firm performance: Evidence from the UK. *The European Journal of Finance*, *15*(4), 385–404.

Herzberg, F. I. (1966). *Work and the nature of man*. Oxford: World.

Hillman, A. J. (2015). Board diversity: Beginning to unpeel the onion. *Corporate Governance: An International Review*, *23*(2), 104–107.

Hillman, A. J., Withers, M. C., & Collins, B. J. (2009). Resource dependence theory: A review. *Journal of Management*, *35*(6), 1404–1427.

Hoobler, J. M., Masterson, C. R., Nkomo, S. M., & Michel, E. J. (2018). The business case for women leaders: Meta-analysis, research critique, and path forward. *Journal of Management*, *44*(6), 2473–2499.

IFC. (2012). *IFC family business governance handbook*. Washington, DC: International Finance Corporation.

Issued based on the provisions of Articles (12/N) and (118/B) of the Securities Law No. (18) for the year 2017 and approved by the Decision of the Board of Commissioners of the Securities Commission No. (146/2017) dated 22/5/2017.

Jaafar, A., & El-Shawa, M. (2009). Ownership concentration, board characteristics and performance: Evidence from Jordan. In *Accounting in emerging economies* (Vol. 9, pp. 73–95). Leeds: Emerald Publishing Limited.

Jensen, M. C. (1993). The modern industrial revolution, exit, and the failure of internal control systems. *The Journal of Finance*, *48*(3), 831–880.

Jensen, M. C., & Meckling, W. H. (1976). Theory of the firm: Managerial behavior, agency costs and ownership structure. *Journal of Financial Economics*, *3*(4), 305–360. doi:10.1016/0304-405X(76)90026-X

Kanakriyah, R. (2021). The impact of board of directors' characteristics on firm performance: A case study in Jordan. *The Journal of Asian Finance, Economics and Business*, *8*(3), 341–350.

Kirsch, A. (2018). The gender composition of corporate boards: A review and research agenda. *The Leadership Quarterly*, *29*(2), 346–364.

Kumar, P., & Zattoni, A. (2016). Institutional environment and corporate governance. *Corporate Governance: An International Review*, *24*(2), 82–84.

Leblanc, R., & Schwartz, M. S. (2007). The black box of board process: Gaining access to a difficult subject. *Corporate Governance: An International Review*, *15*(5), 843–851. doi:10.1111/j.1467-8683.2007.00617.x

Lorsch, J. W., & MacIver, E. (1989). *Pawns or potentates: The reality of America's corporate boards*. Boston, MA: Harvard Business School Press.

Makhlouf, M. H., Laili, N. H., Ramli, N. A., & Basah, M. Y. (2017). Board of directors' effectiveness and firm performance: Evidence from Jordan. *Research Journal of Finance and Accounting*, *8*(18), 23–34.

McGregor, D. (1960). *The human side of enterprise* (Vol. 21, pp. 166). New York, NY: McGraw-Hill.

Mohammad, S. J., Abdullatif, M., & Zakzouk, F. (2018). The effect of gender diversity on the financial performance of Jordanian banks. *Academy of Accounting and Financial Studies Journal*, *22*(2), 1–11.

Nguyen, T. H., Elmagrhi, M. H., Ntim, C. G., & Wu, Y. (2021). Environmental performance, sustainability, governance and financial performance: Evidence from heavily polluting industries in China. *Business Strategy and the Environment*, *30*(5), 2313–2331.

Ntim, C. G., Opong, K. K., & Danbolt, J. (2015). Board size, corporate regulations and firm valuation in an emerging market: A simultaneous equation approach. *International Review of Applied Economics*, *29*(2), 194–220.

Pallant, J. F. (2013). *SPSS survival manual: A step by step guide to data analysis using IBM SPSS*. Crows Nest, NSW: Allen & Unwin.

Pfeffer, J. (1972). Merger as a response to organizational interdependence. *Administrative Science Quarterly*, 382–394.

Pletzer, J. L., Nikolova, R., Kedzior, K. K., & Voelpel, S. C. (2015). Does gender matter? Female representation on corporate boards and firm financial performance-a meta-analysis. *PLoS One*, *10*(6), e0130005.

Post, C., & Byron, K. (2015). Women on boards and firm financial performance: A meta-analysis. *Academy of Management Journal*, *58*(5), 1546–1571.

Qadorah, A. A. M., & Fadzil, F. H. B. (2018). The relationship between board size and CEO duality and firm performance: Evidence from Jordan. *International Journal of Accounting, Finance and Risk Management*, *3*(3), 16–20.

Reguera-Alvarado, N., de Fuentes, P., & Laffarga, J. (2017). Does board gender diversity influence financial performance? Evidence from Spain. *Journal of Business Ethics*, *141*, 337–350.

Rhoades, D. L., Rechner, P. L., & Sundaramurthy, C. (2001). A meta-analysis of board leadership structure and financial performance: Are "two heads better than one". *Corporate Governance: An International Review*, *9*(4), 311–319.

Saidat, Z., Silva, M., & Seaman, C. (2018). The relationship between corporate governance and financial performance: Evidence from Jordanian family and nonfamily firms. *Journal of Family Business Management*, *9*(1), 54–78.

Salancik, G. R., & Pfeffer, J. (1978). A social information processing approach to job attitudes and task design. *Administrative Science Quarterly*, 224–253.

Shanikat, M., & Abbadi, S. S. (2011). Assessment of corporate governance in Jordan: An empirical study. *Australasian Accounting, Business and Finance Journal*, *5*(3), 93–106.

Terjesen, S., Sealy, R., & Singh, V. (2009). Women directors on corporate boards: A review and research agenda. *Corporate Governance: An International Review*, *17*(3), 320–337.

Tulung, J. E., & Ramdani, D. (2018). Independence, size and performance of the board: An emerging market research. *Corporate Ownership and Control*, *15*(2).

Velte, P. (2017). Do women on board of directors have an impact on corporate governance quality and firm performance? A literature review. *International Journal of Sustainable Strategic Management*, *5*(4), 302–346.

Villalonga, B., & Amit, R. (2006). How do family ownership, control and management affect firm value? *Journal of Financial Economics*, *80*(2), 385–417.

Yermack, D. (1996). Higher market valuation of companies with a small board of directors. *Journal of Financial Economics*, *40*(2), 185–211.

Zheng, C., Moudud-Ul-Huq, S., Rahman, M. M., & Ashraf, B. N. (2017). Does the ownership structure matter for banks' capital regulation and risk-taking behavior? Empirical evidence from a developing country. *Research in International Business and Finance*, *42*, 404–421.

Chapter 19

Human Development Based on the Competitiveness of the Peruvian Region of Ancash, 2008–2021

William Dextre-Martinez[a], *Rosario Huerta-Soto*[b], *Eduardo Rocca-Espinoza*[c], *Manuel Chenet-Zuta*[d] *and Luis Angulo-Cabanillas*[a]

[a]Universidad Nacional Santiago Antúnez de Mayolo, Peru
[b]Universidad Cesar Vallejo, Peru
[c]Pontificia Universidad Católica del Peru, Peru
[d]Universidad Nacional Mayor de San Marcos, Perú

Abstract

The study set out to understand how the regional competitiveness index (RCI) in the department of Ancash related to the human development index (HDI) from 2008 to 2021. For a more complete understanding of the findings, each component or dimension of the RCI was analyzed. Ancash's HDI and its competitiveness index over a 14-year period were used as the population for this applied, longitudinal, descriptive-correlational study, which was based on secondary data extracted from the "Instituto Nacional de Estadística e Informática" (INEI) and business school of the Pontificia Universidad Católica del Perú (CENTRUM) statistical databases. Multiple linear regression was used to find the relationship. The research found a strong and positive correlation between regional competitiveness and human development between 2008 and 2021. No correlations were found between the HDI and the health, education, employment, or institutional dimensions of regional competitiveness, but direct and significant correlations were established between the economic environment and the HDI and between the infrastructure dimension and the HDI.

Technological Innovations for Business, Education and Sustainability, 283–296

doi:10.1108/978-1-83753-106-620241019

Keywords: Competitiveness; human development; economic environment; standard of living; employment; sustainability

1. Introduction

Human development is a hidden problem in most societies; ours is no exception. This is especially true in our region, which has benefited for years from the influx of economic resources from the Canon, but this has not translated into an increase in the standard of living of the local population (García-Lirios, 2019). By the same token, competitiveness is a characteristic of any organization operating in a competitive economic or market environment. Thanks to the efforts of technicians and professionals, human development and competitiveness indicators have been developed that allow for more informed decisions on how the limited resources of the Ancash region should be allocated and dispersed for the greater good of the population as a whole.

Since the 1990s, countries around the world have been working on the creation of their own human development indices; in Peru, since 2008, we have been working on a regional competitiveness index (RCI) that covers the entire country and includes a set of variables organized in dimensions that we intend to analyses and interpret in terms of their impact and influence on human development (Huerta-Soto, Huaranga Toledo, Anaya Lopez, & Concepción Lázaro, 2022). Therefore, the Ancash team must measure, investigate, and question these assertions. This study aims to carry out a methodical analysis of the impacts on the impact of the competitiveness of this area of the country with respect to the human development index (HDI), as little is known about the claims that, in regions where opponents of mining activity claim that progress has not been as significant, conceal the fact that mining areas register positive migration while non-mining areas register the opposite situation (Villanueva & Pinchi, 2019).

The challenge is how to explain the large-scale migration of people to regulated mining areas. Possible motivations include the desire to increase their life expectancy, improve their standard of living, and provide a better future for their children and grandchildren through education. For this reason, the competitiveness index and the HDI have been brought together in this study effort (Espinosa-Espinosa, Madero-Jirado, Rodríguez-Puello, & Díaz-Canedo, 2020). Consequently, there is a pressing need to investigate and examine this phenomenon using the methods of scientific research, the concepts of management science, and the theoretical foundations of competitiveness and the HDI.

The main objective of the study is to determine whether or not there is a relationship between the HDI and the regional competitiveness index (RCI), and whether or not there is a relationship between the dimensions of regional competitiveness and the HDI. The data used to evaluate the hypotheses in each of the proposed objectives are presented, as well as the results of a simulation study assessing the impact of the dimensions of regional competitiveness on the HDI. The study set out to answer the question: How does the level of competitiveness in the department of Ancash relate to human development from 2008 to 2022?

2. Literature Review

Many academics and experts in the field use the term "competitiveness" interchangeably. According to Díaz, Alvarez, and Ojeda (2020), a country's level of competitiveness indicates the extent to which it is able to compete with others in the global marketplace by providing superior goods and services, much like multinational companies such as the Nestlé and Kraft Foods. That is, the assumption that nations compete with each other like General Motors and Toyota is widespread, but not entirely accurate. The issue for any nation that aspires to improve the lot of its population is not competitiveness, but productivity; in other words, any nation that aspires to improve the lot of its population must increase its productivity levels, and not just in comparison with other nations. Alvarado and Jiménez (2020) also point out that the relationship between trade, trade balance, and employment rates is unclear. Trade imbalances and employment losses are a cause for concern, but are not fully supported by evidence.

As a consultant to both companies and countries, González (2021) has come to understand that competitiveness is linked to the development of an advantage over the competition, which he calls "Competitive Advantage," and which is the subject of one of the best-selling books on the subject of competitiveness. In his approach, he separates comparative advantage from competitive advantage by underlining the importance of the term "sustainability of advantage" to distinguish between the two. He comes to the following conclusion about what it takes to be competitive in today's market: "Competitiveness is about developing and maintaining a superior competitive position," which is achieved by identifying the value that is obtained for customers and that cannot be imitated by competitors over a long period (Mora-Villamizar, Morales-Pérez, & Barrientos-Monsalve, 2019).

As we have seen, the idea of "competitiveness" has been around for a long time; in fact, it has its roots in trade theories developed almost three centuries ago (Morales-Guerrero & Álvarez-Aros, 2021). Thus, Ráez, Jiménez, and Buitrago (2021) defined a country as having an "absolute advantage" if its exports of a given good or service were the cheapest in the world. On the other hand, Soto, Asis, Figueroa, and Plasencia (2023) stated that a country should export those goods in which it is more productive relative to others and import those in which it is less productive. Sharon Oster states that, Michael Porter argues that a country's ability to cope with this problem depends on the innovative capacity of its industries and that, as a result, "firms gain advantages over the world's best competitors because of pressure and challenge." Over a given period of time, a firm's competitiveness is measured by its performance relative to other firms around the world that make similar things (Porter, 2014).

It follows from these definitions that competitiveness refers to a firm's ability to provide consumers with goods and services that meet or exceed their expectations through superior management of available resources compared to rivals in the same industry. To remain competitive, a firm must master resource management, increase productivity, and anticipate customer needs. Since a company's competitiveness depends on "productivity" and the factors that determine it internally, it is important to understand what this term means. Productivity refers to the efficiency with which a set of resources is used to produce a given output, or the ratio of output to inputs, or output to time spent producing it. Porter defines a firm's competitive advantage as the amount by which the value it provides to its consumers exceeds its expenditures (Chuya, Herrera, Aguirre, & Serrano, 2021).

Improvements that add value to the product are examples of competitive advantages, as are distribution processes that are more efficient and prices that are higher than those offered by competitors, among other factors that give a company an advantage over its rivals in the market. To assess competitiveness, we must first identify its driving forces and quantify their relative importance (Luciani-Toro, Zambrano, & González, 2019). Different techniques attempt to quantify different aspects of competitiveness by considering different conditioning variables, just as there are different definitions of competitiveness. Several scholars are of the opinion that industrial competitiveness does not emerge out of nowhere whenever the macroeconomic environment changes, nor can it be generated solely by entrepreneurship at the microeconomic level. On the contrary, it is the result of the interaction of several factors, such as the state, enterprises, intermediary institutions, and the organizational capacity of society.

In addition to a functioning production mechanism at the micro level and stable macroeconomic conditions at the macro level, successful industrial development also requires the existence of targeted measures by public and private development organizations to improve the competitiveness of businesses at the middle level (Soto, Avalos, Albornoz, & Aguilar, 2022). This means that political and economic structures at the destination level, as well as sociocultural elements and key organizational patterns, determine the extent to which middle- and macro-level policies can be linked. Technology, innovation, marketing, human resources, management capacity, financial resources, culture, quality, production, logistics, internal organization, purchasing, research and development, and interaction with suppliers and customers are just some of the indicators that have been proposed to measure competitiveness by the Organisation for Economic Co-operation and Development (OECD), the World Bank, the Inter-American Development Bank and various authors. If we want to make the kind of decisions that will help our companies to prosper, which in turn will boost national growth and improve people's standard of living, we must have a thorough understanding of how competitive our companies and our country really are (Bárbara & Darcy, 2020).

The World Competitiveness Year book, which has been modified for use in Peru and is cited as such by Zeibote, Volkova, and Todorov (2019), will serve as the instrument used to measure the competitiveness variable. Considering a country's financial markets are a good indicator of the health of the economy because they mediate the flow of capital between households and firms. It is an indicator of the government's influence on a country's economy. Its metrics include real gross domestic product (GDP), real GDP per capita, capital stock per worker, public budget per capita, real monthly household expenditure, annual growth in real household expenditure, availability of financial services, and access to credit. Investment in the nation's physical, technological and human resources (Zia, Rafiq, Saqib, & Atiq, 2022). In addition, a country's ability to attract foreign direct investment and boost private sector productivity is often linked to the quality of its infrastructure: availability of electricity, cost of electricity, availability of water, reliability of water supply, water quality, sewerage access, internet access, mobile phone ownership, and air transport density are some of the metrics used.

It describes the health status of a region's inhabitants and their families: birth weight, infant mortality, child mortality, chronic malnutrition, morbidity, percentage of the population with access to health care, percentage of hospital births, percentage of the population with health insurance (Wibowo & Nurcahyo, 2020). Education expenditure also examines how much money a country spends on the education and training of its inhabitants, both public and private. Illiteracy, primary and secondary enrollment, and the percentage of the population with a postsecondary qualification are some of the indicators used. Academic performance in reading and mathematics classrooms connected to the internet (Soto et al., 2023).

Employment market performance indicates the functioning of the national employment market and its competitiveness. It takes into account indicators of employment market efficiency, basic education, and the degree of distortion of employment taxation, as well as a measure of a country's level of employment expenditure relative to international standards (Roman, Roman, Prus, & Szczepanek, 2020). Employment income, gender wage gap, employment opportunities, employment force formation both formal and informal, youth unemployment in urban areas, and institutions which are products of the growing literature on the impact of various civil and legal institutions on economic development and competitiveness (Cazallo-Antúnez, Meñaca Guerrero, Lechuga Cardozo, & García Guiliany, 2019). Public investment performance, availability of public finances, and trust in government are some of its metrics. Social unrest, lawlessness, bloodshed and police presence.

In contrast, we could look at human development through the lens of developmental psychology, which Sánchez (2019) describes as the identification and understanding of all the changes and continuities that human beings experience throughout their lives. Rodríguez-Miranda, Vial Cossani, and Parrao (2021) mention five different theoretical approaches to the growth of the mind. Psychological speculations of this school of thought focused on the unconscious and instincts. Learning theorization: The idea that most human behavior is learned and that children's actions can be largely autonomous from their understanding of the world. The general aim of cognitive theories is to describe how and why a child's knowledge grows and changes over time. De La Rosa, Toro, Jaén, and Espinoza (2019) comment primarily on their definition of cognitive development as growth of intellectual potential and attribute that support understanding. From an ethologist's point of view, there are two main categories of behavioral explanations: immediate and evolutionary. Since their main goal is to understand the inherent mechanisms that affect growth, they concentrate mainly on the evolutionary ones. Montiel-Méndez and Soto-Maciel (2020) argue that this method focuses on cultural transmission, it follows that children need opportunities for social contact in order to internalize the norms of the society in which they grow up.

According to Olvera's *A Look at the Concept of Poverty*, the HDI was the "great achievement" of the United Nations Development Program (UNDP) and was necessary due to the lack of a specific definition of poverty (Guerra-Carrillo & Castañeda-Núñez, 2020). This index, first established in the late 1980s, is used to quantify the degree of economic hardship of individuals, and has served as a standard for ranking nations according to their progress in human development. The United Nations selected three social indicators that together show high, medium, and low levels of human development; they were used to calculate the logarithm of the HDI. The indicators of life expectancy, educational attainment, and economic prosperity constitute the trifecta of basic HDI components. Using life expectancy as a measure, we can see that those who have easier access to health care live longer than those who do not (Hernández-Ortiz, Ortíz-Medina, & Martínez-Pérez, 2020). In addition to the value people place on longevity per se, there are also many indirect benefits of living longer that contribute to the importance of life expectancy. Health and nutrition are the "valuable gains" alluded to in the phrase; in other words, people can expect to live longer if they have better access to health care and nutrition.

Maroto-Navarro, Ocaña-Riola, Gil-García, and García-Calvente (2021) state that the HDI is widely used as a metric in the social and economic sciences. The Human Development Report (HDR) was created in 1989 and debuted in 1990 with the publication of the first World HDR. The HDI has gained popularity as an alternative measure of a country's level of development to the more conventional GDP per capita. Longevity (measured by the average age at death), education (measured by the adult literacy rate, which has a weighting of two, and the combined primary, secondary, and tertiary enrollment rate, which has a weighting of one), and wealth (measured by GDP per capita in purchasing power parity dollars) are the three components of the international HDI that are proposed to be introduced as a synthetic indicator. All these indicators are averaged and "normalized," or given the same weight, to make them more easily comparable. To the extent possible, the HDI is determined using information collected from the most authoritative national and international statistical agencies and other credible sources. To better reflect disparities in achievement over time, Peru's most recent HDR includes a national HDI (Barreno-Benavides, López-Paredes, & Cabrera-Maya, 2020). Data from the National Institute of Statistics' Living Conditions Survey have been used to ensure uniformity and comparability. Although this index is similar within the categories and time periods described in the Report, it is not necessarily comparable with those reported in other national and global reports.

Household health is measured by a composite score that takes into account factors such as health insurance coverage, the number of people sharing a bedroom, the availability of drinking water and toilets, and soil quality (Villa-Vélez, 2020). Birth rate and longevity reflect this. Education: This indicator takes into account both the level of education attained by young people and those over

25 years of age. Adult illiteracy and primary and secondary school enrollment are two indicators. Quality of life: Internationally comparable estimates (in PPP dollars per capita) of household income from both employment and nonemployment sources were included. Per capita income from both employment and capital (Boraita, Alsina, Ibort, & Torres, 2022). As a normative criterion, the highest attainable levels of health and education, as well as the highest attainable level of income (just over $18,000 per capita per year) are used as comparisons for income and wealth indicators, respectively. GDP per capita is another metric used to assess success.

3. Methodology

The study is correlational because it examined the links between two independent variables (competitiveness and human development) and therefore has an applied purpose. Furthermore, it is longitudinal in nature because it was evaluated over time. Moreover, it analyses each year from 2008 to 2021. The indices and statistics of the dimensions of each variable make up the population. The competitiveness indices include the following categories: economic environment, infrastructure, health, education, employment competence, and institutions. The HDI has quantifiable data for each year of the designated time period (data extracted from the INEI and CENTRUM).

This study employs data analysis based on previously collected information. Information from the National Institute of Statistics and Informatics of Peru will serve as the primary or informant source for the case. According to the parameters of this study, indices were calculated for the independent and dependent variables. Descriptive statistics are used to show aggregate data (Hernández & Mendoza, 2018). They are presented in the form of a frequency table. Each research signal is entered into a database and displayed in separate or cross-tabulated tables as needed. For this, we used the statistical software eViews v10 to transform the collected data into a spreadsheet formatted for the relevant metrics. Tabulation was completed, which will expose the aggregate and individual behavior of the variables over the time period of the study. With these numbers in hand, tables can be produced for each indication and the factors identified in this study.

4. Results

A differential equation technique for a multiple linear regression model is used to compare all observable aspects of the RCI with the HDI of the Ancash area. After eliminating all dimensions and components of the independent variable, their values were compared with those of the dependent variable using linear regression. To identify the specific relationships between the objectives of the study, direct regressions were performed between the HDI and each of the six components of the regional competitiveness variable. The behavior of the variables over time is observed and a descriptive analysis is carried out on the basis of the figures

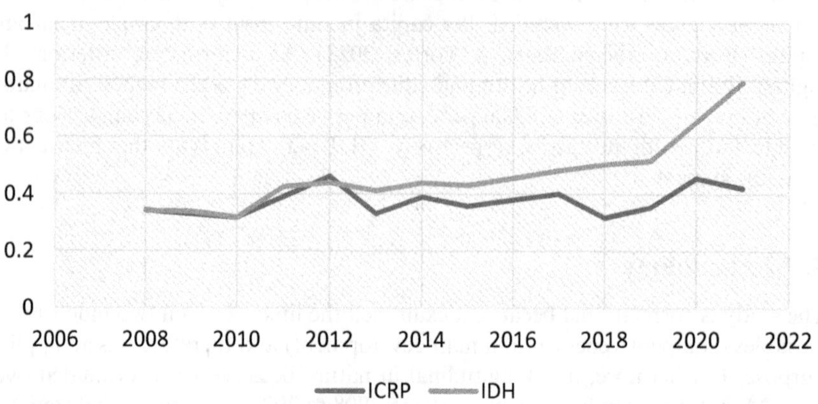

Fig. 19.1. Comparison of the Regional Competitiveness Index (RCI) and Human Development Index (HDI).

provided containing the values acquired. Finally, through a probabilistic simulation process, it is possible to identify or prioritise the dimensions to which resources will be allocated based on the results reported on the degree to which the latent variables or dimensions of the regional competitiveness construct influence the HDI variable.

Comparing the progress of the variables under study over the period of analysis, and a similar pattern of behavior is observed between the two, with both experiencing falls in the indicators or indices in 2010 (3), rises in 2012 (5), and falls in 2013 (6) to rise again in the subsequent period. When comparing 2018 and 2021, the most striking difference is that while the HDI had a small gain in 2018, the Public Relations Council of India (PRCI) experienced a decline in the following year (5). As can be seen in Fig. 19.1.

Tables 19.1, 19.2, and 19.3 show the results of a multiple linear regression analysis of the relationship between the RCI and the HDI. There is a strong, direct, and substantial link between the dimensions of competitiveness and the HDI; the R^2 is 0.949616329 and the adjusted R^2 is 0.817575036, with a p-value of 0.003136921. The β of dimension 5, which corresponds to employment market competitiveness, is negative, providing observational support for the particular null hypothesis.

5. Discussion

We used a multiple regression model in which the dimensions of competitiveness were treated as independent variables to determine the strength of the association

Table 19.1. Multiple Linear Regression.

Regression Statistics	
Multiple correlation coefficient	0.949616329
Coefficient of determination $R2$	0.901771173
Adjusted $R2$	0.817575036
Standard error	0.053820028
Observations	13

Table 19.2. Relationship Between Regional Competitiveness Index (RCI) and Human Development Index (HDI).

	Coefficients	**Standard Error *t***	***t* Statistic**	**Probability**
Interception	0.102921024	0.185934369	0.553534152	0.597125885
Dim1 – Economic environment	1.368986291	0.265387472	5.158443538	0.001311711
Dim2 – Infrastructure	−0.006692406	0.100441827	−0.066629667	0.948739638
Dim3 – Health	−0.007732228	0.225015832	−0.034363041	0.973546995
Dim4 – Education	0.250035939	0.320644667	0.779791356	0.461061098
Dim5 – Employment	−0.404641745	0.271799301	−1.488751967	0.180159707
Dim6 – Institutions	0.17015756	0.146381707	1.162423662	0.28315708

Table 19.3. Analysis of Variance.

	Degrees of Freedom	**Sum of Squares**	**Mean Squares**	***F***	**Critical Value of *F***
Regression	6	0.186141527	0.031023588	10.710363	0.003136921
Residuals	7	0.020276168	0.002896595		
Total	13	0.206417695			

between RCI and HDI. To this end, particular hypotheses were posed, the results of which allow inferences to be drawn in each case. As for the specific hypothesis, which assesses the connection between the economic environment and the HDI, it is clear that there is a direct and substantial connection. Thus, the economic environment is the independent variable that most affects the HDI; however, it is evident that this component has been neglected during the time period considered. This dimension has one of the lowest averages compared to the other dimensions.

Based on the above, we can say that real and per capita GDP, capital stock per worker, per capita public budget, real expenditure per monthly household, and three others suggesting theoretical bases are part of the examination of the economic environment. Specifically, the research by Soto et al. (2022) examines regional competitiveness and economic development, finds that micro and macroeconomic variables significantly influence competitiveness, but are notoriously difficult to measure. From these findings, we can conclude that this condition does not prevent such research in the Ancash area. Additionally, the study of the relationship between the level of road infrastructure development, productive activity, and human development by Ramirez et al. (2022) concludes that road infrastructure has a positive impact on human development in Peru, accounting for all factors that contribute to HDI (electricity, water, drainage, communication, and transport coverage).

Although the health dimension has been shown to be related to the HDI, the results do not point to a direct or significant relationship; the correlation value is rather small and tends to zero, and the level of significance is above 0.05. However, these results should be interpreted with caution because the constituent parts of the health axis could be examined independently to assess the connection. Due to the diversity of indicators included in the health component of the RCI, a more nuanced examination of the variable, such as life expectancy at birth, chronic malnutrition, morbidity, hospital coverage, and access to health insurance, is necessary. It is also important to note that in the Rojas-Vega et al. study (2023), in the ICR and in the other versions that allowed us to do the analysis up to 2017, a 10-year interval or period was used. This suggests that, for an objective discussion for future studies, more years should be taken as a reference to determine whether or not this relationship might occur as expected. As Saehu et al. explain (2022), states that Peru is a developing nation; this association has not been demonstrated, but may be explained by the circumstances of health management, which have persisted for more than a century under the current administration.

But research by Soto et al. (2023) shows that spending money on research and development (R&D) and higher education has a positive effect on measures of competitiveness, and that there is a direct relationship between the two. It follows from these data that competitiveness indices improve living standards to the extent that there is investment in education, making competitiveness indices themselves a moderating variable between educational attainment and human flourishing. With respect to the previous paragraph, the empirical evidence suggests that there is a correlation, but it is not immediately obvious, as the effects of education take time to manifest themselves in the medium and long term, i.e., the connection between school expenditure and the impact on human development may not be detected until it is too late. This leaves room for further research on the topic (Huaranga-Toledo, Ruiz, Vergara, & Rodríguez, 2023).

According to the research of Huerta-Soto et al. (2023), human development and economic growth are intertwined, and productivity is the central issue for advancement, which requires a workforce properly educated in technical and professional skills to make meaningful contributions to society. To the extent that the analysis is to be conducted systemically, meaning that the set of dimensions affects and is related to the dependent variable, but that is not how all of these dimensions should be analyzed, the notion that the HDI is positively correlated with the RCI is supported by a generally recognized correlation and degree of significance in the overall model.

Given that the Ancash area ranks last in the country for the fourth consecutive year in the institutions pillar, this is where most work needs to be done to make it more competitive. Considering that this is the area with the highest number of social clashes (28 in 2017, compared to 24 in 2016). Moreover, barely 56.6% of the region's investment budget was actually spent in 2017, making it the region with the second lowest level of public execution. In 2016, the region ranked last in execution rates, with only 53.2%. Public administration approval has fallen from 16.2% in 2016 to 13.1% in 2017. This puts the area at the third lowest approval rate in the country. The informality of our national, regional, and local reality is largely to blame for the inability to establish a correlation between the competitiveness of our employment market and the HDI. Similarly, linking the institutional competitiveness factor with the HDI has proven to be an unattainable task.

6. Conclusion

From 2008 to 2022, the RCI in Ancash has a direct and strong correlation with the HDI. However, the link and relevance can only be demonstrated by a combined study of the dimensions using multiple linear regression. The study found that the economic environment component had the highest levels of correlation and significance, as well as the highest levels of probabilistic simulation, with the HDI.

The economic environment dimension, despite having the highest impact, was shown to have the lowest average score compared to the other dimensions, suggesting that the most important variable for the benefit of society has improved the least in the Ancash region. Both the economic environment component and the sixth component, which measures institutional competitiveness, are below average. While Peru as a whole has a high HDI, the Ancash area has a relatively low one.

In particular, the research has found that the infrastructure metric and the HDI have a clear and substantial correlation. No correlation has been found between the HDI and the education criterion. However, if the temporal nature of the indices is taken into account, as the antecedents suggest, this link can be demonstrated. Last but not least, the data show that there is no correlation between the health dimension and the HDI despite the fact that this is one of the aspects in which most effort has been invested without the desired result.

References

Alvarado, R., & Jiménez, C. (2020). Relación entre competitividad y desarrollo regional en Ecuador: una aplicación de modelos espaciales. *Revista Economía y Política*, (31), 117–133. doi:10.25097/rep.n31.2020.06

Bárbara, V. K., & Darcy, F. O. S. (2020). Efectos de la inversión extranjera y competitividad en el comercio y productividad de países latinoamericanos. *Economía y Sociedad*, *25*(57), 110–125. doi:10.15359/eys.25-57.6

Barreno-Benavides, L., López-Paredes, H., & Cabrera-Maya, L. (2020). Análisis del impacto del crédito para iniciativas productivas entregados a los beneficiarios del bono de desarrollo humano. Estudio de caso. *Revista Economía y Política*, (31), 3–24. doi:10.25097/rep.n31.2020.01

Boraita, R. J., Alsina, D. A., Ibort, E. G., & Torres, J. M. D. (2022, March). Hábitos y calidad de vida relacionada con la salud: diferencias entre adolescentes de entornos rurales y urbanos. *In Anales de Pediatría*, *96*(3), 196–202. doi:10.1016/j.anpedi.2020.11.022

Cazallo-Antúnez, A. M., Meñaca Guerrero, I., Lechuga Cardozo, J. I., & García Guiliany, J. E. (2019). La Alianza del pacífico y los brics: Dos modelos de competitividad país. *Revista Lasallista de Investigación*, *16*(2), 122–141. doi:10.22507/rli.v16n2a11

Chuya, J. C., Herrera, K. C., Aguirre, P. A. U., & Serrano, L. A. L. (2021). Economía digital, herramienta para mejorar la competitividad y productividad en las PYMES caso: Machala-Ecuador. *593 Digital Publisher CEIT*, *6*(3), 76–86. doi:10.33386/593dp.2021.3.543

De La Rosa, A., Toro, K., Jaén, K., & Espinoza, E. E. (2019). El proceso de enseñanza-aprendizaje en las ciencias naturales: las estrategias didácticas como alternativa. *Revista Científica Agroecosistemas*, *7*(1), 58–62. Retrieved from https://aes.ucf.edu.cu/index.php/aes/article/view/243

Díaz, D. E., Alvarez, B. M., & Ojeda, M. N. (2020). Competitividad regional y desarrollo económico: Una breve Revisión de la literatura ecónomica moderna. *Revista de economía política de Buenos Aires*, (20), 109–153. Retrieved from https://ojs.econ.uba.ar/index.php/REPBA/article/view/1720

Espinosa-Espinosa, A., Madero-Jirado, M., Rodríguez-Puello, G., & Díaz-Canedo, L. C. (2020). Etnicidad, espacio y desarrollo humano en comunidades pobres urbanas: la comuna 6 en Cartagena de Indias, Colombia. *Cuadernos de Economía*, *39*(81), 635–665. doi:10.15446/cuad.econ.v39n81.77333

García-Lirios, C. (2019). Dimensiones de la teoría del desarrollo humano. *Ehquidad: La Revista Internacional de Políticas de Bienestar y Trabajo Social*, *11*, 27–54. Retrieved from https://www.redalyc.org/articulo.oa?id=672174444002

González, S. (2021). Regional competitiveness in Latin America: A comparative study of the key elements for regional performance. *Investigaciones Regionales= Journal of Regional Research*, (50), 125–146. doi:10.38191/iirr-jorr.21.014

Guerra-Carrillo, J. C., & Castañeda-Núñez, E. S. (2020). Impacto de la gestión de inversiones municipales sobre el índice de desarrollo humano en el Valle del Mantaro (Perú). *Revista Visión Contable*, (21), 143–165. doi:10.24142/rvc.n21a5

Hernández-Ortiz, M., Ortíz-Medina, I., & Martínez-Pérez, J. (2020). Producto interno bruto e índice de desarrollo humano: dos variables inconexas. *Revista De Ciencias Sociales*, *29*(44), 97–116. Retrieved from http://www.revistacienciasociales.cl/index.php/publicacion/article/view/155

Hernández, R., & Mendoza, C. (2018). *Metodología de investigación. Las rutas cuantitativa, cualitativa y mixta*. New York, NY: McGraw-Hill.

Huaranga-Toledo, H. L., Ruiz, J. R., Vergara, C. S., & Rodríguez, J. L. (2023). Cultura organizativa y el crecimiento empresarial de la medianas empresa de la ciudad de Huaraz, Perú. *Revista Científica Epistemia*, *7*(1), 01–13. doi:10.26495/re.v7i1.2426

Huerta-Soto, R., Huaranga Toledo, H., Anaya Lopez, C., & Concepción Lázaro, R. (2022). Marketing de influenciadores y su efecto en la intención de compra de los consumidores de prendas ecológicas. *Revista Cientifica Epistemia*, *6*(2), 113–127. doi:10.26495/re.v6i2.2299

Huerta-Soto, R., Ramirez-Asis, E., Tarazona-Jiménez, J., Nivin-Vargas, L., Norabuena-Figueroa, R., Guzman-Avalos, M., & Reyes-Reyes, C. (2023). Predictable inventory management within dairy supply chain operations. *International Journal of Retail & Distribution Management*. doi:10.1108/IJRDM-01-2023-0051

Luciani-Toro, L. R., Zambrano, Á. A., & González, A. I. (2019). MIPYMES ecuatorianas: Una visión de su emprendimiento, productividad y competitividad en aras de mejora continua. *Cooperativismo y Desarrollo*, *7*(3), 313–332. Retrieved from http://coodes.upr.edu.cu/index.php/coodes/article/view/217

Maroto-Navarro, G., Ocaña-Riola, R., Gil-García, E., & García-Calvente, M. D. M. (2021). Análisis multinivel de la producción científica mundial sobre paternidad, desarrollo humano e igualdad de género. *Gaceta Sanitaria*, *34*, 582–588. doi:10.1016/j.gaceta.2019.04.008

Montiel-Méndez, O. J., & Soto-Maciel, A. (2020). Un marco exploratorio para el emprendimiento desde una perspectiva evolutiva. *RETOS. Revista de Ciencias de la Administración y Economía*, *10*(20), 361–373. doi:10.17163/ret.n20.2020.10

Mora-Villamizar, D. A., Morales-Pérez, K. T., & Barrientos-Monsalve, E. J. (2019). Análisis de la competitividad entre las empresas los olivos y la esperanza en Cúcuta, Norte de Santander-según las cinco fuerzas de Michael Porter. *Revista convicciones*, *6*(11), 69–75. Retrieved from https://www.fesc.edu.co/Revistas/OJS/index.php/convicciones/article/view/418

Morales-Guerrero, R. E., & Álvarez-Aros, E. L. (2021). Innovación abierta como acelerador de competitividad y resultados empresariales, un estudio bibliométrico. *Revista Economía y Política*, (34), 1–16. Retrieved from https://www.redalyc.org/journal/5711/571167877002/html/

Porter, M. (2014). *Ser competitivo*. Boston, MA: Deusto.

Ráez, R. N., Jiménez, W. G., & Buitrago, J. D. (2021). Las teorías de la competitividad: una síntesis. *Revista republicana*, (31), 119–144. doi:10.21017/rev.repub.2021.v31.a110

Ramirez, E. H., Rosario, H. S., Laura, N. V., Hober, H. T., Julio, V. A., & Victor, F. L. (2022). Distribution of public service and individual job performance in Peruvian Municipality. *유통과학연구*, *20*(10), 11–17. doi:10.15722/jds.20.10.202210.11

Rodríguez-Miranda, A., Vial Cossani, C., & Parrao, A. (2021). Índice compuesto y multidimensional de desarrollo regional: una propuesta para América Latina. *Revista iberoamericana de estudios municipales*, (23), 1–33. doi:10.32457/riem.v23i1.580

Rojas-Vega, J. A., Brito, E., Medrano, W., & Leiva, O. C. (2023). Relación de la responsabilidad empresarial en los conflictos medioambientales y sociales en una unidad minera de la Región Ancash. *Revista Científica Epistemia*, *7*(1), 69–82. doi:10.26495/re.v7i1.2436

Roman, M., Roman, M., Prus, P., & Szczepanek, M. (2020). Tourism competitiveness of rural areas: Evidence from a region in Poland. *Agriculture*, *10*(11), 569. doi:10.3390/agriculture10110569

Saehu, M. S., Diah, A. M., Julca-Guerrero, F., Huerta-Soto, R., & Valderrama-Plasencia, L. (2022). Environmental awareness and environmental management practices: Mediating effect of environmental data distribution. *Journal of Environmental Management & Tourism*, *13*(5), 1339–1352. doi:10.14505/jemt.v13.5(61).11

Sánchez, J. R. (2019). Desarrollo y calidad de vida. Una perspectiva crítica a partir del pensamiento de Amartya Sen. *Aletheia*, *11*(2), 107–126. doi:10.11600/ale.v11i2.551

Soto, R. H., Asis, E. H., Figueroa, R. P., & Plasencia, L. (2023). Autoeficacia emprendedora y desempeño de micro y pequeñas empresas peruanas. *Revista Venezolana de Gerencia: RVG*, *28*(102), 751–768. doi:10.52080/rvgluz.28.102.19

Soto, R. M., Avalos, M., Albornoz, J. I., & Aguilar, S. J. (2022). Competencias digitales de los profesores universitarios durante la pandemia por covid-19 en el Perú. *Revista Electrónica Interuniversitaria de Formación del Profesorado*, *25*(1), 49–60. doi:10.6018/reifop.500481

Villa-Vélez, L. (2020). Educación para la salud y justicia social basada en el enfoque de las capacidades: Una oportunidad para el desarrollo de la salud pública. *Ciência & Saúde Coletiva*, *25*, 1539–1546. doi:10.1590/1413-81232020254.19052018

Villanueva, A. H., & Pinchi, W. (2019). Crecimiento económico, pobreza y desarrollo humano en el Perú. *Revista Científica Pakamuros*, *7*(1), 68–79. doi:10.37787/pakamuros-unj.v7i1.77

Wibowo, N., & Nurcahyo, R. (2020, March). Competitiveness in global transformation: A systematic review. In *Proceedings of the International Conference on Industrial Engineering and Operations Management* (Vol. 12, No. 10, pp. 718–727). Retrieved from https://scholar.ui.ac.id/en/publications/competitiveness-in-global-transformation-a-systematic-review

Zeibote, Z., Volkova, T., & Todorov, K. (2019). The impact of globalization on regional development and competitiveness: Cases of selected regions. *Insights Into Regional Development*, *1*(1), 33–47. doi:10.9770/IRD.2019.1.1(3)

Zia, B., Rafiq, M., Saqib, S. E., & Atiq, M. (2022). Agricultural market competitiveness in the context of climate change: A systematic review. *Sustainability*, *14*(7), 3721. doi:10.3390/su14073721

Chapter 20

Female Education and Economic Growth in Egypt: An Empirical Study

Samar H. AlBagoury

Cairo University, Egypt

Abstract

Education had proven to be one of the main determinants of economic growth, and it is a reason of the variations in economic growth levels between developed and developing countries. One of the main dimensions in studding the relationship between economic growth and education is the gender dimension or the importance of gender equality or female education in achieving economic growth. This chapter aims to test the hypothesis of the existence of a positive relationship between female education and economic growth in Egypt since 1990.

To address this question, Auto Regression Distributed Lag (ARDL) Bound test approach is conducted to analyze the co-integration between female education and economic growth using Egyptian Data for the period 1990–2022. The Empirical analysis for Egypt suggests the existence of positive significant relationship both in the short run and long run and that the impact of female education on economic growth is larger than the impact of education in general on growth. This could be explained by the existence of gender gap in Egypt, labor market, and thus, more educated girls able to enter the labor market will affect the economic growth more than the education of both sexes, in other words, there is still a room for improvement in the female labor market opportunities than for both sexes. The chapter also confirms the existence of a direct link between education in general and economic growth and thus confirms the hypothesis of the positive impact of education economic growth.

Keywords: Female education; ARDL; economic growth; bound test; cointegration; Egypt

Technological Innovations for Business, Education and Sustainability, 297–308

Published under exclusive licence by Emerald Publishing Limited
doi:10.1108/978-1-83753-106-620241020

1. Introduction

Although education is considered as one of the main determinants of economic growth, in many cases, this link is insignificant. And one of the main reasons or explanation of this insignificance according to many studies is the gender inequality in education.

Gender inequality in general refers to the situation in which gender determine different rights and dignity. In other words, it refers to the situation in which women and men have unequal access to their rights and their participation in labor market, economic and political rights, power and decision-making (European Commission, 2004). And one of the main common aspects of gender inequality is the inequality in education as the female enrollment ratio in different schooling levels tends to be low in developing and less developed countries. For decades, developing countries are known with gender inequality in almost all development and economic indicators, one of which the gender inequality in education especially in higher level of education.

In Egypt, female education is significant part of Egyptian development plane 2030, as it is one of the main sustainable development goals of United Nations. But as many developing countries, there is still a considerable gap between male and female education indicators in Egypt especially in higher level of education. For example, female gross enrollment ration of tertiary education is only 39.8 which is lower than the world average (45.35), while female upper secondary education completion rate is 85.5%, but it is worth to mention that the enrollment rate for both male and female is actually low in Egypt, and thus, the gender parity index of tertiary school enrollment is 1.04. This means that the issue in Egypt is not only the gender gap in education but also the relative low rates of enrollment in higher levels of education (USAID, 2023). The education gender gap is clearer in the adult education indicators. For example, adult women (above 24 years old) illiteracy rate is 41% while it is 29% for males (UNESCO, 2022).

To emphasis the impact of female education on economic growth in Egypt, this chapter is organized as follows: the first section provides a brief review for the theoretical and empirical literature of the link between economic growth and education in general and then between female education and economic growth. The second section discusses the methodology of the chapter, while the third section reports the main results and discussion. The last section is for the conclusion.

2. Literature Review

The education impact on economic growth is well-established in the economic literature since 1960's. The correlation between education and economic growth even had mentioned Adam Smith's thought, when he mentioned human capital as one of four types of capital he recognized in his book "wealth of nations." He defined it as skills dexterity (physical, intellectual, psychological) and judgment (Karatzia-Stavlioti, 2009). Neoclassical economists also identify the role of education in economic growth as Solow argued that, economic growth doesn't depend only on the fiscal factors of production as labor force and capital but it also affected by the technological progress which is directly related to education. The extended Solow model also assures the importance of education or human capital accumulation as one of the main determinants of economic growth (Pegkas, 2014).

Schultz (1961) argued that knowledge and skill are types or forms of capital, and investment in education or human capital increases both economic growth and individuals' or worker earning. And that rich countries' ability to productively use physical capital is determined mainly by the level of human capital in those countries. And that the main difference between rich and poor countries and their ability to devastated after II world war is the difference human capital level or education (Breton, 2013).

New growth theories meaning that human capital is a factor or endogenous growth theories argue that, education is considered as one of the main components of human capital. Romer (1990) and Lucas (1988) pointed out how education affects economic growth through its effect on labor productivity and on technological progress.

Recently, the new growth models and strategies as sustainable growth and inclusive growth also indicate the importance of education in achieving sustainable and inclusive growth. Education is one of the main outputs of sustainable growth. as sustainable development aspects include social development and enhancing the standard of living which is highly correlated with enhancing education. Education could be considered also as an input and output for inclusive growth. Inclusive growth by definition is the growth that distributed fairly on the society and creates opportunities for all. And one of the main measurements of offering these opportunities is education (Rabah AreKzi, 2012).

Empirically, economic literature had broadly discussed the relationship between education and economic growth. Although most of these studies assure the inconclusive impact of education on economic growth, even those studies that conclude the existence of that relationship indicates that in some cases the level of education matter, meaning that not all levels of education are significant *t* economic growth (Abbass, 2001; Chi, 2008). For example, it indicates that only secondary and higher education is significant. While Leoning, 2010; Pereira, 2009; and Petrakis, 2002 argue that lower level of education is more important to economic growth than higher education especially in developing countries, while in developed countries higher education is more significant. On the other hand, (Asteriou, 2001; Gyimah-Brempong, 2006; and Lin, 2006) argue that all levels of education have a positive impact on economic growth.

On the contrary, some literature found that in some cases, education has a nonsignificant impact on economic growth (Zhu, 2014). For example, argue that no significance between all education levels and economic growth in both China and Malaysia. On the other hand, some studies indicates that there is a heterogeneous effect in the short run and long run (Liao, Du, Wang, & Yu, 2019; Mariana, 2015), for example found that there is a bidirectional relationship between education and economic growth, but such relationship exists only in the short run. While in the long run the direction is only from education to economic growth.

In the same context, some studies argue that although there is insignificant impact of education on growth or even negative impact on some cases, there is an indirect effect of education on growth. Hojo (2003) suggested that education may not directly enhance economic growth, it could accelerate economic growth indirectly by improving productivity, and also through its impact on some social aspects as health and population growth which could be called as social externalities of education.

Recently, some literature explained the existence of insignificant relationship between education and economic growth due to the assumption of linear relationship between both variables, these studies argued that the relationship between education and economic growth in fact is not linear, and that the significant positive effect of education can only be realized after an economy crosses a threshold level of growth. Ahsan (2017) and Roger (2008) explained that the existence of this type of relationship could be explained by the characteristics of countries that have low development level as the existence of corruption, brain drain, and black-market premium. Other literature argued that the nonlinearity is in the different impacts of different levels and types of education as (Petrakis, 2002; Self, 2004). These studies argued that lower level of education have a larger contribution in economic growth than higher levels in developing countries.

As education is considered one of the main determinants of economic growth, either through its direct or indirect impact, gender inequality in education could be one of the main factors that may influence this impact. The impact of gender inequality in education had been discussed in many literature as (Cooray, 2014; Dauda, 2013; Khalsen, 2002; Khan, 2016; Sehrawat, 2017; Zaman, 2010). The empirical finding of these studies confirms the existence of a causal relationship between female education and economic growth in different case studies.

In the same context, Jalilian (2012) found that female education doesn't only accelerate growth but also linked to poverty reduction and some other special externalities (compare to males' education) as slowing population growth, improve health conditions, and even enhance democracy in some cases. This idea is also discussed in Hong (2019) who links female education to inclusive growth. The chapter found that reducing gender gap in education is associated with lower infant mortality and poverty rates and improvement in health and environmental conditions. Khalsen (2002) found that female participation in labor force is the main determinant of the significance of the relationship between female education and economic growth. Thaddeus (2022) confirms the existence of a significant impact of female education on economic growth through its effect on increasing female employment.

Some other studies focus on the net returns of education, Ozpolat (2009) argued that female education tends to accelerate growth in all societies especially in developing countries, and that the net returns of female education and training are larger than those for male.

3. Methodology

Following Cooray (2014) and Dauda (2013), the extended version of solo growth model is used to investigate the relationship between female education and economic growth as follows:

$$\ln GDP_t = \beta_0 + \beta_1 \ln INV_t + \beta_2 \ln GOV_t + \beta_3 \ln FEDU_t + \beta_4 \ln EDU_t + \xi_t$$

where:

GDP: Annual gross domestic product (GDP) Growth Rate
INV: Gross Capital Formation as a percentage of GDP
FEDU: Female enrollment in primary and lower secondary education
EDU: Gross enrollment in primary education (both sexes)
GOV: Government Spending on Education

To capture both short-term and long-term relationship between female education, auto regression distributed lag (ARDL) model is used. According to this technique, the estimated error correction model is used to estimate the short-term relationship. While bounds test is used to test the co-integration between the two variables.

3.1 Data Description

This chapter uses Egypt annual time data for the period 1990–2021 gathered from the World Bank online data bank. Table 20.1 shows the statistic description of the data.

3.2 Model

3.2.1 Unit Root Test

As ARDL model assumes that the variables are integrated at the level or at the first level, augmented Dicky Fuller unit root tests should be used to assure the existence of such assumption. Table 20.2 shows the results of the unit root test.

The results of unit root test suggested that both GDP growth rate and investment as a percentage to GDP are integrated at level I(0), while government expenditure on education, gross enrollment, female enrollment, and female employment are integrated at the first level I(1). Since there are no variables integrated at higher level and then ARDL could be conducted.

3.2.2 ARDL Bounds Test

To apply ARDL Bounds test approach for co-integration, the model lag order should first be identified using one of the statistical selection criteria as Schwarz Information Criterion. According to the value of the test, the best optimal lag for the model is ARDL (4, 3, 4) as shown in Fig. 20.1.

Table 20.1. Descriptive Statistics.

	GDP	INV	GOV	EDU	FEDU	FEMP
Mean	4.361541	18.66357	4.042847	98.28667	91.80625	28.69693
Median	4.421882	18.48470	4.064042	97.20071	91.92509	29.72486
Maximum	7.156284	28.91441	4.945630	106.4096	105.0055	39.44389
Minimum	1.125405	13.64319	2.480000	85.28523	73.68350	16.79983
Std. Dev.	1.556023	3.085302	0.642289	6.155591	9.920789	5.528680

Source: E-views outputs.

Table 20.2. Augmented Dickey Fuller Test Results.

	Unit Root Test		
Variable	**Intercept**	**Trend & Intercept**	**Order of Integration**
GDP	−3.292	−4.18	I(0)
INV	−3.906	−3.977	I(0)
GOV	−4.11	−4.147	I(1)
EDU	−9.24	−9.107	I(1)
FEDU	−5.549	−5.713	I(1)

Source: E-views outputs.

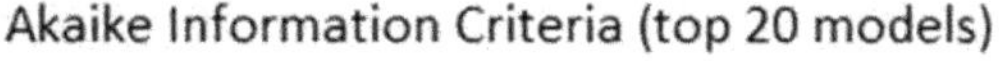

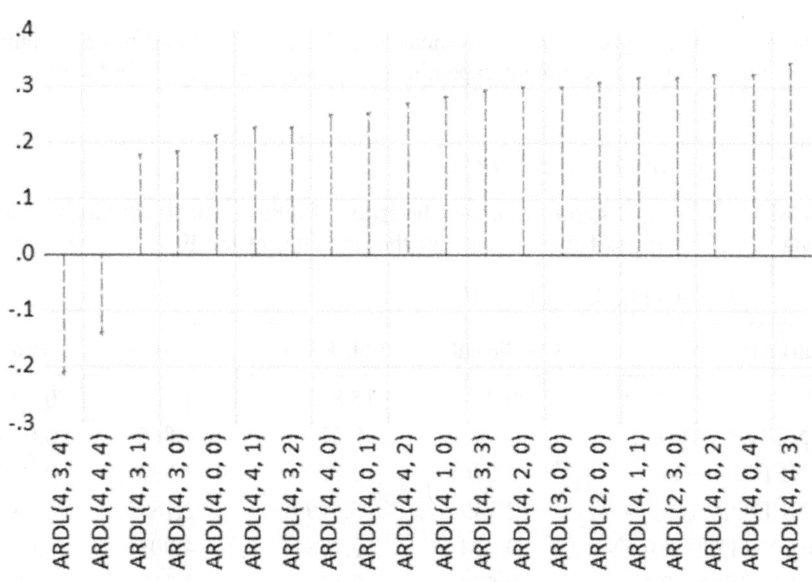

Fig. 20.1. Akaike Information Criteria Selection Graph.
Source: E-views outputs.

To test co-integration between female education and economic growth, ARDL Bounds test approach is used as follow in Table 20.3.

The results confirm the existence of co-integration as F-statistics (12.748) is higher than the upper bound at 5% significance level. This means that in the long run, the variables tend to reach an equilibrium. The ARDL long run form of the estimated model is listed in Table 20.4.

The result of the long run model confirms the significant positive impact of both education and female education to the economic growth at different lags.

Table 20.3. Bounds Test.

Test Statistic	Value	Significance	I(0)	I(1)
			Asymptotic: n = 1,000	
F-statistic	12.74875	10%	2.63	3.35
K	2	5%	3.1	3.87
		2.5%	3.55	4.38
		1%	4.13	5
		10%	2.845	3.623
		5%	3.478	4.335
		1%	4.948	6.028

Source: E-views outputs.

The model also suggests that investment as a share of GDP had positive significant impact while government expenditure on education is not significant.

3.2.3 Error Correction Model (ECM)

ECM is used in this step to estimate the speed of adjustment to equilibrium and long run coefficients. Table 20.5 shows the estimates of the ECM.

Table 20.4. ARDL Long Run Form.

Variable	Coefficient	Std. Error	t-Statistic	Prob.
C	20.26	15.82	1.281	0.2245
LNGDP(−1)*	−1.49	0.217	−6.865	0.0000
LNFEDU(−1)	7.576	2.772	2.733	0.0182
LNEDU(−1)	−12.149	5.5499	−2.189	0.0491
D(LNGDP(−1))	0.874	0.178	4.901	0.0004
D(LNGDP(−2))	0.578	0.174	3.318	0.0061
D(LNGDP(−3))	0.445	0.128	3.491	0.0045
D(LNFEDU)	11.197	4.123	2.7159	0.0187
D(LNFEDU(−1))	−1.064	2.657	−0.400	0.6959
D(LNFEDU(−2))	8.695	2.619	3.319	0.0061
D(LNEDU)	2.977	2.378	1.252	0.2345
D(LNEDU(−1))	12.775	5.1098	2.500	0.0279
D(LNEDU(−2))	8.022	3.1515	2.545	0.0257
D(LNEDU(−3))	5.844	1.919	3.046	0.0102
LNGOV	−0.665	0.548	−1.214	0.2480
LNINV	1.329	0.643	2.067	0.0610

Source: E-views outputs.

Table 20.5. Error Correction Model (ECM).

Variable	Coefficient	Std. Error	*t*-Statistic	Prob.
D(LNGDP(−1))	0.873700	0.149585	5.840842	0.0001
D(LNGDP(−2))	0.578049	0.130743	4.421247	0.0008
D(LNGDP(−3))	0.445533	0.104815	4.250648	0.0011
D(LNFEDU)	11.19724	2.221726	5.039884	0.0003
D(LNFEDU (−1))	−1.063936	1.976917	−0.538179	0.6003
D(LNFEDU (−2))	8.694883	2.112970	4.115005	0.0014
D(LNEDU)	2.976953	1.908003	1.560246	0.1447
D(LNEDU(−1))	12.77514	2.339885	5.459729	0.0001
D(LNEDU(−2))	8.022135	1.829627	4.384574	0.0009
D(LNEDU(−3))	5.844302	1.379047	4.237930	0.0012
LNGOV	−0.665499	0.236553	−2.813321	0.0157
LNINV	1.329257	0.214097	6.208663	0.0000
CointEq(−1)*	−1.492228	0.186903	−7.983970	0.0000
R-squared	0.853295	Mean dependent var	0.004504	
Adjusted *R*-squared	0.735930	S.D. dependent var	0.327091	
S.E. of regression	0.168085	Akaike information criterion	−0.424280	
Sum squared residual	0.423787	Schwarz criterion	0.194243	
Log likelihood	18.93992	Hannan-Quinn criterion	−0.235191	

Source: E-views outputs.

The results reveal significant relationship between female education and economic growth at level and second lag. The error correction term is negative and statistically significant.

3.2.4 Stability Tests

To test the stability of the estimated model, the cumulative sum of the recursive (CUSUM) and the cumulative sum of squares of the recursive residuals (CUSUMSQ) tests are used as shown in Figs. 20.2 and 20.3. As the CUSUM and CUSUMSQ plots are within the critical bounds of 95 confidence level, the null hypothesis of all coefficients in the given regression is stable, cannot be rejected, meaning that both short run and long run coefficients in the ECM are stable.

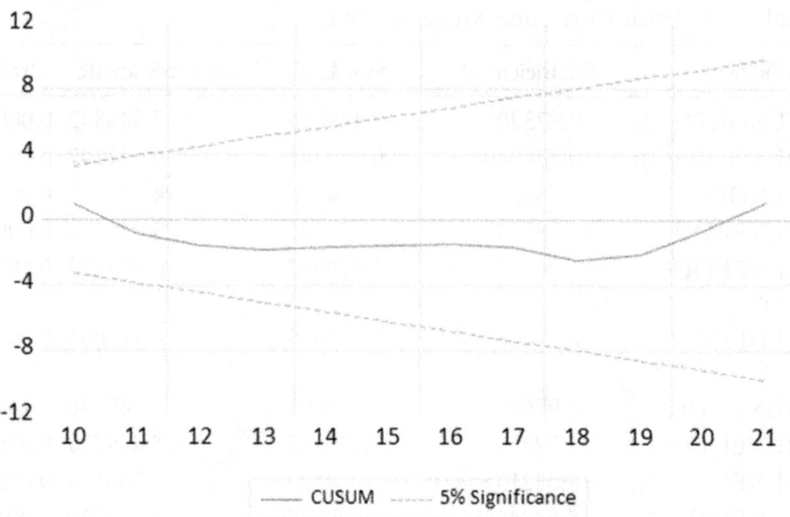

Fig. 20.2. Cumulative Sum Of The Recursive (CUSUM) Test. *Source:* E-views Outputs.

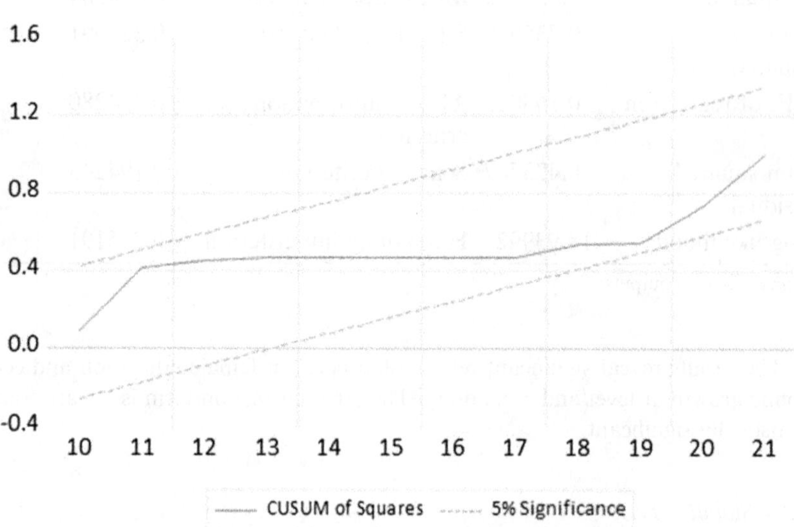

Fig. 20.3. Cumulative Sum Of Squares Of The Recursive Residuals (CUSUMSQ) Test. *Source:* E-views Outputs.

4. Conclusion

To test the hypothesis of a positive impact of female education on economic growth, this chapter adopted ARDL Bound test of co-integration approach. The econometric result suggests the existence of positive significant relationship both in the short run and long run, and that the impact of female education on economic growth is larger than the impact of education in general on growth. This could be explained by the existence of gender gap in Egypt labor market, and thus, more educated girls able to enter the labor market will affect the economic growth more than the education of both sexes, in other words there is still a room for improvement in the female labor market opportunities than for both sexes.

The chapter also confirms the existence of a direct link between education in general and economic growth and thus confirms the hypothesis of the positive impact of education economic growth.

The model also confirms the existence of a positive significant relationship between investment and economic growth however government expenditure on education is insignificant in both short run and long run, suggesting the necessity for public expenditure reform that could make this expenditure more efficient.

References

Abbass, Q. (2001). Endogenous growth and human capital: A comparative study of Pakistan and Sri Lanka. *The Pakistan Development Review*, *40*(4).

Ahsan, H. (2017). Threshold effect of human capital: Schooling and economic growth. *Economic Letters*, *156*.

Asteriou, D. (2001). Human capital and economic growth, time series evidence from Greece. *Journal of Policy Modeling*, *23*.

Breton, T. R. (2013). The role of education in economic growth: Theory, history and current returns. *Education Research*, *55*(2).

Chi, W. (2008). The role of human capital in China's economic development: Review and new evidence. *China Economic Review*, *19*(3).

Cooray, A. (2014). Gender-specific human capital, openness and growth: Exploring the linkage for South Asia. *Review of Development Economics*, *18*(1).

Dauda, S. (2013). Does female education promote economic performance? Evidence from Nigeria. *International Journal of Economics and Finance*, *5*(1).

European Commission. (2004). *Toolkit on mainstreaming gender equality in EC development cooperation*. Retrieved from https://ec.europa.eu/europeaid/sites/devco/files/toolkit-mainstreaming-g

Gyimah-Brempong, K. P. (2006). Higher education and economic growth in Africa. *Journal of Development Studies*, *42*(3).

Hojo, M. (2003). An indirect effect of education growth. *Economics Letters*, *80*.

Hong, G. (2019). Female education externality and inclusive growth. *Sustainability*, *11*(3344).

Jalilian, P. (2012). *The effect of female education on human development and economic growth: A study of human capital formation in developing countries*. Soderton University. Retrieved from https://urn.kb.se/resolve?urn=urn:nbn:se:sh:diva-17466

Karatzia-Stavlioti, E. (2009). Education and economic development: Evaluations and ideologies. In R. K. Cowen (Ed.), *International handbooks of education*. Dordrecht: Springer.

Khalsen, S. (2002). Low schooling for girls, slower growth for all. *The World Bank Economic Review*, *16*(3).

Khan, K. (2016). Contribution of female human capital in economic growth: An empirical analysis of Pakistan (1972–2012). *Quality and Quantity*, *50*(2).

Leoning, J. B. (2010). *Effects of education on economic growth: Evidence from Guatemala*. MPRA Paper 23665.

Liao, L., Du, M., Wang, B., & Yu, Y. (2019). The impact of educational investment on sustainable economic growth in Guangdong, China: A cointegration and causality analysis. *Sustainability*, *11*(766).

Lin, T. (2006). Alternative measure for education variable in the empirical economic growth model: Is primary education less important. *Economic Bulletin*, *15*.

Lucas, R. E., Jr. (1988). On the mechanics of economic development. *Journal of Monetary Economics*, *22*(1), 3–42.

Mariana, D. R. (2015). Education as a determinant of the economic growth: The case of Romania. *Social and Behavioral Sciences*, *197*.

Ozpolat, A. (2009). In developing countries, relationship between women's education and growth. In *Anadolu International Conference in Economics*, Turkey.

Pegkas, P. (2014). The link between educational level and economic growth: A neoclassical approach for the case of growth. *International Journal of Applied Economics*, *11*(2).

Pereira, J. (2009). What level of education matters most for growth? Evidence from Portugal. *Economics of Education Review*, *28*(1).

Petrakis, P. E. (2002). Growth and education levels: A comparative analysis. *Economics of Education Review*, *21*(5).

Rabah AreKzi, C. A. (2012). *Commodities price volatility and inclusive growth on low income countries*. Washington, DC: International Monetary Fund.

Roger, M. (2008). Directly unproductive schooling: How countries characteristics affect the impact of schooling on growth. *European Economic Review*, *52*(2).

Romer, P. M. (1990). Endogenous technological change. *Journal of Political Economics*, *98*(5), 71–102.

Schultz, T. W. (1961). Investment in human capital. *The American Economic Review*, *5*(1), 1–17.

Sehrawat, M. (2017). Does female human capital contribute to economic growth in India? An empirical investigation. *International Journal of Socail Economics*, *44*(11).

Self, S. (2004). Does education at all levels cause growth? India, a case study. *Economics of Education Review*, *23*(1).

Thaddeus, K. B. (2022). Female labour force participation rate and economic growth in sub-Saharan Africa: "A liability or an asset". *Journal of Business and Socio-Economic Development*, *2*(1).

UNESCO. (2022). *Global education monitoring report*. Paris: UNESCO.

USAID. (2023). *Egypt – Gender – Country Dashboard*.

Zaman, K. (2010). Do female enrollment rates cause economic growth in Pakistan. *Asian Social Science*, *6*(11).

Zhu, X. (2014). The effect of education on economic growth – An empirical research based on the EBA model. *Journal of Interdisciplinary Mathematics*, *17*.

Index

Printed in the USA
CPSIA information can be obtained
at www.ICGtesting.com
JSHW051528280424
61906JS00018B/44

9 781837 531073